American Popular Music

Classical

American Popular Music

Blues
Classical
Country
Folk
Jazz
Rhythm and Blues, Rap, and Hip-Hop
Rock and Roll

General Editor: Richard Carlin

Editorial Board:

Barbara Ching, Ph.D., University of Memphis

Ronald D. Cohen, Ph.D., Indiana University-Northwest

William Duckworth, Bucknell University

Kevin J. Holm-Hudson, Ph.D., University of Kentucky

Nadine Hubbs, Ph.D., University of Michigan

Craig Morrison, Ph.D., Concordia University and McGill University

Albin J. Zak III, Ph.D., University at Albany (SUNY)

American Popular Music

Classical

Brad Hill

Foreword by Nadine Hubbs, Ph.D.
University of Michigan

☑®Facts On File
An imprint of Infobase Publishing

American Popular Music: Classical

Facts On File, Inc.
An imprint of Infobase Publishing
132 West 31st Street
New York NY 10001

Library of Congress Cataloging-in-Publication Data

Hill, Brad, 1953–
    American popular music : classical / Brad Hill ; foreword by Nadine Hubbs; general editor, Richard Carlin.
        p. cm.
    Includes bibliographical references (p.   ) and index.
    ISBN 0-8160-5311-1 (hc : alk. paper)
    1. Popular music—United States—Encyclopedias. I. Title.
    ML102.P66H55 2005
    780'.973'03—dc22   2004026425

Facts On File books are available at special discounts when purchased in bulk quantities for businesses, associations, institutions, or sales promotions. Please call our Special Sales Department in New York at (212) 967-8800 or (800) 322-8755.

You can find Facts On File on the World Wide Web at http://www.factsonfile.com

Text design by James Scotto-Lavino
Cover design by Nora Wertz

Printed in the United States of America

VB FOF 10 9 8 7 6 5 4 3 2 1

This book is printed on acid-free paper.

Contents

Foreword

In 1892, the Czech composer Antonín Dvořák sailed to New York to accept a highly paid post at the National Conservatory of Music in America. Dvořák was an eminent nationalist whose symphonies and quartets, vocal and other works presented a proud musical portrait of his native Bohemia. Eager to establish a comparable national tradition in the United States, Dvořák's patrons hoped he would lead American musicians to develop a compelling voice on behalf of their own young country. Indeed, the princely salary offered to Dvořák was one measure of the fervency of this hope—and of the belief, shared among many leading citizens, that the United States was in urgent need of cultural improvement. Although America was by this time a wealthy industrial and global power, it was still deemed a backwater by high-culture standards, having no national arts tradition—and certainly no musical tradition—comparable to the revered traditions of Europe. And as Dvořák's patrons surely knew, continued weakness in this realm could threaten the burgeoning growth of American empire.

Dvořák understood his charge and pursued it in earnest, seeking out distinctly American musical idioms that might form the basis of a characteristic U.S. national style. From 1892 until he returned home in 1895, the Czech composer's oft-solicited advice to his U.S. colleagues was to cultivate a musical language based on certain elements that he found distinctive in African-American spirituals and plantation songs, and in transcriptions of American Indian melodies. Such elements included pentatonic melodies, drone accompaniments, syncopated rhythms, and lowered leading tones (as in blues scales). The directive for would-be U.S. nationalist composers to draw upon African American and American Indian sources was invoked time and again over the ensuing decades, as several generations of U.S. culture boosters repeated the call for a characteristically American classical music.

Despite the concerted efforts of Dvořák and his patrons, no widely embraced "American sound" materialized in the 1890s. Nor did a convincing national idiom surface in the opening decades of the "American century," even though late 19th- and early 20th-century U.S. composers produced an ever broader and deeper range of works. Among these artists were Amy Cheney Beach, John Alden Carpenter, George Whitfield Chadwick, Edward MacDowell, Arthur Farwell, Arthur Foote, Charles Tomlinson Griffes, Edward Burlingame Hill, Horatio Parker, and others who either extended romanticism or blazed modernist trails.

It is not surprising that a distinct American concert music culture never emerged in this period. After all, the United States had only recently seen the birth of high culture on its home terrain. European cultural imports, including Shakespeare's plays, German and Italian opera, and Mozart symphonies acquired "high" status only in the late 1800s, when a high/low cultural hierarchy began to take shape in cultural centers like Boston and New York. Of course, there was musical life in the United States before this time; indeed, two New England colonists, Francis Hopkinson and William Billings, are identified in this volume as America's earliest composers. But the music emanating from diverse American religious, folk, and entertainment centers through the mid-19th century was scarcely professionalized or institutionalized, and musical culture in the United States was judged primitive by comparison with Europe's august classical tradition.

A pivotal moment for American music had come in its late 18th-century shift from sacred to secular, and rural to urban, locations, as described in the introduction to this volume. By the late 19th century, America's blossoming urban cultural centers and escalating industrial wealth would give birth to concert halls, opera houses, and even conservatories—although not to any characteristic American classical musical culture. Indeed, the emphasis was all the more on Europe and, in the wake of Beethoven, on the aura of divine artistic genius, which was ascribed—even by U.S. audiences and critics—only to European artists and works. Hence Americans' native "inferiority complex," noted in the following pages, and Dvořák's generously funded American mission in the 1890s.

By the time of Dvořák's arrival a hushed reverence had settled in around works of art, now deemed the property of an elite class of citizens who alone could understand and appreciate them. This is, of course, what is meant by the phrase "high/low divide," used to describe the cultural scene in the United States around this time. But what was created by late 19th-century culture boosters in (especially) Boston and New York was not simply a cult of veneration of "great" works of art but also a belief that this "greatness" transcended all boundaries. "Greatness" was inarguably and self-evidently great for all places, for all people, and for all times—past, present, and future.

With the stakes of cultural capital thus raised, American music entered the 20th century seeming—by the nation's own increasingly lofty standards—more intolerably backward and underdeveloped than ever. The opening decades of the century witnessed considerable clamor over the question

of how to launch an important music culture "made in America." Newspapers and magazines of the 1910s and 1920s featured frequent commentaries on the "problem" of American music, including speculation on its possible causes and prescriptions for its cure.

While Jim Crow segregation was being established, women agitated for rights and suffrage, and anti-Semitism swelled on both sides of the Atlantic, many culture watchers believed the root of this problem lay in American music having come under "the wrong influences." By these accounts, American music was weak because it was pervaded by immigrants or because it had been feminized, not only by growing numbers of women in the music professions, but by homosexuals. Cultural commentators were anxious for American music to cast off Europe's influence and assert an independent profile. At the same time, they expressed anxiety about any deviations from the virile-white-male identity profile modeled in the European canon, the model for all "great" art.

By the 1920s, forces of backlash had significantly reduced the number of white women in American music. But African-American and Jewish artists remained leaders in U.S. jazz and popular music, which was by now the toast of Europe and much of the rest of the world, and the envy of many European modernists (including Hindemith, Milhaud, Stravinsky). And in U.S. classical music, Jews and homosexuals were numerous and prominent. In fact, despite all the warnings and finger-pointing directed against them throughout the first third of the century, it would be these composers, ironically, who largely saved the day for American concert music.

Beginning with the breakthrough success of Aaron Copland's 1938 ballet *Billy the Kid,* an American national sound was finally established on the domestic and international stage. The Coplandian Americana idiom, as also heard in such works as *Rodeo* (1942), *Fanfare for the Common Man* (1942), and *Appalachian Spring* (1944), featured some of the musical traits Dvořák had flagged decades earlier as distinctly American, including rhythmic syncopation and various folkish pitch characteristics. But it was also distinguished by a modernist harmonic palette and spare leanness that Copland and others in his circle—including Marc Blitzstein, Roy Harris, William Schuman, Virgil Thomson—had honed under the tutelage of Nadia Boulanger at the Conservatoire Américain outside Paris.

At last, the United States could claim a classical music distinctly national and distinctly its own. The Americana sound was one of exuberant joy and simple dignity, evoking Americanness in melancholy cityscapes and in wide-open prairies. This music was audibly American in its fiddle tunes and blue notes, in its jazzy rhythms and the vastness of its spaces. It stood apart from the European high canon through these elements and to the extent that it drew upon French, more than Austro-German, musical traditions. The lean, tonal Americana music created in the century's middle decades by such composers as Thomson, Copland, Blitzstein, Paul Bowles, and Leonard Bernstein was also American by dint of its democratic function and appeal: Engaging popular venues and media—theater, ballet, movies, radio—this was art interwoven with everyday life. America now had its own classical music, though notably it was classical music that, by its nature and from its inception, eroded the very notion of classical music—both as defined in the late 19th-century U.S. high/low cultural divide and as represented by the music's European origins in church hierarchy and imperial court.

The remarkable popularity of tonal Americana would become a liability following World War II, as would the music's minority associations. Stateside cold warriors, like their World War I–era predecessors, now sought American music of muscularity and might to rattle chains of U.S. empire abroad: That music would be spelled *serialism.* Post-Webernian serialism and other abstract, quasi-scientific "complexity music" appeared cosmopolitan by contrast with Americana "regionalism," and it symbolized defiant American freedom by contrast with the Soviet ban on such "elitist" art. Even the difficult reputation of complexity music, its apparent accessibility to only the learned few, struck the right note in this atomic era when all hopes for U.S. supremacy and survival rode on highly technical advances in science and technology.

Serial and, at times, experimental music enjoyed intellectual prestige in the university and the foundation throughout the cold war years, but it never won audience favor. In fact, during this time audiences for concert music overall began to dwindle; in the words of the Introduction, "classical music lost momentum." By the mid-1980s, classical music had all but ceded the high cultural ground it had occupied in America for nearly 100 years: The "eternal" hierarchy of cultural value, it turned out, had both a beginning and an end, and classical music in the United States became simply one among many styles and traditions, including pop-rock, folk, jazz and blues, country, and world music.

But the "descent" of classical music in America may be a boon to musicians and listeners, insofar as it allows them greater freedom to pursue their particular interests and tastes. And classical music can still play an important role in U.S. national culture. Indeed, post–9/11 America has witnessed a revival of Copland's and Samuel Barber's midcentury tonal compositions, and a proliferation of tonal works that emulate their style.

It is this varied, if now relatively level, terrain that we inhabit in American music, and that *American Popular Music* maps throughout its several volumes and many entries. In its focus on U.S. classical music, the present volume surveys a history beginning in colonial times and spanning some 250 years to our own moment, in all its diversity of style and practice. In the light of such a diverse, evolving present and distinct, richly textured past, surely it is impossible to predict the future of American classical music. It is a history yet to be made and yet to be written—very possibly by readers of this encyclopedia. And so, welcome: Read on, engage, and enjoy!

Nadine Hubbs

Preface

American popular music reflects the rich cultural diversity of the American people. From classical to folk to jazz, America has contributed a rich legacy of musical styles to the world over its two-plus centuries of existence. The rich cross-fertilization of cultures—African-American, Hispanic, Asian, and European—has resulted in one of the unique musical mixtures in the world.

American Popular Music celebrates this great diversity by presenting to the student, researcher, and individual enthusiast a wealth of information on each musical style in an easily accessible format. The subjects covered are:

Blues
Classical music
Country
Folk music
Jazz
Rock and Roll
Rhythm and Blues, Rap, and Hip-Hop

Each volume presents key information on performers, musical genres, famous compositions, musical instruments, media, and centers of musical activity. The volumes conclude with a chronology, recommended listening, and a complete bibliography or list of sources for further study.

How do we define *popular music?* Literally, any music that attracts a reasonably large audience is "popular" (as opposed to "unpopular"). Over the past few decades, however, as the study of popular music has grown, the term has come to have specific meanings. While some might exclude certain genres covered in this series—American classical music leaps to mind—we felt that it was important to represent the range of musical styles that have been popular in the United States over its entire history. New scholarship has brought to light the interplay among genres that previously were felt to be unrelated—such as the influence of folk forms on classical music, opera's influence on jazz, or the blues' influence on country—so that to truly understand each musical style, it is important to be conversant with at least some aspects of all.

These volumes are intended to be introductory, not comprehensive. Any "A to Z" work is by its very nature selective; it's impossible to include *every* figure, *every* song, or *every* key event. For most users, we hope the selections made here will be more than adequate, giving information on the key composers and performers who shaped each style, while also introducing some lesser-known figures who are worthy of study. The Editorial Board and other outside advisers played a key role in reviewing the entry lists for completeness.

All encyclopedia authors also face the rather daunting task of separating fact from fiction when writing short biographies of performers and composers. Even birth and death dates can be "up for grabs," as artists have been known to subtract years from their lives in their official biographies. "Official" records are often unavailable, particularly for earlier artists who may have been born at home, or for those whose family histories themselves are shrouded in mystery. We have attempted to draw on the latest research and most reliable sources whenever possible, and have also pointed out when key facts are in dispute. And, for many popular performers, the myth can be as important as the reality when it comes to their lives, so we have tried to honor both in writing about their achievements.

Popular music reflects the concerns of the artists who create it and their audience. Each era of our country's history has spawned a variety of popular music styles, and these styles in turn have grown over the decades as new performers and new times have arisen. These volumes try to place the music into its context, acknowledging that the way music is performed and its effect on the greater society is as important as the music itself. We've also tried to highlight the many interchanges between styles and performers, because one of the unique—and important—aspects of American cultural life is the way that various people have come together to create a new culture out of the interplay of their original practices and beliefs.

Race, class, culture, and sex have played roles in the development of American popular music. Regrettably, the playing field has not always been level for performers from different backgrounds, particularly when it comes to the business aspects of the industry: paying royalties, honoring copyrights, and the general treatment of artists. Some figures have been forgotten or ignored who deserved greater attention; the marketplace can be ruthless, and its agents—music publishers, record producers, concert promoters—have and undoubtedly will continue to take advantage of the musicians trying to bring their unique voices to market. These volumes attempt to address many of these issues as they have affected the development of individual musicians' careers as well as from the larger perspective of the growth of popular music. The reader is encouraged to delve further into these topics by referring to the bibliographies in each volume.

Popular music can be a slave itself to crass commercialism, as well as a bevy of hangers-on, fellow travelers, and others who seek only to make a quick buck by following easy-to-identify trends. While we bemoan the lack of new visionary artists today like Bessie Smith, Miles Davis, Pauline Oliveros, or Bob Dylan, it's important to remember that when they first came on the scene the vast majority of popular performers were journeymen musicians at best. Popular music will always include many second-, third-, and fourth-tier performers; some will offer one or two recordings or performances that will have a lasting impact, while many will be celebrated during their 15 minutes of fame, but most will be forgotten. In separating the wheat from the chaff, it is understandably easier for our writers working on earlier styles where the passing of time has helped sort out the important from the just popular. However, all the contributors have tried to supply some distance, giving greatest weight to the true artists, while acknowledging that popular figures who are less talented can nonetheless have a great impact on the genre during their performing career—no matter how brief it might be.

All in all, the range, depth, and quality of popular musical styles that have developed in the United States over its lifetime is truly amazing. These styles could not have arisen anywhere else, but are the unique products of the mixing of cultures, geography, technology, and sheer luck that helped disseminate each style. Who could have forecast the music of Bill Monroe before he assembled his first great bluegrass band? Or predicted the melding of gospel, rhythm and blues, and popular music achieved by Aretha Franklin during her reign as "Queen of Soul"? The tinkering of classical composer John Cage—who admitted to having no talent for creating melodies—was a truly American response to new technologies, a new environment, and a new role for music in our lives. And Patti Smith's particular take on poetry, the punk-rock movement, and the difficulties faced by a woman who leads a rock band make her music particularly compelling and original—and unpredictable to those who dismissed the original rock records as mere "teenage fluff."

We hope that the volumes in this series will open your eyes, minds, and, most important, your ears to a world of musical styles. Some may be familiar, others more obscure, but all are worthy. With today's proliferation of sound on the Web, finding even the most obscure recording is becoming increasingly simple. We urge you to read deeply but also to put these books down to listen. Come to your own conclusions. American popular music is a rich world, one open to many different interpretations. We hope these volumes serve as your windows to these many compelling worlds.

Richard Carlin,
General Editor

About This Book

Classical music is a field of study and creativity that has evolved over centuries, and it has developed a unique language. Readers who are new to classical music might be confused by the terms and conventions used in the entries of this volume. Knowledgeable readers might wonder why some entries were included and others excluded. It is my intention to clarify these points for all readers.

It is impossible to separate wholly American classical music from its European ancestry. (See the Introduction.) Accordingly, this book includes many European names among its biographical entries. The determining factor for inclusion, where possible, was American citizenship. Naturally, American-born musicians of significance were added. In addition, foreign-born musicians who immigrated to the United States and took citizenship were eligible. Finally, non-U.S. citizens who affected the evolution of American music were considered; Italian conductor ARTURO TOSCANINI, whose conducting of an American orchestra was broadcast nationally every week for years, and ANTONÍN DVOŘÁK, who was invited to teach at the NATIONAL CONSERVATORY specifically to advance the cause of American classical music, are two obvious examples of foreign-born musicians who needed to be represented in these pages.

For the most part, the entries are of four types:

1. Short biographies of individuals
2. Orchestras and performing groups
3. Institutions such as concert halls and music schools
4. Significant compositions

In each of these categories, the American-only rule was applied to whatever extent was possible and meaningful. Just as Dvořák earned a biographical entry, so did his *FROM THE NEW WORLD* symphony, which he wrote in the United States and which spiritually refers to America. Every orchestra, performing ensemble, music school, and concert hall in an entry title is American, without exception. Within the entries, non-American people, places, and institutions are referred to, especially in the context of the career traveling undertaken by American composers and performers. Nearly every important American musician worked or studied in Europe.

Newcomers to classical music might be surprised at the emphasis on education. More than the other volumes of this series, biographical entries focus on each person's educational underpinnings. In classical tradition, the lineage of teachers to which a young musician is exposed is meaningful—not only as a way of establishing credentials, but to identify what type of musician was formed by the training. A young composer who studied with TERRY RILEY or HARRY PARTCH is likely to be more involved with microtonal composing than someone who studied with WILLIAM SCHUMAN or ELLIOTT CARTER.

First performances are also mentioned in many biographical entries, and this convention is more about establishing credentials than anything else. It is also astonishing to read of so many musicians who started their performing lives as children; a prodigious childhood of study and, sometimes, major performances is almost a requirement for an important career. (Major exceptions do exist, though; see the entries for Elliott Carter and HAROLD BAUER, among others.)

Through the centuries, classical composers have written in traditional forms while new forms have occasionally been invented and accepted by the industry generally. The many formal terms for *type* of composition can be baffling to newcomers. Here is a brief rundown of the major music forms encountered in this volume:

- **Symphony:** A symphony is a long piece for orchestra, usually divided into four sections called movements. The number of movements can vary, particularly in works composed after about 1875.
- **Concerto:** A concerto is a long piece for solo instrument with orchestral accompaniment. Like symphonies, concertos are generally divided into movements, but three is more common than four.
- **Sonata:** A sonata is a piece for solo instrument, or solo instrument accompanied by another instrument (such as a sonata for violin and piano). As with concertos, sonatas come in movements—usually three or four.
- **Chamber music:** Chamber music is not a type of piece but a subgenre of classical music. It is composed for small groups of instruments, from two to about 15. Duos, trios, quartets, quintets, sextets, septets, and octets play chamber music. Any group larger than eight instruments is verging on becoming a chamber orchestra, which is a very small orchestra.
- **Opera:** An opera is a musical stage drama or comedy in which all the dialogue is sung. Operas have been composed from the time of Mozart, in the mid-18th century, to the present.
- **Art song:** Art songs are so called to distinguish them from nonclassical songs such as jazz and pop. They are generally scored for one singer and a piano, or sometimes with orchestral accompaniment.
- **Choral music:** Choral music is composed for singing groups—a chorus or church choir.

Along with these types of composition, there are various types of performing group:

- **Orchestra:** Orchestras are large classical groups, containing up to about 110 players of every instrument type. They are often called "Philharmonic" orchestras or "Symphonic" orchestras—or, as with the CLEVELAND ORCHESTRA and the MINNESOTA ORCHESTRA, simply orchestras.
- **Chamber orchestra or chamber group:** As described above, a chamber orchestra is a small orchestra of about 12 to 30 players. The term "chamber group" usually refers to a trio or quartet.
- **Soloist:** Soloists play alone in some sense—either in complete isolation on the stage, as with concert pianists, or playing a solo part in a concerto. Singers performing recitals, accompanied by a pianist (in most cases), are said to be soloists, too. However, when a pianist plays sonatas with a violinist, the violinist is not said to be the soloist; the two performers receive equal billing.
- **Opera company:** Opera companies are real companies, employing a multitude of workers. They usually reside in cities and, occasionally, take productions on tour.

Finally, some explanation of the complex lives of conductors is called for. The men and women who lead orchestras hold uniquely demanding and powerful positions in the classical music industry. To gain the title music director is to become a sort of performing CEO. The job involves rehearsing and performing, of course, and also planning the season's programs, attracting soloists to the conductor's city to play concertos, often handling administrative tasks in the orchestra's operating company, acting as the liaison between orchestra and community, touring, and recording. Amazingly, these maestros often take more than one music directorship at a time, and sometimes the two jobs are on opposite sides of the planet.

The entries in this volume are heavily cross-referenced, specifically to encourage readers to browse beyond the initial point of research. Similarly to following links on the Web, *surfing* this book is the best way to get acquainted with the complex, fascinating, and admittedly ingrown world of classical music.

Brad Hill

Introduction

The American Declaration of Independence was composed in 1776. But American classical music has been struggling for 250 years to gain independence from Europe. From the first documented composition by an American-born musician in 1759 to the Euro-focused orchestras of today, the United States has labored under an inferiority complex.

Classical music is a European invention. Its foundation is the tempered scale, which establishes the system of keys, key signatures, scales, tuning, and notation that underlies all of Western music. The system is taught to every child who begins piano lessons. Developed in the late 1600s, this highly organized set of rules set the stage for a complex type of music whose conventions were passed from generation to generation in formal educational settings. This is the main difference between classical and folk music; classical traditions are much more difficult, expensive, and time-consuming to learn. America came to the classical party late, lacking the generations of knowledge that had been handed down through European society and schools. As a result, America has suffered from a "wannabe" stigma, trying to break away from the European example while, at the same time, relying on it for sustenance.

America started out as a nation of largely European immigrants who organized the country 25 years after the death of Johann Sebastian Bach in Germany, one of the great composers who cast a shadow of influence over centuries of music. By the time America came to grips with its lack of classical music, and its desire for it, whole musical epochs had come and gone in Europe. The baroque era, represented most famously by Bach, Handel, and Vivaldi, came to an end in about 1750 when Bach died. (Musical periods do not have exact start and end dates; they take shape in retrospect. When one lives through them, music styles seem to evolve gradually and without boundaries.) Then came the so-called classicists, represented prominently by Haydn, Mozart, and most of Beethoven's work, covering the second half of the 1700s and into the 19th century. From about 1830 and through that century, the romanticists held sway; composers like Chopin and Liszt valued melodies and emotional impact above all.

Several factors slowed the development of classical music in America. First, the stresses of survival in a new land left little time for the elaborate refinements of such music. Classical music requires a high degree of education and training to compose or perform. Historically, classical music has proved popular in less educated levels of society, but liking it is different from creating it. From the time of the pilgrims until the mid-19th century, America lacked the infrastructure for classical music—no orchestras, not much music education, not many high-level performers, few composers, and undeveloped urban centers in which classical music typically thrives.

By the mid-19th century, major American cities began forming their first orchestras and other music institutions. (Many important orchestras didn't get started until much later.) By the time

America was getting its musical feet on the ground, classically speaking, many European countries (Germany and Austria in particular) had as many as 200 years of musical evolution under their belts. America was playing catch-up and it has been easier to acquire art than to create it. The result was—and continues to be in certain ways—that classical music became an imported product. European personalities, many of whom are represented in this book, became the backbone of talent and experience needed to build a classical music infrastructure. Along the way, several brilliant American-born musicians, educators, and administrators accelerated music's growth in the new country.

During the 20th century America took greater control of its musical destiny. Still, in the United States as in the rest of the world, classical music remained overwhelmingly a European product, dominated by a repertoire hundreds of years old that was (and is still) very much alive in concert halls and recordings. In that context, many American composers and performers have managed to establish enduring legacies. It has been a long and difficult evolution.

Seeds of American Classical Music

American classical music, which started in small towns during the 17th century, was mostly connected to church life. The earliest documented effort to organize and publish music was the BAY PSALM BOOK, a supplement to the Bible that contained standard-meter tunes (all of them European) to which psalms could be sung. This was neither original nor individualized music; the songs were generic and meant to be applied to many different texts. The *Bay Psalm Book* was the first indication of a trend that would dominate the early musical efforts of America (still a British colony) for at least 50 years. During that time American professional music consisted mostly of hymn compilation, a task undertaken by clergy at first, then gradually assumed by nonclerical specialists who can be considered America's first musicians.

Congregational singing was America's first organized music. Thoroughly participatory, there was no performance aspect at first; as in churches today, everyone picked up a book and sang. The books at hand were almost always collections of imported European hymns. America had no composers as such until the mid-18th century. Before then, whoever had the knowledge and initiative to put together a hymn book became the community's leading musical figure. These books were published locally and, as with any other cultural product, became more or less popular and renowned. The best tune books were distributed beyond the local congregation, giving primitive sort of musical stardom to their compilers.

New England developed into a hotbed of congregational singing and tune compilation. There, especially in and around Boston, some sense of artistic standard began to emerge in the early part of the 18th century. In this light, Boston could be regarded as America's first music capital, a distinction it has lived up to many times over, in different ways, ever since. In Boston a reform movement was born to systematize congregational singing, which was a noisy and undisciplined affair despite the tune books. Like many reform movements, especially those that promote change within a church, this one stalled for decades. Many church officials resisted the idea of bringing education into the congregation, fearing (justifiably) that music would take secular flight away from the sacred purpose of worship. Indeed, classical music did fly away from the church, but it took much longer than the musical reformation movement wanted.

Nevertheless, community singing schools sprang up, sometimes forming choirs with their most enthusiastic and naturally skilled members. This development gradually affected the tune books, as compilers started adding slightly more advanced material to their collections—again, mostly in New England. Two events were worthy of note. First, in 1759, FRANCIS HOPKINSON published the first piece of American secular music, an art song (not a church hymn) called "MY DAYS HAVE BEEN SO

WONDROUS FREE." He published a modest collection of seven original songs in 1788, but the 1759 publication marked Hopkinson as America's first composer. Then, in 1770, WILLIAM BILLINGS published a tune book that, startlingly, contained 127 of his own compositions. These pieces were mostly for four-part unaccompanied choir and designed for singing schools. Billings is also sometimes considered America's first composer.

Out of the Churches and into the Cities

The evolution of American music from sacred to secular was matched by an evolution from rural to urban settings. A similar transformation had occurred in Europe. Bach and many of his colleagues in the 18th century were employed by churches, often in small towns dotting the countryside. Their jobs included rehearsing church choirs and playing the organ during services. Many of Bach's immortal compositions (such as the oratorios, the cantatas, and the magnificent Mass in B Minor) were composed during busy days, under tight deadlines, for specific church services and ceremonies. In the second half of the 18th century the patronage of musicians became less constraining, giving composers more time to compose (while also teaching private students and playing live performance dates). But church dignitaries were often, still, their main sponsors. (Mozart was employed by an archbishop for several years.) The government also took some responsibility for underwriting the arts, as emperors employed court composers and commissioned major works from freelance musicians. (Taking that route, Mozart supported himself in Vienna by writing operas for the emperor of Austria.) In the 19th century, European musicians were more at the mercy of the free market. They earned their living through performance and publishing fees, plus patronage, which by then was somewhat taken over by arts-loving philanthropists of the aristocracy. Royal patronage still existed, but career paths were available separate from the comingled power bases of church and state. And those career paths led through major cultural cities such as Paris and Vienna. So, historically, as music moved from the sacred to the secular, it likewise moved from the rural to the urban.

In America, musicians likewise had to find their way from the church and from the countryside. Before that could happen, cities needed to be built, then stocked with concert halls, opera houses, and orchestras. Once the cultural power centers were in place, it was natural for composers to write less music that was sacred. In the meantime, William Billings emancipated tune book compilers, many of whom followed in his footsteps and included original music in their compilations. By some estimates, 250 Americans had composed pieces for religious tune books by 1810. As their music became a bit more advanced, untrained congregations were left behind and the new music was embraced more by independent singing schools and groups. As the best of these groups were located in Boston, the trend toward slightly more refined music inched the tunes not only out of the church, but toward the city.

At the same time, in the late 18th and early 19th centuries, German immigrants of the Moravian Church settled south and west of New England, with concentrations in Pennsylvania, the Carolinas, and Georgia. These settlers connected music and worship as strongly as the British settlers of New England, but they were freer in their musical presentations. Whereas congregational singing in New England was unaccompanied by instruments, the Moravians welcomed instruments during services. And like the New Englanders, Moravian settlers started out importing their hymns from Europe, than increasingly composed their own.

The 19th Century

The 1800s in Europe was a century of stupendous musical evolution. At the beginning, Beethoven was in mid-career, turning out piano sonatas and symphonies that epitomized pre-romantic classicism. At the end, Liszt had changed the piano forever, the romantic epoch had flourished and was fading, Italian opera had given way to German opera and Wagner was already dead, Russia emerged as a powerful music force in both performance and composition, in France the impressionists were altering musical language profoundly, and Arnold Schoenberg was about to storm out of Austria to invent 12-tone music.

In America, musical evolution was so much slower by comparison as to appear stagnant. At the start, small towns were still singing from mostly European tune books, and at the end several orchestras and opera houses had been formed to perform mostly European music. Although some notable composers had emerged, they were known mainly within academic and professional circles. A classical music industry had not taken root appreciably.

The 19th century was divided politically by the American Civil War (1861–65), which also served as a dividing line in American classical music. Before the war, the United States took a few important steps toward the urbanization and secularization of music. A handful of institutions were founded to perform large-scale classical works at a professional level. Notably, in Boston, the HANDEL AND HAYDN SOCIETY offered classical choral works far more ambitious than those attempted by church singing groups, representing an isolated leap forward for choir singing outside the church. But this did not happen until 1858. (The Handel and Haydn Society still operates today.) In New York, orchestras formed that would later merge into the NEW YORK PHILHARMONIC, starting in 1842. Some touring transpired among growing U.S. cities.

During this period one individual, ANTHONY PHILIP HEINRICH, was radically ahead of his time. Called "The Beethoven of America," he was the first American (though not American-born) to compose mature, large-scale symphonic works. Mostly self-taught, he had tried his hand at numerous businesses before turning to music and publishing his first piece in 1820. Ironically, and not too surprisingly, Heinrich received more attention and critical praise in Europe than in the United States. His

majestic and sophisticated orchestral music was a good deal more complex than most Americans were accustomed to, and his scores were too difficult for American groups to play.

A similar pioneer in operatic composing, WILLIAM HENRY FRY had his first opera, LEONORA, produced in 1845 in Philadelphia, and is generally regarded as the father of American opera. Both Heinrich and Fry wrote music of admirable maturity, and many years ahead of their colleagues (if one could even say that they had colleagues), but their scores were deeply derivative of European symphonies and operas. Both composers set examples of serious purpose and attainment, but neither nudged America toward its own style of classical music to compete with European countries. That struggle would not begin to see rewards for at least 50 years.

On the performance front, LOUIS MOREAU GOTTSCHALK became America's best-known classical virtuoso during his too-short life (1829–69). Gottschalk also composed, and some of his piano pieces are played today, but they fit into what might be called the novelty repertoire. During his life Gottschalk's big impact was as a piano virtuoso—America's first. He studied in Europe and met Chopin during the 1840s, when Chopin and Liszt were changing music history in Paris. Gottschalk toured North and South America. As with Heinrich and Fry, Gottschalk had no true colleagues in the United States; each was unique for his time. Only after the Civil War did America's musical life become sophisticated to a degree in which accomplishment was not an anomaly.

In the second half of the 19th century, America awakened to its artistic insufficiency in the realm of classical music. With financial stability and prosperity during the aftermath of the Civil War (in the northern states, at least), institution building got underway on a broader scale than before. Many major American orchestras were founded in these years, as were opera houses and concert halls. CARNEGIE HALL, in New York City, was built by Andrew Carnegie in 1890, and hosted the Russian composer Tchaikovsky as the conductor of its first concert in 1891. The opening of Carnegie Hall served as a template for America's strategy in the classical arts: If you build a grand concert hall or orchestra, master musicians from Europe will come. The first half of that equation (building) dominated the late 1800s; the second part (hosting European musicians) dominated the early 1900s.

As in 19th-century Europe, private patronage came to the fore in financing grand building projects. And another thread appeared in the tapestry of American music, one that distinguished America from Europe more effectively than ever before and that would have profound consequences in the mid-20th century, namely, academic patronage. Dedicated music schools were conceived during this period, modeled after European examples, and a few (NEW ENGLAND CONSERVATORY, Peabody Conservatory [see PEABODY INSTITUTE], OBERLIN CONSERVATORY, NATIONAL CONSERVATORY) began operations well before 1900. But the real forces behind academic patronage of classical music were the Ivy League universities, some of which grabbed native composers and built music departments around them. So JOHN KNOWLES PAINE was installed at Harvard, HORATIO PARKER at Yale, and EDWARD MACDOWELL at Columbia. These appointments sanctioned music education as equal in status to the liberal arts and sciences. The concept, unique to America, instituted a type of training heritage that eventually led to a distinct American composition style. As music education got its formal start in the United States, performance arts (learning to be a piano virtuoso or violin player in an orchestra) became the domain of private music conservatories, and composition was revered at universities. When composers became tenured professors, classical music began receiving the full respect of American society.

The Great American Emergence

Between 1892 and 1895, Czech composer ANTONÍN DVOŘÁK lived in the United States and was a professor at the National Conservatory in New York. He was brought over by a wealthy arts supporter explicitly to jump-start American classical music. It was hoped that the presence of a leading European musical figure would provide inspiration and valuable instruction. Dvořák did excellent work in the United States and composed his FROM THE NEW WORLD symphony while in the country. His main message to American composers was to look within their own nation for inspiration and influences, and stop borrowing traditions from Europe. Finding that homegrown artistic path proved an elusive struggle, but between the turn of the 20th century and World War II, America finally began finding itself musically.

Those years, between roughly 1890 and 1940, brewed an intoxicating and extraordinarily diverse musical life in a nation torn between its ongoing adulation of Europe and preoccupation with its own musical adolescence. During this time America's greatest strides occurred in the fields of composition; performance still lagged sluggishly. If anything, the country's inferiority complex deepened in the performance arena, as European virtuosos discovered touring opportunities and hungry audiences in the United States. America was stunned by a bombardment of heavy-hitting Slavic pianists, including Emil Gilels, Sviastoslav Richter, and especially ARTUR RUBINSTEIN and VLADIMIR HOROWITZ, who became American citizens.

The importation of European virtuosos was even more pronounced on the conductor's podium, where maestro after maestro moved to America and assumed control of its major orchestras. ARTURO TOSCANINI was the most celebrated and influential; after conducting the METROPOLITAN OPERA in New York, the NBC radio network took the astounding step of creating an orchestra expressly for him, which Toscanini led from 1937 through the 1940s. Most of these concerts were broadcast nationally during a time when radio was the dominant entertainment medium in America, elevating classical music appreciation and awareness to a height in American society that has probably never been equaled. Toscanini was hardly alone. SERGE

KOUSSEVITZKY took over the BOSTON SYMPHONY ORCHESTRA in 1924, turning it into one of the great new-music platforms and single-handedly making the careers of several new American composers. Ironically, it took a European maestro to commission important new works from American composers and force-feed them to American audiences (who loved him for it). LEOPOLD STOKOWSKY did much the same in Philadelphia. (The trend continued after World War II as well, with GEORGE SZELL in Cleveland and GEORG SOLTI in Chicago, as well as innumerable other European conductors who made a mark in America.)

Opera houses staked out early ground of classical music for the masses. In cities dense with immigrant populations (New York and San Francisco in particular), Italian and German opera did huge business. Before the 1906 earthquake devastated San Francisco, 20 different opera companies had performed over 5,000 operas in 26 theaters. The SAN FRANCISCO OPERA was founded in 1923. The Metropolitan Opera had been founded in 1883, and its seats filled with New York's German population when it switched from Italian to German opera after the first season. Toscanini conducted there from 1908 to 1915, and the company started broadcasting weekly operas in 1931, continuing for decades.

If some American audiences considered classical music too highbrow, with its European pretensions, GEORGE GERSHWIN became their hero. The first major crossover artist, Gershwin composed with equal fluency for Broadway and the formal concert hall. While other composers tried following Dvořák's admonishment to "look within" by copying Native-American and African-American melodies, Gershwin was the first to successfully integrate jazz, America's own unique art form, into music composed in the classical tradition. His Broadway work was popular, but his 1924 *RHAPSODY IN BLUE* made him an instant international star. *Rhapsody* was a unique piece of American work, but it did not set the tone for other composers to follow. Gershwin was brilliantly apart from the musical

mainstream, and his music did not participate in the ongoing self-discovery of the academic composers.

It was those composers—AARON COPLAND, ROGER SESSIONS, WALTER PISTON, Edward MacDowell—who created a national style. Rugged, extroverted, unsentimental (except for MacDowell), the music of these new masters was pioneer music, more than a century after the American pioneers. But in the United States, composing has always been a slower and less reliable path to stardom than performing. Although the American composers of the early 20th century were forging the country's musical identity, the European imports—lighting up stages with European virtuoso music—were the public's stars.

Modern America

The modern period of American classical music, roughly from 1945 to the present, has been a time in which everything has come together, and fallen apart.

After World War II, the United States became not just a new world in which to tour, but a place for European musicians to settle. Composers and performers alike moved to the East and West Coasts, but the star system still revolved around performers. In that realm, America began holding its own against centuries of European tradition. In 1958, American piano student VAN CLIBURN competed in Moscow in the International Tchaikovsky Competition and took first prize from a mostly European field of competitors and a heavily Soviet panel of judges. In the middle of the cold war, Cliburn became a Soviet idol and an American hero—the only classical artist celebrated with a ticker-tape parade in New York. America had come of age suddenly and ferociously. The Soviet press credited the American music schools (Cliburn went to the JUILLIARD SCHOOL in New York) with surpassing their much older European counterparts, upon which American conservatories had been modeled.

Even so, America was in the thrall of European imports: conductors (Szell and Solti), pianists

(Horowitz and Rubinstein), violinists (JASCHA HEIFETZ), cellists (GREGOR PIATIGORSKY), and opera singers (too many to mention)—the superstars remained European. But the Soviets were right about America's music schools, which were claiming an educational tradition second to none, with the help, it should be added, of innumerable European artists who taught in the United States. Parity was being achieved in the two decades after World War II; America was finally gaining equal stature with Europe and competing effectively on all fronts.

Competing, in fact, became the preoccupation of American music students. Music contests were not new; Liszt and Thalberg battled it out on two pianos in 1835. But it was American instrumentalists whose inborn love of competing reinvigorated top-level music competition and gave rise to many new contests. After Cliburn's victory it became increasingly imperative to accumulate a contest track record, and winning one of the big ones could make a career instantly. Americans love winner-take-all contests. The next important competition warrior was GARRICK OHLSSON, another Juilliard student who won a series of international contests culminating in the 1970 gold medal at the Chopin International Piano Competition in Warsaw, Poland, held every five years. The Warsaw festival is as prestigious as the Tchaikovsky event, and again, Ohlsson was the first American to emerge with the top prize. Headlines ensued but no parade. Indeed, the endless competition season and steady supply of winners dulled the thrill, just as classical music lost momentum in other ways.

Modernism in art is always difficult to appreciate at first. Over time its newness softens and familiarity illuminates previously unrecognized beauty. Beethoven, Chopin, Liszt, Wagner, Scriabin, Copland—all experienced delayed appreciation. But the modernism that imbued classical music in the mid-20th century was more inaccessible to audiences, who never recovered from the onslaught of extreme dissonances and seemingly unfeeling compositions of pure objectivity. Arnold Schoenberg is largely responsible for the 12-tone movement, which discarded the familiar system of keys and scales that is naturally grasped by the Western ear. Schoenberg developed a method of serialism in which he determined note sequences by academic method, not by any attempt to convey feeling or atmosphere. To be sure, Schoenberg was not trying to offend. He was certain that he and his colleagues could develop a new music theory, cultivate a new sense of tonality in the ears of society, and bring atonal music (that is, music without a traditional key—the tonal center) into the natural evolution of music. He sought a new music era, no less beautiful to the ear than classicism or romanticism. Unfortunately, such music sounded chaotic and unpleasant at first, and most people thought it continued to sound that way as time passed.

At this point America's academic patronage of composers, which isolated them from interaction with audiences, insulated the 12-tone movement, deeply alienating audiences and turning them back to European masters of the past. Because composers needed only to please their colleagues to attain university tenure, an ingrown culture developed that disdained audience approval and even approval by a wider circle of colleagues previously required for success. Before academic 12-tone music took on a life of its own, composers needed to impress conductors to obtain premieres of their orchestra pieces; they also needed to impress instrumentalists to get their chamber music and solo works added to recital programs; above all, they needed to impress audiences if they wished their music to be played repeatedly. In the two decades following World War II, composers in American colleges needed only to impress other composers and university deans, all of whom spoke the same obscure musical language that most people could not understand.

Yet alongside the raging academia, some composers continued to produce music beloved by many. SAMUEL BARBER's works were played by Toscanini, and Barber became one of the world's most popular composers. GIAN CARLO MENOTTI wrote an opera for television, *AMAHL AND THE*

NIGHT VISITORS, which became the most performed one-act opera in history. LEONARD BERNSTEIN became a superstar on many fronts—conducting, composing, writing, lecturing, and promoting great music.

Into the Future

American music recovered from its academic hijacking, but the same cannot be said of its audience or the music marketplace.

During the first five years of the 21st century, an epidemic of troubled finances wiped out or reduced more second-tier orchestras than ever before. The classical music recording industry has never been in deeper trouble than it is now. National Public Radio, previously a haven for the classical listener, has systematically eliminated music programming through much of the network. Public grade schools minimize music exposure and education, reducing awareness of the classics and hindering the discovery of talent. Marketing modern classical artists on the basis of pure musical accomplishment is difficult, so record labels and the artists themselves turn to gimmickry, crossing over into jazz, folk music, and bizarre collaborations for attention. A core audience still exists, especially in large cities whose orchestras, opera houses, and concert halls generate excitement and substantial ticket receipts. Patronage of classical music is shouldered increasingly by private citizens, through donations and willingness to pay high ticket prices for music that has become increasingly rare.

Europe remains America's biggest competitor, not so much in the performing arena, where the United States competes effectively with European and Asian virtuosos, but in the realm of repertoire, where American composers still must battle with dead German composers for program space. This, America's centuries-old dilemma, remains as fresh and intractable as it was in 1852 when William Henry Fry complained publicly that the New York Philharmonic was not playing enough of his music.

But if the stodginess of American audiences and conductors were solely to blame, or if music's problems could be laid at the feet of American serialism in the 1950s, classical music would be thriving in other countries. It has similar problems everywhere. At issue is not the winding down of a genre but the multiplicity of competing entertainment. When Toscanini conducted the NBC SYMPHONY ORCHESTRA on the radio in 1947, it was the highlight of the weekend, perhaps along with a baseball game. In the age of digital media, hardly anything could be less true. The entire music industry—not just the classical genre—must compete with movies, digital games, the Internet, and hundreds of television channels.

The good news is that classical music's rich tradition and immense body of immortal music can never be lost. If not another note were ever composed, enough would already exist to keep anyone listening for a lifetime. But new music *is* composed, as the many modern composers in this volume indicate, and the world's most refined and sublime music continues to attract support. America, after centuries of self-doubt, stands on an equal footing in what is now a fully global creative community.

A-to-Z Entries

a

Abravanel, Maurice (1903–1993) *conductor*
Born in Greece, and a stranger to the United States until the age of 33, Maurice Abravanel became one of the most important 20th-century American conductors. Revered in the state of Utah for instituting musical culture almost single-handedly, Abravanel also conducted opera and Broadway in New York, and opera in Chicago. Best known as the music director of the UTAH SYMPHONY Orchestra, Abravanel held that position from 1947 to 1979. The Utah Symphony's current home, Abravanel Hall, was constructed during his retirement year and named after him when he died. Sadly and ironically, Abravanel never conducted in it.

Abravanel spent his childhood in Greece and Switzerland, and studied medicine before considering music as a profession. Eventually he established a close working relationship with Kurt Weill, the German theater composer. At the age of 30 Abravanel was conducting ballet in Paris, and fortified his reputation by conducting a tour of the British National Opera Company. Recommendations from the foremost European conductors of the day led to Abravanel's debut at New York's METROPOLITAN OPERA in 1936. He mixed opera conducting with work on Broadway, and his American career was born.

The Utah Symphony was founded in 1940. Its location, remote from the country's cultural centers, kept the orchestra a local community attraction. During the 32 years of Abravanel's directorship, the Utah Symphony grew to become one of America's most respected orchestras. Adventurous in his programming, Abravanel expanded the orchestra's repertoire while improving its musicianship. Notably, the Utah Symphony was the first orchestra to record the nine symphonies of Gustav Mahler, and Abravanel remains the only conductor to have recorded the entire Mahler symphonic cycle with the same orchestra. Abravanel also brought the

Maurice Abravanel (Courtesy of Utah Symphony and Opera)

orchestra and its audience fully into the 20th century by recording music of NED ROREM, MORTON GOULD, and WILLIAM SCHUMAN.

Abravanel was music director of the Music Academy of the West (Santa Barbara, California) from 1954 to 1980, and taught conducting at TANGLEWOOD, where he was appointed artist-in-residence for life. He served on the National Council of the Arts from 1970 to 1976. Abravanel was the vice chairman of the AMERICAN SYMPHONY ORCHESTRA LEAGUE and received its Golden Baton Award in 1981.

Abravanel Hall

The performing home of the UTAH SYMPHONY Orchestra, Abravanel Hall was built in 1979 and named for MAURICE ABRAVANEL, the iconic music director of the Utah Symphony from 1947. Sadly, Abravanel died soon after the building was completed, and he never conducted in it. Abravanel Hall is part of the Salt Lake County Center for the Arts. The interior was designed by Cyril M. Harris, who also worked on AVERY FISHER HALL in New York's LINCOLN CENTER, and the KENNEDY CENTER in Washington, D.C. Using a box-within-a-box design, Abravanel Hall requires audience members to proceed through sound-lock doors to reach their seats, thereby preventing lobby noise and outside sounds from intruding in the concert space.

Adagio for Strings (1936)

One of the most famous and revered pieces of American music, SAMUEL BARBER's Adagio is an orchestral transcription (made by the composer in 1938) of the second movement of his String Quartet, a relatively early work. The orchestral version was premiered, along with Barber's first Essay for orchestra, by Toscanini and the NBC SYMPHONY ORCHESTRA, at a time when Toscanini programmed very little new music. The concert, broadcast to millions of listeners, put Barber on the

musical map and launched one of the most successful composition careers in American musical history. The piece—slow, grave, and sad—has been used to underscore occasions of national tragedy.

Adams, Claus (1917–1983) *cellist and composer*

Claus Adams was an active ensemble performer in the mid-20th century. He received his early training in Austria, and his family emigrated to the United States in 1929, when Adams was 12. He was the principal cellist of the Minneapolis Symphony Orchestra from 1940 to 1943 under DIMITRI MITROPOULOS, and he played with the JUILLIARD STRING QUARTET from 1955 to 1974. In between, Adams formed the New Music Quartet and performed with that group from 1948 to 1955. Adams taught cello in New York at the JUILLIARD SCHOOL and the MANNES COLLEGE OF MUSIC, and also took students in the summer at the ASPEN MUSIC FESTIVAL. His compositions include a cello concerto and chamber music.

Adams, John (b. 1947) *composer*

John Adams is considered one of the most important composers in the history of American classical music. Adams was raised in Massachusetts, Vermont, and New Hampshire and educated at Harvard University. His work has been influenced by the cultural traditions and institutions of New England. His music has been programmed by every major orchestra in the country. Adams is also an experienced conductor, having led concerts by the CLEVELAND ORCHESTRA, the SAN FRANCISCO SYMPHONY, and the LOS ANGELES PHILHARMONIC.

As a child, Adams learned to play the clarinet from his father and began studying music theory and composition at age 10. He attended Harvard University from 1965 to 1971, where he continued composition studies with LEON KIRCHNER, ROGER SESSIONS, HAROLD SHAPERO, and DAVID DEL TREDICI. Upon graduating, Adams moved to San Francisco and began a 10-year stint teaching at the SAN

FRANCISCO CONSERVATORY. During that time Adams conducted the school's New Music Ensemble, sometimes commissioning new works by avant-garde composers of the day. His advocacy of experimental music led to a position as music adviser to the San Francisco Symphony in 1978. There, with music director EDO DE WAART, Adams created the New and Unusual Music concert series. In 1982, Adams became the San Francisco Symphony's composer in residence. Between 1988 and 1990 he was the conductor and music adviser of the SAINT PAUL CHAMBER ORCHESTRA. In fall 2003 Adams began a three-year term as holder of the Richard and Barbara Deb Composer's Chair at CARNEGIE HALL in New York, the position, essentially that of composer-in-residence, and was previously held by PIERRE BOULEZ.

Adams has won numerous awards for individual compositions and for lifetime achievement. He was awarded the 2003 Pulitzer Prize for his ON THE TRANSMIGRATION OF SOULS, a work premiered in 2002 that is derived from the terrorist attacks of September 11, 2001. The piece is scored for orchestra, chorus, and prerecorded sound.

John Adams is sometimes pigeonholed as a minimalist composer, but his work is more complex, varied, and grounded in Western classical tradition than the music of GLASS and REICH, the two best-known minimalists. Highly virtuosic and dense in some cases, the instrumental work requires extreme levels of performance skill. Adams is unafraid to blend elements of popular music into his work, and his music sometimes conveys a sharp sense of humor. Much of Adams's reputation is based on his three operas, and particularly the first: *Nixon in China*. Based on current events in the early 1970s, *Nixon in China* has been performed all over the world and is firmly established in the modern operatic repertoire. His second opera, *The Death of Klinghoffer*, is concerned with a terrorist hijacking, and suffered from persistent controversy, with protest gatherings forming at some performances. It has been, for the most part, withdrawn from the standard repertoire. Adams's third opera, *I Was Looking at the Ceiling and Then I Saw the Sky*, is a collection of songs that incorporate elements of gospel and funk, and is set in Los Angeles during an earthquake.

Adams's 2003 Pulitzer and Carnegie Hall appointment affirm his standing as the most successful American composer of his generation, and one of the most important of all American composers.

Adler, Kurt Herbert (1905–1988) *conductor*

Born in Vienna, Kurt Herbert Adler began his American career with an appearance as conductor of the CHICAGO SYMPHONY ORCHESTRA in 1938. In 1942 Adler started his most important affiliation when he became chorus master at the SAN FRANCISCO OPERA, rising to music director in 1953 and general director in 1958. He held this last position until 1981, and during this period Adler doubled the length of the company's season, dramatically expanded its repertoire, established community outreach programs, and transformed the San Francisco Opera into an important institution.

Adler's conducting debut came in Vienna in 1925, and he was for a time TOSCANINI's assistant in Salzburg. He received more posthumous awards from European countries than from the United States, but he remains an important part of American opera history.

Adler, Peter Herman (1899–1990) *conductor*

Adler's conducting career spanned two continents and extended from the stage to television. Born in Czechoslovakia, Adler held music directorships in Europe and guest-conducted widely until the age of 40, when he relocated to the United States. His 1940 American debut was with the NEW YORK PHILHARMONIC, and he spent the years between 1940 and 1949 touring the United States as a guest conductor. During the 1950s (1949–59), Adler was music and artistic director of the NBC-TV Opera Company, in an era when classical broadcasts were an important part of television programming. At this post he shared artistic responsibilities with TOSCANINI. Adler got an American orchestra of his own when he became the music director of the BALTIMORE SYMPHONY ORCHESTRA in 1959. He stayed in Baltimore until 1968, and the next year Adler became music director of National Educational Television (WNET). He played a large part in introducing televised opera to American audiences. Notably, Adler commissioned MENOTTI's *AMAHL AND THE NIGHT VISITORS*, which went on to receive thousands of performances worldwide and become the most successful short opera in American history. *Amahl* was first performed on NBC television, on Christmas Eve of 1951.

Adler conducted at the METROPOLITAN OPERA after his debut there in 1971. He directed the American Opera Center at the JUILLIARD SCHOOL from 1973 to 1981.

Adler, Samuel (b. 1928) *composer and conductor*
A German-born American composer and conductor who moved to the United States at age 11, Adler is best known for his substantial compositional output. His published portfolio of over 400 works includes five operas, six symphonies, eight concerti, chamber music, and numerous songs. He has also published three technical books about music and has engaged actively in teaching. Adler has received many grants, prizes, and commissions as a composer. As a conductor, Adler has worked with professional and university orchestras all over the world. Since 1996, Adler has been on the composition faculty of the JUILLIARD SCHOOL.

Adler's music education took place in the United States. He received a bachelor of music from Boston University and a master of arts from Harvard University. His composition teachers included AARON COPLAND, PAUL HINDEMITH, and WALTER PISTON. Several honorary doctorates were later bestowed upon him. After college, Adler founded and directed the Seventh Army Symphony Orchestra, which toured Europe with great success.

Adler received the Army's Medal of Honor for his musical and administrative accomplishments. In 1966 Adler joined the faculty of the EASTMAN SCHOOL OF MUSIC, which was to become his most important teaching affiliation. He was the chairman of the composition department from 1974 to 1994, when he retired from Eastman with the honorary title of professor emeritus. Since then Adler taught briefly at several universities (including the University of Cincinnati, Bowling Green State University, and the University of Utah) before settling at Juilliard.

Adler received National Foundation for the Arts grants in 1975, 1978, 1980, and 1982. He received the Deems Taylor Award for his book *The Study of Orchestration* (1982, second edition 1989). Adler's two other books are *Choral Conducting* (1971) and *Sight-Singing* (1979, 1997).

Aftertones of Infinity (1978)
Winner of the 1979 Pulitzer Prize for JOSEPH SCHWANTNER, *Aftertones of Infinity* is scored for orchestra, whose members must sing at times, and tuned crystal glasses. The work is based on a poem written by the composer, which includes the lines: "celestial voices echo the lost dreams / of the children of the universe."

Air Music (1974)
NED ROREM is best known as a song composer (*Time Magazine* called him "the world's best composer of art songs"), but he won a 1976 Pulitzer Prize for the orchestral suite *Air Music*. It was premiered on December 5, 1975, by the Ohio Symphony Orchestra in Cincinatti, Thomas Schippers conducting.

Albeneri Trio
A performing and recording trio whose members have included Erich Itor Kahn (pianist), ALEXANDER SCHNEIDER (violinist), Benar Heifetz (cellist),

WILLIAM KROLL (violinist), and ARTUR BALSAM (pianist). The group was renamed the Balsam-Kroll-Heifetz Trio in 1960 when Balsam replaced Kahn.

Albert, Stephen (1941–1992) composer

Stephen Albert began his music training with lessons in piano, trumpet, and french horn, and became a Pulitzer Prize–winning composer. His composition teachers included DARIUS MILHAUD and GEORGE ROCHBERG, and he received a bachelor of music from the Philadelphia Music Academy in 1962. Albert was the composer-in-residence of the SEATTLE SYMPHONY ORCHESTRA from 1985 to 1988. His symphony *RiverRun,* inspired by the works of James Joyce, received the Pulitzer Prize in 1985. After that work, Albert's *Cello Concerto,* composed for YO-YO MA, remains his best-known composition. At the time of his untimely death in 1991, Albert had just completed a first draft of the Symphony No. 2, commissioned by the NEW YORK PHILHARMONIC for its 150th anniversary. The symphony was performed in 1994 from Albert's draft score. Albert was on the faculty of the JUILLIARD SCHOOL when he died in a car accident; he had also taught at the Philadelphia Music Academy (1968–70), Stanford University (1970–71), and Smith College (1974–76). Albert's music is universally considered to have a strong lyrical quality, which makes it accessible to average listeners despite the complexity of his scores.

Albrecht, Charles (1760–1848) piano maker

Though much is unknown about the life of Charles Albrecht, he was a successful piano maker in Philadelphia during the 1790s. About 20 Albrecht pianos have endured from this period, four of which are housed in the Smithsonian Institution. Albrecht manufactured instruments of the "square piano" type, which looked like a cross between an upright and a grand. Albrecht continued building pianos into the 19th century (at least one surviving instrument is dated as late as 1848), adding improvements to the action as piano technology developed.

Alice Tully Hall

Located in LINCOLN CENTER, Alice Tully Hall seats an audience of 1,096. That size is large for a recital hall but small for a full-orchestra concert. Accordingly, Alice Tully Hall stages headlining solo musicians giving recitals, leading chamber groups, and chamber orchestras. The hall's namesake was an opera singer and recitalist who helped found the CHAMBER MUSIC SOCIETY OF LINCOLN CENTER and, helped raise the money necessary to build the hall. Heinrich Keilholz was the hall's acoustic designer (he also managed the acoustics during the renovation of Cleveland's SEVERANCE HALL.)

Aller, Eleanor (1917–1995) cellist

Eleanor Aller was a Hollywood specialist, holding principal positions in orchestras run by movie studios. Her first lessons were from her father, the cellist Gregory Aller. She later studied at the JUILLIARD SCHOOL. Aller's first studio orchestra appointment was as principal cellist of the Warner Brothers Studio Orchestra (1936–72), and she was the first woman to hold a principal chair in a Hollywood orchestra. On two occasions, composers wrote film soundtrack music specifically for Aller: Erich Korngold for the movie *Deception* and John Williams for *Close Encounters of the Third Kind.* Aller and her husband, violinist FELIX SLATKIN, founded the HOLLYWOOD STRING QUARTET in 1947. The group disbanded in 1961. Aller was the principal cellist for the orchestra at 20th Century Fox from 1972 to 1985.

Alsop, Marin (b. 1956) conductor

Marin Alsop attended Yale University and received a master of music degree from the JUILLIARD SCHOOL. She won the high-profile Koussevitsky Conducting Prize in 1989 at the TANGLEWOOD MUSIC FESTIVAL. Her conducting teachers have included LEONARD

BERNSTEIN and SEIJI OZAWA. In 1984 she founded the Concordia Orchestra, which continues to issue recordings specializing in American music. Alsop became music director of the Colorado Symphony Orchestra in 1993, a position she held until 2002, when she was appointed music director of the Bournemouth Symphony Orchestra in Poole, England. (Alsop remained involved with the Colorado Symphony Orchestra as music director laureate for a term of two years.) Alsop has been principal guest conductor of the Royal Scottish National Orchestra since 1999, with which she embarked on a recording cycle of Samuel Barber's complete works for orchestra. Alsop has conducted the City of Birmingham Symphony Orchestra and many other European orchestras. Her career has been sustained in Europe as much as or more so than in the United States, but wherever she conducts, Alsop champions American music.

Amahl and the Night Visitors (1951)

A one-act opera by GIAN CARLO MENOTTI commissioned by the National Broadcasting Company, *Amahl* was the first opera written explicitly for television. It is also the most successful short opera in American history—by some counts, it has been seen more than any other opera in the world. Menotti had completed another opera, *The Old Maid and the Thief,* on commission to NBC for radio broadcast. The network asked Menotti for a television opera in 1949, but the composer could not find inspiration to fulfill the commission. He finally found his story in late 1951 and began writing (music and libretto) mere weeks before the broadcast, scheduled for Christmas Eve. Rehearsals began even as Menotti was completing portions of the opera.

Amahl tells the story of a crippled boy and his poor mother one winter night. They are visited in their tiny, bare house by three kings traveling with gifts for a child born in Bethlehem. Amahl's mother, driven by impoverishment, attempts to steal gold coins from the sleeping men, but they awaken and she is caught. The kings offer her the gold, saying that the child they visit will rule the world with love. Humbled, Amahl's

mother returns the gold. Amahl offers to send his crutch along with the men, and in that moment of miracle he is healed and can walk unassisted. He joyfully accompanies the kings on their journey, to offer his crutch to the baby Jesus himself.

The opera is scored for a small orchestra and cast of six. The music is simple and contains no virtuosic demands. Sets are spare. The easy production elements and compelling story create an attractive staging for community houses, making *Amahl* one of the most frequently performed operas in the world.

American Bach Soloists

Founded in 1989, this orchestral/choral group was formed with the explicit purpose of performing Bach cantatas in what its promotional literature refers to as an "historically informed" manner. Since then, the ABS has expanded its repertoire to include other baroque composers and early masters of the classical period. The group started performing in Belvedere, California, and are still the artists-in-residence at St. Stephen's Church in that city. Performances are also given in San Francisco and Berkeley. The founding and continuing music director of the ABS is tenor Jeffrey Thomas. In 2004, Thomas announced the group's intention to perform an ambitious Bach cycle, including an extensive list of oratorios, concertos, and sonatas. In addition to presenting a subscription season, the ABS performs the annual one-week SummerFest at St. Stephens Church.

American Brass Quintet

This performing ensemble founded in 1960, consisting of two trumpets, horn, trombone, and bass trombone, performed for two years before making its official debut in 1962 at CARNEGIE HALL. The American Brass Quintet has played a major role in introducing brass chamber music—both originally scored and in transcription—to American audiences. Several composers, including ELLIOTT CARTER, WILLIAM BOLCOM, WILLIAM SCHUMAN, and others have composed works specifically for the group. They are an ensemble-in-residence at the

JUILLIARD SCHOOL in New York. The group has experienced considerable turnover in its membership; current players include Kevin Cobb and Raymond Mase (trumpets; Mase is the senior member, having joined in 1973), David Wakefield (horn), Michael Powell (trombone), and John Rojak (bass trombone).

American Composers Forum

Founded in 1973 in Minnesota, the American Composers Forum helps connect contemporary composers with audiences and professional resources. The organization operates a recording label (Innova Recordings) and subsidizes recordings.

American Composers Orchestra

Founded in 1977 by composers Francis Thorne and Nicholas Roussakis, and conductor DENNIS RUSSELL DAVIES, the ACO was created to perform music of American composers exclusively. It has premiered over 100 works and performed music by over 500 composers. Two of its commissions (by ELLEN TAAFFE ZWILICH and JOSEPH SCHWANTNER) won Pulitzer Prizes. The ACO has recorded 22 discs, and performances are broadcast over Public Radio International, National Public Radio, and the Voice of America. The ACO has locked up ASCAP's annual prize for "adventurous programming," having won the award every year of its existence. The orchestra presents an annual festival of Latin American music, the Sonidos de las Américas. Based in New York, the ACO operates a subscription series in CARNEGIE HALL. The current music director is Steven Sloane. Robert Beaser is the Artistic director. Dennis Russell Davies continues his association with the ACO as conductor laureate. Cofounder Francis Thorne is the organization's president.

American Festival Overture (1939)

This single-movement piece helped establish WILLIAM SCHUMAN as a major American composer, two years before the Symphony No. 3 won him the New York Music Critics' Circle Award, and four years before he won the first Pulitzer Prize in music.

American in Paris, An (1928)

A tone poem for orchestra, and one of GEORGE GERSHWIN's seminal works in a classical form, the piece was premiered on December 13, 1928, at CARNEGIE HALL by the NEW YORK SYMPHONY SOCIETY Orchestra, conducted by WALTER DAMROSCH. Gershwin was then reaching the height of his influence, prestige, and earning power. The following year, Gershwin conducted an outdoor performance of the piece at Lewisohn Stadium in New York, to an audience of 15,000. The piece was later used in the 1951 film of the same title.

American Music

American Music is a quarterly scholarly journal produced by the SOCIETY FOR AMERICAN MUSIC (previously the Sonneck Society). The journal covers all aspects of North American music and was first published in 1983.

American Music Center

Founded in New York in 1939 by MARION BAUER, AARON COPLAND, and others, the American Music Center is a focal point for American classical music and jazz. The organization brings together composers, presents conferences, publishes a Web magazine, and hosts music selections on its Web site. The group maintains a circulating library of many thousands of scores.

American String Quartet

Formed in 1974 by students of the JUILLIARD SCHOOL, the American String Quartet has enjoyed critical acclaim in New York, nationally, and internationally. The group made its debut at ALICE TULLY HALL in LINCOLN CENTER in 1975. That same year it won a Naumburg Award. Its annual tours are extensive; in 2000, celebrating its 25th anniversary, the quartet played in all 50 states. The group is the resident quartet at the ASPEN MUSIC FESTIVAL (since 1974) and the MANHATTAN SCHOOL OF MUSIC (since 1984), and the Van Cliburn International Piano Competition. The quartet's repertoire is vast and wide-ranging, extending from Mozart to contemporary composers. Current members are Peter Winograd (violin), Laurie Carney (violin), Daniel Avshalomov (viola), and Margo Tatgenhorst Drakos (cello).

American Symphony Orchestra

One of several orchestras founded by conducting powerhouse LEOPOLD STOKOWSKI, the American Symphony Orchestra began its life in 1962 with a mandate to "perform concerts of great music within the means of everyone." That mission has continued in contemporary New York through a subscription series at AVERY FISHER HALL in LINCOLN CENTER, and many community outreach programs that take the orchestra to high schools, colleges, and festivals. Characteristically, the ASO's programming is adventurous and innovative, often resulting in themed programs that tie music to literature and other aspects of modern culture. The orchestra has toured outside the United States, giving the inaugural concert at São Paolo's (Brazil) concert hall and traveling in Asia more than once. Leon Botstein is the current music director. The Stokowski-founded ASO is distinct from another American Symphony Orchestra, founded in 1894 by conductor Sam Franko.

American Symphony Orchestra League

The ASOL is an advocacy organization that provides organizational and financial support to American orchestras. It was founded in 1942. Membership is open to individuals, conductors, orchestra administrators, students, and, of course, orchestras. Offices are located in New York and Washington, D.C. The ASOL founded the Conductors Guild in 1975. The house publication is the bimonthly magazine *Symphony.*

Ancient Voices of Children (1970)

The best-known work of GEORGE CRUMB, *Ancient Voices of Children* is a song cycle set to words by Federico García Lorca. The music is scored for mezzo-soprano and boy soprano, accompanied by a small ensemble of melody and percussion instruments. It was premiered at the Library of Congress in Washington, D.C.

Anderson, June (b. 1952) *opera singer*

Soprano June Anderson began singing lessons at age 11 and was a finalist in the METROPOLITAN OPERA National Auditions when she was 17. After

June Anderson (Courtesy of Jonathan Letts)

attending Yale University, where she majored in French, Anderson made her operatic debut at the NEW YORK CITY OPERA. Her European debut occurred in Rome in 1982. Anderson debuted at the Metropolitan Opera in 1989. She has sung throughout Europe, as well as in Chicago and San Francisco. Anderson's voice is heard during opera sequences in the film *Amadeus*.

Anderson, Laurie (b. 1947) *multimedia performance artist*

Laurie Anderson is more often considered a pop artist than a classical one. But avant-garde composers often find their audiences in the same underground venues that emerging pop artists inhabit, and Anderson's career to date is that of a serious and trained musician, writer, and visual artist. She studied violin as a child and received arts degrees from Barnard College (B.A., 1969) and Columbia University (M.F.A., 1972). During the 1970s Anderson brought together the disparate elements of sound, visuals, movement, and technology that would characterize her work for the next three decades. In her early performances in small venues, Anderson could easily be viewed as a social critic and, at the same time, admired as a technologist who often synthesized sounds from devices of her own invention. Her first major performance installation, which brought Anderson a fair degree of notoriety and acclaim, was *United States, I-IV*, performed at the Brooklyn Academy of Music in 1983. She had already scaled pop music heights with the song *O Superman*, which was a hit on the British pop charts. Encouraged in the direction of music recording, Anderson released two albums in quick succession: *Big Science* (1982) and *Mister Heartbreak* (1984). She secured a larger and more diverse audience with the release of a feature film, *Home of the Brave*, in 1986.

Anderson's popularity as a composer is the result of her crossover appeal, which attracts diverse audiences. Just as important, she has, with the exception of her record releases, propagated her music as part of large-scale, immersive multimedia performanc-

es. Her work receives near-global recognition. In 2003, the city of Düsseldorf, Germany, hosted a retrospective exhibition entitled "Record of the Time: Sound in the Art of Laurie Anderson." She is the first artist-in-residence at the National Aeronautics and Space Administration (NASA). Anderson has engaged in strictly musical tours in Europe and the United States, sometimes focusing on her more traditional classical output. In September 2003 she performed with the Stuttgart Chamber Orchestra. A solo tour of American college campuses was planned for 2004.

Anderson, Marian (1897–1993) *singer*

Generally acknowledged as one of America's greatest singers, contralto Marian Anderson was also a civil rights ambassador whose career mirrored America's striving for social equality, helped move the country toward that ideal, and broke barriers for every African-American opera singer to follow. She was the first black singer to appear in a leading role on the stage of the METROPOLITAN OPERA. In what was to become her defining moment, Anderson performed a concert on the steps of the Lincoln Memorial after she was prevented from singing in Constitution Hall in Washington, D.C.

Anderson began singing at a young age in her local church. More advanced studies were funded by benefit concerts and other fund-raising efforts within her church community. Anderson was denied entrance to the Philadelphia Music Academy because of her race. After more fundraising, Anderson studied with Giuseppe Boghetti and gave her debut concert in New York's Town Hall in 1924. The reviews of that concert were not altogether favorable, partly because of Anderson's lack of mastery over the foreign languages in which much of the classical song repertoire is written. Still, the next year Anderson won first prize in a competition sponsored by the NEW YORK PHILHARMONIC, and she performed a concert with the orchestra on August 27, 1925. Despite that promising start, Anderson found further career

Marian Anderson (Marian Anderson Collection, Rare Book and Manuscript Library, University of Pennsylvania)

doors mostly closed to her, and in 1930 she ventured to Europe with the hope of developing more performing opportunities.

In Europe during the early 1930s, Anderson's career found its footing, and she toured with great success. The Finnish composer Jean Sibelius dedicated a song ("Solitude") to her, and TOSCANINI famously remarked, "A voice like yours is heard once in a hundred years." Anderson returned to America in 1935. She was reluctant to test the waters again in her native country, but impresario and manager Sol Hurok persuaded her to perform a second debut in TOWN HALL. The concert was a resounding success, and the *New York Times* called her "one of the great singers of our time." From that point onward, Anderson gave about 70 concerts a year in the United States, including the legendary Lincoln Memorial appearance in 1939. Organized by the U.S. Department of the Interior and First Lady Eleanor Roosevelt, it was attended by a throng of 75,000 and heard by millions of radio listeners. Images of that concert became symbols of the American civil rights movement. In 1943, the Daughters of the American Revolution, which owned Constitution Hall and had refused Anderson in 1939, invited her to participate in a benefit concert, and Anderson finally sang on that stage. She would later begin her farewell tour in Constitution Hall.

Anderson sidestepped the prejudices of the opera world by constructing a career as a recitalist. So it continued until RUDOLPH BING, then head of the Metropolitan Opera, asked Anderson to sing the character Ulrica in Verdi's *A Masked Ball* on January 7, 1955. Anderson was by then a respected and beloved performer, and her voice was past its prime. But her technical performance didn't matter to the moved and cheering audience, which, aware of the historical significance of her appearance on the Met stage, gave her ovations before she even sang a note. After this landmark event, Anderson toured India, Australia, and the Far East, sometimes accompanied by documentary and television news crews. She sang at the inaugurations of Presidents Eisenhower and Kennedy. Anderson's last performance was at CARNEGIE HALL on April 18, 1965.

Anderson's voice was often described as "rich" and "velvety." Her singing demonstrated enormous range, flexibility, and heartfelt emotion. She sang repertoire from Bach to the late romantic composers and was especially noted for giving American spirituals equal footing with the classics in her concerts. She received innumerable awards, including the Presidential Medal of Freedom, Kennedy Center Honors (in the first year they were given), National Arts Medal, and the first Eleanor Roosevelt Human Rights Award of the City of New York. Anderson was an alternative representative in the Human Rights Committee of the United Nations.

Antes, John (1740–1811) composer

Usually acknowledged as the first American-born composer of chamber music, John Antes thought of himself as a musical dilettante, sometimes even signing his scores as such. Antes was an inventor and instrument maker who built violins, violas, and designed piano hammers. He left America in 1769 as a missionary in the Moravian Church, his most personally important calling. He lived in Egypt for 12 years, where, for unknown reasons, he was captured and tortured by followers of anti-Semitic leader Osman Bey. The injuries Antes sustained during this ordeal plagued him for years afterward but didn't prevent him from composing chamber music while in Egypt. Antes enjoyed a more placid life in Germany, where he lived beginning in 1782. The church called him to England in 1785, where he worked until his retirement in 1808. Antes died in England without returning to America, but he is regarded as a pioneer American composer who wrote in the style of Haydn.

Antheil, George (1900–1959) composer and pianist

During the course of a relatively short life, composer and pianist George Antheil engineered two separate careers and created several distinct compositional phases. He was, at one time, considered the most important avant-garde composer in Europe; at his lowest point he was regarded as a fraud in his own country. His music experienced a revival in the 1990s, but Antheil's posthumous reputation does not approach the legendary status among American composers of a COPLAND or MACDOWELL.

Antheil began playing the piano when he was six years old. He studied composition with ERNEST BLOCH at the Philadelphia Conservatory, but in 1922 he decided that his best path lay as a pianist and traveled to Europe to begin a concert career. There, Antheil toured with stupendous success and controversy. Playing a mixture of standard repertoire and his own pieces, and sometimes devoting entire recitals to original compositions, Antheil gave performances that sparked riots among audiences. His compositions were influenced by the modern, anti-romantic aspects of his personal hero, Russian composer Igor Stravinsky, and featured propulsively rhythmic, impersonal blocks of music. While audiences literally fought over the merits of Antheil's concerts, he was befriended by the most famous and influential artistic community in Paris, which included luminaries Stravinsky, Ezra Pound, James Joyce, Eric Satie, Man Ray, and Pablo Picasso. As the darling of the creative jet set, Antheil began composing larger forms and for bigger ensembles. BALLET MÉCANIQUE culminated this phase; with it, he intended to summarize his compositional style. Not an actual ballet, *Ballet mécanique* is a pure-music work originally scored for a massive percussion ensemble including 20 player pianos, a few airplane propellers, and a siren. The piece premiered on June 19, 1926, was a tumultuous success in Europe, and established Antheil firmly as the composer of the hour.

Antheil did not rest long on this pinnacle. He turned to a different, more conservative composition style, a neoclassicism that introduced modern elements to classical forms, with a more accessible and less challenging sound than the modernist work on which he had built his fame. European critics charged Antheil with imitating Stravinsky, where earlier he was merely influenced by him. In America, where Antheil's fame was secondhand, his reputation was blackened by the New York premiere of *Ballet mécanique* at CARNEGIE HALL in 1927. Sloppily promoted, badly staged, and underrehearsed, the performance was one of the most comical disasters in concert history, capped by a stubborn siren that refused to play its part until the piece ended, at which point the malfunctioning instrument burst into full wail. Roundly rejected in New York, and losing his status in Paris, Antheil moved to Germany in 1928, where he wrote his opera *Transatlantic,* a satire of American life.

Antheil returned to the United States in 1933 and settled in Hollywood in 1936. There, he scored over 30 films and wrote articles. This sort of work for hire was a discouraging development to Antheil, but he acknowledged that film music brought him a larger audience than he would have gained otherwise. He continued composing pure music, and in 1942 his career was revived by the publication and subsequent premiere (on February 13, 1944, by the NBC SYMPHONY ORCHESTRA under STOKOWSKI) of his Symphony no. 4. This symphony's easy melodies and memorable climaxes are far removed from the avant-garde work that caused riots in Paris 20 years earlier. Both this symphony and the following Symphony no. 5 were critical and popular successes. In the early 1950s, Antheil composed five operas. His entire output includes a piano concerto, the *Jazz Symphony,* many other orchestral works, dozens of songs, a collection of chamber music, and quite a bit of piano music written during and after his controversial Parisian phase.

Apollo's Fire

Founded in 1992 by harpsichordist Jeannette Sorrell, Apollo's Fire is a baroque chamber orchestra that performs on period instruments. Based in Cleveland, Ohio, the group early received a start-up grant from the Cleveland Foundation. The group's debut occurred in June 1992, and they have since performed in several states. Apollo's Fire has recorded several discs and is often heard in holiday programs over National Public Radio. The group won the Noah Greenberg Award from the American Musicological Society in 1995.

Appalachian Spring (1944)

Perhaps AARON COPLAND's most famous work, *Appalachian Spring* is a single-movement piece for orchestra, originally conceived as a ballet score, that evokes a pastoral America. The piece was commissioned by Martha Graham, and its working title was "Ballet for Martha." Graham herself bestowed the final title after hearing the piece. Copland quoted the Shaker hymn "Simple Gifts" in the piece. *Appalachian Spring* won the Pulitzer Prize in 1945.

Argento, Dominick (b. 1927) *composer*

Dominick Argento was primarily an opera and song composer, some of whose works are established in the modern stage repertoire. He took piano lessons as a child and entered the Peabody Conservatory, from which he took a bachelor of music degree in 1951. Argento received a Fulbright grant for postgraduate study at the Cherubini Conservatory in Florence, Italy. He returned to the United States and Peabody, earning a master of music degree in 1954. He received a Ph.D. from the EASTMAN SCHOOL OF MUSIC in 1957. From 1958 to 1997, Argento taught at the University of Minnesota, Minneapolis.

Argento composed mostly operatic and song material; much of his orchestral output was conceived for opera, then reworked. His best-known and most firmly established work is the one-act opera *Postcard from Morocco,* which received its premiere in Minneapolis on October 14, 1971. He won a Pulitzer Prize in 1975 for a song cycle entitled *From the Diary of Virginia Woolf.*

Ashley, Robert (b. 1930) *composer of opera and mixed-media performance art*

Robert Ashley is considered by some critics to be a groundbreaking visionary whose historical contribution to opera has yet to be assessed. Ashley attended the University of Michigan from 1948 to 1952, then received a master of science degree from the MANHATTAN SCHOOL OF MUSIC in 1953. His early staging experiments occurred with regional touring groups through which Ashley tested his work in the United States and abroad. Ashley organized the ONCE Festival in Ann Arbor, Michigan, to showcase modern music. From 1969 to 1981 he was the director of the Center for Contemporary Music at Mills College in Oakland, California. Ashley gained a degree of renown through his 1980 commissioned work, *Perfect Lives,* an opera composed for television, stretched over seven half-hour episodes. The production has been aired in Austria, Germany, Spain, and the United States, and has also been staged as a live theater production.

Babbitt, Milton (b. 1916) *composer and theorist*
The foremost American-born 12-tone composer and theorist, Babbitt began his college career with every intention of becoming a mathematician. His affinity with numbers and formulas informed his later musical work. As a child, Babbitt played violin, clarinet, and saxophone, and he gravitated toward jazz. He started college at the University of Pennsylvania in 1931, then transferred to New York University, where he studied composition with Marion Bauer. In New York Babbitt grew acquainted with and devoted to the emerging 12-tone school developed by the Austrian composers Schoenberg, Berg, and Webern. He received a bachelor of arts degree in 1935 and moved to Princeton University for graduate work. During this time Babbitt studied with Roger Sessions. He received a master of fine arts degree from Princeton in 1942. He later served on Princeton's mathematics faculty. He became director of the Columbia-Princeton Electronic Music Center in 1959.

Babbitt was named Conant Professor of Music at Princeton in 1960. In 1973 he joined the composition faculty of the Juilliard School. His received honors include a National Institute of Arts and Letters Award in 1959, a Guggenheim Fellowship in 1960, and a Pulitzer Prize Special Citation in 1982. Babbitt has been awarded honorary degrees from at least six institutions.

Bacon, Ernst (1898–1990) *composer and pianist*
Bacon is best remembered for his original compositions, especially his songs. Raised by an Austrian mother and an American father, Bacon composed work rooted in European tradition and inspired by American language, landscapes, and lore. Bacon attended Northwestern University and the University of Chicago, and received a master of arts degree from the University of California. Along the way he taught at the Eastman School of Music (1925–28) and the San Francisco Conservatory (1928–30). After receiving a graduate degree, Bacon spent time on the faculty of Converse College in Spartanburg, South Carolina (1938–45) before settling into Syracuse University in New York State, where he directed the music school from 1945 and was named professor emeritus in 1964. Bacon was awarded a Pulitzer Prize for his Symphony no. 1 in 1932. He is the author of two popular books on music, *Words on Music* (1960) and *Notes on the Piano* (1963).

Bali (1933)
An orchestral work by Henry Eichheim, *Bali* was remarkable for its time in the use of gamelan instruments. It was preceded by Eichheim's other gamelan-enhanced piece, *Java* (1929).

Ballad of Baby Doe, The (1956)
Douglas S. Moore's most popular opera, it established the composer as primarily a stage composer. It was premiered in Central City, Colorado, on July 7, 1956.

Ballet mécanique (1924)

A seminal work by GEORGE ANTHEIL, scored for large percussion ensemble, the *Ballet mécanique* caused a furor in Europe and America, in different ways. This piece was the culmination of Antheil's avant-garde period, during which he lived in Paris, and was anointed by literary and musical celebrities as the most progressive composer of the day. The Paris premiere of *Ballet mécanique* was a great success in 1926. The American premiere, at New York's CARNEGIE HALL in 1927, was a disaster rarely matched in the annals of concert catastrophes. The large airplane propellers, written into the score for the sound they emit, were mistakenly turned toward the audience, sending programs, gloves, and toupées flying through the hall. The siren part was flubbed, thanks to a defective siren that didn't make a sound until the piece had just concluded. American critics flocked to characterize Antheil's European success as undeserving by American standards. Antheil's American career did not recover for nearly 20 years, and *Ballet mécanique* was not performed again for over 60 years.

Ballet mécanique (whose full translated title is *Ballet for Mechanical Percussion Instruments*) was originally scored for 20 player pianos in addition to a large complement of other percussion tools and gadgets. In 1953 Antheil revised and rescored the piece without player pianos, their popularity having dwindled. The work was originally conceived as the soundtrack to a film, but synchronization difficulties forced the two products, music and film, to be released separately. They remained autonomous works until the late 1990s, when Paul Lehrman, who had revived the piece in MIDI format, and Bruce Posner, used modern synchronization techniques finally to put the two together. The film, with Antheil's *Ballet mécanique* soundtrack, premiered in 2001 in Moscow.

Balsam, Artur (1906–1994) *pianist*

One of the 20th century's great chamber music pianists, Balsam collaborated with almost every important violinist and cellist of his day. As a classical-era specialist, he also recorded all the solo repertoire of Mozart and Haydn. Balsam debuted in Berlin at the age of 12 and won that city's International Piano Competition in 1930. His career as an accompanist began suddenly, when violinist YEHUDI MENUHIN (then 14 years old) asked Balsam to tour with him through North America. Following that opportunity was a tour with violinist NATHAN MILSTEIN. In the 1940s, Balsam was the house pianist for the NBC ORCHESTRA under TOSCANINI. He joined the ALBENERI TRIO in 1960, and it was soon renamed the Balsam-Kroll-Heifitz Trio.

Balsam's penetrating touch on the piano, and uncanny ability to perform complex music perfectly at first sight, made him famous as an ensemble pianist. Hardly a faceless performer, he combined sensitivity with a distinctive force of personality. Throughout his career, he preached that all participants in any chamber music setting are equally important. Balsam served on the faculties of the MANHATTAN SCHOOL OF MUSIC and Boston University, and spent summers between 1956 and 1992 leading chamber music courses at KNEISEL HALL in Blue Hill, Maine. MURRAY PERAHIA, the headlining concert pianist, was Balsam's most distinguished student.

Baltimore Symphony Orchestra

Founded first in 1916, then again in 1942, the Baltimore Symphony is an orchestra with two histories. The first founding was unprecedented in America: the orchestra was started by appropriations of the city government. Gustav Strube was the first conductor, and he remained on the podium until 1930. Strube was followed by George Siemonn (1930–35), Ernest Schelling (1935–37), Werner Janssen (1937–39), and Howard Barlow (1939–42). At that point the orchestra was dissolved and reorganized as a private institution under the management of Reginald Stewart, the director of Baltimore's Peabody Conservatory. After Stewart, the new orchestra's music directors have included

Massimo Freccia (1952–59), Peter Herman Adler (1959–68), Brian Priestman (1968–69), Sergiu Comissiona (1968–84, the orchestra's most influential leader), D. J. Zinman (1985–98), and the current music director, YURY TEMIRKANOV. The Baltimore Symphony Orchestra toured Europe, including Russia, in 1987, and East Asia in 1994 and again in 1997 with violinist ISAAC STERN. As a recording ensemble, the Baltimore Symphony has won multiple Grammy Awards and enjoys a particularly fertile association with cellist YO-YO MA. In 2004 the orchestra moved to a new Strathmore Hall Performing Arts and Education Center in North Bethesda, Maryland.

Barber, Samuel (1910–1981) *composer*

For almost 30 years in the mid-20th century, Samuel Barber was the most successful American composer. Almost all his works became standard concert material soon after he wrote them, and many have remained so. He was awarded two Pulitzer Prizes and was elected to the American Academy of Arts and Letters. Barber was especially drawn to writing songs and, on a larger scale, operas; even his instrumental music has a lyrical, songlike quality. Yet, ironically, it was the failure of one of his operas that sent Barber's career and psychological health spiraling downward.

Barber was a precocious composer, writing an operetta when he was 10 years old. He was the nephew of contralto Louise Homer and composer Sidney Homer. According to some biographical accounts, Barber wrote a childhood note to his mother: "I was meant to be a composer and will be I'm sure. Don't ask me to try to forget this unpleasant thing and go play football." Barber entered the CURTIS INSTITUTE OF MUSIC in 1924 at age 14, where he studied piano, composition, conducting, and singing. At Curtis, Barber met fellow composer GIAN CARLO MENOTTI, with whom he was to form a nearly lifelong personal and professional partnership. The school's founder, Mary Curtis Bok, became a staunch and supportive ally

during these years and continued to assist Barber after he graduated.

Barber's early career met with instant success. He won the Joseph H. Bearns prize from Columbia University at the age of 18 for a violin sonata that remained unpublished and is now lost, and received a second Bearns prize in 1931 for his orchestral overture to *The School for Scandal*. By 1938 Barber had completed his first Essay (of three composed for orchestra) and the string quartet from which the famous ADAGIO FOR STRINGS was extracted and orchestrated. Both the Essay and the Adagio were premiered in live broadcasts by TOSCANINI and the NBC SYMPHONY ORCHESTRA, at a time when Toscanini, late in his career, was mostly uninterested in new music. This exposure put Barber on the American cultural map.

After the Toscanini premieres, demand for Barber's music intensified, and nearly all his large-scale compositions through 1966 were produced on commission from the foremost American conductors and institutions. His opera, *VANESSA*, was premiered at the METROPOLITAN OPERA (1938), was the first American opera staged at the Salzburg Festival, and won Barber his first Pulitzer Prize. Barber taught briefly at Curtis (1939–42) but did not join any faculty after that. In 1943, partly with the financial assistance of Mary Curtis Bok, Barber and Menotti purchased an estate in Mt. Kisco, New York, which they named Capricorn. Barber composed most of his middle-period work living there, while acting as reluctant host to the many creative luminaries attracted to the place.

Barber regarded his least successful work to be his Symphony no. 2, commissioned by the U.S. Army Airforce. Hoping to instill a military state of mind, the army shuttled Barber from base to base on a kind of inspirational tour. This distraction inhibited Barber's work, and after his death the *New York Times* obituary reported that Barber had visited his publisher's warehouse to personally destroy all existing copies of the symphony.

But it was a disastrous opera commission that turned the tables on Barber's career. As the new

LINCOLN CENTER FOR THE PERFORMING ARTS was nearing completion in New York during the mid-1960s, the Metropolitan Opera commissioned an operatic staging of Shakespeare's *Antony and Cleopatra* from Barber. (In 1962 Barber's new Piano Concerto, likewise commissioned by Lincoln Center, had opened PHILHARMONIC HALL and won Barber his second Pulitzer Prize.) *Antony and Cleopatra* would be performed at the gala opening of the new METROPOLITAN OPERA HOUSE, a $45 million edifice that was a focal point of the entire music world. The epic visionary Franco Zeffirelli designed the set production, and LEONTYNE PRICE sang the role of Cleopatra. The grand opening took place on September 16, 1966, and on September 17 the horrific reviews began dismantling Barber's world. Obvious technical difficulties (Price got stuck inside a pyramid) attracted the scorn of critics, but Barber's role in the fiasco was brought to task as well. Intellectual, academic music had taken hold in the 1960s, and Barber's adamantly conservative, lushly romantic musical styling was considered as much a part of the problem as Zeffirelli's overblown sets. Barber insisted that the opera contained some of his best work and engaged in sporadic attempts over the years to revise and revive the opera. A new version was performed at the JUILLIARD SCHOOL in 1975, but the opera never entered the standard repertoire.

From 1966 until his death in 1981, Barber continued receiving and completing commissions, though his stubbornly unmodern style was not as urgently sought by the music power centers as it had been. He struggled with depression, alcoholism, and creative dry spells. In the year of his death, Barber had just started composing again after a six-year drought, and he left an incomplete oboe concerto, the second movement of which was published posthumously.

Barbirolli, John (Sir) (1899–1970) *conductor*

Englishman Sir John Barbirolli made his mark on American classical music when he succeeded TOSCANINI as music director of the Philharmonic-Symphony Orchestra of New York (later to become the NEW YORK PHILHARMONIC). He was a third-generation musician in a family of Italian musicians settled in London, and he received his training at London's Trinity College of Music and the Royal Academy of Music also in London. He first conducted while serving in the army and, upon his discharge in 1919, pursued a career as an orchestral cellist. Barbirolli's conducting career picked up in 1928 when he was invited to lead the British National Opera Company. In 1931 he became permanent conductor of the Scottish Orchestra.

Barbirolli's directorship of the Philharmonic-Symphony of New York came after a 10-week stint as a guest conductor. When Toscanini moved on to lead the NBC SYMPHONY ORCHESTRA, the Philharmonic quickly appointed Barbirolli to replace him—after another respected European conductor with more experience, Wilhelm Furtwängler, refused the assignment. Barbirolli's first three-year contract was followed by another two-year term, but his tenure wasn't as happy as it might have seemed. Most observers at the time, and later historians, viewed these years as a period of deterioration for the orchestra, whose members were perhaps pining for the glamorous, exacting, departed Toscanini. Barbirolli left New York in 1943 and took control of the Hallé Orchestra in Manchester, England, an ensemble to which he devoted the rest of his career. He declined two invitations (1946 and 1950) to lead the BBC Symphony, a high-profile directorship that could be considered a British parallel to Toscanini's position with the NBC Symphony. Barbirolli's legacy remains primarily associated with the Hallé Orchestra, which he transformed from a small ensemble into one of Europe's finest full-sized orchestras.

Bard Music Festival

Founded in 1990 at Bard College in Annandale-on-Hudson, New York, the Bard Festival focuses on a single composer every year. The format is eclectic, involving multiple groups of performers in single concerts, and presentations of biographies, literature, painting, and theater. The main venue for the Bard Music Festival is the Richard B. Fisher Center for the Performing Arts. The festival was founded by LEON BOTSTEIN, who serves as its codirector.

Barenboim, Daniel (b. 1942) *pianist and conductor*

An Israeli pianist and conductor, Daniel Barenboim is currently the music director of the CHICAGO SYMPHONY ORCHESTRA. Barenboim studied piano with his parents as a child and made his concert debut in Vienna at the age of eight. His interest in conducting took hold early in life, and in 1954 Barenboim became the youngest conducting student of Russian composer and conductor Igor Markevich. At this time the legendary German conductor Wilhelm Furtwängler took Barenboim under his wing, helping the boy through the prodigy years. Barenboim was also taught and assisted by NADIA BOULANGER, ARTHUR RUBINSTEIN, and LEOPOLD STOKOWSKI. He made his New York piano debut with Stokowski and the Symphony of the Air. In 1960, at age 18, Barenboim performed the complete cycle of Beethoven Sonatas—a difficult feat at any age. During the 1960s Barenboim established his conducting career in Europe. During this time he met cellist Jacqueline du Pré, whom he later married.

Barenboim's conducting career began with the English Chamber Orchestra, with which he performed Mozart piano concertos in the dual roles of pianist and conductor. The English Chamber Orchestra provided his main conducting platform well into the 1970s. From 1975 to 1989, Barenboim was the music director of the Orchestre de Paris, with which he performed an extensive modern repertoire, he also founded the chorus of that orchestra.

Barenboim conducted the Chicago Symphony Orchestra for the first time in 1970, in four concerts. Between 1975 and 1989 he was music director of L'Orchestre de Paris. Then, in 1989, the CSO named Barenboim as successor to SIR GEORG SOLTI, who had led the orchestra for 20 years in a legendary collaboration. Barenboim took over as the ninth music director in Chicago in the fall of 1991. Also in that year, Barenboim's autobiography, *A Life in Music,* was published.

Barere, Simon (1896–1951) *pianist*

Simon Barere was a great, if underrecognized, piano virtuoso of the 20th century. Born in Odessa, Russia, the 11th of 13 children, Barere took lessons from siblings and a neighbor, then helped support the family from an early age playing in restaurants and movie houses. After playing for the composer Aleksandr Glazunov in St. Petersburg, Barere entered the music conservatory of that city, while continuing to play casual music for money. Barere won the Rubinstein Prize upon his graduation in 1919, at which point he made his well-known remark, "Barere is Franz Liszt in the one hand and Anton Rubinstein in the other." Out of school, Barere taught at the Kiev Conservatory while establishing himself as a concert artist. He was not permitted to tour outside the Soviet Union but, in 1932, succeeded in moving with his wife to Berlin. There, affected by the persecution of Jews, Barere was not able to perform as a classical artist, and again resorted to playing in restaurants.

Barere's career took off after his British debut in 1934, which resulted in a recording contract. He made his American debut in CARNEGIE HALL on November 9, 1936, and received glowing notices. Barere moved his family to the United States, and from this base he toured globally. When the Philips record company released its 200-CD series, *Great Pianists of the 20th Century,* some observers complained that Barere was excluded. The pianist's legacy is mixed: an undeniable technical wizard who did not always offer interpretive depth. He was best in showpieces by Liszt and Godowski. Writing in the *New York Times* after a Barere piano recital in 1949, Noel Straus exclaimed over "one of the most amazing feats of pianism heard in this city in many a year." Other critics agreed but also noted that Barere's Chopin and Beethoven were unconvincing. During his life, Barere played in the top concert halls to general acclaim. He died suddenly of a cerebral hemorrhage while performing in Carnegie Hall.

Barili, Alfredo (1854–1935) *musician*

Generally identified as the first professional musician in Atlanta, Georgia, who introduced a wide range of classical works to that city, Alfredo Barili was a pianist, conductor, and teacher. He was born to a family of musicians and made his New York playing debut at age 11, before his family moved to Philadelphia, where Barili continued studying. He attended the Cologne Conservatory in Germany, then moved to Atlanta in 1880. In 1883 he founded the Atlanta Music Festival, which hosted orchestras from other cities.

Barzin, Leon (1900–1999) *conductor*

Not a legendary but an influential conductor, Leon Barzin is best remembered as a teacher of conducting and orchestral playing, and as a founder of the New York City Ballet. He moved to the United States as a two-year-old and became a citizen in 1924. His father, the first violist of the Metropolitan Opera Orchestra, taught Leon violin and viola. Barzin continued instrumental studies with a series of violin masters, including EUGÈNE YSAŸE. He played in the house orchestra of the Hotel Astor as a teenager with the NATIONAL SYMPHONY ORCHESTRA, and he eventually earned the first viola chair of the NEW YORK PHILHARMONIC, where he played from 1925 to 1929. A career turning point occurred when TOSCANINI, the orchestra's music director, asked Barzin to conduct during a rehearsal while Toscanini listened from the back of the hall. When Toscanini took back the baton, he advised Barzin to concentrate on a conducting career.

Barzin became music director of the National Orchestral Association, a training orchestra for young instrumentalists, in 1930. He remained at this position for nearly 30 years, until 1959, and returned to it from 1969 to 1976, when he retired. Barzin is credited, during this tenure, of training the largest group of instrumentalists ever influenced by a single conductor, thousands of whom moved into positions—sometimes first-chair positions—with major metropolitan orchestras. Barzin was invariably kind to young musicians, while exposing them to exacting standards and unstinting critiques of their playing. He was also the music director of New York's Ballet Society (1948–58), which became the New York City Ballet.

Bassett, Leslie (b. 1923) *composer*

A Pulitzer Prize–winning composer, Leslie Bassett early studied piano, trombone, and cello. He spent three years in the army during World War II as a

Leslie Bassett (Courtesy of Leslie Bassett; Photo by Richard Singleton)

musician, playing trombone in orchestras, conducting, and arranging music. Later he was the principal trombonist of the Fresno Symphony Orchestra in California. Bassett studied composition with ROSS LEE FINNEY, his greatest influence, and also with NADIA BOULANGER, Arthur Honegger, and MARIO DAVIDOVSKY. Associated with the faculty of the University of Michigan since 1952, he became the chair of the composition department in 1970; he was named Albert A. Stanley Distinguished University Professor of Music in 1977 and Henry Russel Lecturer in 1980. Bassett won the 1966 Pultizer Prize for his Variations for Orchestra. He has been awarded two Guggenheim Fellowships, a Naumberg Foundation Award, and a Rockefeller Foundation grant.

Battle, Kathleen (b. 1948) *opera singer*

Kathleen Battle attended the University of Cincinnati College Conservatory, and for a time after graduation she became a public school teacher. While teaching she auditioned for various productions and, in 1972, sang the soprano solo in Brahms's A German Requiem at the SPOLETO FESTIVAL. She met conductor JAMES LEVINE and began a collaboration that furthered both their careers. In 1976 she sang at the NEW YORK CITY OPERA. Battle's METROPOLITAN OPERA debut followed five years after the Spoleto appearance, when she sang in Wagner's *Tannhäuser.*

One of the most popular sopranos of her time, Battle has had a career marked by accolades on stage contrasted with trouble behind the scenes. In an extraordinary 1994 incident, Battle was fired from the Metropolitan Opera due to "unprofessional actions" during rehearsals for an upcoming production in which she was hired to star. A year earlier, Battle had quit another Metropolitan production in midrehearsal. Reports of temperamental behavior have followed Battle through much of her later career; an entertainment magazine once referred to her as "arguably the most hated person in the music business." Industry turmoil notwith-standing, Battle has remained a favorite among audiences and music collectors.

Bauer, Harold (1873–1951) *pianist*

Born in England, Harold Bauer took American citizenship in 1924. As a child, Bauer received lessons in both piano and violin, and continued pursuing both instruments to the age of 15, when he gave a concert featuring both. Concentrating during his later teen years on the violin, Bauer did not turn wholeheartedly to the piano until encouraged to do so by pianist Ignacy Paderewski, when Bauer was in his early twenties. Thinking himself too old for conventional lessons, Bauer became a self-taught virtuoso, developing a novel technique and an intellectual approach to music. After 1896 he lived in Paris for four years, acquainting himself with composers Debussy, Ravel, and Saint-Saëns, cellist Pablo Casals, and violinist FRITZ KREISLER. Later, Bauer was one of the first touring pianists to introduce the impressionistic music of Debussy and Ravel to American audiences. Ravel dedicated his "Ondine" (one movement of the piano suite *Gaspard de la Nuit*) to Bauer.

Bauer made his American debut in 1900, playing the first piano concerto of Brahms with the BOSTON SYMPHONY ORCHESTRA. In 1918 he founded the Beethoven Society in New York; the organization promoted a wide range of classical music in its concerts. Bauer wrote on musical subjects and edited scores for the music publisher G. Schirmer. He was head of the piano department at the MANHATTAN SCHOOL OF MUSIC. His autobiography, *Harold Bauer, His Book,* was published in 1948.

Bauer, Marion (1882–1955) *composer*

One of the most successful female composers of the early 20th century, Marion Bauer was also an educator, writer, and institutional administrator. Her writings about music are better remembered today than her musical compositions. She studied composition in America and abroad, and was reportedly the first

American student of NADIA BOULANGER in Paris. Her early work tended toward small-scale pieces for piano and songs; as her career matured she explored larger forms, eventually composing a string quartet, a violin sonata, and a symphony, among other works. Her piano concerto was commissioned by the High School of Music and Art in New York. Her *Sun Splendor* was premiered by the NEW YORK PHILHARMONIC under STOKOWSKI. Bauer was a regular summer visitor to the MACDOWELL COLONY, an artist residency program at which she met other pioneering women musicians, including AMY BEACH. Throughout her mature career, Bauer was an advocate of other (especially younger) American composers, introducing them to powerful musicians and critics who could help their careers.

Bauer was one of the first music historians of American birth. Her magnum opus was the now-dated *Twentieth Century Music* (1933, second edition 1947). Other books include *How Music Grew* (1925, rev. 1939) and *Music Through the Ages* (1932). She consistently championed modern music in her teaching and promotional work. As a music critic, Bauer contributed to the journals *Modern Music* and *Musical Quarterly,* and edited *Etude.* Bauer was cofounder of both the AMERICAN MUSIC CENTER and the American Music Guild. She taught history and composition at New York University from 1926 to 1951, and joined the faculty of the Juilliard School of Music (later the JUILLIARD SCHOOL) in 1940.

Bauer, Ross (b. 1951) *composer*

Ross Bauer is head of the music department at the University of California, Davis. Trained at the NEW ENGLAND CONSERVATORY, Bauer helped found the Griffin Music Ensemble. He also founded the Empyrean Ensemble at Davis. Bauer's awards and grants include a Guggenheim Fellowship, the Walter Hinrichsen Award from the American Academy of Arts and Letters, Fromm Foundation commissions, and a Koussevitsky commission. His work has been performed by the SAINT PAUL CHAMBER ORCHESTRA and the New York New Music Ensemble, among other groups. At least three CDs of Bauer's music have been released. A review of Bauer's *Icons,* a concerto for bassoon and orchestra, stated: "Bauer's style is quite international—somewhat reminiscent of the works of Schoenberg and Berg, but with an American love of percussion and percussive sounds in the manner of Edgard Varese."

Bay Psalm Book

Perhaps the earliest music publication in America, the full title of this tune book was *The Psalms, Hymns, and Spiritual Songs of the Old and New Testament.* The book contained generic tunes to which biblical psalms could be sung. The tunes were set to common meters that fit the psalms' words and were of European origin. These tunes were not American music by any definition; they represented America's earliest attempt to organize and publish music. Various editions of this book were published in the late 17th century.

Beach, Amy (born Cheney; aka Mrs. H. H. A. Beach) (1867–1944) *composer*

A true pioneer and prodigy, Amy Beach is the most prominent woman in the history of American composers. Childhood feats include being able to sing a repertoire of songs with perfect pitch at the age of one, singing in harmony at age two, and playing four-part hymns on the piano at age four. Beach's mother began teaching her piano formally at age six. The following year, Beach played Beethoven, Handel, Chopin, and her own pieces in public. She played her solo debut in Boston in 1883 and her concerto debut with the BOSTON SYMPHONY ORCHESTRA in 1885. That year she married Henry Harris Aubrey Beach and, at his request, curtailed her public performances for the most part. She resumed her concert career after her husband's death in 1910.

During her married years, Beach became the first American woman to create large-scale works, including a symphony, piano concerto, and the Mass in E-flat. Her first published work was a song ("The Rainy Day"), issued in 1883. Many of her works were performed, sometimes by top-ranked ensembles such as the Boston Symphony. She was largely self-taught as a composer and learned the fundamentals of orchestration by laboriously translating a tutorial on the subject by French composer Hector Berlioz. After 1910, Beach toured Europe before settling in New Hampshire. Her annual work cycle included touring as a piano recitalist in winter and composing in summer. She was an energetic promoter of her work. She cofounded and presided over the Society of American Women Composers.

Beach, John Parsons (1877–1953) *pianist and stage composer*

John Beach was one of the composers published in the WA-WAN PRESS, founded by ARTHUR FARWELL. Beach studied piano in Boston and in Europe; his teachers included HAROLD BAUER. He studied composition with GEORGE CHADWICK and CHARLES MARTIN LOEFFLER. Beach composed two small-scale operas, *Pippa's Holiday* (staged in 1915) and *Jorinda and Jorindel* (1909).

Beaser, Robert (b. 1954) *composer*

A composer who has been compared to Samuel Barber, Robert Beaser attended Yale University, obtaining a doctor of musical arts degree in 1986. His composition teachers included JACOB DRUCKMAN and EARLE BROWN. He studied conducting at TANGLEWOOD. He was the composer in residence with the AMERICAN COMPOSERS ORCHESTRA and joined the faculty of the JUILLIARD SCHOOL in 1993. He was the youngest recipient of the Prix de Rome (1977), was awarded Guggenheim and Fulbright fellowships, and received a Grammy nomination for a recording of his best-known work, *Mountain Songs*, in 1985. Beaser has composed commissions for the Saint Louis Symphony ORCHESTRA, CHICAGO SYMPHONY ORCHESTRA, BALTIMORE SYMPHONY ORCHESTRA, and NEW YORK PHILHARMONIC. As one of the anti-academic composers of the 1980s and 1990s, Beaser merges European tradition with American styles that developed through the 20th century.

Beaux Arts Trio

This internationally lauded performing and recording trio was founded as a convergence of virtuosos in 1955. The original members were Menahem Pressler (piano), Daniel Guilet (violin), and BERNARD GREENHOUSE (cello). Pressler remains the pianist nearly 50 years later. Other current members are Daniel Hope (violin) and Antonio Meneses (cello). The group's discography, recorded over five decades, is exhaustive and unadventurous. The group is not known for commissioning new works or championing contemporary composers. Virtually the entire standard trio repertoire, including complete piano trios of Beethoven, Haydn, Mozart, DVOŘÁK, Fauré, Schubert, and Ravel have been committed to disc.

Beck, Johann H. (1856–1924) *conductor, composer, and violinist*

Johann Beck studied in Germany, where he gave his violin and compositional debut. Upon returning to the United States, Beck formed both the Schubert String Quartet and the Beck String Quartet. He was music director of the DETROIT SYMPHONY ORCHESTRA for the 1895–96 season and guest-conducted many orchestras in Cleveland and elsewhere. Though most of his music remained unpublished, it was readily performed, frequently under his baton. He specialized in chamber music (four string quartets and a sextet) and vocal music.

Becker, John J. (1886–1961) *composer and teacher*

John Becker was one of the so-called American Five (with IVES, RUGGLES, COWELL, and RIEGGER), though the least remembered of that avant-garde alliance of composers. Becker studied at Cincinnati University, from which he graduated in 1905, and he attained a doctorate in composition from Wisconsin University in 1923. He taught at the college level for many years, from 1917 nearly to his death, mostly at Catholic colleges in the Midwest. He was an energetic proponent of modern music, introducing the works of his fellow American Five composers to middle-America audiences. He was especially close to Charles Ives. However, Becker's own music was largely neglected. His early work was neo-romantic, but Becker was profoundly influenced by progressive American styles, and after 1920 his music became more dissonant and experimental.

Belcher, Supply (1751–1836) songwriter

In an era before music was considered a realistic full-time profession, Belcher owned and ran a tavern, served as town clerk of Farmington, Massachusetts, worked as a schoolteacher, and was also known as a singer and violinist. The main compositional activity of that time in New England was sacred songwriting. Composers typically compiled the songs of others into "tune books," in which their own songs might be placed. Belcher is known to have written 75 songs, all of which appear in his 1794 compilation, *The Harmony of Maine.*

Bell, Joshua (b. 1967) violinist

Joshua Bell's talent reportedly attracted his parents' attention when, at the age of four, he picked out tunes on rubber bands stretched around the handles of his dresser drawers. As a child he studied with Mimi Zweig, then with JOSEPH GINGOLD at the University of Indiana, Bloomington. He made his debut with the Philadelphia Orchestra in 1981. Bell has since performed with numerous top orchestras, as well as with a variety of chamber ensembles. He signed his first recording contract in 1979, at age 18. He also conducts, and in 2002 took the Academy of St.-Martin-in-the-Fields on a

Joshua Bell (Courtesy of JAG Entertainment; Photo by Timothy White)

13-city tour. His discography as a violinist is extensive, covering most of the standard repertoire. Bell is an active crossover artist, performing in nonclassical genres with WYNTON MARSALIS, Bela Fleck, and others. He contributed as composer and player to the soundtrack of the movie *The Red Violin,* which won an Academy Award for Best Original Score (composed by JOHN CORIGLIANO). He has made a video and appeared on numerous talk shows. Bell is an adjunct professor at MIT's Media Lab.

Bennett, Robert Russell (1894–1981) arranger and composer

Though listed in reference books as a composer, Robert Russell Bennett specialized in arranging the music of other composers, and he was the most prolific and successful orchestrator in the history of American music. He studied with NADIA

BOULANGER in Paris—a résumé point that generally led in its time to a career in classical music. But like many musicians, Bennett took whatever work he could find early in his career. He worked as a copyist and arranger at the music publisher G. SCHIRMER. After fulfilling a commission to orchestrate some of popular songwriter Cole Porter's songs, Bennett's reputation as a naturally skillful arranger grew quickly. Broadway was the obvious venue for his talent, as theater orchestras are small and it is difficult to arrange music effectively for them. For over 40 years, Bennett orchestrated other composers' music to some or all of about 300 Broadway shows, including *Kiss Me Kate, Oklahoma!, The Sound of Music,* and *Camelot.* This work included writing pieces of incidental music for entrances, exits, dance numbers, and overtures. Bennett worked as a film arranger in Hollywood from 1936 to 1940. After 1945 he executed commissions for NBC television, both as an arranger and a composer.

During the course of this high-volume contract work, Bennett composed art music—pure classical music—on the side. His portfolio includes seven symphonies and a handful of operas. His best-remembered opera, *Maria Melibran,* was premiered at the JUILLIARD SCHOOL to mixed reviews. But it is his Broadway and film work that anchors Bennett's posthumous legacy. His book *Instrumentally Speaking* (1975) remains the definitive treatise on arranging and orchestrating for theater orchestras.

Berger, Arthur (1912–2003) *composer, critic, scholar, and educator*

Arthur Berger was closely associated with Russian composer Igor Stravinsky, whose work he defended when it was going out of style, and AARON COPLAND, with whom he studied at TANGLEWOOD and who was a mentor to Berger's generation of composers. Copland called Berger, IRVING FINE, and HAROLD SHAPERO the "Stravinsky School." He studied piano as a boy and attained his music degree from New York University. He joined Copland's Young Composers Group and received a master's degree from Harvard University (1936). At Harvard he studied composition with WALTER PISTON, in whose classes he met Fine and Shapero, all of whom were influenced by Piston's lessons and writing style. He was in Paris from 1937 to 1939 for the obligatory lessons with NADIA BOULANGER (many American composers studied in her Parisian studio), and he also worked with French composer DARIUS MILHAUD.

Berger's teaching career began early, with a 1939 appointment to the faculty of Mills College in Oakland, California. He worked at Brooklyn College, the JUILLIARD SCHOOL, and Brandeis University in Waltham, Massachusetts (hired at the latter by his friend Shapero, who founded the music school at Brandeis). Berger joined the faculty at the NEW ENGLAND CONSERVATORY in 1979. As a music critic, Berger's articles appeared in the *Boston Transcript, New York Sun, New York Herald Tribune,* and *Perspectives in New Music.*

As a composer, Berger won a Fulbright Scholarship in 1960 and a Guggenheim Fellowship in 1975. He was a member of the American Academy of Arts and Sciences.

Bergmann, Carl (1821–1876) *conductor*

Born in Germany and a lifelong champion of the music of his countryman Richard Wagner, Carl Bergman became an American conductor who directed three important Wagner premieres in the United States. He emigrated to the United States in 1849, after gaining conducting experience in Europe. In Boston he led the Germania Musical Society until its dissolution in 1854, at which time he settled in New York. Bergmann was chief conductor of the PHILHARMONIC SYMPHONY SOCIETY OF NEW YORK intermittently from 1855 to 1876. He directed the first performance of Wagner's opera *Tannhäuser* on April 4, 1859—the first American performance of a complete Wagner opera. In 1852 Bergmann conducted the first U.S. performance of

Wagner's music, and the following year he led America's first all-Wagner concert.

Bergsma, William (1921–1994) *composer and teacher*

William Bergsma studied at the University of Rochester and the Eastman School, obtaining degrees in 1942 and 1943. He taught composition at the Juilliard School of Music (later JUILLIARD SCHOOL) from 1946 to 1963, then joined the faculty of the University of Washington, where he was director of the School of Music from 1963 to 1971. A conservative composer who never veered toward the academic genre of 12-tone composition, Bergsma received two Guggenheim Fellowships, an American Academy of Arts and Letters award, and the Bearns Prize from Columbia University. He left two ballets, two operas, several orchestral works, a handful of songs, and solo and chamber music.

Berman, Boris (b. 1948) *pianist*

An American of Russian birth, Boris Berman emigrated to the United States via Israel, where he lived from 1973 to 1979. His formal study was at the Moscow Conservatory from 1965 to 1971, where he worked with Lev Oborin. Berman teaches piano at Yale University, where he headed the piano department from 1984 to 1997. During this period Berman founded and directed the Yale Music Spectrum series. An eager recording artist with a large discography, Berman was the first pianist to record all the piano music of Russian composer Sergey Prokofiev, and he has also recorded all of Aleksandr Scriabin's piano sonatas. His book *Notes from the Piano Bench* was published in 2000. As of the 2003-season, Berman actively toured internationally, as a concerto performer and recitalist.

Berkshire Music Center See TANGLEWOOD MUSIC CENTER.

Bernstein, Leonard (born Louis) (1918–1990) *conductor*

Arguably the most famous American-born classical musician, Leonard Bernstein certainly was the first to gain global renown. Primarily identified with his conducting work, Bernstein was also a pianist, composer, educator, and musical ambassador.

Born to a family of Russian émigrés with strong religious ties to Talmudic Judaism, Bernstein began piano lessons at age 10. Two years later he started piano studies with Susan Williams at the NEW ENGLAND CONSERVATORY OF MUSIC. He gave his first piano recital in his high school at 16 years, and that same year he appeared in his first radio broadcast in Boston. Attending Harvard University, Bernstein studied composition with EDWARD BURLINGAME HILL and WALTER PISTON. During his student years he met AARON COPLAND, who was to become an important influence, mentor, and colleague. At Harvard Bernstein tried his hand at stage composition, which was to become a staple of his composition work, when he wrote music for a production of the ancient Greek comedy *The Birds,* and conducted the performance (1939, his first appearance as a conductor).

Bernstein graduated from Harvard in 1939. In 1940 he spent the first of many summers at the Berkshire Music Center in TANGLEWOOD, studying conducting with SERGE KOUSSEVITZKY, Tanglewood's founder and conducting icon for many years. That year he also completed a short course of postgraduate work at the CURTIS INSTITUTE OF MUSIC, where his teachers included FRITZ REINER (conducting) and RANDALL THOMPSON (composing). In 1942, Bernstein became Koussevitzky's assistant at Tanglewood. Like many young composers, Bernstein put in time working for a publishing company, Harms (1942–43), where he transcribed the playing of jazz pianists and wrote arrangements under the name Lenny Amber.

In 1943, Bernstein's seminal relationship with the NEW YORK PHILHARMONIC (at that time still usually called the Philharmonic-Symphony Society of New York) began when he was named Assistant

Conductor under ARTUR RODZINSKI. On November 14, scheduled conductor Bruno Walter fell ill, and Bernstein's fame was launched. Notified in the morning that he would be conducting that afternoon's nationally broadcast concert, Bernstein spent a few hours studying the Schumann, Rozsa, Strauss, and Wagner scores on the program and took the podium with no outward sign of nervousness. The audience was on his side by intermission, and was cheering by the end. Reviews on page one of the *New York Times* and elsewhere notified the musical world that a new luminary had arrived. Rodzinski was quick to capitalize on this opportunity for Bernstein and scheduled him to rehearse and conduct the orchestra in four concerts the following month.

At this time Bernstein had been composing seriously and with some recognition; the premiere of his first symphony (entitled *Jeremiah*) was already

Leonard Bernstein (Bettmann/Corbis)

scheduled in Pittsburgh later that season (January 28, 1944). It won the New York Music Critics' Circle award for best American work. That year saw the divergence of Bernstein's classical and popular stage career: his music for the ballet *Fancy Free* was premiered at the METROPOLITAN OPERA HOUSE, and his musical *On the Town* opened on Broadway. Through the remainder of the 1940s, Bernstein guest-conducted in the United States and Israel, and continued composing works for the concert and popular stages. He was conductor of the New York City Symphony from 1945 to 1948, where he worked without salary.

In the 1950s, Bernstein attained international recognition and continued diversifying his talent. He and Koussevitzky took the Israel Philharmonic on a three-month European tour in 1951. When Koussevitzky died on June 5, Bernstein took his mentor's place as head of the orchestra and conducting departments at Tanglewood. He was the first American to take the podium for an opera production at Italy's La Scala (1953, *Medea*). In 1954 he wrote the film score to *On the Waterfront*. In 1955 he was appointed to the composition faculty at Brandeis University. In 1956 he was named one of two principal conductors of the New York Philharmonic, sharing the job with DMITRI MITROPOULOS. During this eventful decade Bernstein became a family man, marrying the Chilean actress Felicia Montealegre Cohn in 1951; the couple would raise three children.

West Side Story premiered in 1957 at the Winter Garden Theater in New York. This dramatic musical has become Bernstein's identifying composition. It was conceived six years before its eventual opening; the original version was titled *East Side Story*. Bernstein had originally planned to write the music lyrics himself, but in the end he turned to the then-unknown Stephen Sondheim. The Winter Garden production ran for 732 performances before starting its touring life. A 1961 film version starred Richard Beymer and Natalie Wood.

Inevitably (in 1958), Bernstein became the sole music director of the New York Philharmonic, the first American-born conductor (and the youngest conductor) to earn that post in the 116-year history of the orchestra. He remained at the job until 1969, at which time he was named laureate conductor for life. He returned frequently to guest-conduct. Bernstein's tenure with the Philharmonic was notable for his energy, commitment to modern music, and emphasis on music appreciation, education, and community outreach. He immediately began the long-running televised series of *Young People's Concerts* (1958–71) and was not shy about addressing the audience with informal lectures from the podium. When he stepped down in 1969, he had conducted more concerts than any of his predecessors and had programmed 36 world premieres. Some observers believe the orchestra has never, before or since, programmed such a balanced blend of standard and unconventional repertoire.

After retiring from the directorship of the Philharmonic, Bernstein became a musical celebrity-at-large. He conducted all over the world, attended festivals in his honor, and wrote books. On September 8, 1971, his Mass was performed at the gala inaugural of the KENNEDY CENTER FOR THE PERFORMING ARTS. He made his Metropolitan Opera debut in 1972, conducting Bizet's *Carmen*. A concert celebration of his 60th birthday, at WOLF TRAP, Virginia, was televised internationally. He took temporary residential teaching positions at Harvard and Indiana Universities and gave conducting master classes at the Los Angeles Philharmonic Institute. Immediately following his 70th birthday, Bernstein took the Vienna Philharmonic and the London Philharmonic on European tours. His final New York concert was at Carnegie Hall on March 11, 1990, leading the Vienna Philharmonic. His final conducting appearance was at Tanglewood on August 19. Bernstein died on October 14 in New York.

Along with popular adulation, Bernstein suffered through mixed reviews from sometimes savage critics. His irrepressible populism and unorthodox training as a conductor were the easiest targets for music traditionalists. Critics thought he should concentrate on one field, whether it be conducting, composing, writing for theater, educating, or concertizing on the piano. To the end, Bernstein remained staunch and unapologetic in his diversity. "I don't want to spend my life as Toscanini did, studying and restudying the same 50 pieces of music," he once wrote in the *New York Times*. Bernstein's outsized and crowd-pleasing conducting style, full of grand gestures and leaps that occasionally sent him tumbling off the podium, displeased purists and thrilled audiences. While he revivified the New York Philharmonic, which had declined in quality and popularity when he took over in 1958, some colleagues resented Bernstein's uncanny ability to generate publicity for himself.

Throughout a long and varied career, Bernstein seemed constitutionally incapable of slowing down or refusing to conquer new fields of endeavor. At the end, even his harshest, most puritan critics had to concede that his classical work contained points of lasting value to the musical world. His performances and recordings of Mahler's symphonies, representing years of near obsession, helped launch a Mahler revival of global scope. And he introduced the music of many American composers, including ELLIOTT CARTER, MILTON BABBITT, JOHN CAGE, and Gunther Schuller, to U.S. concert audiences. If his legacy is mixed, it is just as enduring, and Bernstein will likely remain a permanent iconic figure in American classical music.

Bethune, Thomas (Blind Tom) (1849–1908)
musician

Blind from birth, Thomas Bethune was an autistic savant and musical prodigy of remarkable dimensions. From a young age, he could play pieces after hearing them once and could mimic almost any sound. Reportedly one of 21 siblings, and raised in a slave family owned by James N. Bethune, Tom received piano lessons from Bethune's daughter. When he was eight years old, Tom was exhibited locally by Bethune. From the age of nine, Tom was toured for several years throughout the South by an

Blind Tom Bethune (Public Domain)

entrepreneur named Perry Olliver, who, in effect, rented Tom from Bethune. In addition to performing the standard virtuoso repertoire, Tom's act featured stunts such as repeating any piece performed once by an audience member and playing with his back to the keyboard. During this period he played for President Buchanan in the White House, garnering renown that would lead to European travels. In Europe, Tom heard Josef Hofmann and Ignacy Paderewski play, and met and played for Hofmann.

During Tom's career, which lasted into his forties, his promoters earned hundreds of thousands of dollars, very little of which was paid to Tom or his parents. Otherwise he was not badly treated by the Bethunes (who, after the Civil War, became his legal guardians). Between concert tours he lived on a large estate in Virginia, where he had a Steinway concert grand piano. In 1887 the Bethunes lost a custody case brought by Tom's mother and the widow of John Bethune, James Bethune's son. Tom moved from Virginia to New York against his will and continued to be exhibited on tours. His popularity eventually waned through overexposure, and Tom's retirement passed in a comfortable home, with caretakers and a piano, in New Jersey. Tom composed several parlor pieces for piano, some of which attempted to convey sounds of nature. None of them entered the standard repertoire.

Billings, William (1746–1800) *composer*

Often regarded as America's first native-born composer, William Billings was one of several New England musicians who wrote hymns and songs in the last few decades of the 18th century. Most songbooks of the day compiled music from many composers; Billings was the first composer to publish a book exclusively of his own music. Mostly self-taught as a composer, Billings was a career singing teacher whose work took him through New England and affiliated him with Boston's most prosperous churches. Financial difficulties beset him, though, and by 1790 Billings was desperately seeking a new publisher. In 1795 his wife died, leaving him the care of their six children. The circumstances of his last years are unknown.

Billings composed well over 300 pieces for four-part chorus. Some of his pieces experiment with fugue, which, in Billings's time and place, was an esoteric and advanced art form. His landmark book of Billings-only music, *The New England Psalm-Singer,* was published in 1770. Billings attempted to copyright the book, but officials in England (still America's sovereign nation) blocked his effort. According to the prevailing practice, Billings's work was freely reprinted in other compilations, reducing his income. In 1778 he published *The Singing Master's Assistant,* a compilation of his most popular work. His hymn "An Anthem for Easter" is Billings's best-remembered single work.

Billy the Kid (1938)

One of three major ballet scores composed by AARON COPLAND, this one for the Ballet Caravan of Lincoln Kirstein. Its first performance was on

November 9, 1940, in New York, by WILLIAM STEINBERG leading the NBC SYMPHONY ORCHESTRA.

Bilson, Malcolm (b. 1935) *pioneering fortepianist*

Bilson's research and recordings helped establish a movement toward using authentic period instruments when performing music of the late 18th and early 19th centuries. He received a bachelor of arts from Bard College in 1957, then a doctor of musical arts from the University of Illinois in 1968. (Bilson was awarded an honorary doctorate from Bard in 1991.) He formed the Amadé Trio in 1974. Bilson's discography includes the complete Beethoven piano sonatas, the complete Mozart piano sonatas, the complete Mozart piano concertos, the complete Schubert piano sonatas, and much chamber music—all on historically accurate instruments. Bilson received a Fulbright Scholarship (1957–59) and a Harriet Hale Woolley Fellowship (1959–60). He has given master classes on several continents and joined the faculty of Cornell University in 1968, where he is currently the Frederick J. Whiton Professor of Music.

Bing, Rudolf (Sir) (1902–1997) *manager*

Born in Austria and later a British citizen, Rudolf Bing was the general manager of the METROPOLITAN OPERA in New York for 22 years, exerting tremendous influence over the staging and perception of opera in America. He held executive positions in European opera houses from 1930 to 1949 and, in 1946, helped found the Edinburgh Festival. Bing took charge of the Metropolitan Opera in 1950, quickly integrating the historically all-white company. He implemented sophisticated ideas and techniques in set design and direction, and once said, "We are similar to a museum. My function is to present old masterpieces in modern frames." He appeared on the cover of *Time* magazine on September 23, 1966. Bing's reign at the Met was the second-longest in the company's history.

Bliss, Anthony (1913–1991) *director and manager*

Anthony Bliss was executive director of the METROPOLITAN OPERA in New York from 1974 to 1981, then general manager (succeeding John Dexter) from 1981 to 1985.

Blitzstein, Marc (1905–1964) *seminal American composer*

Marc Blitzstein merged music with political activism. Growing up in Philadelphia and California, Blitzstein studied piano and performed a Mozart piano concerto when he was seven. A more professional debut occurred when he was 21; he played a Liszt piano concerto with the PHILADELPHIA ORCHESTRA. Blitzstein studied composition at the CURTIS INSTITUTE OF MUSIC, then embarked for Europe in 1926. There, he worked with Austrian composer Arnold Schoenberg and NADIA BOULANGER. In 1928, having returned to the United States, Blitzstein married Eva Goldbeck, despite his open homosexuality. With Goldbeck, Blitzstein found a true meeting of minds and political inclinations. During this time he composed for the piano, including the Piano Sonata (1927) and the Percussion Music for Piano (1929), the latter of which featured sounds created by slapping and slamming the keyboard lid.

Blitzstein composed pure music and was also an important theater composer and producer. His most successful theater piece was not entirely original; Blitzstein translated *The Threepenny Opera* (words by Bertold Brecht, music by Kurt Weill), which enjoyed a six-year run on Broadway. This production represented an about-face of Blitzstein's musical ideology, from snobbish intellectualism to new-found populism. Earlier in his career he had publicly scorned Weill and his less-than-highbrow work; the *Threepenny* translation marked a repudiation of his earlier attitude. From the late 1920s, Blitzstein was a card-carrying American communist, and was investigated more than once in the late 1950s. His ideology didn't prevent him from serving in World War II, which, in his mind, was sanctioned when the Soviet Union joined the Allies after being attacked by Germany in 1941. Musically, Blitzstein's extreme leftism was reflected in harsh criticism of opulent music; he called Ravel's *Bolero* an "opium package." In his own work, particularly the stage pieces, Blitzstein popularized and championed the common person against forces of industry and capitalism. The premiere of his play-with-music, *The Cradle Will Rock,* was delayed because its union-thumping was considered too inflammatory. His best-remembered opera, *Regina,* a rewrite of a play called *The Little Foxes* by Lillian Hellman, is set in the American South and is less political.

Goldbeck died in 1936. In 1939, Blitzstein met LEONARD BERNSTEIN, and the two formed a close personal and professional relationship.

Bloch, Ernest (1880–1959) *composer*
A composer of music derived from philosophical and religious (Jewish) themes, Ernest Bloch was born in Switzerland and settled in the United States in 1916. He studied violin and composition in

Ernest Bloch (Courtesy of G. Schirmer)

France and Germany. Bloch first traveled to the United States as the second violinist in the Flonzaley Quartet, and when the tour ended Bloch accepted a teaching position at the MANNES COLLEGE OF MUSIC in New York. He quickly established himself as a composer, especially of Jewish-themed music. From 1916 to 1918 Bloch saw the premieres of his String Quartet no. 1, the orchestral piece *Trois poèmes juifs* by the BOSTON SYMPHONY ORCHESTRA, and one of his best-known works, *Schelomo,* for cello and orchestra. The music publisher G. SCHIRMER signed Bloch to a publishing deal in 1918.

Bloch was a founder of the CLEVELAND INSTITUTE OF MUSIC, and he directed that school from 1920 to 1925. He was then appointed director of the SAN FRANCISCO CONSERVATORY OF MUSIC (1925–30). Though he had been naturalized as an American citizen in 1924, Bloch moved to Switzerland in 1930, composing there with the support of a grant from the University of California at Berkeley. He returned in 1940 to teach at Berkeley. Bloch was awarded the Gold Medal in Music from the American Academy of Arts and Sciences, and the Henry Hadley Medal. Bloch wrote emotional, neoromantic music that ignored the academic and atonal movements in fashion during his career. When it came to the ethnoreligious quality of his music, Bloch stated he was more interested in conveying the Jewish soul than Jewish music per se.

Blood on the Fields (1994)
An oratorio by jazz-classical trumpeter and composer WYNTON MARSALIS, *Blood on the Fields* won the 1997 Pulitzer Prize. The work is scored for large jazz band and treats the subject of American slavery. It was premiered at Yale University on January 28, 1997.

Blossom Music Center
Founded in 1968, the Blossom Music Center is the summer home of the CLEVELAND ORCHESTRA. Blossom is located in the Cuyahoga Valley National

Blossom Music Center (Courtesy of the Cleveland Orchestra)

Park. The facility is named for the Dudley S. Blossom family, which was a supporter of the Cleveland Orchestra for many years. The orchestra hosts a summer festival, directed by Jahja Ling since 2000. The Blossom Pavilion, the centerpiece of the facility, is an outdoor, roofed venue of striking design that seats over 5,000 people beneath the roof and over 13,000 more on the surrounding lawns. The entire Blossom campus was renovated at a cost of $17 million in 2003.

Bolcom, William (b. 1938) *composer*
One of the most award-winning composers of his generation, William Bolcom started piano and composition lessons at the University of Washington while still a child. He earned a bachelor of arts from that school in 1958 and studied with composer DARIUS MILHAUD in California. Bolcom received a doctorate in composition from Stanford University in 1964. The following year, he won the second prize in the composition competition at the Paris Conservatoire.

Interested in music of popular genres as well as pure classical music, Bolcom specialized in playing ragtime and composing piano rags. His classical style began in the atonal world of serialism, then became less academic and more accessible to wider audiences. He has written seven symphonies, a violin concerto, a great deal of piano music, and many songs. His awards include the BMI Award (1953), two Guggenheim Fellowships (1965 and 1968), multiple Rockefeller Foundation Awards, the Marc

William Bolcom (Courtesy of William Bolcom; Photo by Steve Leonard)

Blitzstein Award, two Koussevitzky Foundation Awards (1976 and 1993), and the 1988 Pulitzer Prize for 12 NEW ETUDES FOR PIANO. He has fulfilled commissions for major orchestras, concert halls, and chamber ensembles, and has composed major works for some of the most prominent performers of the day, including RICHARD STOLTZMAN, YO-YO MA, EMANUEL AX, GARY GRAFFMAN, and MARILYN HORNE. He is married to mezzo-soprano Joan Morris.

Bolet, Jorge (1914–1990) *Cuban-American pianist*
Jorge Bolet was a throwback performer to the late 19th century, in which virtuosos were bent on exploiting the piano for all it was worth. He specialized in operatic transcriptions of Liszt and other bygone virtuosos, while also recording and playing the standard romantic repertoire. Bolet entered the CURTIS INSTITUTE OF MUSIC in 1927, when he was but 13 years old. He also studied in Paris and returned to Curtis for conducting classes with FRITZ REINER. He won the Naumberg International Piano Competition in 1937. He taught at Curtis (1939–42) and at the University of Indiana, Bloomington (1968–77). During World War II he was a military attaché to Cuba and conducted some service orchestras. Bolet's performance career was slow to launch, despite winning the Naumburg. But by the mid-1970s, he was recognized as the leading exponent (along with HOROWITZ) of the grand virtuoso style, and he received uniformly enthusiastic reviews in the *New York Times*. Generally, Bolet's clippings praised his dazzling technique, control of pianistic color, and nobility of line, while remaining mostly silent on the question of interpretive originality. He was a technician more than a poet, but with great control over the piano's tonal resources.

Boosey & Hawkes
An English music publishing company, Boosey & Hawkes grew out of a bookstore established in 1792. A music division was founded in 1816, at first importing music, then publishing European composers such as Hummel, Rossini, Bellini, Donizetti, and Verdi. A New York office, opened in 1892, grew into a major American publisher of new music, including that of composers ELLIOTT CARTER, DAVID DEL TREDICI, WALTER PISTON, and NED ROREM.

Borge, Victor (1909–2000) *music humorist*
One of the two foremost music humorists in America (the other being PETER SCHICKELE), Victor Borge was born in Denmark and moved to the United States in 1940, becoming a U.S. citizen in 1948. He was a talented pianist who attended the music conservatory in Copenhagen on scholarship after making a performing debut at age eight. He studied with Egon Petri in Germany. His early bent for satire got him in trouble when he caricatured Hitler in Germany, and he moved to Sweden, then to the United States. He arrived in America not knowing a word of English and later claimed that he taught himself the language by spending hours in movie theaters.

His first U.S. appearances were on a radio series hosted by popular singer Bing Crosby in 1940, and he soon was given his own radio program. He began a long run on Broadway in 1953 at the Golden Theater, performing a one-man comedy show framed as a serious piano recital. He gave 849 performances. Borge's trademark routine involved continually interrupting his own playing and veering into semi-improvised satires of composers and famous classical pieces. He enjoyed playing verbal games with the audience, and he combined famous melodies from different pieces into amusing medleys. Many of his comedy routines were not musical in nature, bearing more resemblance to stand-up comedy. One famous routine described a fictitious grandfather who invented a soft drink called 3-Up, then attempted to market improved versions 4-Up and 5-Up, but died penniless and brokenhearted after 6-Up failed. Borge also conducted (serious) opera in Boston and Cleveland. An insatiable performer, Borge staged 60 comedy shows when he was 90. He was eventually knighted by every Scandinavian country.

Borowski, Felix (1872–1956) *composer*

Felix Borowski composed a handful of large-scale works, including a piano concerto, three string quartets, various orchestral pieces, and three sonatas for organ. He is best remembered for two early American reference books about classical music: *The Standard Operas* (1928) and *The Standard Concert Guide* (1932). He taught for many years at the Chicago Musical College (now part of Roosevelt University) and was its president from 1916 to 1925. He taught musicology at Northwestern University from 1937 to 1942.

Boston Baroque

A full-sized baroque orchestra and the first such ensemble established in North America, the Boston Baroque was founded in 1973 as Banchetto Musicale. The founding music director, Martin Pearlman, continues to lead the group today. Started as an eight-member ensemble, the Boston Baroque today places 55 musicians on the stage. During its growth, it has gained a reputation as one of the leading period-instrument groups in America. The group has recorded on the Telarc label and garnered three Grammy Award nominations. The Boston Baroque made its European debut in 2003, performing in Warsaw and Kraków, Poland.

Boston Camerata

One of the country's best-known groups performing ancient music, the Boston Camerata was founded in 1954 by Narcissa Williamson. Joel Cohen has been the ensemble's director since 1968. The group's first European tour came in 1974, and Camerata has traveled widely since then. The group has played three times in the summer season of the TANGLEWOOD FESTIVAL, and toured Japan in 1995 and Scandinavia in 1996. The Boston Camerata has recorded an extensive discography of early music and won the Grand Prix du Disque in 1989.

Boston Composers String Quartet

Founded in 1985, the Boston Composers String Quartet performs mostly modern music, much of it composed by Boston-area musicians. They have recorded the complete string quartets of LEON KIRCHNER and were artists in residence at the All Newton Music School in Massachusetts. Current members are Clayton Hoener (violin), Sue Rabut (violin), Scott Woolweaver (viola), and Nathaniel Parke (cello).

Boston Pops Orchestra

America's foremost light-classical orchestra, the Boston Pops has been recorded more than any other orchestra in the world and has played to the single-largest live audience in classical music history. The orchestra was founded in 1885, when Adolf Neuendorff conducted the Boston Symphony Orchestra in the first of many promenade concerts in the Old Boston Music Hall. Promotions for the event advertised "light music of the best class." The orchestra was institutionalized as a distinct performing group in 1900 when its name was changed to Boston Pops by the management of its parent organization, the BOSTON SYMPHONY ORCHESTRA. In 1930, ARTHUR FIEDLER was named conductor of the Boston Pops, beginning one of the most remarkable and enduring collaborations of orchestra and director in history. Fiedler assumed the post after a public outcry against the incumbent director, Alfred Casella (1927–29), who programmed standard classical repertoire such as Beethoven symphonies. Fiedler held the director's position until his death in 1979. The reputation of both Fiedler and the orchestra grew with the advent of regular broadcasts of Pops concerts, in 1952, and especially when the *Evening at Pops* public-TV series started in 1970. The Boston Pops traditionally performs on July 4, and it was the 1976 concert, celebrating America's bicentennial, that attracted the record-shattering live audience of 400,000. After Fiedler's death, composer and conductor JOHN WILLIAMS assumed the Pops directorship. Williams was succeeded in 1995 by Keith Lockhart.

Boston Symphony Orchestra

One of the oldest American orchestras, the Boston Symphony Orchestra was, for many years after its founding, without equal in the United States. Although the Philharmonic Society of New York (later to become the NEW YORK PHILHARMONIC ORCHESTRA) was the older organization, the BSO took the lead in programming, touring, professional conditions for its players, and community outreach.

The Boston Symphony was founded in 1881 on the patronage of Henry Lee Higginson, who single-handedly established the ensemble and paid the musicians' salaries. Georg Henschel conducted the first concert in the Old Boston Music Hall, the BSO's home until 1900, when Symphony Hall was inaugurated. Henschel remained on the podium until 1884 and was succeeded by a series of European maestros: Wilhelm Gericke, Arthur Nikisch, and Emil Paur. In 1906 CARL MUCK arrived on the scene and led the BSO in its first recordings. Muck was succeeded by Max Fiedler, but only temporarily; he returned in 1912 before being forced out of the country by anti-German feeling during World War I. Muck led the BSO on its first national tours, traveling as far afield as San Francisco. After Muck's second tenure, the orchestra shifted its Eurocentric allegiance from Germany to France, hiring many French-trained players. Henri Rabaud became conductor for a year (1918), followed by PIERRE MONTEUX.

The "Koussevitzky era" began in 1924, when Russian maestro SERGE KOUSSEVITZKY began a 25-year term as music director. During this epochal collaboration, the BSO began its summer residency at Tanglewood (starting in 1937), and in 1940 it started the Berkshire Music Center (later to become the TANGLEWOOD MUSIC CENTER). Koussevitzky was a relentless champion of new music, introducing new works by SAMUEL BARBER, LEONARD BERNSTEIN, HOWARD HANSON, WALTER PISTON, WILLIAM SCHUMAN, and others. This adventurous programming stood in sharp contrast to the conservative and Europe-infatuated leaning of the BSO's competition in New York, the NEW YORK PHILHARMONIC,

and the BSO's boldness was not lost on grumbling New York critics of the time. For the BSO's 50th season (1930–31), Koussevitzky commissioned new works by Stravinsky, HINDEMITH, COPLAND, Honegger, Prokofiev, Respighi, and Roussel. Koussevitzky's forward-looking legacy continues through the endowments of the Koussevitzky Music Foundation. Partly through the financial assistance of this foundation, the BSO commissioned a tremendous amount of new music for its 75th and 100th anniversary seasons.

Koussevitzky was succeeded by CHARLES MUNCH in 1949. Subsequent music directors were ERICH LEINSDORF (1962–73), SEIJI OZAWA (1973–2004), and JAMES LEVINE (starting in fall 2004). Levine is the first American-born music director of the Boston Symphony Orchestra.

Botstein, Leon (b. 1946) *conductor and violinist*

Leon Botstein is currently the music director of the American Symphony Orchestra and president of Bard College (since 1975). He founded and codirects the BARD MUSIC FESTIVAL, which explores the repertoire of a single composer every summer. Botstein has recorded with the London Philharmonic Orchestra. He studied violin with polish violinist Roman Totenberg. Botstein's career has been fairly evenly divided among performance, music administration, and writing. In 1996 he received Harvard University's Centennial Award for scholarly work. He is the editor of the *Musical Quarterly* and has contributed articles to *The Grove Dictionary of Music and Musicians.*

Boulanger, Nadia (1887–1979) *teacher, lecturer, composer, and conductor*

Nadia Boulanger's contribution to American music, though indirect, was staggering. She conducted in the United States and, more important, she was the foremost composition teacher of the 20th century. Though most of her teaching transpired in Paris, nearly every significant American composer studied with her. The composer NED ROREM said of her, "So far as musical pedagogy is concerned—and by extension of musical creation—Nadia Boulanger is the most influential person who ever lived."

Boulanger taught at the Conservatoire Femina-Musica from 1907, then at the École Normale de Musique from 1920 to 1939. She helped found the American Conservatory at Fountainebleu, France, in 1921, where she became director in 1948. She taught at the Paris Conservatoire from 1946 to 1957. Her legendary master classes and private lessons occurred mostly in her Paris home. Her American students included MARC BLITZSTEIN, ELLIOTT CARTER, AARON COPLAND, LEONARD BERNSTEIN, ROY HARRIS, WALTER PISTON, ROGER SESSIONS, VIRGIL THOMSON, PHILIP GLASS, and many others. Her emphasis on ear training, counterpoint, and basic harmony skills laid the foundation for American classical composition in the 20th century. In the United States, Boulanger taught at the JUILLIARD SCHOOL and conducted the BOSTON SYMPHONY ORCHESTRA, the PHILADELPHIA ORCHESTRA, and the NEW YORK PHILHARMONIC. Boulanger composed early in her career and won second prize in the Grand Prix de Rome in 1906. She stopped writing music after the death of her sister Lili, who, Nadia thought, was a better composer. Boulanger received honorary doctorates from Oxford and Harvard Universities and was a member of the American Academy of Arts and Sciences.

Boulez, Pierre (b. 1925) *composer and conductor*

Pierre Boulez is a French composer, conductor, and modernist best known for his work on the podium. Much of his career has transpired in Europe, but he made his mark on American classical music beginning in the early 1970s, when he was music director of the NEW YORK PHILHARMONIC (1971–77). He has frequently guest-conducted the CLEVELAND ORCHESTRA, beginning in 1967, and has recorded frequently with that group. As a composer, Boulez peaked early. An aggressive modernist, he felt that the avant-garde of the mid-1940s wasn't nearly avant enough. Impressed by the rhythmic innovations of Stravinsky and the groundbreaking new harmonic language of Schoenberg, Boulez sought to synthesize those two influences by writing atonal music that was rhythmically unpredictable. The musical world lost interest in the avant-garde movement before Boulez did, though, stranding him on an island of modernism and forcing his career toward conducting. As an orchestra leader, Boulez's intellect and rigor hold forth as much as in his compositions. He is masterful conductor of French impressionism (Debussy, Ravel, and others), and his recording set new standards of clarity, eliciting a crystalline palette of colors from the orchestra. He has not held a musical directorship since the New York days but is an active and international guest conductor.

Bowles, Paul (1910–1999) *composer and critic*

A remarkable figure in 20th-century arts and letters, Bowles was an author, composer, and music critic. He studied with AARON COPLAND, NADIA BOULANGER, ROGER SESSIONS, and VIRGIL THOMSON. Most of his music remained unpublished, though some of it was performed before and after his death. He wrote many small-scale pieces that incorporated musical elements of other countries. Bowles left perhaps his most enduring legacy in the archives of the *New York Herald Tribune,* where he was a music critic and wrote hundreds of reviews. He is probably most famous for his novel *The Sheltering Sky.*

Brailowsky, Alexander (1896–1976) *pianist*

Born in Russia, Alexander Brailowsky was an American pianist who specialized in Chopin and whose repertoire extended over the romantic period of piano literature. He took first lessons from his father, a professional pianist, then studied with Polish pianist Theodor Leschetitzky. He made his debut in Paris in 1920. Brailowsky's first claim to fame was a six-concert recital of Chopin's complete output for solo piano, which he performed multiple times with great success in Europe and imported to the United States. He is not generally regarded as a great interpreter but a fine, controlled pianist.

Brandenburg Ensemble

Founded by manager Frank Salomon and violinist ALEXANDER SCHNEIDER in 1973, the Brandenburg Ensemble was originally directed by Schneider, who died in 1993. The ensemble has performed in the United States and Japan, often in collaboration with JAIME LAREDO and PETER SERKIN. The group has appeared in the Great Performers series at LINCOLN CENTER.

Branscombe, Gena (1881–1977) *composer*

An advocate of women's arts, Gena Branscombe studied at the Chicago Musical College, winning prizes there in composition. She moved to New York in 1910. There, she founded the Branscombe Chorale, a woman's chorus specializing in the music of women composers. She was known primarily for her songs and choral pieces but also wrote works for piano and chamber ensembles.

Brant, Henry (b. 1913) *composer*

A popular and successful avant-garde composer, Henry Brant is a pioneer in "spatial music," which features two or more performing groups widely separated. He began composing as a child, creating performance pieces with household implements. Born in Canada, he moved to New York in 1929. He taught orchestration at the Juilliard School of Music (later the JUILLIARD SCHOOL) from 1947 to 1955, and composition at Bennington College, in Vermont, from 1957 to 1980. In 1981 Brant moved to California.

Brant's work in spatial music began in 1950, and nearly everything he has written since then involves spatially separated groups. He regards space as a

Henry Brant (Courtesy of Henry Brant; Photo by Chris Gardener)

fourth dimension of music, along with melody, harmony, and rhythm. Though his work is experimental and his outdoor performances are always at the mercy of weather and environmental noise, almost all Brant's spatial works have been composed on commission. There are recordings of his pieces, but the spatial aspect is diminished when removed from a live venue. Brant won a Pulitzer Prize in 2002 for *ICE FIELD*, scored for large orchestral groups and organ. Other pieces feature exotic scoring elements such as jazz bands, gamelan ensembles, and African drummers. Brant's *500: Hidden Hemisphere* (1992), commissioned by LINCOLN CENTER in New York, was premiered in the Lincoln Center Plaza and required four conductors. His music has been performed by the SAN

FRANCISCO SYMPHONY, the Royal Concertgebouw Orchestra, the AMERICAN COMPOSERS ORCHESTRA, the DALLAS SYMPHONY ORCHESTRA, and many others. Brant attracted attention with his orchestration of the CONCORD SONATA by CHARLES IVES, originally composed for the piano.

Bristow, George Frederick (1825–1898)
conductor, violinist, and composer

George Frederick Bristow led an active musical life in New York. His first professional job was violinist with the Olympic Theatre orchestra—a sextet, despite the grand name. He joined a real orchestra (the New York Philharmonic Symphony Orchestra) in 1843, the year after it was founded. He stayed with the orchestra until 1879, performing part-time with other orchestras during that period. He also conducted the New York Harmonic Society and the Mendelssohn Society, both New York choral groups. Bristow composed in the European style, inspired by American folklore and landmarks. Not all his music was published, but much of it was performed, and most of it survives in manuscript form. He wrote two operas, the more famous being *Rip Van Winkle,* at least three symphonies, many sacred and secular choral works with organ accompaniment, chamber music, and piano pieces.

Brooklyn Academy of Music

Not a conservatory but a performance theater, the Brooklyn Academy of Music (conversationally referred to in New York as BAM) was inaugurated in 1861. The building burned down in 1903, and a newly built facility opened in 1908 with a gala presentation by the METROPOLITAN OPERA, which continued presenting its company in BAM until 1921. BAM enjoys prestige in New York as a cultural center that presents concerts and film festivals. Its two main performance spaces are the Howard Gilman Opera House and the Harvey Lichtenstein Theater.

Brooklyn Philharmonic Orchestra

Founded in 1954 by conductor Siegfried Landau, the Brooklyn Philharmonic sustains a robust reputation as a fine orchestra operating in the shadow of the NEW YORK PHILHARMONIC. LUKAS FOSS succeeded Landau as music director and now holds the title of conductor laureate. Foss stepped down in 1991, yielding to DENNIS RUSSELL DAVIES, who was music director until ROBERT SPANO took over in 1996. (Spano is also music director of the ATLANTA SYMPHONY ORCHESTRA.) Throughout its history, the Brooklyn Philharmonic has provided a platform for the introduction of new music, and especially American music. The orchestra has premiered works by ELLIOTT CARTER, PHILIP GLASS, JOHN ADAMS, Stephen Sondheim, STEVE REICH, and many others. The orchestra performs at the BROOKLYN ACADEMY OF MUSIC.

Brooks, Patricia (b. 1937) *opera singer*

An operatic soprano, Patricia Brooks studied at the MANHATTAN SCHOOL OF MUSIC and worked in New York as a dancer and actress. She became a member of the NEW YORK CITY OPERA in 1960 and has appeared in major opera houses in the United States and abroad. She sings with notable range, able to reach a high E-flat.

Brown, Earle (1926–2002) *composer*

Earle Brown was one of the most innovative avant-garde composers among the group that emerged in the 1950s. He studied mathematics in addition to composition and trumpet, and worked with artists Jackson Pollock and Alexander Calder. His artistic studies probably contributed to Brown's ground-breaking, completely original, and much imitated style of graphical music notation. He painted and composed while living in Denver from 1950 to 1952. He worked with JOHN CAGE at the Project for Music for Magnetic Tape in 1952 and 1953. He was a producer and sound engineer for Capitol Records from 1955 to 1960. Brown held a long and distinguished

Earle Brown (Courtesy of Earle Brown Music Foundation)

series of composer-in-residence positions at universities in the United States and Europe, including the California Institute of the Arts, the Peabody Conservatory, the Rotterdam Kunstichting, the Basel Conservatory of Music, Yale University, Indiana University at Bloomington, and the American Academy in Rome. He was awarded a Guggenheim Fellowship (1965–66) and an American Academy and National Institute of Arts and Letters Award (1972).

Brown's music is characterized by new styles of notation and an unusual degree of choice bestowed on the performers. Though his work cannot be called improvisational, the ordering of musical blocks is sometimes left to the performers' discretion. His *Available Forms I* (1961) and *Available Forms II* (1962) are notated in unbound scores that allow the conductor to choose, on the fly, the order of its composed portions. Brown often integrated art in his scores; in *Calder Piece* a custom-built mobile by Alexander Calder is present during the performance, and the score of *Summer Suite '95* is a computer transcription of Brown's semi-improvised performance.

Browning, John (1933–2003) *pianist*

The pianist for whom SAMUEL BARBER wrote his Piano Concerto, John Browning started lessons at age five and gave his debut, with the Denver Symphony, at 10. He studied with ROSINA LHEVINNE at the JUILLIARD SCHOOL, where he received a master of music degree in 1956. Browning won the Steinway Centennial Award in 1954 and the ultra-prestigious Levintritt Award in 1955. This led to a New York debut with the NEW YORK PHILHARMONIC in 1956. He also took second prize in the Queen Elisabeth International Competition in Brussels in 1956. He received honorary doctorates from Ithaca College and Occidental College.

Browning was closely associated with the Barber Piano Concerto and gave its world premiere in 1962 at the inaugural celebration of LINCOLN CENTER in New York. He recorded the complete piano works of Barber in 1993, a disc that earned Browning a Grammy Award. He received another Grammy for a recording (his second) of the Barber concerto with the Saint Louis Symphony Orchestra under LEONARD SLATKIN. Browning was known for his virile piano technique and muscularly American interpretive style. His open playing style, in contrast to the dark introversions of the Russian pianists who influenced American students in the first half of the 20th century, presaged the emerging class of American competition warriors led by GARRICK OHLSSON. Browning continued performing busily up to his death; he had a full concert season scheduled in 2002–03.

Buffalo Philharmonic Orchestra

The Philharmonic Society of Buffalo, founded in 1908, sponsored appearances by visiting orchestras but did not have an ensemble of its own until 1935. In that year the Buffalo Philharmonic Orchestra Society was founded, and the orchestra performed a series of light-classical concerts in its first season. Further financing was forthcoming in 1937, enabling the hiring of additional musicians and, more important, the hiring of Franco Autori from the DALLAS SYMPHONY.

In 1940, the orchestra moved into its permanent home, Kleinhans Music Hall. WILLIAM STEINBERG, then associate conductor of the NBC SYMPHONY under TOSCANINI, succeeded Autori as music director in 1945. Steinberg held the position until leaving for the PITTSBURGH SYMPHONY in 1952; JOSEF KRIPS took his place in Buffalo until 1963, when LUKAS FOSS became music director. Succeeding appointments to the Buffalo podium have been MICHAEL TILSON THOMAS (1971), JULIUS RUDEL (1979), Semyon Bychkov (1984), Maximiano Valdes (1989), and JOANNE FALLETTA (1998). The Buffalo Philharmonic traveled on its first European tour in 1988.

Burkholder, Peter J. (b. 1954) *musicologist*

A musicologist with research interests in American classical music, Peter Burkholder received degrees from Earlham College (B.A., 1975) and the University of Chicago (M.A., 1980; Ph.D., 1983). He has worked on the faculties of the University of Wisconsin, Madison (since 1982, musicology chair 1987–88), and Indiana University from 1988. He is currently professor of music and associate dean of the faculties at Indiana University, Bloomington. Burkholder's specific area of expertise is the music of CHARLES IVES, and he has been president of the Charles Ives Society since 1992. He has written two books about Ives (*Charles Ives: The Ideas Behind the Music* [1985] and *All Made of Tunes: Charles Ives and the Uses of Musical Borrowing* [1995]) in addition to numerous journal articles.

Burleigh, Henry (1866–1949) *composer*

Born just after the Civil War, Henry Burleigh was one of the first, and most important African-American composers in America; he also enjoyed a long singing career. He was 26 before beginning serious training; he won a scholarship to the National Conservatory in 1892. He entered that institution during the period in which ANTONÍN DVOŘÁK was director, and the young baritone impressed the legendary European maestro with his singing of American spirituals. Burleigh was the baritone soloist at St. George's Episcopal Church in New York. He wrote 265 vocal compositions; they include original songs and many arrangements of traditional spirituals. His work can be found on modern compilation CDs of American spiritual music.

Busch, Adolf (1891–1952) *violinist*

Adolf Busch was a renowned German violinist who took Swiss nationality in 1935. His work in America focused on the creation of the Marlboro Music Festival and his ongoing collaboration with American (of Austrian birth) pianist RUDOLF SERKIN, who was also Busch's son-in-law. Serkin and Busch formed a chamber duo and performed together for 32 years. Busch was a child prodigy who began learning the violin at age three and entered the Cologne Conservatory when he was 11. He lived in the United States for many years between 1936 and his death in 1952; he died in Vermont just two years after founding Marlboro.

Cabrillo Festival of Contemporary Music

Founded in Santa Cruz, California in 1961, Cabrillo is a preeminent platform for the exposure of contemporary music. Since its founding, the festival has produced 78 world premieres and 50 U.S. premieres. Cabrillo's music directors have included Gerhard Samuel (1963–68), Carlos Chávez (1970–73), DENNIS RUSSEL DAVIES (1974–90), and JOHN ADAMS (appointed in 1991). The current director is MARIN ALSOP.

Cadman, Charles Wakefield (1881–1946)
composer and musicologist

Charles Wakefield Cadman's work derived inspiration from his study of traditional Native American music. His studies were not associated with any university, though he took advanced lessons in piano, organ, and music theory. Early in his career (1909), Cadman published arrangements of four American-Indian songs, which became popular and moved his career in that direction. His opera *Shanewis or the Robin Woman* was produced by the METROPOLITAN OPERA in 1918 and 1919. He composed film scores in Hollywood. Cadman is linked with ARTHUR FARWELL and a few other American composers whose composition careers were based on borrowing and adapting American Indian melodies and moods.

Cage, John (1912–1992) *composer*

John Cage was one of the most controversial American composers. His life spanned most of the 20th century, and his work formed the leading edge of avant-garde music after World War II. Cage was the first minimalist composer, and he took that sensibility beyond the mere reduction of scale and complexity. Cage's most egoless work removed the composer almost entirely from the role of determining what a piece would sound like. By championing chance, rather than intention, Cage left it to the performers and the environment to determine what sounds would fill the spaces of his pieces. Besides chance, silence was the great touchstone of Cage's compositions and philosophy. The two qualities combined—chance and silence—found their most potent expression in Cage's most famous piece, *4'33"* (1952).

Cage took piano lessons as a child but was not a prodigy. In later life, he derided his music skills, claiming he had no sense of harmony, and once writing, "I can't keep a tune. In fact I have no talent for music." Cage spent two years in Pomona College but pursued most of his advanced education with individuals. He worked with HENRY COWELL and received enormous influence and inspiration from Arnold Schoenberg. For his part, Schoenberg did not particularly respect Cage as a musician; he publicly referred to Cage as "not a composer but an inventor," a characterization that pleased Cage.

Cage's first pieces were produced in the mid-1930s and were based on Schoenberg's serial-music underpinnings. Cage moved quickly away from Schoenberg's coattails, though, when he started composing for "prepared piano"—pianos with various objects and materials inserted between and atop their strings. This development was an extension of Cage's interest in composing for varied percussion instruments, at a time when percussion ensembles were not available to him. As he turned the piano into a new instrument capable of making unprecedented sounds, he also scored pieces for standard drums from around the world, tin cans, turntables, automobile parts, and other strikable objects. Much of this work was intended for dance performances; Cage worked as an accompanist for the modern dance ensemble of the University of California at Los Angeles, then for dance classes at the Cornish School of the Arts in Seattle. In 1937 Cage met dancer and choreographer Merce Cunningham at the Cornish School, and the two began a collaboration that lasted decades. Many of Cage's prepared piano works and other percussion pieces were performed by Cunningham's dance company. In 1938 he joined the faculty at Mills College in California.

A seminal moment of Cage's career occurred in February 1943, when he staged a performance of three percussion pieces, as well as works of other composers, in New York. A brusque review in the *New York Times* called the music "inexplicably childish" and declared that it "could not be taken seriously enough to require detailed comment." Cage had hoped for a blazing start of a New York career; instead he began a period of relative impoverishment. Nevertheless, he continued writing for Merce Cunningham, and the two toured together during the mid-1940s.

Also during this decade, Cage discovered Eastern spiritual traditions, the writings from which sent his creative work in new directions that would endure for the rest of his life. His studies of Zen Buddhism deeply influenced his conception of the role of music and the importance of silence. His discovery of the I Ching inspired his reliance on chance in determing the order of sounds in his pieces. One of his first works to be directly influenced by Asian mysticism was *Music of Changes* (1951), which requires performers to throw I Ching coins to determine musical events. In *Imaginary Landscape 4,* from the same year, performers manipulate the dials of 12 radios according to specific instructions; the ensuing sound is determined by whatever is currently being broadcast. The infamous *4'33,"* which came in 1952, is scored for any instrument or combination of instruments, though it is usually performed at the piano. Lacking any sound notation whatsoever, the piece is divided into three movements and requires utter stillness from the performer. The resulting composition consists of audience noises, other environmental sounds, and, of course, silence.

Highly controversial though Cage's work was in the early years of its performances, his persistence, self-effacement, and the intellectual rigor of his musical experiments built a foundation of international respect over the years, not to mention a rabid cult following. His 60th and 70th birthdays were celebrated with extensive retrospective performances. He taught experimental music in the United States and Germany. He was elected to the American Academy of Arts and Sciences in 1978, and he received the New York Mayor's Award of Honor for Arts and Culture in 1981. Cage's semiprofessional hobbies included photography, painting, and mushroom identification. He continued composing to the end of his life, leaving a portfolio of hundreds of compositions. His book, *Silence: Lectures and Writings* (1961), is Cage's greatest philosophical statement; it helped establish him globally as a serious experimental composer.

John Cage did not advance the melodic, rhythmic, or harmonic vocabulary of music. His great contribution was in refreshing the modern perception of sound. In Cage's view, traditional assignments of "beauty" and "nonbeauty" were meaningless, and he forced audiences to adopt, or at least sample, his neutrality. Cage once wrote, "The first question I ask myself when something doesn't seem to be beautiful is why do I think it's not beautiful. And very shortly you discover that there is no reason."

Callas, Maria (1923–1977) *opera singer*

One of the great sopranos in the history of opera, Maria Callas sparked a revival in Italian bel canto operas, which had been deemed irrelevant before she took an interest in them. The florid, ornamental, difficult singing parts featured in Italian bel canto were a perfect match for Callas's precise and highly interpretive voice technique. Her blazing success with forgotten operatic styles forged new career paths for later stars Australian Joan Sutherland and Americans MARILYN HORNE and BEVERLY SILLS.

Callas was born of Greek parents who had moved to New York just months before. She lived in Manhattan until age 13, when her family moved back to Greece. There, she studied with Elvira de Hilgado at the Athens Conservatory. She sang the lead role in *Tosca,* in Athens, when she was 19—an astonishingly young age for an operatic debut. She made her American debut in 1947, and demand grew for her appearance in operas both light and heavy. Important international debuts included La Scala (1950), Covent Garden (1952), the Lyric Theatre of Chicago (1954), and the METROPOLITAN OPERA (1956). As her fame expanded, so did a notoriety for backstage difficulties. RUDOLF BING, general manager of the Metropolitan, terminated her contract, then invited her back in 1965. She was accused of breaking contracts and canceling engagements. Of her reputation as a prima donna, Callas spoke of her devotion to the highest standards of art and refused to be associated with inferior productions. Vocal difficulties also caused her to cancel some appearances. Among colleagues, Callas was known as an exceptionally hard worker who was willing to rehearse more than expected, and who demanded perfection of herself as much as of everybody else.

Her return to the Metropolitan Opera in 1965 (singing *Tosca*) was Callas's final operatic performance. During the last 12 years of her life, she taught master classes at the JUILLIARD SCHOOL and elsewhere, tried her hand at opera production (with a

Maria Callas (Hulton/Deutsch Collection/Corbis)

lack of critical success), and sang some concerts. She made an international singing tour in 1974 with tenor Stefan di Stefano, and those concerts were her final public performances. Her last New York concert was in February of that year, in CARNEGIE HALL. By that time her vocal ability was greatly diminished, but her interpretive skills were as compelling as ever. Critical appraisal reached consensus along those lines throughout Callas's career. Her voice was regarded as having three distinct ranges—low, middle, and high—and they were not as integrated in Callas as would be ideal in an opera superstar. Her upper notes were said to be shrill, and her sweet spot was located in midrange, especially during soft passages. It was her heartfelt interpretations, matched with superlative dramatic acting skill, that propelled Callas to staggering popularity despite shortcomings in her voice quality. In a short career lasting less than 20 years, Callas reinvigorated opera as popular theater. HAROLD C. SCHONBERG, music critic of the *New York Times,* wrote, "No singer of her time, and very few in history, could so dominate an audience."

Cantata Singers

Founded in Cambridge, Massachusetts in 1964 with a mission to perform the cantatas of J.S. Bach, the Cantata Singers have since broadened their horizons and repertoire. The current ensemble performs music from the baroque era to contemporary pieces. The group won the ASCAP/Chorus America Award for Adventurous Programming of Contemporary Music in 1995. The Cantata Singers present an eight-concert subscription series in Jordan Hall of the NEW ENGLAND CONSERVATORY in Boston. The music director of the Cantata Singers is horn player and conductor David Hoose.

Canticle of the Sun, The (1944)

Winner of the Pulitzer Prize in 1946 for LEO SOWERBY, the cantata *The Canticle of the Sun* was first performed in New York by the Schola Cantorum in April, 1945.

Canti del Sole (1984)

Scored for tenor and 11 instruments, *Canti del Sole* won the Pulitzer Prize in 1984 for BERNARD RANDS. It premiered on June 8, 1983, played by the NEW YORK PHILHARMONIC. The piece sets to music poems by several writers, all concerning the sun. The descriptive text progresses from dawn to dusk. *Canti del Sole* is generally regarded as a postromantic work.

Caramoor

The Caramoor Estate, located in Katonah, New York, was built by Walter and Lucie Rosen in 1928 as a summer home, where they kept a large private art collection. When their son died in 1945, the Rosens planned to bequeath their house as a center for music and art. By 1970 the house had opened to the public as a museum, and the International Music Festival was instituted as a summer series bringing performers from all over the world. YO-YO MA and Pinchas Zuckerman have performed at Caramoor. The festival maintains an in-house chamber group, the Caramoor Virtuosi.

Carlos, Wendy (b. 1939) *composer*

An American composer and, secondarily, a transsexual who was known until 1979 as Walter Carlos, Wendy Carlos is a composer, technologist, and record producer who received her degrees from Brown University (1962) and Columbia University (1965). Her breakthrough moment came in 1968 with the release of her LP album *Switched-On Bach,* which re-created scores of Johann Sebastian Bach using a Moog synthesizer. Carlos had served as an adviser to Robert Moog during the previous year as he perfected his new instrument. Carlos rode the success of her initial album with three more records featuring other baroque composers, and the entire four-disc set was issued as a box set in 1999. Her original masterpiece was refashioned using modern digital instruments in 1992 and released as *Switched-On Bach 2000.* Carlos's work enhanced awareness of both Bach and synthesizers.

Carnegie Hall

Built by Andrew Carnegie in 1890, Carnegie Hall hosted its first concert on May 5, 1891, with Russian composer Pyotr Tchaikovsky conducting. Since then it has proved to be one of the most famous and enduring concert halls in the world, staging virtually every great orchestra, chamber group, and soloist of the 20th and 21st centuries. The Carnegie family sold the building to a real estate developer in 1924. In 1960, as construction began on New York's new LINCOLN CENTER, Carnegie Hall was slated for demolition. The city's main orchestra, the New York Philharmonic, had used Carnegie Hall as its home base, sharing the space with visiting orchestras from around the country and the world. The Philharmonic planned to move to Lincoln Center (and did in 1962), so there seemed little reason to maintain Carnegie Hall as a municipal theater. Violinist ISAAC STERN prevailed on the city to purchase the building, which is now protected as a historical landmark.

Carnegie Hall's main auditorium is named Isaac Stern Auditorium; it seats 2,804 people in what most professionals regard as a nearly perfect listening space. Though the auditorium extends upward five levels, there is famously not a bad seat in the house. Two other performance spaces complete the venue. The Joan and Sanford L. Weill Recital Hall (usually called WEILL RECITAL HALL) seats 268 people. The Weill Recital Hall was an original part of the layout, and was first called Chamber Music Hall; it was renamed in 1986 after the chairman of Carnegie's board of directors. The Judy and Arthur Zankel Hall (usually called ZANKEL HALL) was opened in fall 2003 as a midsize recital hall (599 seats) that features all kinds of music. The first two seasons at Zankel Hall emphasized alternative programming in several genres. Zankel Hall, located beneath street level, was called Recital Hall until 1960, when it was converted to a cinema. Reclamation of the space for music, and extensive renovation, started in 1997.

Carnegie hall's history is documented in the Carnegie Hall Archives, portions of which are displayed in the Rose Museum within the building. Amazingly, the archives were in disarray as late as 1986, with no systematic collection having occurred to that date. A general call for artifacts was issued, and the response was a global inpouring of programs and other memorabilia. The archives now contain 12,000 photos, vast numbers of fliers, nearly every program in the hall's history, thousands of recordings, and various autographs, paintings, and drawings.

Carnegie Hall's status as a musical showcase is towering. Since 1891, an artist heading for fame might make a performance debut anywhere in the world, an event secondary to a Carnegie Hall debut, even if it comes first. From the start, the hall was prestigious; by 1895, pianist Ignacy Paderewski, JOSEF HOFFMAN, and ANTONÍN DVOŘÁK had performed American debuts on the Carnegie stage. The luminous list continued with RUBINSTEIN, HEIFITZ, GERSHWIN, Stern himself, and many others. Farewell concerts are as important to the Carnegie tradition: TOSCANINI and MARIA CALLAS each bade farewell there. Andrew Carnegie's words, upon the laying of the building's foundation stone, have proved true: "It is built to stand for ages, and during these ages it is probable that this hall will intertwine itself with the history of our country."

Carpenter, John Alden (1876–1951) *composer*

Like Charles Ives, John Alden Carpenter divided his time between composition and a corporate career. He attended Harvard University, where he studied composition with JOHN KNOWLES PAINE. He travelled in 1906 to Rome and studied with British composer Edward Elgar. Carpenter's many art songs brought him a good measure of success, but larger-scale works have given him lasting renown. They include a "jazz pantomime" called KRAZY KAT, based on a comic strip; the ballet SKYSCRAPERS; and the orchestra piece *Sea Drifters*.

Carr, Benjamin (1768–1831) *composer and organist*

Born in London, Benjamin Carr had emigrated to America by the time he was 25, in 1793. He worked as a composer, accompanist, and arranger for local theater companies. He lived in New York from 1994 to 1997, then moved back to Philadelphia for the remainder of his life. He taught singing, was organist for at least two Philadelphia churches, and composed. He is sometimes regarded as having founded musical culture in Philadelphia. Carr published dozens of songs, and his most famous piece was the *Federal Overture* for orchestra.

Carter, Elliott (b. 1908) *composer*

A dominating American composer in influence, stylistic range, and sheer longevity, Elliott Carter was something of a late bloomer. Born to a family that imported lace, Carter spent much of his childhood in Europe. Though he took piano lessons early, his musical maturity started as a teenager in the early 1920s, when the then-modern European music of Igor Stravinsky and others made its way across the ocean. Carter also became aware of American modern music, and was brought under the mentorship of CHARLES IVES. The great composer encouraged the young man's appreciation of the arts, but Ives did not recognize Carter's compositional potential. Carter developed his technique in harmony and structure slowly, entering Harvard in 1926 and gaining a master of arts in music in 1932. While in school, Carter studied with Walter Piston, EDWARD BURLINGAME HILL, and composer Gustav

Elliott Carter (Courtesy of G. Schirmer)

Holst. Leaving Harvard, Carter, like so many other American composers, studied with NADIA BOULANGER in Paris from 1932 to 1935. Up to 1935, when he was 27, Carter had yet to compose any music he felt worth preserving.

Carter returned to the United States in 1935 and settled in New York. He wrote articles, positioned himself as the music director of the Ballet Caravan, and started composing in earnest. During a long and restless teaching career, Carter held faculty positions at St. John's College (1939–43), the Peabody Conservatory (1946–48), Columbia University (1948–50), City University of New York, Queens College (1955–56), Yale University (1960–62), and Cornell University. He taught at the JUILLIARD SCHOOL for 20 years (1964–84). His portfolio of awards is too long to list comprehensively. Carter won two Pulitzer Prizes: for the Second String Quartet (1960) and for the String Quartet no. 3 (1973). He received the Gold Medal of the National Institute for Arts and Letters in 1971, and the National Medal of Arts in 1985.

Carter cannot be considered a lyric composer, and audiences do not leave the concert hall humming his melodies. Rhythmic vitality, thematic ingenuity, and structural innovation are the hallmarks of Carter's music. Carter might be termed the Einstein of music, in that he destroys the concept of a single, absolute framework of time; in his hands, music transpires along several rhythmic paths simultaneously. In this way, Carter is as important as Arnold Schoenberg, who destroyed the idea of a single, absolute farmework of tonality (or key). Carter is often credited with reinventing and reinvigorating the string quartet form, and his composing career first gained recognition in 1951 with his String Quartet no. 1. The composer's deep study of counterpoint, with Boulanger, shows through his fiercely independent yet synergistic parts. Challenging to performers, Carter's string quartets and orchestral works (notably the famous *Concerto for Orchestra*, 1969) sometimes require opposing ensembles to play in different styles and rhythms. He is one of the few modern composers to score a major work for harpsichord (the Double Concerto for Harpsichord and Piano, 1961). As of this writing, Carter is an active composer in his 90s who attends many New York concerts featuring his music.

Cary, Annie Louise (1841–1921) *opera singer*

A contralto, Annie Louise Cary was one of the first American opera singers to gain international recognition. She studied in Boston and Milan, Italy, and made her operatic debut in Copenhagen, Denmark, in 1867. She returned to America in 1870 and gave her concert debut in New York that year. Cary performed in Russia from 1875 to 1877, then again returned to the United States. She was the first American woman to sing a Wagner role when she performed Ortrud in *Lohengrin* in 1877. Cary retired in 1882, in her prime.

Centennial Hymn (1876)

Composed by JOHN KNOWLES PAINE for the Centennial Exposition in Philadelphia of that year, the *Centennial Hymn* is scored for orchestra, chorus, and organ.

Chadwick, George Whitefield (1854–1931) *composer*

One of the most important American composers of the pre–World War II era, George Chadwick led what is sometimes called the Second New England School of composition. (JOHN KNOWLES PAINE and AMY BEACH are also associated with this movement.) Though his works were popular and critically acclaimed during his life, they fell out of favor quickly after his death, as new composers advanced more modern musical styles. Chadwick's most enduring legacy derives from his work as a teacher and administrator. He was mentor to HORATIO PARKER, EDWARD BURLINGAME HILL, ARTHER FARWELL (who rebelled against his traditionalism), WILLIAM GRANT STILL, and others— next-generation composers who would, in turn,

help forge the creative talents of ELLIOTT CARTER, AARON COPLAND, LEONARD BERNSTEIN, and others. As an administrator, Chadwick directed the NEW ENGLAND CONSERVATORY OF MUSIC from 1897, transforming it from a local school for piano teachers to a widely recognized music school with a full course of study.

Chadwick had an unsettled childhood following the death of his mother. His father tried to discourage a career in music, but Chadwick played organ publicly by age 15 and was the regular organist at a local church in 1872. He became a music professor at Olivet College in 1876. The next year he traveled to Europe and enrolled as a composition student at the Leipzig Conservatory in Germany. There he composed his *Rip Van Winkle* overture, which won the school's annual composition contest and became one of his trademark compositions. Chadwick returned to Boston in 1880, where he resumed playing organ, began teaching, and continued composing. His orchestral pieces were performed by several Boston ensembles, including the BOSTON SYMPHONY ORCHESTRA. At the start of his tenure with the New England Conservatory, Chadwick wrote a textbook entitled *Harmony: A Course of Study,* which became standard in the field.

The 1890s, before he took the reins at the New England Conservatory, were Chadwick's heyday as a composer. He was commissioned to write a large-scale work for the World's Columbian Exposition in Chicago; the resulting symphony was scored for orchestra, three bands, and chorus, and was performed by a total ensemble of 5,500 performers. While directing the New England Conservatory, Chadwick composed mostly during the summers, but he found time to finish many new orchestral works, several of which (*Euterpe*, 1903; *Cleopatra*, 1904; *Aphrodite*, 1910) were based on ancient and mythological characters. His opera, *The Padrone*, about an American immigrant family under the thumb of organized crime, was not performed until a long-posthumous 1997 staging at the New England Conservatory. Chadwick composed 137 songs for solo voice and piano.

Chamber Music Society of Lincoln Center

Founded in 1965 by WILLIAM SCHUMAN (then president of Lincoln Center), CHARLES WADSWORTH (pianist and chamber music specialist), and ALICE TULLY (retired soprano and active philanthropist), the Chamber Music Society of Lincoln Center has a mandate to commission and perform music for small groups of instruments and singers. Performing for the most part in ALICE TULLY HALL, the recital hall of LINCOLN CENTER, the Society has sponsored thousands of concerts and commissioned hundreds of new works. The Society's success has motivated the creation of similar organizations around the country and furthered the popularity of chamber music more than any other single cultural institution. In June 2004, the Society named David Finckel and Wu Han artistic directors.

Chang, Sarah (b. 1980) *violinist*

A young violinist who survived the prodigy years to become an internationally recognized artist, Sarah Chang began studying music at age four and attended the preparatory division of the JUILLIARD SCHOOL, where she worked with DOROTHY DELAY. Her debut, at the remarkable age of eight, was with the NEW YORK PHILHARMONIC in 1988, playing Paganini's first violin concerto. As a teenager she played with major orchestras internationally. At this writing Chang has released nearly a dozen CDs, covering standard concerto repertoire and shorter pieces.

Chapin, Schuyler (b. 1923) *director and manager*

Best known as the general manager of the METROPOLITAN OPERA (1972–75), Schuyler Chapin held several important music administration positions. He never attended college and did not complete high school, though he was born to an educated family of professionals. Seeking a career in music, Chapin began studies with NADIA BOULANGER

during one of her American teaching stints. Boulanger assessed his prospects plainly: "My dear, you have no talent," and encouraged Chapin to pursue a backstage occupation in music. He worked at NBC in a variety of jobs from copy boy to advertising salesman. Chapin married Betty Steinway, of the piano company, in 1947, and through in-law connections became the tour manager for violinist JASCHA HEIFITZ and, later, for VAN CLIBURN. In 1959, Chapin became director of the Masterworks department of Columbia Records and supervised now-legendary recordings of Glenn Gould, VLADIMIR HOROWITZ, ISAAC STERN, RUDOLF SERKIN, and many others. Wearying of corporate politics, Chapin became director of programming at the newly opened Lincoln Center in New York in 1964. He remained at Lincoln Center until his position was eliminated in 1968, at which point LEONARD BERNSTEIN invited Chapin to run Amberson Enterprises, Bernstein's creative office.

Chapin had added another position by 1972—that of assistant manager of the Metropolitan Opera. The reigning general manager, RUDOLF BING, was set to retire that year, and his replacement was Goeran Gentele, who took over on July 1. On July 18, Gentele was killed in an automobile accident, and Chapin took over as general manager. His tenure was difficult, and he left the job in 1975, but not before appointing JAMES LEVINE music director. In 1976, Chapin became the first dean of Columbia University's School of the Arts. He has published an autobiography entitled *Musical Chairs: A Life in the Arts* (1977).

Chase, Gilbert (1906–1992) *musicologist and teacher*

Cuban-born Gilbert Chase specialized in American music. He studied at Columbia University and received a bachelor of arts from University of North Carolina. He was director of the School of Music of the University of Oklahoma (1955–61) and founded the Inter-American Institute for Musical Research at Tulane University. He was professor of comparative studies at the University of Texas, Austin, from 1975 to his retirement in 1979. Chase wrote four books about Latin American music. Concerning classical music of the United States, his enduring books are *The American Composer Speaks: A Historical Anthology, 1770–1965* (1966) and *America's Music, from the Pilgrims to the Present* (1955, 3 ed. 1987).

Cherkassky, Shura (1909–1995) *pianist*

An American pianist, Shura Cherkassky was born in Russia and lived much of his life in London. He received his advanced musical training in the United States after moving to America in 1923, a 14-year-old prodigy. Cherkassky's dream was to study with Sergey Rachmaninov, who lived in New York at that time. He auditioned in the great pianist/composer's apartment, and Rachmaninov accepted him as a student, with the stipulation that he cease performing for two years. This restriction was unsatisfactory, and Cherkassky ended up studying with JOSEF HOFMANN at the CURTIS INSTITUTE in Philadelphia—Hofmann had also been a performing prodigy, and he encouraged Cherkassky to continue concertizing as he matured. Cherkassky played in America, Australia, and South Africa as a teenager.

Often considered a throwback to the grand style of romantic piano playing, along the lines of pianists Chopin, Liszt, Alfred Cortot, and Ignaz Friedman, Cherkassky was treasured for his idiosyncratic interpretations, large technique, and total command of pianistic color. His performances were nuanced and full of unpredictable personality—Cherkassky disliked playing a piece the same way twice. This type of playing began going out of favor in America following World War II, when a more disciplined and literal sensibility took hold. Cherkassky's career migrated to Europe, whose audiences were kinder to romantic individualism. Cherkassky stayed away from the United States in the ensuing decades, for the most part, though he did perform an 80th-birthday concert in CARNEGIE

HALL. Meanwhile, his recording career flourished, despite his distaste for the "cold" atmosphere of recorded music. Cherkassky was under contract to Nimbus during the 1980s, and in 1990 he signed with Decca/London. Cherkassky's legacy remains touched by the stigma of old-fashioned playing, but his memory and his recordings are beloved by piano connoisseurs.

Chicago Symphony Orchestra

The CSO's predecessor, the Chicago Orchestra, was founded in 1891 and gave its inaugural concert in October of that year at Chicago's Auditorium Theatre. The new orchestra immediately embarked on its first tour that fall, visiting other parts of Illinois and surrounding states. Later in the first season, the Chicago Orchestra toured the South. In its second season, the Chicago Orchestra gave the American premiere of Pyotr Tchaikovsky's *Nutcracker Suite.* During the rest of the decade, the Chicago Orchestra performed premieres of Richard Strauss's *Also Sprach Zarathustra* and *Ein Heldenleben,* and the second symphony of Jan Sibelius. During this time it visited New York and Boston, becoming recognized as a major musical force in the United States. Conductor THEODORE THOMAS was the orchestra's first conductor. In 1904 the orchestra moved to its new permanent home, Orchestra Hall. It was renamed the Theodore Thomas Orchestra following Thomas's death in 1905, and the name was changed again in 1912 to the Chicago Symphony Orchestra.

The Chicago Symphony Orchestra has been led by nine musical directors since its founding. FREDERICK STOCK replaced Theodore Thomas in 1895, remaining at the orchestra's helm for 37 years until 1942. Stock's tenure is the longest directorship in the CSO's history. He founded the Civic Orchestra of Chicago and instituted subscription concerts for children. When Stock retired, three conductors took over the Chicago Symphony Orchestra during the next 10 years: Désiré Defaux

(1943–47), ARTUR RODZINSKI (1947–48), and RAFAEL KUBELIK (1950–53). FRITZ REINER led the orchestra from 1953 to 1963, followed by JEAN MARTINON between 1963 and 1968.

SIR GEORG SOLTI, a Hungarian-born maestro who had been guest-conducting the CSO since 1954, became music director between 1969 and 1991; he continued beyond then conducting many concerts each season as music director laureate until his death in 1997. Solti is widely identified with the Chicago Symphony Orchestra, and it with him. In one of the great music partnerships in history, Solti took the CSO overseas for its first international tours. Solti won a lifetime achievement award from the National Society of Recording Arts and Sciences during his laureate tenure. He was succeeded in 1991 by DANIEL BARENBOIM, who first conducted the orchestra in 1970, the year after Solti took over. Barenboim has continued to tour the CSO internationally and often performs as both conductor and piano soloist.

The Chicago Symphony Orchestra now performs in Symphony Center, an expansion of Orchestra Hall built in 1996–97. The orchestra comprises 110 musicians, and performs 200 concerts a year. It is universally regarded as one of a handful of the world's finest orchestras.

Chihara, Paul (b. 1938) composer

An avant-garde composer who also worked on films Paul Chihara has gained both academic respect and high-profile soundtrack commissions in Hollywood. He attained his masters and doctoral degrees from Cornell University (1961 and 1965, respectively) and studied with NADIA BOULANGER in Paris during 1962–63. He was associated with the faculty of the University of California at Los Angeles (UCLA) from 1966 to 1976, then rejoined the faculty in 1966. He has been composer in residence for the LOS ANGELES CHAMBER ORCHESTRA (1971–74) and the San Francisco Ballet (1980–90). Chihara scored his first Hollywood film (*Death Race 2000*) in 1974, and has composed soundtracks

for *Prince of the City, The Morning After,* and *Crossing Delancey,* as well as television shows and Broadway productions.

Chung, Kyung-Wha (b. 1948) violinist

Sister of cellist Myung-Wha, Chung is an internationally lauded violinist who was born in South Korea and received most of her training in the United States. Before moving to America, the nine-year-old Chung debuted in Seoul with the Mendelssohn violin concerto, then toured Japan. Arriving in New York at age 13, Chung studied with Ivan Galamian at the JUILLIARD SCHOOL. In 1967 she was cowinner of the prestigious Levintritt Award, with Pinchas Zuckerman, and made her NEW YORK PHILHARMONIC debut the following year, per Levintritt tradition. A London debut followed in 1970. Chung records on the EMI label, and her recording of the Bartók Violin Concerto no. 2, with the City of Birmingham Orchestra conducted by Simon Rattle, won a Grammy Award.

Chung, Myung-Wha (b. 1944) cellist

Sister of violinist Kyung-Wha, Myung-Wha Chung is an American (Korean-born) cellist who made her debut with the Seoul Symphony Orchestra at age 11. Two years later she was the youngest performer to win the Korean National Competition. Moving to the United States with her family in 1961, Chung studied with LEONARD ROSE at the JUILLIARD SCHOOL. Her U.S. debut occurred in San Francisco in 1967. Chung's breakthrough came in 1971, when she took first prize in the Geneva International Music Competition. She is a professor at the Korean National Institute for the Arts, and is a Goodwill Ambassador for UNICEF.

Cincinnati Chamber Orchestra

A 32-piece orchestra founded in 1974, the Cincinnati Chamber Orchestra made its debut in 1974 at the College of Mount Saint Joseph. It was founded by conductor Paul Nagler. The CCO became a fully professional organization in 1976 and offers a subscription season.

Cincinnati Opera

One of the largest opera companies in the United States, the Cincinnati Opera was founded (as the Cincinnati Opera Association) in 1920. The company performed in the Cincinnati Zoo Pavilion until 1972, when it moved to Music Hall, where it is established still. James de Blasis was the director from that time until 1995. Nicholas Muni became the new artistic director, and holds that post today.

Cincinnati Symphony Orchestra

The fifth-oldest symphony orchestra in the United States and the first to embark on a world tour, the Cincinnati Symphony grew from its precursors, the Philharmonic Society and the Cincinnati Orchestra. The former gave concerts intermittently between 1857 and 1872. The Cincinnati Orchestra gave its first concert in 1872; in 1894 the Cincinnati Orchestra Association was founded. The following year, on January 17, the first concert of the Cincinnati Symphony Orchestra was presented by conductor Frank Van der Stucken. In that first season the orchestra staged 48 players—somewhere between a chamber orchestra and a full orchestra. The orchestra's first home was Pile's Hall, and in 1896 it moved to Music Hall. Frank Van der Stucken remained as music director until 1907. At that time, despite prestigious appearances by Richard Strauss and EDWARD MACDOWELL, financial difficulties forced the orchestra (but not the Association) to disband temporarily. Performances resumed in 1909, with LEOPOLD STOKOWSKI as music director. By this time the orchestra numbered 77 players. Stokowski moved the orchestra to Emery Auditorium in 1911.

Stokowski left in 1912, succeeded by Ernst Kunwald, who directed the Cincinnati Symphony in its first recordings in 1917. Kunwald was followed by EUGÈNE YSAŸE (1918–22), who was succeeded by FRITZ REINER (1922–31). Reiner conducted the American premiere of Bartók's Piano Concerto no. 1, with the composer as soloist. Eugene Goossens took the podium after Reiner, from 1931 to 1947. During his tenure, the Cincinnati Symphony left Emery Auditorium and returned to Music Hall. It was Goossens who commissioned Aaron Copland's famous *Fanfare for the Common Man,* one of a series of fanfares Goossens elicited from contemporary composers. Goossens was succeeded by Thor Johnson (1947–58), who was followed in turn by MAX RUDOLF (1958–70). Johnson took the Cincinnati Symphony on its first world tour in 1966 (assisted by the U.S. Department of State, this venture was the first world tour attempted by any American orchestra), and on its second in 1969. Also in 1969, the Music Hall was refurbished in celebration of the orchestra's 75th anniversary.

THOMAS SCHIPPERS was music director from 1970 until his death in 1979. Walter Susskind then took over, leading the orchestra until 1980, when Michael Gielen was named music director (1980–86). Jesús López-Cobos assumed the podium in 1986 and remained for 15 years—the longest tenure for a music director in the history of an orchestra whose directorship had been a stepping-stone for so many great conductors. López-Cobos retired and became music director emeritus in 2001. He had taken the orchestra on its first European jaunt since 1969, first in 1995, then again in the 2000–01 season. PAARVO JÄRVI became the Cincinnati Symphony's 12th music director in 2001.

Cleveland Chamber Symphony Orchestra

Founded by Edwin London in 1980, the Cleveland Chamber Symphony Orchestra has a mission to perform contemporary music exclusively. The group has performed over 170 world premieres, many of them commissioned by the orchestra. Beyond merely premiering pieces, the CCSO incorporates new music into an ongoing repertoire, continuing to expose its commissions and premieres to multiple audiences.

The group sponsors composing competitions among regional universities to discover new composers. The CCSO has received grants from the National Endowment for the Arts, the Cleveland Foundation, and the Aaron Copland Fund for Music, among many other organizations. It is a repeated winner of the ASCAP John S. Edwards Award for Adventuresome Programming of Contemporary Music. The CCSO makes its home in the Drinko Recital Hall of Cleveland State University.

Cleveland Institute of Music

An important American conservatory, the Cleveland Institute of Music was founded in 1920, with composer Ernest Bloch as its first music director. Beryl Rubinstein, later to become an important figure in the school's history, joined the piano faculty in 1921. In 1922 the school established a preparatory division for music study at the high-school level. Mrs. Franklyn Sanders took over directorship of the school in 1926. The next year, a School of Opera was added. Rubinstein became music director in 1932, the same year the school moved into new quarters on Euclid Avenue, and he remained at the helm until his death in 1952. Ward Davenny took over in 1954. The institute moved into a new building at University Circle for the fall of 1961. Pianist GRANT JOHANNESEN led the school from 1974 to 1985. David Cerone is now president of the institute.

The Cleveland Institute of Music acts as a feeder school for the Cleveland Orchestra, in which some 30 graduates hold chairs. At the same time, solo artists such as Judith Ingolfsson, Frank Huang, and Ning Kam, all violinists, have won major international competitions after studying in Cleveland.

Cleveland Orchestra

Though not one of America's oldest symphonic institutions, the Cleveland Orchestra is universally regarded as one of the world's outstanding symphonic ensembles. The orchestra has been under the stable leadership of seven A-list music directors since its first concert in 1918. Founded as the Cleveland Symphony Orchestra by the Hughes and Musical Arts Association (itself founded in 1915), the first concert, on December 11, 1918, was conducted by Nikolai Sokoloff. The Cleveland Orchestra leapt immediately into the media age, bypassing decades of live-only concertizing withstood by the orchestras of New York, Boston, and Cincinnati. Sokoloff put the orchestra on the radio and began recording immediately. Performances were held in Grays Armory for the first season, then in the Masonic Auditorium; the orchestra moved to its permanent home, SEVERANCE HALL (still the main performance venue) in 1931. Severance Hall was built by John Long Severance, president of the Musical Arts Association. Emphasizing the organization's media-savvy operation, Severance Hall was one of the first American concert halls to include broadcasting facilities.

Beginning in 1933, the Cleveland Orchestra was led by a succession of stellar conductors: ARTUR RODZINSKI (1933–43), ERICH LEINSDORF (1943–46), GEORGE SZELL (1946–70), LORIN MAAZEL (1972–84), CHRISTOPH VON DOHNÁNYI (1984–2002), and FRANZ WELSER-MÖST (starting in 2002). Szell is undoubtedly the conductor who forged the most historically potent collaboration with the Cleveland Orchestra. Besides the unequaled length of his tenure, Szell buffed the orchestra's sound to a high sheen, solidified its reputation as America's premier orchestra of its day, and locked in its status as one of the preeminent classical institutions of global reach. Szell expanded the size of the orchestra and began taking it overseas for the first time. The Cleveland Orchestra Chorus was established during Szell's reign (with ROBERT SHAW as music director), and in 1968 the BLOSSOM MUSIC CENTER opened during the summer season, lengthening the orchestra's performing schedule. It took a while for the Cleveland Orchestra to regain its footing after Szell's death. PIERRE BOULEZ, who had begun guest-conducting the orchestra in 1965, acted as principal guest conductor and musical adviser until Maazel took over in 1972. Christoph von Dohnányi took the honorary position of music director laureate upon his retirement.

Cleveland Women's Orchestra

The oldest women's orchestra in the country, the Cleveland Women's Orchestra was founded in 1935 by Hyman Schandler, a (male) member of the CLEVELAND ORCHESTRA. Traditionally, women's orchestras have provided otherwise scarce opportunities for the employment of skilled women instrumentalists, and that was the purpose of this group. The first concert took place on November 17, 1936, in Severance Hall, home of the Cleveland Orchestra. In addition to spotlighting the musical skills of women, the Cleveland Women's Orchestra has engaged in the ongoing mission of providing community access to fine music and has performed over 500 free concerts. Schandler conducted the orchestra until his death in 1990, at which time Robert L. Cronquist was named music director. The orchestra has never had a woman chief conductor.

Van Cliburn (Courtesy of the Cliburn Foundation)

Cliburn, Van (b. 1934) *pianist*

Perhaps the most celebrated of all American pianists, Van Cliburn is best remembered for winning the first International Tchaikovsky Competition in 1958. His first teacher was his mother, an accomplished pianist. At age 17, Cliburn began advanced studies with ROSINA LHEVINNE at the Juilliard School of Music (later the JUILLIARD SCHOOL). By then he had won a local music contest in Texas. At Juilliard, Cliburn claimed nearly every award in sight, including the school's concerto competition, the Carl M. Roeder Memorial Award, and the Frank Damrosch Scholarship. In 1954, Cliburn won the Levintritt Award, one of the most prestigious distinctions for young musicians at that time.

It was in 1958 that Cliburn's star became a supernova. At the height of the cold war, mere months after the Soviet Union launched *Sputnik* to begin the space race, Cliburn was one of several American pianists who traveled to Moscow for the Tchaikovsky Competition. Cliburn himself had no political sentiments about the event; he admired the Russian classics of Tchaikovsky and Rachmaninov, and was unabashedly thrilled to visit their homeland. The Russian audiences returned his adoration, creating scenes of bedlam during the final phase of the contest. Cliburn's performance of Rachmaninov's Piano Concerto no. 3 was stupendously received, effectively halting the contest until competition officials broke their own rule and sent Cliburn onstage for a second bow, calming the audience. The head of the contest's jury, legendary Soviet pianist Emil Gilels, rushed backstage in an unprecedented abandonment of protocol to embrace Cliburn. Cliburn's victory was considered a political triumph by many Americans; Russians viewed the result as a shift in the musical power balance, crediting American training institutions such as Juilliard with having eclipsed their own centuries-old music schools. Cliburn was celebrated with a ticker-tape parade in New York upon his return to the United States.

Cliburn's performing and recording career was extremely active into the mid-1960s. Like some other pianists whose stardom was intense and sudden, Cliburn retired from the stage for extended periods and never returned to full-time performing. In addition to his discography, especially early recordings from the 1950s, Cliburn's most enduring legacy might derive from the work of the Cliburn Foundation. In 1962 the foundation established the quadrennial Van Cliburn International Piano Competition, which has evolved to become one of the most important musical events in the world. The Cliburn Foundation also promotes concerts and operates an amateur version of the main competition, designed for outstanding nonprofessional pianists.

Coerne, Louis (1870–1922) *composer*

Primarily an opera composer, Louis Coerne is remembered for having been the first recipient of a doctoral degree, in music, from an American university, Harvard. During his undergraduate years (also at Harvard), Coerne studied violin with Fritz Kneisel and composition with John Knowles Paine. He studied organ playing in Germany and held various American posts as organist. He taught at Smith College for the 1903–04 year. His most successful opera was *Zenobia,* which, in 1905, became the first American opera produced in Europe (Bremen, Germany).

Colgrass, Michael (b. 1932) *composer and percussionist*

Michael Colgrass is associated with classical and jazz music in roughly equal measure. He graduated from the University of Illinois in 1956 and studied

Michael Colgrass (Courtesy of Michael Colgrass)

with Darius Milhaud and Lukas Foss. During the 1950s he freelanced as a percussionist, playing with symphony orchestras and jazz ensembles in America and abroad. His compositions, many of which are scored for percussion instruments with orchestra, or a percussion ensemble by itself, have been performed in numerous major venues of the United States and Europe. His orchestral piece *Déjà vu,* commissioned by the New York Philharmonic, won a 1978 Pulitzer Prize. The Public Broadcasting System produced a documentary (*Soundings: The Music of Michael Colgrass*), which won an Emmy Award in 1982.

Columbia-Princeton Electronic Music Center

The oldest music lab of its type, the Columbia-Princeton Electronic Music Center was founded at New York's Columbia University by OTTO LUENING, VLADIMIR USSACHEVSKY, MILTON BABBITT, and ROGER SESSIONS, with a grant from the Rockefeller Foundation in 1958. Ussachevsky directed the center until 1980; he was succeeded by MARIO DAVIDOVSKY. Princeton dropped out in 1996, and the name was changed to Columbia University Computer Music Center.

Concerto for Flute, Strings and Percussion (1998)

Winner of a Pulitzer Prize in 1999 for Linda Wagner, this concerto for flute plus small orchestra was commissioned and premiered (May 30, 1998) by the Westchester Philharmonic Orchestra.

Concerto for Orchestra (1981)

Winner of a Pulitzer Prize in 1982, ROGER SESSIONS's Concerto for Orchestra was premiered by the BOSTON SYMPHONY ORCHESTRA under SEIJI OZAWA on October 23, 1981. This Pulitzer was Sessions's second, the first being awarded as a special lifetime achievement award in 1974.

Concerto for Two Pianos and Orchestra (1953)

Winner of the Pulitzer Prize in 1954, QUINCY PORTER's two-piano concerto was commissioned by a grant from the Rockefeller Foundation and was premiered by the Louisville (Kentucky) Symphony Orchestra on March 17, 1954.

Concerto in F (1925)

This piano concerto was composed by GEORGE GERSHWIN just after his success with *Rhapsody in Blue*. Originally titled the *New York Concerto*, the piece was commissioned by WALTER DAMROSCH for the NEW YORK SYMPHONY SOCIETY and was premiered by that orchestra on Christmas Day, 1925, in CARNEGIE HALL, with Gershwin at the piano.

Concord Sonata (1840–1860)

The second of three piano sonatas by CHARLES IVES, the *Concord Sonata* is the most famous and enduring, and was one of Ives's most successful pieces during his lifetime. As with many other of his works, Ives revised the *Concord Sonata* during his retirement from new composition; the bulk of the *Concord*'s material was composed between 1916 and 1919. The piece is scored in four movements, titled *Emerson, Hawthorne, The Alcotts,* and *Thoreau*. Far from expressing the placidity that those titles might suggest, the sonata is marked by extended passages of dense, dissonant writing. The pianist JOHN KIRKPATRICK premiered the work twice: First in Cos Cob, Connecticut (1937), then in New York (1938).

Cone, Edward T. (b. 1917) *musicologist, music editor, and teacher*

Edward Cone is closely associated with Princeton University. He received bachelor and masters degrees from that institution (1939 and 1942, respectively) and joined its faculty in 1947. He became professor emeritus in 1985. Cone published numerous journal articles about form and structure of music. His book *Musical Form and Musical Performance* was published in 1968.

Conlon, James (b. 1950) *conductor*

Currently the principal conductor of the Paris Opera and general music director of the Cologne Opera in Cologne, Germany, James Conlon is an American conductor who studied at the JUILLIARD SCHOOL. An active opera conductor, Conlon made his debut at the METROPOLITAN OPERA in 1976. He first conducted the NEW YORK PHILHARMONIC in 1974. In 1979 he became music director of the

Cincinnati May Festival, succeeding JAMES LEVINE, a position he still holds.

Consul, The (1950)

One of the most performed American operas, GIAN-CARLO MENOTTI's *The Consul* received its premiere in New York's Ethyl Barrymore Theater and remained there for eight months. Olin Downes, writing in the *New York Times,* delivered one of that newspaper's most unqualified raves for a classical production, saying Menotti "produced an opera of eloquence, momentousness, and intensity of expression unequaled by any native composer" and calling the performance "an unquestioned and overwhelming success." Written during the cold war, the opera tells of a family's struggle against totalitarianism. *The Consul* won the Pulitzer Prize in 1950 and the Drama Critics' Circle Award. It has been widely translated and produced around the world.

Converse, Frederick (1871–1940) *composer*

Frederick Converse was one of the most important composers in early 20th-century America. Born to a large family, he began piano lessons at age 10. He received a music degree from Harvard in 1893, then studied composition for two years in Europe. Converse taught at the NEW ENGLAND CONSERVATORY, then at Harvard, between 1900 and 1907. He resigned from teaching to spend more time composing. He concentrated on opera, his first being *The Pipe of Desire*, which was critically unsuccessful. Later operas fared better and included *The Sacrifice, Beauty and the Beast,* and *The Immigrants.* His best-remembered piece is *FLIVVER TEN MILLION.* Converse was elected to the American Academy of Arts and Letters.

Copland, Aaron (1900–1990) *composer*

Aaron Copland was one of the most successful, influential, popular, and respected composers in American musical history. He was also a pianist,

writer, and conductor, but his creative body of work sustains his legacy.

Copland took his first lessons from a sister, one of five siblings. He composed as a child, too, and began formal piano lessons at the age of 13. Compared with piano and composition prodigies, Copland's early development was not remarkable. After graduating from the Boys' High School in New York (1918), Copland continued private studies rather than attending college or a music conservatory. At that time he was honing his composing skills with RUBIN GOLDMARK, who became head of the composition department of the Institute of Musical Art (later the JUILLIARD SCHOOL) when it was founded in 1924. Copland played various piano gigs to support himself during this period of private study. In 1921, he traveled to France to attend the American Conservatory at Fountainebleau, where he met and worked with NADIA BOULANGER. He studied with other teachers as well, but, as with countless other American composers, Boulanger was Copland's greatest influence in the fields of harmony and composition. Throughout this post–high school era, Copland was like a cultural sponge, frequently attending concerts, drama, and ballet on two continents. By 1924, among works that have not remained in the repertoire, Copland had completed the Piano Sonata, the *Three Moods* for piano, and the *Scherzo Humoristique (The Cat and the Mouse)* for piano. The last of these became Copland's first published work (1921). Also in 1921, Copland wrote his first articles for the journal *Modern Music.*

It is not too much to say that Boulanger launched Copland's career. In addition to productive instruction, Boulanger arranged for the premiere of Copland's Symphony for Organ and Orchestra by the NEW YORK PHILHARMONIC, with Boulanger herself playing the solo organ part. Later, the piece was performed by the BOSTON SYMPHONY ORCHESTRA under SERGE KOUSSEVITZKY, who became an enduring collaborator with Copland. The conductor eventually commissioned several major pieces from Copland and premiered them in Boston. Commissions and grants sustained Copland more than did popular acclaim during this early phase of his career. As with most new classical music in the 20th century, popular (and even critical) success was slow to develop. However, his Concerto for Piano and Orchestra received its premiere in Boston (1927) under the stalwart Koussevitzky, and Copland received the first Guggenheim Fellowship in music for the 1925–26 season; it was renewed for the next season as well. He won the RCA Victor Composition for his *Dance* symphony. Copland did not assume a full-time university position during the 1920s but wrote articles and gave lectures. He also engaged himself as a composers' activist through his association with New York's LEAGUE OF COMPOSERS and by promoting concerts. With composer ROGER SESSIONS, Copland organized a contemporary music series called the Copland-Sessions concerts, which ran in New York between 1928 and 1932. He also helped establish the Cos Cob Press, whose mandate was the publication of recently composed American music.

Copland's career remained varied and intensive during the 1930s, with some measure of popular acclaim arriving toward the end of the decade. He wrote the Piano Variations, a thorny and thoroughly modern work even by today's standards, in 1930. In 1935 he taught composition at Harvard University, filling in for the absent WALTER PISTON. In 1937 he cofounded the American Composers Alliance. The following year he supervised the incorporation of Arrow Music Press, successor of Cos Cob Press, and remained as its treasurer for 35 years. Also in 1938, Copland's famous ballet suite *Billy the Kid* was first performed. His still respected book, *What to Listen for in Music,* was published in 1939. During this decade and into the 1940s, Copland lived and traveled with photographer Victor Kraft.

Unlike some avant-garde composers who become more "avant" with age, Copland seemed to mellow in the late 1930s and early 1940s, producing far more accessible music than the stern and dissonant Piano Variations of 1930. The popular *El Salón México* was finished in 1936, and APPALACHIAN SPRING (which, along with the FANFARE FOR THE COMMON MAN, is one of Copland's two iconic compositions) was completed in 1944. The lyrical and evocative *Appalachian Spring* received the Pulitzer Prize and the New York Music Critics' Circle Award. The year 1942 also saw the completion of the *Fanfare,* the LINCOLN PORTRAIT, and the ballet *Rodeo.* This entire cluster of major works has remained firmly established in the popular orchestral repertoire. In 1940, Copland accepted Koussevitzky's request to teach composition at the Berkshire Music Center in Tanglewood, Massachusetts. The center's operation was interrupted by World War II, and after the war Copland remained associated with Tanglewood until 1965.

In the 1950s Copland experienced political trouble, which had no effect on the upward trajectory of his career. With his socialist leanings, Copland was targeted by the anticommunist alarmists of the early 1950s. A performance of the *Lincoln Portrait,* scheduled for a presidential inauguration, was canceled. Copland was interrogated by the House Committee on Un-American Activities in 1953. He avoided any lasting indictments. At the same time, Copland continued working in all his established venues, plus adding a new one: Hollywood. Copland scored six feature films, received four Academy Award nominations, and won an Oscar for his score to *The Heiress* (1949). In 1951 he was appointed the Charles Eliot Norton Professor of Poetics at Harvard, and was the first American composer to sit in that chair. His Harvard lectures were collected in the book *Music and Imagination,* published in 1952. In 1956 he won a Gold Medal from the National Institute and American Academy of Arts and Letters and the first of many honorary doctorates, this one from Princeton University. A short list of Copland's later awards includes the MacDowell Medal (1961), the Presidential Medal of Freedom (1964), a Kennedy Center Honor (1979), and a Congressional Gold

Aaron Copland (Hulton-Deutsch Collection/Corbis)

Medal (1986). He was the recipient of innumerable fellowships internationally.

Copland made his conducting debut with the New York Philharmonic in 1958, after which he became more devoted to that aspect of his career. He never became the music director of an orchestra but guest-conducted internationally. In most concerts he led the orchestra in his own music while exploring other orchestral repertoire and championing American music generally. His *Connotations* (1962) was commissioned by the New York Philharmonic for the gala opening of Philharmonic Hall (later AVERY FISHER HALL) in LINCOLN CENTER. The orchestra again turned to Copland for its 125th anniversary in 1967, for which the composer produced *Inscape.*

In 1972, Copland's creative energy fizzled in one of the most sudden career conclusions in the history of music. He commented on the abrupt end of his composing by saying, "It was exactly as if someone had simply turned off a faucet." Far from bitter or perplexed over this development, Copland seemed primarily grateful for his long career and commented in a 1980 interview, "You'd think if you had spent 50 years at it you'd have the feeling that something was missing, and I really don't. I must have expressed myself sufficiently." Memory distortions and other health problems began appearing in the mid-1970s, and Copland's last 15 years were unproductive musically. Still, he continued receiving awards, notably the National Medal of Arts from President Ronald Reagan in 1986.

Copland's music conveys an indisputably American atmosphere without clumsy appropriations of Native American and African-American elements, the downfall of earlier and lesser American composers. While he was not above adopting American themes and settings for BILLY THE KID, *Rodeo, Appalachian Spring,* and *Lincoln Portrait,* it was Copland's style of open harmonies and evocative dissonance that forged a connection to the American psyche. All the same, Copland sometimes explicitly quoted American melodic material, especially hoedown tunes and, famously in *Appalachian Spring,* a Shaker hymn. His piano music, notably the Piano Variations, the Piano Sonata, and the Piano Fantasy, is more abstract and rigorous than many of the orchestral pieces and the ballet music. In fact, his stylistic explorations range from American popular music to academic 12-tone compositions. John Rockwell, writing about Copland in the *New York Times* just after the composer's death, said, "Mr. Copland's greatest gift was his ability to be both serious and popular." Beyond his personal legacy, Copland's concert work helped revive the music of CHARLES IVES and boosted the visibility of a generation of American composers, including LEONARD BERNSTEIN, LUKAS FOSS, DAVID DIAMOND, and DAVID DEL TREDICI.

Corigliano, John (b. 1938) *composer*

A composer of unusually broad range, John Corigliano's work extends from Hollywood scores to formal orchestral pieces with atonal and electronic elements. He received a Bachelor's degree from Columbia University in 1959 and proceeded to a series of broadcasting jobs. He was program director for the classical music radio station WQXR in New York and music director of WBAI. He worked as a producer for the Columbia Masterworks label in 1972 and 1973, and assisted the production of LEONARD BERNSTEIN's *Young People's Concerts* at CBS until 1972. Corigliano taught at the MANHATTAN SCHOOL OF MUSIC from 1971 to 1986 and joined the faculty of the JUILLIARD SCHOOL in 1992. Between 1987 and 1990 he was the composer in residence of the CHICAGO SYMPHONY ORCHESTRA. He was awarded a Guggenheim Fellowship in 1968 and was elected to the American Academy and Institute of Arts and Letters in 1991.

Corigliano received an Academy Award nomination for *Altered States* in 1981, and he won the award in 2000 for his score of *The Red Violin*. Corigliano spun off a major concert work from that film score: Concerto for Violin and Orchestra (*The Red Violin*), which was premiered by its three commissioning orchestras (Baltimore, Dallas, and Atlanta) during the 2003–04 season. A choreographed version was scheduled by the San Francisco Ballet for a 2005 premiere. Yet another derivative work, *The Red Violin: Chaconne for Violin and Orchestra*, has been performed internationally. Corigliano's Symphony no. 2 won the Pulitzer Prize in 2001.

John Corigliano (Courtesy of G. Schirmer)

Cowell, Henry (1897–1965) *composer*

Arguably the first world music composer, Henry Cowell revolutionized American classical music not only by his multiculturalism, but through pioneering harmonic and structural techniques. He was born to an intellectual and idiosyncratic family; his parents homeschooled the boy in a cottage near San Francisco. He started violin lessons at age five but discontinued that instrument and later studied piano. Cowell's parents divorced, and he traveled around the country with his mother, returning to the San Francisco area in about 1910. Cowell supported himself and his mother with a series of odd jobs; she died of cancer in 1916. By then Cowell's unusual range of talents, musical and otherwise, had come to the attention of more than one sponsor, and a fund for his formal education was established by a Stanford University professor. Cowell gave his first concert in 1913, featuring his own music, and he began composition study at the University of California, Berkeley, in 1914.

In the 1920s, Cowell was a professional avant-garde composer. While his music seems tame now, audiences at his concerts were scandalized by his

Henry Cowell (Courtesy of G. Schirmer)

tone clusters (a trademark harmonic device Cowell is famous for pioneering) and by his experiments with brushing and striking directly upon piano strings. Between 1923 and 1932, Cowell traveled on five European tours, promoting his music. His official New York debut occurred in 1924 at CARNEGIE HALL, where he received a sarcastic brush-off in the *New York Times.* The paper's anonymous reviewer, describing Cowell's tone clusters and string plucking, clarified: "He did not, however, sit on the keyboard, nor did he use his feet in this capacity." The brief review ended by stating that Cowell's music "does not inspire comment."

Cowell founded the New Music Society of California in 1925. He taught at the New School for Social Research in New York and accepted private composition students, among them JOHN CAGE, LOU HARRISON, and GEORGE GERSHWIN. During the 1930s, Cowell broadened his scope, diverting his ultramodernist path to incorporate a study of world music traditions. In particular, he became the first

composer to consider gamelan music seriously. His compositions during this period sought to synthesize musical elements common to many cultures. This decade also brought catastrophic personal developments. Cowell was bisexual—not an uncommon characteristic among 20th-century American composers; COPLAND, BARBER, and MENOTTI, among others, sustained homosexual relationships with a fair degree of openness. But Cowell committed an indiscretion with a 17-year-old boy in 1936, was arrested, and spent four years in jail. He continued composing while incarcerated, and wrote two books behind bars (*The Nature of Melody* and *Rhythm*). He was paroled in 1940 and pardoned by the governor of California in 1942.

Moving on, Cowell taught at the Peabody Conservatory (1951–56) and Columbia University (1949–65). His landmark book, *Charles Ives and His Music,* was published in 1955. He was elected to the National Institute of Arts and Letters in 1951. He composed through the last years of his life, ending with an enormous portfolio that includes 20 symphonies. As is often the case with composers, his music experienced surges of recognition and revival after his death.

Crawford (Seeger), Ruth (1901–1953)
composer

A formidable composer and perhaps the most important female American composer, Ruth Crawford was a colleague of AARON COPLAND and HENRY COWELL in modern music of the 1920s and 1930s. As a second career, Crawford was a folk-music anthologist.

Crawford began piano lessons at 11 years of age and attended the American Conservatory of Music in Chicago (1921–24). She continued advanced piano work with Djane Lavoie Herz, through whom Crawford met Cowell. When Cowell created the New Music Society of California in around 1925, he named Crawford to the organization's board. Her first important works were a series of piano preludes, in which Crawford demonstrated her advanced harmonic sense and structural security. A critic once said that Crawford could "sling dissonances like a man," and her work dissolved the idea that women couldn't compose with the same rigor and unsentimentality as men. In 1929, Crawford studied harmony with Charles Seeger, through whom she met the composer CARL RUGGLES. She married Seeger in 1932 and became the stepmother of folk singer Pete Seeger. Crawford was the first woman recipient of a Guggenheim Fellowship in music, which she used for European study; she attempted unsuccessfully to work with Austrian composer Arnold Schoenberg.

Crawford's compositions were uncompromising in their academic exactness. She not only absorbed and practiced 12-tone serialism, but extended it in new directions. In this way she was more progressive than either Cowell or Copland, the two most prominent modernist composers during her heyday.

Creston, Paul (1906–1985) composer

Mostly self-taught, Paul Creston became a popular composer of the mid-20th century. A conservative musician, Creston claimed his greatest influences to be long-dead composers. The hallmark of his style was rhythmic inventiveness. Harmonically, he might be called an American impressionist. Creston achieved renown when his Symphony no. 1 won the New York Music Critics' Circle Award in 1941. He had already received a Guggenheim Fellowship in 1938. His work was performed widely in the aftermath of World War II, but it faded from the concert repertoire with the rise of academic music in the 1960s. His *Principles of Rhythm* was published in 1964, and another book, *Rational Metric Notation,* was released in 1979.

Crucible, The (1961)

By far ROBERT WARD's most successful of six operas *The Crucible* won the Pulitzer Prize in 1962. It was premiered in New York on October 26, 1961.

Crumb, George (b. 1929) composer

A composer whose work mixes influences in a pastiche style, George Crumb was exposed to music from birth. He studied at the Mason College of Music in Charleston, West Virginia and received an advanced music degree from the University of Illinois, Urbana-Champaign, in 1953. He engaged in postgraduate studies in Germany thanks to a Fullbright Scholarship, then returned to America and obtained a doctorate in music from the University of Michigan, Ann Arbor, in 1959. By that time, Crumb was assistant professor in piano and composition at the University of Colorado, Boulder. In 1965 he joined the faculty of the University of Pennsylvania, Philadelphia, where in 1983 he was named Annenberg professor of humanities. Crumb

Paul Creston (Bettmann/Corbis)

retired from teaching in 1997. His fame stems mostly from compositions of the 1960s and 1970s, his best-known piece being ANCIENT VOICES OF CHILDREN (1970). His *Black Angels* (1970) is scored for electric string quartet. His longest work, *Star Child,* was commissioned by PIERRE BOULEZ and the NEW YORK PHILHARMONIC in 1977.

Curtis Institute of Music

One of the preeminent music conservatories in the world, Curtis is an all-scholarship school located in Philadelphia, with extraordinarily high admission standards. Though students may enter at any age, and certain celebrated alumni (such as American pianist Gary Graffman, currently the school's director) began their Curtis career as children, the institute is essentially a college-level training ground for professional performers. Curtis was founded by Mary Louise Curtis Bok in 1924. From the start it has attracted a faculty roster more luminous than any other in the world. Currently the Curtis faculty numbers 85 teachers, most of whom perform actively and internationally. Curtis maintains an international student body of about 160—enough to fill out the Curtis Symphony Orchestra, an opera theater, plus a few piano and composition students. Matriculation at Curtis does not follow standard accreditation agendas; students graduate "when their teachers decide they are ready." It is not unusual for a student's tenure at Curtis to last a decade. Curtis alumni include LEONARD BERNSTEIN, SAMUEL BARBER, RICHARD GOODE, GARY GRAFFMAN, NED ROREM, PETER SERKIN, and HILARY HAHN.

Dahl, Ingolf (1912–1970) *composer, conductor, teacher*

After early studies in Germany, Ingolf Dahl fled the Nazi regime to Switzerland, then to the United States. In America, Dahl became a busy composer, conductor, writer, and teacher. He was closely associated with the University of Southern California, with whose orchestra he introduced a great deal of modern music to West Coast audiences. He taught there from 1945 until his death. As a composer, Dahl was greatly influenced by Igor Stravinsky, and he assisted in the translation of Stravinsky's book *Poetics of Music,* the English version of which was published in 1947. Dahl received two Guggenheim Fellowships (1954 and 1958). The University of Southern California established the Ingolf Dahl lecture series in 1981.

Dallas Symphony Orchestra

The history of the Dallas Symphony tells a troubled story of an orchestra with intermittent financial troubles and no adequate venue for many years. But since 1994 the orchestra's situation has been stable and successful. Founded as the Dallas Symphony Club in 1900, under the direction of Hans Kreissig, the orchestra was more like a chamber ensemble at first, comprising 40 musicians. Its early music directors included Walter Fried (1905–11, then 1918–24), Carl Venth (1911–14), Paul Van Katwijk (1925–38), and Jacques Singer, (1938–42). In 1942 ANTAL DORATI assumed the podium. By this time the Dallas Symphony was a full-size professional orchestra, and Dorati began recording with it while lengthening the performance season. Dorati was succeeded by Walter Hendl (1949–58), who gave way to Paul Kletzki (1958–61). In 1961 GEORG SOLTI, who later forged a legendary collaboration with the CHICAGO SYMPHONY ORCHESTRA, became music director for a single season. Donald Johanos took Solti's place and remained until 1970. Anshel Brusilow enjoyed a short tenure in the early 1970s, to be replaced by MAX RUDOLF for one season. In 1974 the Dallas Symphony was forced by debt to suspend operations. It resumed a year later under the directorship of Louis Lane.

The Dallas Symphony came into its own starting in 1977, when Eduardo Mata was appointed music director. Mata recorded extensively, traveled with the orchestra to Washington, D.C., KENNEDY CENTER, New York's CARNEGIE HALL, and to Europe. Mata retired in 1993, becoming conductor emeritus. He was succeeded by the current music director, ANDREW LITTON.

The orchestra has assumed homes in Fair Park Music Hall (for two stints) and McFarlin Memorial Auditorium, a university facility. In 1982, a civic appropriation approved by voters authorized the construction of the Morton H. Meyerson Symphony Center, which opened in 1989. The Meyerson Center is widely regarded as one of the finest acoustic environments for symphonic concerts in the world.

Damrosch, Leopold (1832–1885) *conductor*

Leopold Damrosch was a successful European conductor who moved to New York and became an important influence in late 19th-century American classical music. He founded the Oratorio Society in 1873, and the NEW YORK SYMPHONY SOCIETY in 1878. In 1881, Damrosch conducted the American premiere of the Berlioz *Requiem*. In 1882 and 1883, he led the Symphony Society on tours in the United States—the first New York orchestra to tour. While directing the Symphony Society, Damrosch conducted the competing PHILHARMONIC SYMPHONY SOCIETY OF NEW YORK for one season (1876–1877). When Leopold Damrosch died in 1885, directorship of the Symphony Society was inherited by his son, Walter, who was in charge when the orchestra merged with the Philharmonic Society in 1928. The resulting merged organization continued as the NEW YORK PHILHARMONIC, America's oldest orchestra.

Damrosch, Walter (1862–1950) *conductor*

Son of Leopold Damrosch, Walter Damrosch followed in his father's footsteps while contributing his own distinct influence on early 20th-century American music. Primarily a conductor and administrator, Damrosch succeeded his father as director of German operas at the METROPOLITAN OPERA in New York, conductor of the Oratorio Society, and director of the NEW YORK SYMPHONY SOCIETY. (The last two organizations were both founded by Leopold Damrosch.) Damrosch managed the Symphony Society's merger with the New York Philharmonic Society (1928), the combined entity that became the New York Philharmonic. He also was instrumental in Andrew Carnegie's decision to build CARNEGIE HALL as the orchestra's home.

Danielpour, Richard (b. 1956) *composer*

A neo-romantic composer, Richard Danielpour is one of a generation of American composers divorced from the academic school of serialism. Best known for his orchestral music, Danielpour has written work that is accessible, colorful, and atmospheric. He received a bachelor of music degree from the NEW ENGLAND CONSERVATORY (1980), where he studied with flutist and composer John Heiss. Danielpour obtained advanced degrees from the JUILLIARD SCHOOL (master of music in 1982; doctor of musical arts in 1986), where he worked with VINCENT PERSICHETTI and PETER MENNIN. He has won the Bearn's Prize from Columbia University (1982) and the Charles Ives Fellowship from the American Academy and Institute of Arts and Letters (1983). He was the composer in residence at the SEATTLE SYMPHONY ORCHESTRA for the 1991–92 season. He has received commissions from the NEW YORK PHILHARMONIC (*Toward the Splendid City*), the PHILADELPHIA ORCHESTRA (*Concerto for Violin and Orchestra: A Fool's Paradise*), the SAN FRANCISCO SYMPHONY

Richard Danielpour (Courtesy of G. Schirmer)

(Symphony no. 2 and the Cello Concerto), the NATIONAL SYMPHONY ORCHESTRA (*Voices of Remembrance*), and many others. He is the only composer besides Igor Stravinsky and AARON COPLAND to be signed exclusively by the record label Sony Classical. Danielpour teaches at the MANHATTAN SCHOOL OF MUSIC and at the CURTIS INSTITUTE OF MUSIC.

Davidovich, Bella (b. 1928) *pianist*
Russian-born Davidovich is known in America mostly as a cornerstone of the piano faculty at the JUILLIARD SCHOOL, with which she has been associated since 1982. She gave her debut in Baku, in present-day Azerbaijan, at the age of nine, playing a Beethoven piano concerto. Her high-profile concert career began in 1949, when Davidovich won first prize in the International Chopin Competition in Warsaw. She performed with the Leningrad Philharmonic for 28 consecutive seasons and was appointed to the faculty of the Moscow Conservatory in 1962. She emigrated to the United States in 1978 and has performed with all major American orchestras. She records on the Philips label.

Davidovsky, Mario (b. 1934) *composer*
An American of Argentinian birth, Mario Davidovsky specializes in compositions for acoustic instruments accompanied by prerecorded sounds. His series of *Synchronisms* represents his best-known work; the Synchronism no. 6 won a Pultizer Prize in 1971. He was associate director of the COLUMBIA-PRINCETON ELECTRONIC MUSIC CENTER from 1960, and he remained a professor at Columbia until 1993, when he joined the faculty at Harvard University. He has also taught at the MANHATTAN SCHOOL OF MUSIC and Yale University.

Davies, Dennis Russell (b. 1944) *conductor*
Dennis Davies is regarded as a preeminent orchestral and chamber conductor. He has lived and worked in Germany since 1980 but continues to wield some influence on the American musical scene. Starting out as a pianist, Davies studied with Gorodnitzky at the JUILLIARD SCHOOL; during his time there, Davies cofounded the Juilliard Ensemble. From 1972 to 1980, Davies directed the SAINT PAUL CHAMBER ORCHESTRA, single-handedly raising the prestige of that ensemble to the current high level it enjoys today. He was a cofounder of the AMERICAN COMPOSERS' ORCHESTRA in 1977 and was that group's music director until 2002. Davies is a relentless champion of contemporary music; he sits on the board of Harvard University's Fromm Music Foundation.

Davis, Andrew (Sir) (b. 1944) *conductor*
British-born Davis became music director of the LYRIC OPERA OF CHICAGO in 2002. His European posts have included the associate conductorship of the BBC Scottish Symphony Orchestra (1970–72) and the principal guest conductorship of the Royal Liverpool Philharmonic Orchestra (1974–77). He was music director of the Toronto Symphony Orchestra from 1975 to 1988, and chief conductor of the BBC Symphony Orchestra from 1988 to 2000.

Davis, Ivan (b. 1932) *pianist*
Ivan Davis has built an international piano career specializing in the music of Liszt and Grieg. A rare student of HOROWITZ, Davis won second prize in the Busoni International Competition in 1958 and the Liszt Prize in 1960. Davis made his debut in 1962 with the NEW YORK PHILHARMONIC in CARNEGIE HALL. His discography is recorded by Audiofon, Sony Classics, New World, and the Musical Heritage Society labels.

Déjà vu for Percussion Quartet and Orchestra (1977)
Winner of the 1978 Pulitzer Prize for MICHAEL COLGRASS, *Déjà vu* was commissioned by the NEW

York Philharmonic and premiered on October 20, 1977.

DeLay, Dorothy (1917–2002) *violinist*

Dorothy DeLay founded the Stuyvesant Trio in 1942. Though she was an active performer in her younger years, DeLay is best remembered as a teacher (of Itzhak Perlman, among other viruosi). She taught at the Juilliard School, Sarah Lawrence College, the New England Conservatory, and the Cincinnati College Conservatory.

Delfs, Andreas (b. 1939) *conductor*

German Andreas Delfs has made a high profile in the United States through two significant appointments. He became music director of the Milwaukee Symphony Orchestra in 1997 and has remained in that position under a contract extending through 2005. In 2000 he was named director of the Saint Paul Chamber Orchestra, succeeding Hugh Wolff. Ironically, an artistic and administrative decision led to Delfs's termination at St. Paul. The orchestra had for years discussed becoming a musician-directed orchestra, and Delfs encouraged the group to take that step, eliminating his musical directorship in the process. He was replaced by a five-member international advisory committee.

Dello Joio, Norman (b. 1913) *composer*

Descended from Italian church organists, Norman Dello Joio experienced an unusually musical childhood. His father was a vocal coach to singers of the Metropolitan Opera. Dello Joio's first job in music, at 14 years of age, was organist and choir director of a church in New York City. He had started piano lessons at four and later began organ studies with his godfather Pietro Yon, the organist of St. Patrick's Cathedral. He attended the College of the City of New York and the Institute of Musical Art, then pursued graduate studies at the Juilliard School of Music from 1939 to 1941.

During his Juilliard days, Dello Joio was organist of St. Anne's Church in New York. In 1941, he began studies with the composer Paul Hindemith. The encounter sparked an epiphany and shifted Dello Joio's career away from organ playing toward composition.

Dello Joio began winning awards for his compositions soon after his student years. He received the Town Hall Composition Award for *Magnificat* (1942), two Guggenheim Fellowships (1943 and 1944), a grant from the American Academy of Arts and Letters (1945), the New York Music Critics' Circle Award (1948 and again in 1962), and the Pulitzer Prize (1957) for *Meditation on Ecclesiastes*. He won an Emmy Award (1965) for his soundtrack to a television documentary, *The Louvre*.

Dello Joio's portfolio includes three operas, eight ballets, nine television soundtracks, 45 choral works, about 30 orchestral pieces, a handful of concertos, many piano pieces, and about 20 chamber pieces. He has taught at Sarah Lawrence College (1945–50), and the Mannes College of Music (1956–72), and was dean of the School of Fine and Applied Arts at Boston University (1972–78). From 1959 to 1973 he was director of the Ford Foundation's Comtemporary Music Project.

Del Tredici, David (b. 1937) *composer*

An influential and wide-ranging composer, David Del Tredici adopted serialism as a young composer, then gradually worked away from it. He received a bachelor of arts from the University of California, Berkeley (1959), and a master of fine arts from Princeton University (1965). He joined the music faculty at Harvard University in 1965 and later taught at the Manhattan School of Music and the Juilliard School. Del Tredici received a Guggenheim Fellowship in 1966. He won a Naumburg Award in 1972, and the Pulitzer Prize for *In Memory of a Summer Day* in 1980. His work became increasingly tonal after the academic-music era of the 1960s, of which Del Tredici's alma mater, Princeton, was in the forefront. Many of Del Tredici's best-known and most accessible works were inspired by the writings of Lewis Carroll, including *An Alice Symphony* (1969) and *Final Alice* (1975).

DePreist, James (b. 1936) *conductor*

Until 2003 the music director of the Oregon Symphony (and still the laureate music director), James DePreist was the first African-American conductor to fill permanent positions with American orchestras; he overcame nearly insurmountable health difficulties. He was the nephew of the contralto MARIAN ANDERSON, and his family nudged DePreist away from a music career toward law. As a result, DePreist had virtually no musical training by the time he graduated from the University of Pennsylvania in 1958. At that point he began studying harmony and composition with composer VINCENT PERSICHETTI, and in 1959 his first large-scale work, *Vision of America,* was performed by the Philadelphia Dance Academy, DePreist conducting.

In 1961 DePreist took an overseas job with the State Department, relocating to Bangkok, Thailand, as the drummer in a band led by the king of Thailand. During this phase he sometimes conducted a local orchestra and developed a voracious appetite for reading orchestral scores. DePreist contracted polio while abroad, and the disease eventually paralyzed his legs. Having learned to walk with crutches, he stunned observers and challenged himself by entering the Dimitri Mitropoulos Conducting Competition in 1963. He reached the semifinals that year and was one of the top prizewinners the following year, conducting from a wheelchair. The Mitropoulos victory led to a year as LEONARD BERNSTEIN's assistant at the NEW YORK PHILHARMONIC, but after that year DePreist's career stalled. Like DEAN DIXON (the pioneering African-American conductor) before him, DePreist moved to Europe in 1967. He guest-conducted there until ANTAL DORATI invited him to be associate conductor of the NATIONAL SYMPHONY ORCHESTRA, a position he filled from 1971 to 1974. He became

principal guest conductor of that group for the 1975–76 season and was music director of the Quebec Symphony Orchestra from 1976 to 1983. He began his signature appointment as music director of the Oregon Symphony in 1980, lifting that orchestra's stature to the first rank. Beginning in 2005, DePreist took the post of Permanent Conductor of the Tokyo Metropolitan Symphony Orchestra.

Detroit Symphony Orchestra

Although orchestra groups had performed in Detroit during the last quarter of the 19th century and into the 20th, it was in 1914 that the Detroit Symphony came into existence, organized by a group of Detroit women who chipped in modest funding and hired Weston Gales, a young church organist, to conduct. The orchestra's first performance took place on February 26 of that year. Gales lasted only one season and was succeeded by the Russian pianist OSSIP GABRILOVICH. Gabrilovich motivated and oversaw the construction of Orchestra Hall, into which the orchestra moved in fall 1919. Thanks to Gabrilovich's connections and the increasingly fine reputation of the orchestra, the Detroit Symphony attracted stellar guest artists such as pianist Serge Rachmaninoff, singer Enrico Caruso, violinist JACHA HEIFETZ, cellist Pablo Casals, and composer Igor Stravinsky. In 1922, the Gabrilovich-conducted orchestra paired with pianist Artur Schnabel for the world's first radio broadcast of a symphony orchestra. Extending its radio-friendly image, the Detroit Symphony became the house orchestra of the Ford Symphony Hour, on national radio, from 1934 to 1942.

Gabrilovich died in 1936, and Franco Ghione succeeded him on the podium. Financial troubles beset the orchestra during World War II, and the 1942–43 season was canceled. Resuming operation in 1943, with Karl Krueger as music director (and renamed the Detroit Orchestra), the organization continued for six years, then dissolved again. The Detroit Symphony Orchestra was resuscitated in

1951 under Paul Paray, who retired in 1963. The orchestra moved to new Ford Auditorium in 1956. During Paray's tenure, the orchestra recorded 70 discs in 11 years. A succession of luminaries followed Paray: SIXTEN EHRLING (1963–73), Aldo Ceccato (1973–77), and the ever-circulating ANTAL DORATI (1977–81). Dorati organized festivals, recorded often, and toured the orchestra through Europe for the first time. The orchestra was at loose ends for a few years after Dorati left, relying primarily on guest conductors. Finally, Gunther Herbig became music director (1984–90), followed by NEEME JÄRVI, the current conductor. After Orchestra Hall received extensive renovations, the Detroit Symphony moved back into that venue, where it remains. The orchestra performs a 26-week subscription season, as well as various special events, young people's concerts, and a pops series. An irregular summer season is spread among several venues.

De Waart, Edo (b. 1941) *conductor*

Edo De Waart is a Dutch conductor who held two important positions in the United States. He was the music director of the SAN FRANCISCO SYMPHONY ORCHESTRA from 1977 to 1985, and was music director of the MINNESOTA ORCHESTRA from 1986 to 1995. During both tenures, but particularly in San Francisco, De Waart promoted contemporary music.

Diamond, David (b. 1915) *composer*

Usually regarded as an American classicist, composer David Diamond never wrote a 12-tone piece during a long career that spanned virtually all of the 20th century's composing trends. The violin was Diamond's first instrument, and he also studied music theory as a child. He briefly attended the EASTMAN SCHOOL OF MUSIC in his hometown of Rochester, New York, then transferred to the New Music School in New York for study with composer ROGER SESSIONS. In the mid-1930s he traveled to Paris, where he was inspired by composers Maurice

Ravel, Darius Milhaud, and Albert Roussel. Like many American composers, Diamond studied with NADIA BOULANGER (1937–39). The thorough grounding in theory, harmony, and counterpoint imparted by Boulanger made Diamond into one of the most disciplined and exacting composers of his generation, and one of the best teachers.

During the 1940s, Diamond received a succession of awards and composed actively. He won a Guggenheim Fellowship in 1941, the Prix de Rome in 1942, the Paderewski Prize in 1943, and a grant from the National Institute of Arts and Letters in 1944. He also played orchestral gigs on the violin. During the 1950s, Diamond lived and worked mainly in Europe, partly motivated by professional opportunity and partly driven by the political discomfort of the emerging McCarthyism in the United States. He became a professor at the University of Rome in 1951 and lived in Florence for many years. Between 1951 and 1965, Diamond visited the United States only three times: once to assist his ailing mother, and twice for short professorships at the State University of New York, Buffalo (1961 and 1963). He returned to the United States in 1965 and was quickly swept up in a busy teaching and composing career. Several important premieres were performed by the NEW YORK PHILHARMONIC, directed by LEONARD BERNSTEIN. He was chair of the composition department at the MANHATTAN SCHOOL OF MUSIC in 1966–67 and taught at the JUILLIARD SCHOOL from 1973 to 1986. He received a Gold Medal from the American Academy of Arts and Letters in 1991 and the National Medal of Arts from President Clinton in 1995.

Dixon, Dean (1915–1976) *conductor*

One of the first African-American conductors in the grand European tradition, Dean Dixon forged a path of artistic equality for younger black conductors (JAMES DEPRIEST and others) to follow. Although he did not reach the level of international acclaim of contralto MARIAN ANDERSON and became a quietly embittered man whose career at home never equaled his European successes, Dixon's accomplishments and important "firsts" created a groundbreaking legacy.

Dixon grudgingly began violin lessons at the age of three and a half, and resisted his mother's enforced five-hour daily practice regimen throughout his childhood. When he was 17, Dixon's violin teacher attempted to discourage him from turning professional, but by then the boy's musical ambition had been awakened and he set his sights on conducting. As a teenager he founded an amateur orchestra, funding it himself until a local women's group whipped up community support. Later, he founded the New York Chamber Orchestra. Dixon studied at the Juilliard School of Music (later the JUILLIARD SCHOOL) and at Columbia University. His conducting debut was at TOWN HALL in 1938. He was the first African-American conductor to lead the NBC SYMPHONY ORCHESTRA (1941) and the NEW YORK PHILHARMONIC (1942).

His engagements with the Philharmonic were a long-standing source of bitterness for Dixon, not because his concerts were badly received—on the contrary, he gained ovations and critical raves. But his 1942 concerts were during the summer, not during the regular subscription season when the world's great conductors were routinely invited to guest-conduct. This prestige-lowering displacement was the case in 1942, then again in the summer of 1970, before Dixon was finally engaged during the season as a replacement for GEORGE SZELL, who had died suddenly in the fall of 1970. The Philharmonic concerts of 1942 were milestone events of a young career that seemed on the verge of taking off. Dixon founded yet another ensemble in 1944—the American Youth Orchestra—and guest-conducted the BOSTON SYMPHONY ORCHESTRA. But no permanent conducting position was forthcoming, and in 1949 Dixon moved to Europe, like many young American musicians before and since, hoping to build a career abroad.

Dixon's European years between 1949 and 1970 were routinely referred to in the musical press as a period of exile. He traveled all over Europe as a guest conductor, breaking down preconceptions and skepticism at every stop. Audiences and critics assumed he was a jazz musician, or they simply couldn't believe, until the concerts proved otherwise, that a black man could express refined musicianship in the traditional European repertoire. As a freelance conductor in Europe, Dixon conducted over 150 concerts a year. He accepted the principal conductorship of the Göteburg Symphony Orchestra in Sweden (1953–69) and held the same position with the Radio Symphony Orchestra of Frankfurt, Germany (1961–74). During the latter tenure, Dixon was also the principal conductor of the Sydney Symphony Orchestra in Australia from 1964 to 1967.

Throughout his career, Dixon championed new music, sometimes daringly so. He was not afraid to program unheard music by unknown composers at important debuts. His musical courage was more than matched by his professional determination and perseverance.

Dodge, Charles (b. 1942) *composer*

One of the first American composers to experiment with sound synthesis, particularly as applied to speech and singing, Charles Dodge's music is renowned for its wit. He received an undergraduate degree in music from the University of Iowa (1964) and a master's and a doctorate from Columbia University (1966 and 1970). He spent time at Princeton University in 1969 and 1970; Columbia and Princeton were then at the forefront of electronic music. Dodge taught at Columbia from 1970 to 1980, and later directed the Center for Computer Music at Brooklyn College of the City University of New York. In 1993 he became a visiting professor at Dartmouth College. He won the Bearns Prize from Columbia University twice, in 1964 and 1967. Two Guggenheim Fellowships followed, in 1972 and 1975. He won an American Academy of Arts and letters Award in 1975. Dodge was president of the American Composers Alliance from 1971 to 1975, and chairman of the board of directors of that organization from 1975 to 1980. He was president of the AMERICAN MUSIC CENTER from 1979 to 1982. Dodge is coauthor of a leading textbook on sound synthesis, *Computer Music: Synthesis, Composition, and Performance* (1996).

Dohnányi, Christoph von (b. 1929) *conductor*

German Christoph von Dohnányi is the grandson of Hungarian composer Ernö Dohnányi. His early career ascendance occurred in Europe, most notably in German opera houses. He made his debut at the METROPOLITAN OPERA in New York in 1972. In 1984, Dohnányi began his signature appointment as music director of the CLEVELAND ORCHESTRA; he was the latest in a succession of distinguished maestros including ARTUR RODZINSKI, ERICH LEINSDORF, GEORGE SZELL, and LORIN MAAZEL. Dohnányi remained at this position until 2002, when he became music director laureate. During his tenure, Dohnányi recorded extensively and oversaw the renovation of SEVERANCE HALL, the orchestra's home.

Dorati, Antal (1906–1988) *conductor*

Born in Hungary, Dorati became an American citizen in 1947 and was one of the most important American conductors of the 20th century. He studied with Béla Bartók and Zoltán Kodály in Hungary, and made his debut at the Hungarian State Opera when he was 18. His American debut was with the NATIONAL SYMPHONY ORCHESTRA in Washington, D.C., in 1937. He became music director of the American Ballet Theater in 1941. Dorati's first permanent appointment with an American symphony orchestra was as music director of the DALLAS SYMPHONY from 1945 to 1949. He moved to the Minneapolis Symphony in 1949, residing there as music director until 1960. He worked mostly in Europe during the 1960s, then resumed his succession of American directorships in 1970, with the National Symphony. In 1977 he became music director of the DETROIT SYMPHONY.

He also conducted the Royal Philharmonic Orchestra in London during this period. When he retired from active conducting, Dorati was lifetime conductor laureate of three orchestras: the Royal Philharmonic, the Stockholm Philharmonic, and the Detroit Symphony. He epitomized and helped create the globe-trotting style of the superstar conductor.

Druckman, Jacob (1928–1996) *composer*

Jacob Druckman studied composition at the JUILLIARD SCHOOL, where his teachers included PETER MENNIN and VINCENT PERSICHETTI. He won a Fulbright Scholarship to study composition in Paris in 1954. He received a masters degree in music from Juilliard in 1956. Druckman's work covers an exceptionally wide range. He was an orchestral colorist, whose *Aureole* (1979), commissioned by LEONARD BERNSTEIN and the NEW YORK PHILHARMONIC, was praised in the *New York Times* for its "shimmering, vaporous, iridescent textures." He also wrote 12-tone music and was involved in electronic music. He directed the electronic music department at Yale University during the 1971–72 school year; before that he was associated with the COLUMBIA-PRINCETON ELECTRONIC MUSIC CENTER. He returned to Yale as chairman of the composition department in 1976. Druckman taught at Juilliard from 1956 to 1972, and at Bard College from 1961 to 1967.

Druckman's most important association might have been with the New York Philharmonic. He was artistic director of that orchestra's three consecutive Horizons festivals, in which many American composers received much-needed exposure. He was also appointed the Philharmonic's composer in residence in 1982. In 1981 the METROPOLITAN OPERA commissioned an opera (*Medea*), but Druckman was unable to complete the work and the commission was canceled in 1986. In 1991 Druckman was appointed president of the Aaron Copland Fund for Music. When he died, he had begun work on a piano concerto for pianist EMANUEL AX.

Dudley, Buck (1839–1909) *composer and organist*

Buck Dudley, a prominent organist and composer, helped establish organ music and choral music for American audiences. He studied organ and piano in the United States and Germany. One of America's first touring organists, he introduced music of Bach and Mendelssohn. Dudley was on the faculty of the New England Conservatory of Music in Boston and was choirmaster of the Holy Trinity Church in that city. His book, *Illustrations in Choir Accompaniment,* was an important teaching reference. He composed 12 secular cantatas that, though out of the repertoire now, enjoyed repeated performances while Dudley was alive.

Duplicates: A Concerto for Two Pianos and Orchestra (1990)

Commissioned by the Koussevitzky Foundation, *Duplicates,* by MEL POWELL, won the Pulitzer Prize in 1990. It was premiered by the LOS ANGELES PHILHARMONIC on January 26, 1990.

Dvořák, Antonín (1841–1904) *composer*

Often regarded as the greatest Czech composer, Antonín Dvořák was among a small handful of the greatest (with Bedřich Smetana and Leoš Janácek). His brief residence in America (1892–95) had a profound impact on the musically young nation, even if his influence on American composers was not as potent as he would have liked.

In the late 19th century the United States generally, and New York City in particular, were culturally mature enough to realize their own cultural deficiencies. The American classical music scene relied almost entirely on European performers, composers, and influence. In 1891 a wealthy arts patron, Jeannette Thurber, hoped to recruit a prominent European musical figure, install that individual semipermanently in an American institution, and attempt to cultivate a uniquely American strain of music. That musical luminary

Antonín Dvořák (Bettmann/Corbis)

turned out to be Dvořák, who was lured by the promise of a salary some 15 times what he was earning at the Prague Conservatory. Thurber hired Dvořák to be president of the NATIONAL CONSERVATORY OF MUSIC in New York; his job would comprise a combination of administrative duties, ceremonial appearances, professorship, and composing. Dvořák arrived on September 15, 1892, and was quickly honored by a series of welcoming concerts and honorary events.

Dvořák's impact on American culture during the next three years was twofold: he composed several important works in a style that blended European classicism with a newly invented American vernacular, and he lectured American composers en masse on the requirements of creating a national musical style. On the latter point, Dvořák believed that American composers were too reliant on European traditions, and that their best path lay in appropriating indigenous musical elements—especially black American spirituals and popular tunes. Dvořák himself seemed to leapfrog ahead of his American contemporaries in this direction, quickly absorbing native song elements and incorporating American-sounding harmonies in his own music. His best-known work from this period is the Symphony no. 9 (*From the New World*), usually known as the *New World Symphony.* He also wrote several chamber pieces and songs while in America, all of which were received by critics with praise and gratitude. The symphony, when debuted by the PHILHARMONIC SYMPHONY SOCIETY OF NEW YORK in December 1893, was probably Dvořák's greatest professional triumph.

An economic recession in 1893 threw a wrench into Thurber's plans to keep Dvořák in America. With her family suddenly facing bankruptcy, Thurber failed to pay Dvořák's salary completely. Still, the composer stayed for two more seasons of partial payment before dissolving his contract and moving back to Böhmen, as Czechoslovakia was known before 1918. In his wake, American music lovers had major new works written explicitly for them, but American composers were not quick to follow Dvořák's advice. New American classical music continued to sound imitative of European music, until the early compositions of MACDOWELL and COPLAND provided evidence of an emerging national style.

Dwight, John Sullivan (1813–1893) *music critic*
The first American-born music critic, John Sullivan Dwight, through his writings, immeasurably elevated music appreciation and the level of cultural discourse. He founded a music criticism journal, *Dwight's Journal of Music,* which he edited and contributed to for nearly 30 years (1852–81). Archives of *Dwight's Journal* were produced and published by the publisher U.M.I. in 1991.

Eastman School of Music

A distinguished music school and the cultural center of Rochester, New York, Eastman was founded in 1912 as the Dossenbach-Klingenberg School of Music, named for its founders. Two years later the name was changed to the DKG Institute of Musical Art. The school was acquired by George Eastman in 1918, and he installed it in a new building, which he gave to the University of Rochester. The Eastman Theater, which, with 3,100 seats has a larger capacity than CARNEGIE HALL, is the main concert venue in Rochester.

Eaton, John (b. 1935) *composer*

An innovator of microtonal composition, which divides the Western music scale into more than the traditional 12 semitones, John Eaton studied with ROGER SESSIONS at Princeton University. He studied extensively abroad, receiving five travel grants (three Prix de Rome and two Guggenheim Fellowships). In 1990 he received a MacArthur Fellowship. He has fulfilled numerous commissions and was one of the first composers to use portable synthesizers in his performance pieces. Eaton is a professor of composition at the University of Chicago.

Echoes of Time and the River (1967)

Winner of the Pulitzer Prize in 1968 and one of GEORGE CRUMB's most famous works, this orchestral suite was commissioned by the University of Chicago and premiered by the CHICAGO SYMPHONY ORCHESTRA on May 26, 1967.

Ehrling, Sixten (b. 1918) *conductor*

Swedish conductor Sixten Ehrling was the music director of the DETROIT SYMPHONY from 1963 to 1973. He was appointed director of the conducting department at the JUILLIARD SCHOOL in 1973 and has conducted the complete *Ring* cycle of Wagner at the METROPOLITAN OPERA.

Eichheim, Henry (1870–1942) *composer*

Remembered as a composer, Henry Eichheim made his early career as a violinist with the THEODORE THOMAS Orchestra, then with the BOSTON SYMPHONY ORCHESTRA from 1890 to 1912. He turned to composing in later years and was one of the first of many American composers to draw inspiration from Asian music. He traveled intermittently through Japan, Korea, China, Bali, and India in the 1920s and 1930s. He transcribed local folk melodies for later appropriation and collected native instruments. His orchestral pieces *JAVA* (1929) and *BALI* (1933) incorporate use of gamelans—Indonesian percussion ensembles. He also composed traditional European-style music for the violin and songs based on English poetry.

Einstein on the Beach (1976)

PHILIP GLASS's first opera resulted in quick fame for its composer. The work was premiered in Europe, then presented by the METROPOLITAN OPERA in November 1976. The New York performances drew a mixed response from the audience, which sat through the production without intermission. The piece is a four-hour extension of minimalism. Clive Barnes, penning a generally positive review of the opera in the *New York Times,* wrote, "Special congratulations to the audience," and advised prospective attendees of the second performance, "You will never forget it, even if you hate it."

Elman, Mischa (1891–1967) *violinist*
Russian-born Mischa Elman became an American citizen in 1923, after living primarily in the United States for 12 years. He played his New York debut in 1910 and founded the Elman String Quartet in 1926. His most influential training came from Leopold Auer. Elman's stardom was founded first on his gorgeous tone and passionately subjective interpretations, and secondarily on technique. His reputation suffered somewhat, both while he was playing and posthumously, by the impact of JASCHA HEIFITZ on the concert scene—Heifitz was technically spectacular, more objective in his interpretations, and helped lead critical standards in that direction.

Eschenbach, Christoph (b. 1940) *conductor and pianist*
German Christoph Eschenbach's influence on American music has mostly been as a music director of two major orchestras. He led the HOUSTON SYMPHONY ORCHESTRA from 1988 to 1999. In 2003 he was appointed music director of the PHILADELPHIA ORCHESTRA.

Face of the Night, the Heart of the Dark, The (1991)

Winner of a Pulitzer Prize in 1992 for WAYNE PETERSON, this orchestral piece was premiered by the SAN FRANCISCO SYMPHONY on October 17, 1991.

Falletta, JoAnne (b. 1954) *conductor*

A pioneer in the mostly male field of conducting, JoAnne Falletta attended the MANNES COLLEGE OF MUSIC and received a doctorate from the JUILLIARD SCHOOL in 1989. While a student she served as associate conductor of the Milwaukee Symphony Orchestra (1985–88) and music director of the Queens Philharmonic in New York (1978–88). She was music director of the Denver Chamber Orchestra from 1983 to 1992. She has worked in a long association with the Virginia Symphony Orchestra, to which she was appointed music director in 1991. In 1998 she became music director of the BUFFALO PHILHARMONIC ORCHESTRA, and she currently runs both the Virginia and Buffalo groups. She has guest-conducted the orchestras of Philadelphia, Los Angeles, Houston, and the NATIONAL SYMPHONY, in addition to innumerable second-tier U.S. orchestras. In Germany, Falletta became the first woman to conduct the Mannheim Orchestra in that group's 200-year history. Falletta received a National Endowment for the Arts Conductor Award, the Stokowski Competition award, a Toscanini Award, a Ditson Award from Columbia University, and a Bruno Walter Award. She has recorded in Buffalo and Virginia, and with

the London symphony Orchestra and the English Chamber Orchestra.

Fanfare for the Common Man (1942)

Only three minutes long, this piece scored for brass and percussion has become one of the best-known fragments of American classical music and one of AARON COPLAND's most enduring pieces. Copland incorporated the *Fanfare* theme in his Symphony no. 3 (1946).

Farberman, Harold (b. 1929) *percussionist, conductor, and composer*

Harold Faberman graduated from the Juilliard School of Music (later the JUILLIARD SCHOOL) in 1951, then became the youngest member of the BOSTON SYMPHONY ORCHESTRA when he joined the percussion section. He studied with AARON COPLAND and has written numerous pieces for percussion ensembles, with and without other instruments. But his most influential works have been composed on commission from major institutions. His opera *The Losers* was commissioned by LINCOLN CENTER for the opening of the Juilliard Opera Theater in 1971. He has composed symphonies for the Oakland and Denver Symphony Orchestras and for the Bournemouth Sinfonietta in England. His commissioned dance music includes assignments from the Murray Lewis Company and the Emily Grankel Dance Drama Company. He scored music for the Hollywood film *The Great American Cowboy*

(1974). Farberman founded the American Conductors' Guild in 1975 and instituted a conducting school at the University of West Virginia in 1981. Likewise, Farberman started the Conductors Institute at Bard College, where he is on faculty. As a conductor, Farberman has visited many orchestras around the world and was the conductor of the Oakland Symphony Orchestra from 1971 to 1979.

Farwell, Arthur (1872–1952) *composer and music publisher*

Although Arthur Farwell was a prolific composer, famous in his time, his legacy is based on his innovative music-publishing ventures. He was the founder and editor of the WA-WAN PRESS, a subscription publication that released new works of leading composers between its founding in 1901 and 1912, when it was acquired and discontinued by the publishing house G. SCHIRMER. Farwell also founded the American Music Society in 1905, during a period when he was promoting American music nationwide in lectures and concerts.

Farwell became a musician late in life, having graduated from the Massachusetts Institute of Technology with a degree in electrical engineering in 1893 before beginning studies with GEORGE WHITEFIELD CHADWICK, a leading composer of the so-called Second New England School (a composing trend, not an institution). Farwell rebelled against Chadwick's traditionalism, veering off on an artistic path that would see fairly radical compositions in his later years. Farwell studied briefly in Europe and lectured on music history at Cornell University from 1899 to 1901. After his Wa-Wan period, Farwell taught at the University of California, Berkeley (1918–19), and Michigan State College (1927–39).

The Wa-Wan Press was named after a peace ceremony performed by Omaha Indians. Indeed, Farwell was profoundly influenced by Native American ("Amerindian") music and appropriated many native tunes in his compositions. The press was an extraordinary accomplishment in every way; a PBS biography of Farwell called Wa-Wan "one of the most significant and idealistic efforts of our cultural history." The near-monthly issues contained two volumes each—one of vocal music and one of instrumental music. They were produced beautifully and included elaborate, scholarly introductions by Farwell. Wa-Wan provided exposure to an entire generation of emerging composers—37 in all. The venture eventually lost steam due to a drop in subscribers, and G. Schirmer, while offering the catalogue of previously published pieces for sale, did not continue publishing new pieces. A reprint of the entire Wa-Wan Press output was published by Arno Press in collaboration with the *New York Times* in 1970.

Farwell's own Amerindian-inspired works, some of which were published in the Wa-Wan Press, started by treating folk material in the classic European tradition, arranged with European harmonies. As Farwell's sophistication evolved, along with his determination to present indigenous music in a uniquely appropriate harmonic setting, his pieces became more modern, even avant-garde. In this way Farwell might be considered an artistic brother to Béla Bartók, the folk-inspired Hungarian composer. Farwell also composed many examples of pure music, of which his piano pieces have remained on the fringe of the standard repertoire. Notable among these are *Impressions of the Wa-Wan Ceremony* (1905) and the Piano Sonata (1949). He could be daringly original, as in his *What's in an Octave?*, which is scored entirely within a single 12-note span. Farwell is sometimes compared to CHARLES IVES, for both his willingness to experiment and his intense interest in many forms of American folk music as applied to classical forms.

Fay, Amy (1844–1928) *pianist*

A musical feminist, Amy Fay studied with Carl Tausig in Berlin. Of greater historical interest was her apprenticeship with Franz Liszt in Weimar, Germany, as a participant in the legendary pianist's summertime master classes. Published collections of her letters have remained essential sources for Liszt scholars, while painting a vivid picture of European music study in the late 19th century. Of these, *Music Study in Germany* is the most important; it was published in 1880, with modern editions released by Dover Publications in 1965 and 1991. At home in America, Fay concertized brilliantly and was president of the New York Women's Philharmonic Society from 1903 to 1914.

Feldman, Morton (1926–1987) *composer*

Morton Feldman was one of the most important experimental composers of the 20th century. He began piano lessons at 12 and began composing immediately. He studied composition with WALLINGFORD RIEGGER and was deeply influenced by JOHN CAGE. Feldman described Cage's influence on him as that of a "green light," giving him the confidence to set down in music his inner aural landscape. He was dean of the New York Studio School from 1969 to 1971, then lived in Germany for two years composing for European ensembles. In 1973, Feldman was appointed Edgar Varèse Professor of Music at the State University of New York, Buffalo, a position he held for the remainder of his life. Feldman's music is minimalist and even more spacious and sparse than the compositions of pop minimalists like STEVE REICH and PHILIP GLASS. Some of his works are extremely long and require great concentration by performers and audience alike; the String Quartet no. 2 (1983) is over four hours long.

Feltsman, Vladimir (b. 1952) *pianist*

A Russian-born pianist who emigrated to the United States, Vladimir Feltsman performs a broad repertoire from a specialty in Bach to 20th-century music. He played with the Moscow Symphony at age 11 and studied at the Moscow Conservatory. He appeared on the international music map in 1971 by winning the Marguerite Long International Piano Competition in Paris. When he applied for an exit visa in 1979, the Soviet government banned him from all public performance. He finally prevailed in 1987, and his unofficial American debut took place that year at the White House. A more formal debut occurred, also in 1987, in CARNEGIE HALL. He has recorded and toured actively since. Feltsman holds the Distinguished Chair of Professor of Piano at the State University of New York at New Paltz, and he also teaches at the MANNES COLLEGE OF MUSIC. He founded the International Festival-Institute Piano Summer at New Paltz, an intensive training program for pianists that draws an international student body.

Festival of Two Worlds

Founded by GIAN CARLO MENOTTI in Spoleto, Italy, in 1958, this music festival spun off a U.S. version in Charleston, South Carolina, in 1977. Both festivals, especially the Charleston incarnation, are often known as the SPOLETO FESTIVAL.

Fiedler, Arthur (1894–1979) *conductor*

One of the most beloved conductors in American history, Arthur Fiedler is best remembered as leader of the BOSTON POPS, the country's foremost light-classical orchestra, a position he held for nearly 50 years. Fiedler was the son of violinist Emanuel Fiedler, a member of the BOSTON SYMPHONY ORCHESTRA. Arthur took his advanced training (in violin, piano, and conducting) in Germany, then joined the Boston Symphony on his return to the United States. In 1924 he formed the Boston Sinfonietta, a chamber orchestra spun off from the BSO. His appointment to lead the Boston Pops came in 1930, and he directed that group until his death. During this legendary tenure, Fiedler was also hired to lead the San Francisco Pops Orchestra (1951–78). Fiedler's Boston Pops was recorded more than any other orchestra in the world, and his outdoor July 4, 1976, concert was attended by 400,000 people, the largest single live audience for a classical concert in history. Fiedler received the Presidential Medal of Freedom in 1977 and was awarded honorary doctorates by Yale and Harvard Universities.

Fifty-four Studies for Player Piano (1948–1992)

The ongoing project of CONLON NANCARROW's life, the 50-plus studies for player piano are impossible for humans to play, so complex and dense are their passages. Freed of the constraint of performability, Nancarrow composed a remarkably original set of pieces whose rhythmic and harmonic innovations inspired later composers. Working with a roll-punch that created the player-piano "score," Nancarrow created pieces that use up to 12 simultaneous tempos and extremely complicated contrapuntal techniques. Besides the theoretical interest of these works, the tornado of notes conveys a uniquely vibrant and joyful listening experience.

Fine, Irving (1914–1962) *composer*

A tonal composer who turned to 12-tone techniques late in his career, Irving Fine had an impeccable musical pedigree. He studied with EDWARD BURLINGAME HILL and WALTER PISTON at Harvard University, where he received music degrees in 1937 and 1938. He worked with NADIA BOULANGER in Paris on harmony and composition, and with SERGE KOUSSEVITZKY on conducting. He taught music theory and history at Harvard from 1939 to 1950; there, he built close associations with AARON COPLAND, a fervent admirer of Fine's carefully composed music, and LEONARD BERNSTEIN. In 1950 he moved from Harvard to Brandeis University in Waltham, Massachusetts, where he taught until 1962. Fine's compositional output was small but finely wrought and universally respected. The String Quartet composed in 1952 was a milestone work, as it signaled a turn toward atonalism previously lacking in Fine's self-described "amiable" music of earlier years. Fine received two Guggenheim Fellowships, a National Institute of Arts and Letters Award, and a New York Music Critics' Circle Award.

Fine, Vivian (1913–2000) *composer*

A startling prodigy of music composition, Vivian Fine dropped out of high school at age 15 and devoted herself to writing music. She enjoyed an uninterrupted composing and teaching career until her death. She studied composition with RUTH CRAWFORD during her teen years and with ROGER SESSIONS during her twenties. Composer HENRY COWELL did not teach her but offered influential encouragement. The first public performances of her compositions occurred when she was 16 (Solo for Oboe, 1930) at the Pan American Association of Composers. From the start, Fine was a dedicated atonalist, committed to the leading edge of the avant-garde. She taught at New York University from 1945 to 1948, and taught briefly at the Juilliard School of Music (later the JUILLIARD SCHOOL) during that time. Fine joined the faculty of Bennington College in Bennington, Vermont, in 1964, remaining there until her retirement from teaching in 1987. She wrote a total of 140 compositions.

Finney, Ross Lee (1906–1997) *composer and teacher*

Ross Lee Finney grew up playing many kinds of music, including folk and jazz. His advanced composition studies make up a star-studded résumé of teachers in vogue during the 1920s and 1930s: NADIA BOULANGER in Paris, EDWARD BURLINGAME HILL at Harvard University, Alban Berg in Vienna, and ROGER SESSIONS in the U.S. Finney taught at Smith College starting in 1929, then moved to Mount Holyoke College in 1940. From 1949 to 1974 Finney was on the faculty at the University of Michigan, where he influenced younger composers LESLIE BASSETT, GEORGE CRUMB, and others. He received a Guggenheim Fellowship in 1937. Finney moved with the times when 12-tone atonalism became fashionable during the 1950s, but even his atonal pieces had a romantic flair and were more accessible than the more academic work of other composers. Finney published two books of essays and biographical material, *Thinking About Music:*

The Collected Writings of Ross Lee Finney and *Profile of a Lifetime*, both first published in 1992.

Firkusny, Rudolf (1912–1994) *pianist*
A Czech who became an American citizen in 1948, Firkusny exceeded an early reputation as a specialist in Czech-composed music to become a favored pianist of elegance and warmth. All his training occurred in Europe, at the Brno and Prague Conservatories, in Czechoslovakia. He made his American debut at New York's Town Hall in 1938, to lukewarm reviews. Critics warmed to his undemonstrative style over the years, though, and Firkusny performed innumerable times in New York and other major music centers. While he did bring the Czech repertoire to the forefront, especially Dvořák's piano concerto, Firkusny also played the general piano repertoire. He returned to Czechoslovakia in 1990 for a concert series.

Fleisher, Leon (b. 1928) *pianist*
Before 1965, Leon Fleisher was known as a robust and fiery interpreter of Liszt and Brahms. He had studied with the legendary pianist Artur Schnabel. He played a Liszt piano concerto with the SAN FRANCISCO SYMPHONY ORCHESTRA at age 16 and gave his New York debut with the NEW YORK PHILHARMONIC, playing the Brahms Piano Concerto in D Minor, two years later. He was the first American to win the Queen Elizabeth International Piano Competition in Brussels, in 1952. In 1965, Fleisher's career suffered a devastating setback when his right hand was afflicted with a type of repetitive stress syndrome, rendering it useless for high-level pianism. Fleisher turned to conducting, making his baton debut at the Mostly Mozart Festival in New York, in 1970. Fleisher learned the small repertoire that exists for the left hand—Ravel and Prokofiev wrote piano concertos for the left hand, and several solo pieces have been composed for the left hand. His recordings of that repertoire have been successful. Fleisher

taught at the Peabody Conservatory of Music from 1959, where Lorin Hollander and ANDRÉ WATTS were among his students. Time and therapy had some healing effect on his right hand, and since 1995, when he performed a Mozart concerto with the CLEVELAND ORCHESTRA, Fleisher has resumed performances of selected two-hand material while continuing to promote left-hand repertoire. He has received honorary doctorates from several institutions and is a fellow of the Amercian Academy of Arts and Sciences.

Fleming, Renée (b. 1959) *opera singer*
Soprano and operatic superstar Renée Fleming studied at the State University of New York, Potsdam, where she worked with Patricia Misslin. She took her graduate work at the EASTMAN

Renée Fleming (Robbie Jack/Corbis)

SCHOOL OF MUSIC, then attended the American Opera Center of the JUILLIARD SCHOOL from 1983 to 1987, studying with Beverley Johnson. She made her debut in Salzburg in 1986 and the next year won the Eleanor McCollum Competition in Houston. Her New York debut followed in 1989, and she first sang at the METROPOLITAN OPERA in 1991, after winning that company's Audition Award. On opening night at the Metropolitan in 1995, Fleming was paired with Placido Domingo in a landmark performance of Verdi's Otello that gained her lasting fame and established her as one of the sought-after voices in contemporary opera. Unusual among opera singers, Fleming is prized for both lyric and dramatic roles. Her range of venues is equally broad, as she is comfortable on the concert stage, in the opera house, and in the recording studio.

Flight into Egypt, The (1986)

Scored for chorus, organ, orchestra, and vocal soloists, this work won JOHN HARBISON a Pulitzer Prize in 1987. It was premiered by the Cantata Singers and Ensemble and the NEW ENGLAND CONSERVATORY in Boston, on November 21, 1986.

Flivver Ten Million (1926)

An orchestral tone poem, *Flivver Ten Million* was FREDERICK CONVERSE's most attention-getting composition and remains the work he is remembered for. As a product of the early automotive age, the piece gave musical expression to America's burgeoning industrial maturity.

Floyd, Carlisle (b. 1926) composer

A successful opera composer, Floyd Carlisle wrote two mid-20th-century operas that have entered the standard repertoire. Starting as a pianist, he received bachelor and master degrees in that instrument from Syracuse University (1946 and 1949, respectively). He joined the piano faculty of Florida State University in 1947, and during a long tenure there he switched from the piano department to the composition department. His first operatic hit was *Susannah,* produced locally in 1955, then mounted at the NEW YORK CITY OPERA the next year. Reviews were uniformly superlative, and Floyd won the New York Critics' Circle Award. *Susannah* was chosen as America's operatic entry in the Brussels World Fair in 1958. It has been produced internationally. Floyd's other trademark opera is *Of Mice and Men,* premiered by the Seattle Opera in 1970. This work, too, has been performed internationally. Floyd wrote his own librettos, making him the most resourceful operatic composer of his generation. He has also written purely orchestral works. Floyd received a Guggenheim Fellowship in 1956 and the National opera Institute's Award for Service to American opera in 1983. That same year he was granted an honorary doctorate from Dickinson College in Carlisle, Pennsylvania.

Foote, Arthur (1853–1937) composer

Arthur Foote received the first master of arts degree awarded by an American University. He entered the music profession as a pianist, having studied at the NEW ENGLAND CONSERVATORY and Harvard College (later Harvard University). He studied harmony, counterpoint, and composition at both institutions—with JOHN KNOWLES PAINE at Harvard. He obtained a bachelor's degree from Harvard in 1874, and the unprecedented masters, also from Harvard, the following year. He played his piano debut in Boston in 1876. As a composer, Foote was a member of the so-called Boston Six, sometimes known historically as the Second New England School. (Other composers affiliated with the Boston Six were Paine, HORATIO PARKER, GEORGE CHADWICK, EDWARD MACDOWELL, and AMY BEACH.) Foote is regarded today as a conservative composer, but his musical activities were considered radical. He traveled to Bayreuth, Germany, to attend new productions of Richard Wagner's operas, and he promoted "advanced" music such as Brahms and Saint-Saëns at home. Foote wrote a treatise on harmony, *Modern Harmony in Its Theory and Practice* (1905), which is now of only historical interest.

Foss, Lukas (b. 1922) *composer and conductor*

German-born American Lukas Foss has created a body of work that follows the legacy of LEONARD BERNSTEIN in its diversity and record of accomplishment. He studied in Berlin and Paris until his family moved to the United States in 1937. He enrolled at the CURTIS INSTITUTE OF MUSIC, where he studied piano, conducting, and composition. His first published work (issued by music publisher G. SCHIRMER) was brought out when he was 15. He graduated from Curtis at 18 and, from 1939 to 1943, studied alternately with SERGE KOUSSEVITZKY at the Berkshire Music Center (conducting) and PAUL HINDEMITH at Yale University (composing). He received a Fulbright Scholarship to study in Rome, from 1950 to 1952. Foss also won a Guggenheim Fellowship. He was the pianist of the BOSTON SYMPHONY ORCHESTRA from 1944 to 1950; this ensemble position didn't stop Foss from pursuing a solo career amid his conducting and composing, and he performed concertos with many American orchestras. His musical directorships have been many and distinguished: the BUFFALO PHILHARMONIC (1963–70), his signature position as leader of the BROOKLYN PHILHARMONIC (1971–90, then conductor-laureate for life), the Milwaukee Symphony (1981–86, then conductor-laureate for life). He has guest-conducted all over the world. Foss currently resides on the faculty of Boston University, which he joined in 1991.

As a composer, Foss has been prolific, adventurous, original, and universally respected. His early work, of which a popular milestone was *The Prairie* (1944, winner of the New York music Critics' Circle Award), was accessible and conservative. In the 1950s, Foss experimented with improvisational elements. He also dabbled in 12-tone atonality but

never committed to it; likewise with electronic parts in his pieces. His receptivity to new ideas makes his total body of work peculiarly American and representative of 20th-century culture. AARON COPLAND gave tribute to Foss's pieces as "among the most original and stimulating compositions in American music."

Foster, Lawrence (b. 1941) *conductor*

Currently music director of the Gulbenkian Orchestra in Lisbon, conductor Lawrence Foster has held directorships of several orchestras in America and Europe. His career started with the Young musicians Foundation Debut orchestra in Los Angeles, which he took over in 1959 at the age of 18. He continued as associate conductor of the San Francisco Ballet from 1961 to 1964. He studied at the Berkshire Music Center (later TANGLEWOOD) and won the Koussevitzky Prize there in 1966. From 1965 to 1968, Foster was the assistant conductor of the LOS ANGELES PHILHARMONIC Orchestra. Across the Atlantic, he debuted in London with the English Chamber orchestra in 1967. His career became solidly grounded in 1972 with his appointment as music director of the HOUSTON SYMPHONY ORCHESTRA. Resigning from that position in 1978, Foster moved to Europe for the most part, engaging in a series of appointments in France, Germany, Spain, and, in the Middle East, Israel. Foster conducted the premiere of Paul McCartney's oratorio *Standing Stone* with the London Symphony orchestra in 1997.

Foster, Sidney (1917–1977) *pianist*

The first pianist to win the Leventritt Award (1940), Sidney Foster studied with Isabelle Vengerova and David Saperton at the CURTIS INSTITUTE OF MUSIC, from which he graduated in 1938. His debut, with the New York Philharmonic, came in 1941. He toured Europe and the Soviet Union aggressively. Foster taught at Florida State University (1949–51) and at Indiana University (1952–77).

4'33" (1952)

JOHN CAGE's marquee composition, and probably his most controversial work in a career marked by controversy, *4'33"* contains no notation or instructions to the performer except to maintain strict silence. The piece is divided into three movements. The audience's listening experience consists of environmental sounds that transpire during the performer's silence. Cage was fascinated by silence and chance in music, and this piece represents his boldest experiment in both those directions at once.

Frank, Claude (b. 1925) *pianist*

Born in Germany, Claude Frank became an American citizen in 1944. He studied piano with Artur Schnabel in the United States during the 1940s, and composition with Paul Dessau. He made his New York debut in 1947. A thoughtful artist, Frank plays a good deal of chamber music, having been associated with the Boston Symphony Chamber Players and the JUILLIARD STRING QUARTET. He has performed the complete cycle of Beethoven sonatas. Frank's unadventurous repertoire rarely extends into modern music. His playing is highly regarded for its intelligence and integrity.

Freeman, Lawrence (1869–1954) *composer and conductor*

The first black American to compose prolifically for the operatic stage, and the first to conduct his own works, Lawrence Freeman started out as a church organist, later devoting himself to composition. He composed 14 operas. Freeman taught at Wilberforce University in Ohio from 1902 to 1904. In 1911 he founded the Freeman School of music in New York.

Freeman, Paul (b. 1936) *conductor*

Founder of the Chicago Sinfonietta, Paul Freeman received his Bachelor's, Masters, and Doctorate from the EASTMAN SCHOOL OF MUSIC (1956, 1957, 1963). While at Eastman, Freeman conducted the Opera Theater of Rochester. He received a Fulbright Scholarship for two years of study abroad, which he took in Berlin. He was associate conductor of the Dallas and Detroit Orchestras, and was principal guest conductor of the Helsinki Philharmonic orchestra. His first music directorship was with the Victoria Symphony in Canada, from 1979 to 1989. In 1996, Freeman was appointed music director of the Czech National Symphony orchestra. He currently maintains both that position and the directorship of the Chicago Sinfonietta.

Free Song, A (Secular Cantata no. 2) (1942)

Scored for four-part chorus and orchestra by composer WILLIAM SCHUMAN, *Free Song* received a Pulitzer Prize in 1943—the first Pulitzer awarded in music. It was first performed by the BOSTON SYMPHONY ORCHESTRA.

From the Diary of Virginia Woolf (1974)

Scored for mezzo-soprano and piano by DOMINICK ARGENTO (and written specifically for mezzo Janet Baker), this work won a Pulitzer Prize in 1975. It consists of eight songs whose words were drawn from journal entries of English writer Virginia Woolf. It was commissioned by the Schubert Club of St. Paul, Minnesota, and was premiered by that group in Minneapolis on January 5, 1975.

From the New World (1893)

The most famous Symphony of Czech composer ANTONÍN DVOŘÁK, and that composer's work most associated with his time in America. *From the New World* was first published as his Symphony no. 5, but it is actually his ninth symphony. It is colloquially known as the *New World Symphony*. The premiere was played in New York in a CARNEGIE HALL concert conducted by Anton Seidl, on December 16, 1893. The piece was a huge popular and critical success. Although it is steeped in

European structural and harmonic tradition, the symphony's melodic and spiritual content evoke the fresh, exploratory, and triumphant qualities of a new and vibrant country. The *New World Symphony* is securely lodged in the standard orchestra repertoire; if anything, it has been overexposed compared with Dvořák's other eight symphonies.

Fry, William Henry (1813–1864) *composer*

Sometimes regarded as the father of American opera, William Henry Fry was one of the first American composers to compose large stage works and the first to produce a full-scale opera in the United States. That opera, *Leonora,* received its premiere in Philadelphia in 1845, and it remains Fry's magnum opus. His music, while ambitious in scale and professional intent, was extremely derivative of Italian opera. None of his works remains in the standard repertoire. Fry was an influential writer and critic; he admonished American composers to work toward an originality perhaps missing from his own composing, and he advised looking for native sources of influence.

Fuchs, Joseph (1899/1900–1997) *violinist*

Called the "greatest American-trained violinist" by colleague NATHAN MILSTEIN, Joseph Fuchs studied with FRANZ KNEISEL at the Institute of musical Art (later the JUILLIARD SCHOOL) in New York. He joined the CLEVELAND ORCHESTRA in 1926 and resigned in 1940. He made his New York debut as a violin soloist in 1943 and afterward toured around the world. He used a Ford Foundation grant (1960) to commission a violin concerto from WALTER PISTON. Fuchs joined the faculty of the Juilliard School of music in 1946, remaining there—and teaching actively—until his death 43 years later. During these years of residency in New York, Fuchs enjoyed an artistic collaboration with pianist ARTUR BALSAM; the two were nearly inseparable on New York concert stages until Balsam's death in 1994. Fuchs gave his final recital at age 93, in CARNEGIE HALL.

Fuleihan, Anis (1900–1970) *composer, pianist, conductor, and administrator*

Anis Fuleihan was born in Greece and became an American citizen in 1925. He made his piano debut in New York in 1919. Touring followed until 1930, when Fuleihan began to diversify his activities. He worked as a radio conductor and started composing. Mostly self-taught, he finished a number of stage works and pure-music compositions, and received a Guggenheim Fellowship in 1939. Major premieres with the NEW YORK PHILHARMONIC were performed during this period. He taught at Indiana University from 1947 to 1953.

Gabrilovich, Ossip (1878–1936) *pianist*
A Russian who settled in the United States in 1914, Ossip Gabrilovich toured successfully as a pianist. He made his most lasting mark as a conductor, leading the DETROIT SYMPHONY ORCHESTRA from 1914 to his death, raising that group's quality and prestige. He married Mark Twain's daughter, Clara Clemens, in 1909.

Galamian, Ivan (1903–1981) *teacher*
Born on Persia, and better known as a teacher than a performer, Ivan Galamian made his playing debut in Paris (1924) and moved to New York in 1937. One of the great celebrity music teachers of the 20th century, Galamian operated primarily at the CURTIS INSTITUTE, which he joined in 1944, and at the Juilliard School of music (later the JUILLIARD SCHOOL), which he joined in 1946. His diverse and luminary roster of students included Itzakh Perlman, MICHAEL RABIN, JAIME LAREDO, Pinchas Zuckerman, and many others. Galamian stressed mental control of physical movements, was famously demanding and detailed in his approach, and protected his students' individualities.

Garbousova, Raya (1906–1997) *cellist*
An American of Russian birth, Raya Garbousova began her American career with a blazingly successful New York debut in TOWN HALL on December 3, 1935. Her first debut was in Moscow in 1923; she immigrated to the United States in 1939 after estab-lishing her reputation in Berlin, Paris, and London. Garbousova was a member of the Vermeer Quartet. SAMUEL BARBER composed his cello concerto for Garbousova, as did Bittorio Rieti. (She recorded the Barber concerto on the American Decca label.) Pablo Casals, one of Garbousova's teachers, called her "the best cellist I have ever heard." After Garbousova's death, cellist MSTISLAV ROSTROPOVICH gave a concert in her memory at the International Cello Congress in 1997.

Garden, Mary (1874–1967) *opera singer*
Born in Scotland and relocated to America as a child, Mary Garden was a beloved and controversial opera singer. She spent most of her career in Scotland but was closely associated with the Chicago Civic Opera, which she directed for a sin-gle season (1921–22). Garden made an unscheduled debut when she filled in for an ailing singer of the Paris Opéra-Comique in mid-opera. In 1902, com-poser Claude Debussy picked her to sing Mélisande in the premiere of his opera, *Pelleas et Mélisande*. Her association with the Chicago Civic Opera, which began in 1910, was marked by controversy. She refused to sing with certain performers for rea-sons that remained obscure. The company's execu-tive manager, artistic director, and some company members quit. Turnover increased during Garden's short reign as general director.

Garden's entire career was controversial. She was primarily an actress, and her voice was criticized often and harshly. Interpretively, her performances were considered beyond peer, even by her detractors. So committed was Garden to her characterizations that, after performances in which her character died, she would not take a curtain call. She returned to Scotland in 1931 and retired from the opera stage to a large extent. She published a biography, *Mary Garden's Story,* in 1951. She last visited the United States in 1954, to audition singers for the National Arts Foundation.

Gatti-Casazza, Giulio (1869–1940)
administrator and director
An Italian impresario and music administrator, Giulio Gatti-Casazza was director of the METRO-POLITAN OPERA in New York from 1908 to 1935 (codirector, with Andreas Dippel, from 1908 to 1910)—the longest tenure in that position's history. He had been director of La Scala in Milan (1898–1908), where, as at the Metropolitan, he collaborated with ARTURO TOSCANINI.

Gebhard, Heinrich (1878–1963) *pianist*
Born in Germany, Heinrich Gebhard made his American debut with the BOSTON SYMPHONY ORCHESTRA in 1899 and performed annually with that orchestra for the next three decades. He composed a handful of works, instrumental and vocal. His book, *The Art of Pedaling,* was published in 1963.

Gershwin, George (1898–1937) *composer, songwriter, and pianist*
George Gershwin was one of America's best-known, financially successful, and widely recognized musicians. As if driven by an inner knowledge of the short lifetime before him, Gershwin left high school at age 15 to work in New York's Tin Pan Alley—the music publishing district. There, he earned $15 a week from Jerome H. Remick as a "song plugger," playing the publisher's material to recording artists. Already having a grounding in classical pianism, Gershwin gained expertise in practical piano playing, learning

to play a song in any key and any style on demand. He also developed his legendary improvisational skills during this period. He began recording solo piano rolls; eventually he made more than 100.

Gershwin's first big leap, from Tin Pan Alley to Broadway, was accomplished as rehearsal pianist for the musical *Miss 1917.* He had been composing for years but without a sale. In 1918 Gershwin accepted a retainer from the Harms Publishing Company for the rights to any original songs. His resulting songs made their ways into Broadway musicals, and in 1919 Gershwin's first fully-composed musical, *La La Lucille,* opened. In 1920, Gershwin's song "Swanee" was recorded by singer Al Jolson and became a hit record and Gershwin's first lucrative music property. During the early 1920s his Broadway career shifted into high gear, and he contributed songs to eight musicals by 1924, three of which were composed entirely by Gershwin. The production of *Lady Be Good!* in 1924 starred dancer Fred Astaire and was the first full-length collaboration between Gershwin and his older brother Ira, George's most steadfast lyricist. By 1930 Gershwin had completed *Oh Kay!, Rosalie, Show Girl, Strike Up the Band, Funny Face,* and *Girl Crazy,* in which musicals the enduring songs "Fascinatin' Rhythm," "How Long Has This Been Going On," "Embraceable You," " 'S Wonderful," "Someone to Watch Over Me," and many others were included.

During this eventful decade, Gershwin's career took a formal turn with the spectacular success of RHAPSODY IN BLUE, a classical-jazz piece for piano and orchestra that premiered in New York on February 12, 1924. More than just a new successful piece of music, *Rhapsody* installed Gershwin as an historical figure who placed the jazz idiom in a classical context, elevating a native expression of American music to concert status and blending it with European tradition. *Rhapsody in Blue* was immediately embedded in the standard classical repertoire, and Gershwin became an international celebrity on every level—popular, critical, and among the creative illuminati on both sides of the Atlantic. Gershwin did not recognize any genre division among theater music, classical music, popular music, and jazz. But his respect for classical forms held sway, and after the spectacular success of *Rhapsody,* Gershwin's theatrical composing slowed. During his remaining years, his landmark accomplishments were generally considered to be the Concerto in F (1925), *AN AMERICAN IN PARIS* (an orchestral tone poem completed in 1928), and the "folk opera" *PORGY AND BESS* (completed in 1935 and opened on Broadway, in the Alvin Theater).

Gershwin's sudden death at age 38 was one of the stunning curtailments of musical life. He was a few years older than Mozart when that composer died, and a year younger than Chopin. Gershwin slipped unexpectedly into a coma after complaining of dizziness; a brain tumor was discovered and Gershwin died just after emergency surgery. He was an ambitious, social, and popular man, and it seemed as if his brilliant star had just begun to rise. Memorial services were held bicoastally; in New

George Gershwin (Underwood & Underwood/Corbis)

York, the governor and mayor were pallbearers, along with WALTER DAMROSCH (conductor of the New York Philharmonic), pianist LEOPOLD GODOWSKY, and producer/director Arthur Hammerstein. Gershwin's obituary was carried on page one of the *New York Times*.

Giants in the Earth (1949)

Not DOUGLAS S. MOORE's most popular or enduring opera, *Giants in the Earth* did win a Pulitzer Prize in 1951. It was premiered by the Columbia opera Workshop on March 28, 1951.

Gilbert, Henry F. B. (1868–1928) *composer*

One of the early 20th-century composers struggling to forge a national style from indigenous musical influences, Henry Gilbert wrote a handful of dramatic works, over a dozen orchestral pieces, many songs, and a smattering of chamber music. He was born to a musical family and studied violin, piano, and theory as a boy. Gilbert studied composition with EDWARD MACDOWELL for several years. He was also closely associated with ARTHUR FARWELL's WA-WAN PRESS, the groundbreaking new-music publishing company. As was the case with other Wa-Wan composers, Gilbert was interested in American Indian music and incorporated elements of that tradition in his own works. He also borrowed extensively from black American music, especially in the first half of his career (*Comedy Overture on Negro Themes*, 1906.) Gilbert's works were popularly performed in Europe. He was the author of numerous articles in the Wa-Wan Press and *New Music Review* on subjects ranging from jazz to recollections of MacDowell to American Indian music.

Gilchrist, William W. (1846–1916) *composer and conductor*

William Gilchrist enjoyed an active career in Philadelphia around the turn of the 20th century. The organ was Gilchrist's main instrument, and he served as organist of a succession of Philadelphia churches. As a conductor, he led the Symphony Society of Philadelphia from 1892 to 1899, and the Mendelssohn Club (which he founded) from 1874 to 1914. Gilchrist won the Cincinnati Festival Association Prize in 1882 and the Mendelssohn Club Prize three times. As a composer, his most important premiere was of his Symphony in C by the PHILADELPHIA ORCHESTRA in 1901. Gilchrist did not create an extensive portfolio of compositions, but most of his work was published in his lifetime. He wrote two symphonies, two other works for orchestra, and many vocal works, some of which are liturgical.

Gilman, Lawrence (1878–1939) *music essayist and critic*

Lawrence Gilman was fairly conservative in his tastes, championing past composers more than present ones of his day. However, his most famous review was that of CHARLES IVES's *CONCORD SONATA* for piano—a dense, dissonant, challenging work composed between 1910 and 1915. Gilman called it "The greatest music composed by an American," and his superlative review helped immeasurably to galvanize greater recognition of Ives, and certainly of the sonata. Gilman was editor of *Harper's Weekly* from 1911, then he wrote for *Harper's Magazine* and the *North American Review*. He was closely associated with the *New York Tribune*, where he was music critic from 1923 until his death in 1939. He wrote program notes for major orchestras in New York and Philadelphia. Gilman authored several books on music, including *Phases of Modern Music* (1904), *Aspects of Modern Opera* (1909), and *Toscanini and Great Music* (1938).

Gingold, Joseph (1909–1995) *teacher*

Joseph Gingold emigrated from Poland to the United States (New York) in 1920. One of the outstanding violin teachers of the 20th century, Gingold taught at Indiana University, Bloomington, where future luminaries JAIME LAREDO, JOSHUA BELL, and others passed through his teaching studio. Gingold also taught at Western Reserve University in Cleveland from 1950 to 1960, Meadowmount School of Music from 1955 to 1981, and MANHATTAN SCHOOL OF MUSIC (Mischa Elman Chair) during the 1980–81 year, and he gave frequent master classes at the Paris Conservatory during the 1970s. While living in Bloomington, Gingold cofounded the International Violin Competition of Indianapolis. As a performer, Gingold was an orchestra principal and occasional soloist. He was a first violinist with ARTURO TOSCANINI in the NBC SYMPHONY ORCHESTRA (1937–43), then concertmaster of the DETROIT SYMPHONY and the CLEVELAND ORCHESTRA.

Giulini, Carlo Maria (b. 1914) *conductor*

Italian Carlo Maria Giulini started in opera then shifted to the concert repertoire. He conducted orchestras in Europe and made his career primarily in London until the late 1960s. He became the principal guest conductor of the CHICAGO SYMPHONY ORCHESTRA in 1969 and was chief conductor of the LOS ANGELES PHILHARMONIC ORCHESTRA from 1978 to 1984.

Glass, Philip (b. 1937) *composer*

A cult favorite of mainstream proportions, Philip Glass established minimalism as a popular genre. Performing with his own PHILIP GLASS ENSEMBLE and extending his work into Hollywood movies, Glass is considered more a pop composer than a classical one, in some quarters.

Glass studied violin and flute as a child, and started composing around age 12. He received a bachelor of arts from the University of Chicago in 1956. During his college studies Glass learned and adopted 12-tone composition techniques. He went on to the JUILLIARD SCHOOL, where he received a master of arts in composition in 1961. By this time Glass had abandoned 12-tone writing and was influenced by

AARON COPLAND and WILLIAM SCHUMAN. He studied with VINCENT PERSICHETTI, DARIUS MILHAUD, and WILLIAM BERGSMA. He received a Ford Foundation grant in 1961, enabling his continued composing. Glass then used a Fulbright Scholarship for two intensive years of study with NADIA BOULANGER in Paris. During this time Glass was exposed to Indian music for the first time, and he began researching musical traditions of North Africa and India, traveling until his return to New York in 1967. At that time he met Steve Reich, another pioneer of minimalism, and the two performed together sporadically until the early 1970s.

A series of three New York concerts in 1968 brought Glass's music to public attention and launched his reputation as an avant-garde minimalist. The Philip Glass Ensemble was formed during this period, with a core group of wind and keyboard players, sometimes supplemented by singers and string players. Glass was a prolific composer for his group, turning out a multitude of abstractions with titles such as *Music in Contrary Motion, Music in Fifths, Music in Similar Motion,* and *Music in Twelve Parts*—the last a summation of his work up to that point (premiered at TOWN HALL in 1974). Glass composed exclusively for the Philip Glass Ensemble for several years and withheld performance rights to his works to keep the ensemble touring.

Glass's opera EINSTEIN ON THE BEACH, premiered by the METROPOLITAN OPERA on November 21, 1976, put the composer on the musical map. The piece required five hours to perform, and the audience was invited to drift around the hall and lobby at will. His film music likewise catapulted Glass to new levels of cultish stardom. In particular, KOYAANISQATSI (1982), which featured Glass's repetitive propulsions underscoring otherwise soundless images, garnered much publicity. It was followed by two films that contributed to an eventual trilogy: *Powaqqatsi* and *Naqoyqatsi.* In these and other works, Glass's trademark style is repetitive, slowly additive, and generally trance-inducing. He has been a prolific composer, completing dozens of dramatic works, vocal pieces, and a huge portfolio of instrumental music.

Gleason, Frederick G. (1848–1903) *composer, writer, and teacher*

Frederick Gleason based his career in Chicago for the most part. He was head of the theory department at the American Conservatory from 1891 to 1900, when he assumed the directorship of that school. Gleason composed two operas and a handful of orchestral works. His criticism appeared in the *Chicago Tribune,* and he edited the journal *Music Review* from 1891 to 1894.

Godowsky, Leopold (1870–1938) *pianist*

A Polish-born pianist who visited the United States in 1884 and moved to the United States in 1890, Leopold Godowsky was one of his generation's great virtuosos who also composed. His original works have not entered the standard piano repertoire, but they are notable for their technical demands. Godowsky's pianism contained more depth than flash, though, and he propounded a method of playing that involved shifts of weight rather than muscular efforts. He composed a famous series of studies on Chopin's Études—as if the originals weren't difficult enough without the additional notes Godowsky imposed upon them! He also transcribed works of Bach for the piano. Godowsky taught at the New York College of Music when he first immigrated to this country. He recorded a good deal of the repertoire but suffered a debilitating stroke during a recording session. He was partially paralyzed during the remaining eight years of his life.

Goetschius, Percy (1853–1943) *teacher*

A musical academic and teacher of composition, Percy Goetschius held positions at Syracuse University, the NEW ENGLAND CONSERVATORY OF MUSIC, and the Institute of Musical Art (later the JUILLIARD SCHOOL) in New York, where he headed the composition department. His two most renowned pupils were HOWARD HANSON and HENRY COWELL. Goetschius edited musical scores and did some composing of his own, including a Symphony, piano pieces, and various vocal works. He was the author of several textbooks and many articles.

Goldmark, Rubin (1872–1936) *composer and composition teacher*

Rubin Goldmark studied in Europe (Vienna Conservatory, 1889–91) and America (City University of New York, 1887–89; National Conservatory 1891–93). He held teaching positions at the National Conservatory, Colorado College, and the New York College of Music. Goldmark chaired the composition department of the Juilliard School of music from 1924 to 1936. Composers AARON COPLAND and GEORGE GERSHWIN studied with Goldmark. Goldmark is remembered for a small portfolio of works, including *A Negro Rhapsody* (1922) and *The Call of the Plains* (1924).

Goldovsky, Boris (1908–2001) *conductor*

Boris Goldovsky was a Russian conductor who first moved to the United States to study at the CURTIS INSTITUTE OF MUSIC in 1930. Although he did not express an early love of opera, Goldovsky became known primarily as an operatic conductor and administrator. He was head of the opera department at the NEW ENGLAND CONSERVATORY OF MUSIC from 1942 to 1964, and during most of that period he also led the opera workshop at the Berkshire Music Center at TANGLEWOOD. He founded and directed the Goldovsky opera Theater, which operated until 1984. He hosted opera broadcasts on the radio during a time when such programs were tremendously popular. Goldovsky was the author of books about opera, including *Bringing Opera to Life* (1968).

Golschmann, Vladimir (1893–1972) *conductor*

A French conductor of Russian descent, Vladimir Golschmann gave his American debut in 1923.

He is best remembered for his 25-year tenure as music director of the St. Louis Symphony, a position he undertook immediately following his first encounter with that orchestra in 1931. He became an American citizen in 1947. He was named conductor emeritus in St. Louis in 1957, after which he held the podium at the Tulsa Symphony orchestra (1958–61) and the Denver Symphony Orchestra (1964–70).

Goode, Richard (b. 1943) *pianist*

Best known for his interpretations of the classic pre-1900 repertoire, especially Mozart, Beethoven, and Schubert, Richard Goode studied with Nadia Reisenberg of the MANNES COLLEGE OF MUSIC and Rudolf Serkin of the CURTIS INSTITUTE. His official debut came in 1962 in New York, when he was 19 years old. In 1973, Goode won the Clara Haskil Competition. He was the first American pianist to record the complete cycle of 32 Beethoven piano sonatas. He received the Avery Fisher Prize in 1980. Goode is currently codirector (with Japanese pianist Mitsuko Uchida) of the MARLBORO FESTIVAL. He concertizes busily and is most recognized for performances of Mozart and Beethoven.

Gorodnitzky, Sascha (1904–1986) *teacher*

Born in the Ukraine, Sascha Gorodnitzky became one of the most famous American piano teachers of the 20th century. He moved to the United States as a child and grew up mainly in New York City. He studied with Josef Lhevinne at the Juilliard School of Music (later, JUILLARD SCHOOL), where he would eventually teach. His concert debut came with the New York Philharmonic in 1930, and the next year Gorodnitzky made his recital debut in CARNEGIE HALL. He joined the Juilliard faculty in 1948, and while Gorodnitzky continued performing, his main legacy is as a pedagogue. An icon at Juilliard, he helped launch the career of GARRICK OHLSSON and others.

Gottschalk, Louis Moreau (1829–1869)
composer and pianist

During his life, Louis Moreau Gottschalk was known as a piano virtuoso—one of the best and brightest of American origin. Since his death, however, Gottschalk's legacy has been based mostly on his compositions, most of which express a virtuosic pianism. He also composed a handful of operatic and instrumental (nonpiano) works, but his portfolio of piano pieces far outweighs everything else combined. His music was popular in its day, accessible to most tastes, and as worldly as one might expect from a man who lived in other countries for extended periods. After ANTHONY PHILIP HEINRICH, Gottschalk was the most popular and successful composer in America up to his time.

Gottschalk was born in New Orleans and reportedly showed musical talent by age five. He was exposed to Creole music from a young age, which, though its exact influence is hard to trace, might have instilled a musical open-mindedness at the very least. Remarkably, Gottschalk decided at age 13 to move to Europe, on his own, to study music classically. He was rejected by the Paris Conservatoire and studied instead with private teachers. In his teens he built a European career as a piano virtuoso, impressing among others, Chopin. Gottschalk was one of the few Americans to engage fully in the intense European music scene during the 1840s, a period during which Franz Liszt was changing performance history with his piano touring and Chopin had recently published his groundbreaking Études for Piano. Gottschalk made his performing debut at the Salle Pleyel, one of the most fashionable performance spaces in Paris.

He returned to America in 1853 and immediately began touring. His often breathtaking pace, was reminiscent of Liszt's grueling, continent-spanning concert tours. Famously, Gottschalk once gave 85 recitals across 15,000 miles in a span of four and a half months. His illustrious life veered in a new direction in 1865, when he was forced to leave the United States in the wake of a false accusation of sexual impropriety with a female student. The pianist played his way out, embarking on a vast South American tour. Gottschalk never returned to the United States, though his supporters eventually cleared his name. He collapsed during an 1869 concert and died three weeks later.

Gould, Morton (1913–1996) *composer*

Morton Gould considered himself a composer first and foremost, though he also attained prominence as a pianist and a conductor. "Composing is my life blood," he said. He won a Pulitzer Prize in 1995 for *Stringmusic,* commissioned by the National Symphony Orchestra. Like Gershwin, Gould became a professional musician at a startlingly young age, parlaying naturally fluent piano skills into jobs on and around Broadway. By age 21 he was the house pianist at Radio City Music Hall. He became nationally famous through his arranging and conducting work on radio. Gould composed music for Broadway shows, including *Billion Dollar Baby* and *Arms and the Girl.* He also worked for film, television, and ballet. Paralleling Gershwin again, Gould was a fearless integrator, weaving strains of jazz, gospel, and folk music into his classical orchestrations. His *Chorale and Fugue in Jazz* was a breakthrough work in his career, premiered by LEOPOLD STOKOWSKI and the PHILADELPHIA ORCHESTRA. In 1993 the Van Cliburn International Piano Competition commissioned a new work, *Ghost Waltzes,* as a required contest piece. Gould was honored with multiple lifetime-achievement awards near the end of his life, including a Kennedy Center Honor and *Musical America*'s Composer of the Year in 1994. Gould was a member of the American Academy and Institute of Arts and Letters.

Graffman, Gary (b. 1928) *pianist*

One of the great piano virtuosos of the mid-20th century, Gary Graffman suffered a disability to his right hand beginning in 1979 that altered, but did not entirely curtail his career. This infirmity limited Graffman's repertoire to left-hand works during the intervening years. Before 1979, he was world renowned as one of the great romantic pianists, and one of the few pianists offered an invitation to study privately with VLADIMIR HOROWITZ. (Graffman did work with Horowitz during the early 1950s.) He got a quick start out of the gate, entering the prestigious CURTIS INSTITUTE OF MUSIC at age 10, graduating a few years later, winning the Rachmaninoff Prize in 1947, and the Levintritt Award in 1949, the latter of which led to high-profile debuts with the CLEVELAND ORCHESTRA and the NEW YORK PHILHARMONIC. Although Graffman is one of the few pianists to record with each of the "Big 5" American orchestras (New York, Boston, Cleveland, Philadelphia, and San Francisco), he became particularly associated with the Cleveland due to many recordings of the concerto repertoire. After the curtailment of his performing career, Graffman concentrated on teaching, joining the faculty at Curtis. In 1986 he became the school's eighth president, and he continues in that position as of this writing. Graffman published a memoir in 1981 entitled *I Really Should Be Practicing.*

Grainger, Percy (1882–1961) *composer and pianist*

Born in Australia and raised in Australia and Europe, Percy Grainger was a pianist, composer, and eccentric who became an American citizen in 1918. He was known for an athletic and virtuosic playing style, a handful of popular original compositions, and an outspokenness about art, racial purity, and sex. No less provocative than Richard Wagner's anti-Semitic proclamations, Grainger's self-described "all-roundedness" detracted from his music career for long periods, and his tendency toward self-admiration also hindered his musical evolution. At the same time, his progressive thinking about music was ahead of its time, and toward the end of his life Grainger experimented with what he called "free music," liberated from the constraints of rhythm and formal structure.

Grainger received his early training from his mother, Rose Grainger, with whom he experienced an exceptionally close relationship. His father left the family while Grainger was nine years old, further bonding the boy and his mother. Grainger gave a formal piano debut in Melbourne, Australia, at age 12, then moved to Germany with Rose to study at the Hoch Conservatory in Frankfurt from 1895 to 1901. After this German phase Grainger lived in London until 1914. He published his first musical works in 1911 and played a concert devoted to his own pieces in 1912. When he moved to the United States in 1914, Grainger's dual career took off. He made piano recordings on piano rolls and gramaphone discs, and signed a publishing agreement with G. SCHIRMER. During this period he composed *Country Gardens,* a piece with which he was identified for the rest of his life, and which he came to detest.

Grainger's mother committed suicide in 1922 by leaping from the 18th story of a New York building. Following this tragic event Grainger traveled in Europe collecting folk songs and continuing to perform. The rest of his life was marked by fitful alternations among the three main aspects of his career: performing, composing, and teaching. He reportedly earned up to $200 an hour for lessons, a fantastic sum in 1925. His personal and intellectual eccentricities kept him in the news, and he was financially secure for the rest of his life, though he suffered from a cancerous condition for several years before he died in 1961. His career drizzled out toward the end, and Grainger's final recordings were made at his home in White Plains, New York, on an upright piano.

Grand Canyon Suite (1931)

Emblematic of FERDE GROFÉ's series of light orchestral works with American themes, the *Grand Canyon Suite* helped popularize concert orchestral repertoire among audiences that had little interest in the standard symphonic fare. Grofé's other works of this sort included *Mississippi* (1925) and *Metropolis* (1928).

Greenburg, Noah (1919–1966) conductor and musicologist

Noah Greenburg is best remembered as the cofounder and chief promoter of the New York Pro Musica early-music group, which originated under the name Pro Musica Antiqua. He started the ensemble in 1952 with Bernard Krainis, a recorder player.

Greenhouse, Bernard (b. 1916) cellist

Bernard Greenhouse chose music over a premed education, and he attended the JUILLIARD SCHOOL. Later he studied with cellist Pablo Casals. Greenhouse made his professional debut in New York in 1946. He was a founding member of the BEAUX ARTS TRIO in 1955, and taught actively in New York during the 1950s and 1960s, at both Juilliard and the MANHATTAN SCHOOL OF MUSIC. Greenhouse was a founder and first president of the Violincello Society (1956–61).

Green Mansions (1937)

Composed during an era in which broadcast opera was popular entertainment, *Green Mansions,* by LOUIS GRUENBERG, was commissioned by CBS Radio and completed soon after Gruenberg moved from Chicago to California.

Griffes, Charles T. (1884–1920) composer

Charles Griffes was a recognized but deeply troubled American composer who died just as he was beginning to reap acceptance from the mainstream musical community. His early musical influences were his sister and his first formal teacher, Mary Selena Broughton. Broughton was influential in enabling Griffes to travel to Germany in 1903 for advanced study. The intent of this trip was to prepare Griffes for a career of concert pianist, but after two years he found himself concentrating on composition.

Griffes returned to America in 1907 and took on the responsibility of supporting his widowed mother (his father died in 1905). He took a position teaching music at the Hackley School in Tarrytown, New York, a job Griffes thought would be temporary. He remained at this post until his death in 1920. During these years Griffes mixed composition with campus duties, not without considerable frustration at his small salary, alienation from the musical scene transpiring in New York and other cities, and the grinding awareness that his circumstances did not match his talent. On the positive side, the school's pastoral setting and Griffes's modest responsibilities offered quiet and time for composition. He spent summers in New York City.

The first breakthrough came in 1917 when Griffes's orchestral arrangement of a piano piece, *The Pleasure-Dome of Kubla Kahn,* was performed by the New York Symphony orchestra to wild praise from the audience and critics alike. The piece was quickly picked up and performed by the BOSTON SYMPHONY ORCHESTRA. Griffes consolidated his position as one of America's important composers with his startlingly advanced and mature Piano Sonata of 1918, which moved beyond the romantic inclinations of his earlier work.

Griffes had not experienced robust health for several years when he collapsed at Hackley from accumulated heart and lung ailments in December 1919 and died several months later.

Grofé, Ferde (1892–1972) *musician*

One of the most successful American journeymen musicians, Ferde Grofé got his start at the turn of the 20th century with a cluster of musical jobs. He was a pianist, violinist, horn player, and arranger, playing both jazz and classical music. Before 1920 Grofé held down positions with the LOS ANGELES PHILHARMONIC and the SAN FRANCISCO SYMPHONY. In 1920 his life and career hinged on a meeting with Paul Whiteman, leader of a popular jazz orchestra. Whiteman hired Grofé as the band's arranger, and the result was a succession of hit recordings. Grofé's talent was composing jazz arrangements with the formality and attention to detail of the classical tradition. The two worked together and toured internationally for about 12 years, then Grofé left Whiteman's ensemble to make his own way.

Widely recognized for arranging *Rhapsody in Blue* and other well-known works, Grofé tried his hand at original composition, writing American-themed orchestral works such as *Mississippi, Metropolis,* and what is probably his most enduring composition, the *Grand Canyon Suite* (1931). After his break with Whiteman, Grofé resumed his itinerant career style, working as a radio arranger, composer, and teacher. He scored a handful of movies (his soundtrack for the 1944 film *Minstrel Man* received an Academy Award nomination), and taught orchestration at the JUILLIARD SCHOOL summer session from 1939 to 1942.

Gruenberg, Louis (1884–1964) *composer*

An American opera and film composer, Louis Gruenberg first wanted to be a concert pianist. Born in Russia, raised in the United States, and a student of pianist Ferruccio Busoni in Berlin, Gruenberg enjoyed success after his debut with the Berlin Philharmonic in 1912 at the relatively advanced age of 26; Busoni nudged him toward composition. Gruenberg returned to America in 1914 and won the Flagler Prize in 1920 for his symphonic poem *The Hill of Dreams.* He helped found the LEAGUE OF COMPOSERS in 1923. During this time Gruenberg dabbled in conducting, introducing modern works to American audiences. He taught at the Chicago Music College from 1933 to 1936, where he headed the composition department. He worked in Hollywood during the 1940s, garnering three Academy Award nominations for his soundtracks

The Fight for Life, So Ends Our Night, and *Commandos Strike at Dawn.* Gruenberg was elected to the National Institute of Arts and Letters.

G. Schirmer

The largest and most influential American music publisher, G. Schirmer (often known simply as Schirmer) started in 1861 when Gustav Schirmer took over the publishing company in New York for which he worked, Kerkseig & Bruesing Company. In 1866 Schirmer bought out his partner and renamed the company G. Schirmer. In 1891 the company installed its own engraving and printing facility. The company passed to Gustav's sons and grandson, and a book division was added to the company's music publication. In 1968 Schirmer was acquired by book publishing conglomerate Macmillan, and in 1986 Macmillan sold off everything except the book division, which remained as Schirmer Books.

Schirmer's catalog is vast, covering music through the centuries from many countries. Its American music publications include works by SAMUEL BARBER, PHILIP GLASS, ERNEST BLOCH, JOHN CORIGLIANO, HENRY COWELL, GIAN CARLO MENOTTI, and dozens of others. No other publisher in American history instantly evokes the rich and prestigious tradition of music publishing as does G. Schirmer.

Gutiérrez, Horacio (b. 1948) *pianist*

A Cuban, Horacio Gutiérrez was a child prodigy who performed with the Havana Philharmonic at age 11. He became an American citizen in 1967. He continued his youthful performing career, playing with both the LOS ANGELES PHILHARMONIC and the NEW YORK PHILHARMONIC—the latter after being personally chosen by LEONARD BERNSTEIN. As a teenager he won a piano competition in San Francisco and studied at the JUILLIARD SCHOOL in New York. Gutiérrez came to prominence by winning the silver medal (second prize) at the Tchaikovski International Competition in Moscow in 1970. International tours followed. He won the Avery Fisher Prize in 1982. Though Gutiérrez is mostly identified with the romantic repertoire, he has championed modern music to some extent and is especially connected to the Piano Concerto of WILLIAM SCHUMAN and the Piano Concerto of ANDRÉ PREVIN.

Hahn, Hilary (b. 1979) *violinist*

The prodigious violinist Hilary Hahn started playing at age three and was admitted to the Curtis Institute of Music at age 10. By the time she was 15, Hahn had played concerto debuts with the Baltimore Symphony Orchestra (her first limelight performance in 1981), Philadelphia Orchestra (1993), Cleveland Orchestra, New York Philharmonic, and Pittsburgh Symphony Orchestra. Her European debut followed in 1995, and that same year she received an Avery Fisher Career Grant. She maintains a strong interest in chamber music and has spent summers pursuing ensemble studies at the Marlboro Music Festival in Vermont. Hahn signed an exclusive recording contract with Sony Classical, for which company she recorded five discs. As of this writing, Hahn records exclusively for Deutsche Grammaphon.

Handel and Haydn Society

One of the oldest classical performing groups in the country, the Handel and Haydn Society was founded in 1815. The group performed the American premiere of Handel's *Messiah* in 1818. Other blockbuster American premieres included Haydn's *Creation* (1819), Verdi's *Requiem* (1878), and Bach's Mass in B Minor (1887). While the group's mission clearly extends beyond performance of Handel and Haydn, over time it has become a foremost ancient music ensemble, developing both a chorus and a period-instrument chamber orchestra. Noted music historian Christopher Hogwood focused the society's mandate during his musical directorship from 1986 to 2001. Grant Llewellyn assumed the directorship after Hogwood and continues in the position. The group performed a modern premiere of the long-lost *Hymn of Thanks and Friendship* by C. P. E. Bach and received a Grammy Award for its recording of Sir John Tavener's *Lamentations and Praises*. The Handel and Haydn Society performs a yearly subscription series at multiple venues in Boston and adds free public concerts. The group tours, mostly in the United States, and records on the Arabesque label.

Hanson, Howard (1896–1981) *composer*

Though not a progressive composer, perhaps because of his conservative and accessible music, Howard Hanson was one of the prominent American composers of the early and mid-20th century. He studied at Northwestern University, where he earned a bachelor of arts degree in 1916. Hanson got an early start as a teacher and administrator, becoming dean of the Conservatory of Fine Arts at the College of the Pacific in 1919. After winning the Rome Prize for composition in 1921, Hanson settled in Italy for three years. When he returned to America, he took over as director of the Eastman School of Music, a post he held for 40 years. Hanson elevated Eastman to world-class status as a music school. The composer's Symphony no. 3 (the "Romantic") is probably his best-known work, but it was the Symphony no. 4 that won Hanson a Pulitzer Prize. Hanson also gained renown for his opera *Merry Mount*, which was staged by the

METROPOLITAN OPERA in 1934. He was elected to the National Institute of Arts and Letters in 1935.

Harbison, John (b. 1938) *composer*

A resourceful and successful composer, John Harbison was influenced as a child by music as varied as jazz, Bach, and Stravinsky. He attended Harvard University for his undergraduate studies, where he studied with WALTER PISTON. He earned a masters degree at Princeton, studying with EARL KIM. His composition style stretches widely from neo-romanticism to academic serialism, and his work sometimes contains jazz elements. He was the composer in residence at the PITTSBURGH SYMPHONY ORCHESTRA between 1981 and 1983, and he held the same position with the LOS ANGELES Philharmonic ORCHESTRA from 1985 to 1988. He has been installed in similar positions with the Tanglewood Music Festival, the Marlboro Music Festival, and the Santa Fe Chamber Music Festival. As a conductor, Harbison has worked with the Scottish Chamber Orchestra and the SEATTLE SYMPHONY.

Harbison joined the faculty of the Massachusetts Institute of Technology and was named Institute Professor there in 1995. He has taught and lectured at Boston University and Duke University. Harbison won the 1987 Pulitzer Prize for his cantata *The Flight Into Egypt*. He was also awarded a MacArthur Fellowship (1989) and the Heinz Award (1997).

John Harbison (Courtesy of G. Schirmer)

Harrell, Lynn (b. 1944) *cellist*

As has been the case with most cellists besides YO-YO MA, Lynn Harrell began his career as an orchestra player, then moved to the solo stage. A student of LEONARD ROSE at the JUILLIARD SCHOOL, Harrell made his debut in CARNEGIE HALL with the NEW YORK PHILHARMONIC at age 17. The following year he joined the Cleveland Orchestra, becoming principal cellist in 1964. He began teaching at Juilliard in 1976. He won the first Avery Fisher Prize in 1975. Harrell held the Gregor Piatigorsky chair as professor of cello at the University of Southern California, from 1987 to 1993. He was associated with the Royal Academy of Music in London from 1986 to 1995. He has recorded chamber music with Vladimir Ashkenazy and Itzhak Perlman.

Harris, Roy (1898–1979) *composer*

One of the most important American composers of the 20th century, Roy Harris is credited with furthering a distinctive American style of composition that was simultaneously imbued with European symphonic traditions. His first music lessons were on the piano under the tutelage of his mother. His higher studies took place on various campuses in the California university system, and he worked individually with ARTHUR FARWELL. He met AARON COPLAND, who was to become a great supporter, in 1926. Copland sent him on to NADIA BOULANGER, who taught so many American composers for decades in Paris. Harris received two Guggenheim Fellowships, in 1927 and 1929. He married Buela Duffey in 1936; the bride changed her first name to Johana to honor Harris's reverence for Johann Sebastian Bach. Later, rumors surfaced that Johana's help in preparing Harris's manuscripts actually extended to composing under his name; but such rumors have been extinguished for the most part by research.

Harris taught in several colleges; his most enduring affiliation was with the University of California at Los Angeles, where he had been composer in residence and a professor for 10 years at the time of his death. In his obituary in the *New York Times,* Donal Henahan wrote, "Mr. Harris's admirers came to identify his music with the mythic simplicity and honesty of heartland America. And, in fact, there is a plainspoken ruggedness in the best of his scores that supports the notion." Harris's most lasting work is the Symphony no. 3 (1936). Overall he composed nine symphonies and an extensive portfolio of works in other formats.

Harrison, Lou (1917–2003) *composer*

A prolific composer, Lou Harrison explored many styles. In part, he was a classical world music composer who experimented with synthesizing Asian and Western influences. He was identified for his compositions for percussion ensembles. His multiple creative phases included work with dense dissonances, as well as periods in which he composed in simple harmonies and airy atmospheres. As a boy he studied piano and violin. Harrison's first

great personal influence was HENRY COWELL, an older composer who also blended traditional styles, at the University of California at San Francisco. Cowell became a friend and mentor for life. Harrison was also connected to CHARLES IVES, who shared his manuscripts with the younger composer. Avid study of the Ives manuscripts contributed to Harrison's more abstract and dissonant flavorings. Harrison edited the score of Ives's Symphony no. 3, and conducted the premiere of that work in 1946, leading to a Pulitzer Prize (1947) for Ives. The composer insisted on sharing the award with Harrison. John Cage was another modernist composer connected to Harrison; both careers were enhanced by the association. Yet another influence was the 12-tone pioneer Austrian-born Arnold Schoenberg, with whom Harrison studied in Los Angeles.

Harrison was for a time music critic for the *Herald Tribune* in New York. Although New York life didn't agree with him, he expanded his writing assignments to *Modern Music, Listen,* and *View.* A nervous breakdown followed his stint in New York, and Harrison was hospitalized for many months. That period of recuperation formed a sort of boundary between creative periods, and his music henceforth contained softened edges and more accessible harmonies. He became even more productive than previously. Retreating to a more rural environment, Harrison taught for two years (1951–53) at Black Mountain College in North Carolina. During the 1950s he became fiercely experimental, inventing instruments for his music and creating new styles of notation and performance. A certain reliance on chance crept into his music, perhaps influenced by John Cage, and he developed a composition system called "Free Style" in which notes were determined by mathematical relationships to previous notes.

Ever seeking artistic kinship, Harrison met William Colvig in 1967, and they collaborated in devising and building "junk instruments" made from odds and ends, and integrating these homemade noisemakers with traditional instruments. Harrison wrote music based on Buddhist texts (*La Koro Sutro,* 1972) and songs written in Esperanto. As unhindered by tradition as Harrison was, he also found it productive to impose artificial limits on himself, such as writing pieces using only certain pitch intervals.

Harrison was elected to the National Institute of Arts and Letters (1973), won two Guggenheim Fellowships (1952 and 1954), a Rockefeller Grant (1961), a Fulbright Scholarship (1983), and the Edward MacDowell Medal (2000). He was an accomplished painter and designer who designed computer fonts. Harrison died while traveling to a festival in his honor.

Hauk, Minnie (1851–1929) *opera singer*

One of the first American opera singers to gain international renown, Minnie Hauk sang both soprano and mezzo-soprano roles. She studied in New Orleans and New York, and made her New York debut a few weeks shy of her 14th birthday. She continued studies in Paris on a financial grant from music publisher G. SCHIRMER and made a London debut in 1869. She landed roles in various European cities during the next two years and centered her career in Germany during most of the 1870s. In 1878 and into the 1880s, Hauk migrated to New York and London. She was the first internationally recognized American singer to specialize in the role of Carmen, which she sang (by some accounts) over 600 times. She is generally recognized with having created the role in America. Her vigorous acting, as much as her singing, helped propel her career. Her last performance came in 1893, in Philadelphia. Hauk's later years were dimmed by increasing blindness and stressed by financial debt inherited from her husband. Hauk was the recipient of the first pension bestowed by the Music Lovers' Foundation of New York, and she also benefited from a fund-raising drive in her honor organized by soprano Geraldine Farrar.

Heifetz, Jascha (1901–1987) *violinist*

A Russian-born violinist who became an American citizen in 1925, Jascha Heifetz earned a reputation as perhaps the world's greatest violinist since Paganini, father of modern violin virtuosity. Very few musical artists achieve the degree of supremacy in their chosen field as did Heifetz. He began playing at age three, coached by his father. He entered a local music school at age five. His family moved from Lithuania to St. Petersburg with the hope of putting the young Heifetz under the training of Leopold Auer, a tactic that eventually worked after many refusals from Auer even to hear the boy. By age 10, Heifetz had given a recital in St. Petersburg that galvanized Russia and performed with the Berlin Philharmonic. He was 21 when he gave four sold-out concerts in New York's Carnegie Hall; at the final performance police were called to cope with near-riot conditions created by throngs of admirers jamming into the hall without tickets.

Heifetz was a tireless and adventurous touring musician. He visited places where classical violin playing had never been heard. Of stern demeanor onstage, Heifetz performed with minimum movement and utmost concentration. Over and over, his playing was (and still is, thanks to a large discography) described as "intense." His bow technique pressed hard on the violin strings, and he used a rapid, deep vibrato. The result was a melodic style that soared without sentimentality; most critics thought his playing conveyed nobility. With the integrity Heifetz brought to music making, his technique was ferocious and he tended toward fast tempos. Still, he was not a show-off in his performing gestures or attitudes, and his detractors wished he would be more forthcoming of his personality both onstage and with the media. A shoulder injury and subsequent surgery in 1975 brought an end to touring and most recording, but Heifetz still taught. To the end, he apparently wished to be remembered for his music alone—not for the superficial trappings of personality or publicity. His death was mourned on the front page of the *New York Times.*

Heinrich, Anthony Philip (1781–1861) *composer*
Called "the Beethoven of America" by a critic of his time, Anthony Philip Heinrich was an original and groundbreaking composer who worked in a time when composing was not an established profession in America. He was born in Germany and inherited a fortune that was destroyed by political and financial events in Europe before 1811. He came to America (for the second time) in 1816, failed to establish a business, and remained in the United States. In a startling epiphany, Heinrich simply decided that he must be a composer, despite a lack of formal training and, apparently, as a result of the emotional impact of walking over a thousand miles from Philadelphia to Kentucky. The powerful effect of nature influenced his decision to pursue music and imbued his compositions. Many of his works were roughly programmatic of nature's beauty and force. He settled at first in a simple log cabin and turned out astonishingly sophisticated, complex (if derivative of European traditions) music. He called himself the "loghouse composer."

Heinrich's first published work, in 1820, was entitled *The Dawning of Music in Kentucky, or The Pleasures of Harmony in the Solitudes of Nature*. It was a collection of pieces for piano, voice, and violin. Though Heinrich's opus did not represent the first American compositions (FRANCIS HOPKINSON is usually credited there, with a song composed in 1859), it was nonetheless unprecedented as a creative and entrepreneurial effort.

Heinrich eventually moved out of the log cabin and resumed cosmopolitan life; he lived in Boston and New York and enjoyed a substantial reputation both in America and abroad. He helped form the New York Philharmonic Society. He played his music for President John Tyler. He embarked on three extended visits to Europe (1826, 1833, and 1856), each time staying for at least three years, and his orchestral works were played from London to Prague.

Heinrich died in poverty, his days of fame in the past, and he is generally unknown today. Yet he might well be considered one of America's most astounding musical geniuses. With little training, no connections, living in an era when there was virtually no musical infrastructure in the United States upon which a composer might build a career, he produced large-scale, complex orchestral works as finely structured as the creations of Europe's finest composers. He was an accomplished symphonist in a land without orchestras. As a composer ahead of his time, Heinrich might be compared to CHARLES IVES.

Heinz Hall

The concert venue of the PITTSBURGH SYMPHONY ORCHESTRA.

Herbert, Victor (1859–1924) *musician and composer*
Victor Herbert was one of America's most successful composers of operetta, as well as an accomplished instrumentalist and serious classical composer. He completed over 50 operettas, comprising an

Heinz Hall (Courtesy of the Pittsburgh Symphony Orchestra)

astounding portfolio of stage work. After his death the *New York Times* wrote, "His place in light opera has been such that his biography would almost be a history of light opera in America." Herbert's attempts to write and produce serious opera were, for the most part, disappointing, but his *Madelaine* (a one-act comedy that, at its premiere in 1914, was paired with *Pagliacci,* one of the most beloved classical operas) enjoyed the unprecedented distinction of being published in full score by G. SCHIRMER. Herbert's operettas, for the most part, were composed in an era in which the boundary between light and serious opera was less pronounced than it would become later in the 20th century. Herbert composed music for highly trained singers accompanied by fully realized orchestral scores.

Herbert grew up in England and Germany, living with his grandfather (Samuel Lover, an Irish poet) after the early death of his father. His first choice of profession was medicine, but Herbert eventually attended the Stuttgart (Germany) Conservatory. A cellist, he played in the orchestra of Eduard Strauss in Vienna, then joined the court orchestra of Stuttgart (1881). He composed the Suite for Cello and Orchestra and the Cello Concerto, premiering both works with the Stuttgart orchestra with himself as soloist. Herbert and his wife, soprano Therese Foerster, moved to the United States in 1886 when Foerster was engaged to sing with the METROPOLITAN OPERA, and Herbert was hired by the company's orchestra. When in New York, Herbert joined the New York String Quartet and became active as a conductor. He joined the faculty of the NATIONAL CONSERVATORY OF MUSIC. In 1894 he completed a second cello concerto.

Between 1898 and 1904, Herbert was the principal conductor of the PITTSBURGH SYMPHONY ORCHESTRA. Musically, Herbert's reign in Pittsburgh was not universally described as an unqualified success, though his energy as a music popularizer gave the orchestra a lift at the box office and catalyzed tours to other cities. He was unafraid to expand the repertoire beyond the standard classical repertoire, and he cared more about building audiences than in

hewing to formal classical traditions. Disagreements with orchestra management led to Herbert's resignation in 1904, whereupon he formed the Victor Herbert Orchestra, which he managed and conducted for the rest of his life, playing mostly light classics. Before and during Herbert's Pittsburgh stint, he met with success on the operetta stage, having created *The Serenade* (1897) and *The Fortune Teller* (1898). His most enduring stage work, *Babes in Toyland,* was completed in 1903. He was elected to the National Institute of Arts and Letters in 1908.

Herbert's theater career lasted from 1894 to 1924—an amazingly short period considering his output and influence. An important side note of Herbert's active career was his work on behalf of artists rights. His lobbying played a role in the revision of American copyright law in 1909, which addressed the emergence of recording technology by giving royalties to composers whose works were commercially recorded. On the performance side, he won a Supreme Court lawsuit giving composers royalty rights to public performances of their work. Herbert helped found ASCAP in 1914, and remained a director there until his death. His obituary was printed on page one of the *New York Times.*

Hill, Edward Burlingame (1872–1960)
composer and educator

Edward Burlingame Hill followed in the footsteps of his Harvard University mentor, JOHN KNOWLES PAINE. Like Paine, who was Harvard's (and America's) first college music professor, Hill taught at Harvard, becoming a full professor in 1928 and later accepting the position of department chair. Continuing the artistic lineage started by Paine, Hill taught LEONARD BERNSTEIN, ELLIOTT CARTER, VIRGIL THOMSON, and ROSS LEE FINNEY. His compositions indicated an infatuation with French impressionism, and Hill wrote the book *Modern French Music* in 1924. He composed a respectable collection of music, including three symphonies, most of which is almost never programmed today. Hill's greatest influence was in the teaching studio, not at his composer's desk. Still, the BOSTON SYMPHONY ORCHESTRA performed 18 of his pieces over the years, and he was a member of the National Institute of Arts and Letters.

Hill, Ureli Corelli (1802–1875) *violinist and conductor*

Ureli Corelli Hill is regarded as the organizer of the PHILHARMONIC SOCIETY OF NEW YORK, which later became the NEW YORK PHILHARMONIC. He conducted the Philharmonic Society's first concert, and though there was no such formal position, Hill is historically considered to be the orchestra's first music director. He served as president of the new orchestra from 1842 to 1848. Previously he had led the New York Sacred Music Society. Hill left New York for Ohio in 1847 but returned in 1850 and was a violinist in the Philharmonic Society until 1873.

Hillis, Margaret (1921–1998) *choral leader*

Though she was never as famous as ROBERT SHAW, Margaret Hillis was an influential choral leader who improved the standard of American choral performance. Her three most significant appointments were with the choruses of the CHICAGO SYMPHONY ORCHESTRA, the CLEVELAND ORCHESTRA, and the SAN FRANCISCO SYMPHONY. With GEORG SOLTI as music director in Chicago, Hillis collaborated on important recordings of Beethoven's Symphony no. 9 and Handel's *Creation* oratorio. She attended Indiana University and the Juilliard School of Music (later the JUILLIARD SCHOOL). She mentored with Robert Shaw and later taught at Juilliard (1951–53) and at New York's Union Theological Seminary (1950–60). Hillis founded the American Choral Foundation.

Hindemith, Paul (1895–1963) *composer and educator*

Paul Hindemith was a German composer and educator who never became an American citizen but was extraordinarily influential on the U.S. music scene in the 1940s and early 1950s. Hindemith was an accomplished instrumentalist (violin and viola), conductor, composer, theorist, writer, and lecturer whose career flourished only after he reluctantly came to the United States for what he thought would be a short visit. He stayed for 13 years.

Hindemith had worked as violinist and concertmaster in European orchestras and had composed since he was a young man. Creatively, his work evolved through many styles, and Hindemith demonstrated an unusual facility with all kinds of composing techniques. He was subject to discouragement and pessimism, a trait that never left him even after his success was well under way. It was with a cautious spirit that he considered visiting the United States at the encouragement of friends, in 1940, as World War II was erupting in Europe. Living in Switzerland at the time, Hindemith finally yielded to numerous teaching requests from U.S. institutions, including the Tanglewood Music Center and Cornell University. Once in America, Hindemith found his home at Yale University.

Yale's initial invitation to Hindemith was based on a single lecture series in 1940. These talks proved so successful, both in content and their effect in lifting Hindemith out of his current depression, that talks proceeded quickly toward installing the composer on the permanent faculty. He had accepted Tanglewood's invitation in the summer of 1940 and made such a strong impression there that some of the center's emerging composition stars (LUKAS FOSS, NORMAN DELLO JOIO, HAROLD SHAPERO) attended Yale to continue working with Hindemith. Yale gave Hindemith broad latitude in creating his music curriculum, and he more than merely continued Yale's distinguished legacy in music education. During his Yale years, Hindemith wrote *A Concentrated Course in Traditional Harmony* (1943) and *Elementary Training for Musicians* (1946). He also founded the Yale Collegium Musicium, an early-music performing group. Hindemith became one of America's most successful composers during his time in the United States. He wrote in traditional formats—concertos, symphonies, string quartets— and although his techniques were advanced, he always wrote music meant to be felt emotionally, as opposed to academic styles that were beginning to emerge.

Hindemith made two visits to Europe while teaching at Yale in response to many invitations emanating from his homeland. He was tentative about moving back to Europe permanently, partly because of his fragile emotional disposition and partly because he was reluctant to rearrange his life yet again while things were going so well for him in the United States. Finally, though, he received an offer he couldn't refuse from the University of Zürich in Switzerland. For a couple of years (1951–53) Hindemith actually commuted between Zürich and Yale until he resettled in Switzerland. He retired from teaching altogether in 1957, and his interest in composing seemed to fade as well. Hindemith's passion turned to conducting for much of his later life.

Hindemith's list of composed works is large and varied, with the most concentration in orchestral and choral music. He is considered more a harmonist than a melodist; in his *New York Times* obituary music critic HAROLD C. SCHONBERG wrote, "He represents harmonic daring and acerbity rather than melodic genius."

Hoffman, Richard (1831–1909) *pianist*

Richard Hoffman was an American pianist born in England who became a respected New York performer associated with the Philharmonic Society of New York (later the NEW YORK PHILHARMONIC). He moved to the United States in 1847, making his debut that year with the Philharmonic. He performed concert recitals with JENNY LIND. Hoffman wrote several salon pieces for piano. His reputation was that of a tasteful, skilled, and fastidious musician.

Hofmann, Josef (1876–1957) *pianist*

Josef Hofmann was a Polish-born American pianist and one of the great piano prodigies. His first piano lessons were from his sister, who quickly passed the fast-learning Josef to their father, who managed the boy's training until the age of 10. During this time Hofmann also showed unusual talent in mathematics and science. He toured Europe by age seven, but his breakthrough performance came at age 11, on November 29, 1887, when he played a Beethoven concerto and several solo pieces at the Metropolitan Opera House in New York before an enthusiastic audience and critics. His mature musicianship and already dazzling technique caused a sensation rarely seen even in New York. A tour that followed was curtailed by intervention from the Society for the Prevention of Cruelty to Children. Hofmann retreated somewhat for more study, including lessons with legendary pianists Mortiz Moszkowski and Anton Rubinstein. In 1926 Hofmann became director of the CURTIS INSTITUTE, remaining at that position until 1938.

As a pianist, Hofmann was universally considered to be peerless in every regard. It is difficult to find any negative criticism of his playing in any quarter. His technical skills were encompassing; his tone, often called "limpid," penetrated through large concert venues with no apparent effort. He was famous for his command of the piano's tonal resources; perhaps the quality his admirers valued above all others was his mastery as a colorist. He was an overwhelmingly romantic pianist in temperament and repertoire; although he played Bach, Mozart, and Beethoven, the bulk of his repertoire focused on Chopin, Schumann, Liszt, and other romantics. He recorded precious little, claiming distaste for making any interpretation permanent. Indeed, Hofmann was characteristically spontaneous on the recital stage, rarely playing a piece the same way twice—another trait of the grand romantic school. Ironically, Hofmann was the first musician to record at the birth of Edison's recording technology, in a visit to the inventor's lab. But he stayed away from commercial recordings.

Hofmann was a prolific composer, but not an important one. He also invented compulsively and held more than 60 patents. His death was front-page news in the *New York Times*.

Hoiby, Lee (b. 1926) *composer and pianist*

Lee Hoiby gave one of the oldest-age debut piano recitals in history in 1978, at 52 years of age. The reason was that Hoiby, who had planned to be a concert pianist, was distracted by a significant composing career. He was first diverted when composer GIAN CARLO MENOTTI invited him to study at the CURTIS INSTITUTE, and Hoiby focused for the first time on writing music, rather than playing it, as a profession. Previously, Hoiby had attended the University of Wisconsin and Mills College in Oakland, California. Since 1978, Hoiby has occupied himself with both composing and performing, but his legacy as a composer is shaping up the more strongly of his two professions. Hoiby has concentrated on opera, with his important works being *The Scarf* (1958), *A Month in the Country* (1964), *Summer and Smoke* (1971), and *The Tempest* (1986). He has composed numerous songs, choral works, some chamber music, and two piano concertos. He has won a Fulbright Scholarship and Guggenheim Fellowship, and the National Institute of Arts and Letters Award.

Hollywood String Quartet

A studio ensemble that worked primarily in film studios, the Hollywood String Quartet was founded in 1947 and disbanded in 1961. Its founding members were FELIX SLATKIN (violin), Paul Shure (violin), Paul Robyn (viola), and ELEANOR ALLER (cello). The quartet gained an exemplary reputation outside the film studio and engaged in modest touring during its last few years. The New Hollywood String Quartet takes its name from the old quartet, but there is no other affiliation.

Hopkinson, Francis (1737–1791) *composer*

Francis Hopkinson holds a unique place in American music history, as the composer of the first American secular piece of music. Composers of his period compiled, adapted, and occasionally composed hymns, but pure art music was not yet an American tradition. Hopkinson's landmark song was "My Days Have Been So Wondrous Free," scored for voice and harpsichord in 1759. It was established as a breakthrough work of American culture, and the first of its type, according to OSCAR SONNECK, the father of American musicology.

Hopkinson was, rather like his contemporary Benjamin Franklin, a man of wide interests and abilities. He was a statesman who signed the Declaration of Independence, a writer, poet, designer, artist, and inventor who developed a shaded candlestick and technical improvements to the harpsichord. The harpsichord was Hopkinson's first instrument, which he began studying at age 17. At that time, in 1750, Bach died and the European classical tradition was making its transition from elaborate baroque dances and fugues to the classicist formalism of Haydn, early Mozart, and Bach's sons. Surviving pieces of Hopkinson's music library (much of which he copied by hand) indicate that he played Handel, Corelli, and other composers. He was an amateur musician, there being no such thing as a professional musician outside of the church, and as such Hopkinson was a respected musical figure in Philadelphia. Like his contemporaries, Hopkinson trafficked in sacred music in the usual ways: compiling hymn tunes and occasionally serving as church organist.

The completion of "My Days Have Been So Wondrous Free" occurred 17 years before America declared its independence. In 1788 Hopkinson published a collection of seven original secular songs (*Seven Songs*), with a dedication that indicates his awareness of his place in history: "I cannot, I believe, be refused the Credit of being the first Native of the United States who has produced a Musical Composition."

Hora Novissima (1893)

Written for the Church Choral Society of New York by HORATIO PARKER, *Hora Novissima* is scored for chous, soloists, and orchestra. It was premiered on May 3, 1893, and frequently performed throughout the decade in America and England. The work helped bring Parker to national recognition as a composer.

Horne, Marilyn (b. 1929) *opera singer*

A preeminent mezzo-soprano of the 20th century, Marilyn Horne took her first professional job in a movie, overdubbing the singing parts in the film *Carmen Jones*, in 1954. That same she made her operatic debut in Los Angeles. Her father, a primary influence and source of support, died in 1956, after which Horne attempted to build her career in Europe, spending three seasons singing roles in Germany. Her San Francisco debut occurred in 1960. The following year Horne began an association with Australian diva Joan Sutherland, singing mezzo roles to Sutherland's soprano parts. Horne made her METROPOLITAN OPERA debut in 1970. During the 1970s and 1980s Horne sang in leading opera houses all over the world and also maintained an extensive recital career. Her biography, *My Life,* was published in 1984. Horne retired from performing in 1998.

Horowitz, Vladimir (1903–1989) *pianist*

An American of Russian birth (he received U.S. citizenship in 1944), Horowitz is regarded by many as the greatest pianist of the 20th century. His legacy is not simple, however, even beyond the normal controversies of exorbitant fame. His mother and sister were his first piano teachers, until Horowitz entered the Kiev Conservatory in Russia at age nine. He studied with Felix Blumenfeld, who had been taught by the legendary Anton Rubinstein. Horowitz began concertizing at the age of 17 by necessity, he and his family having been impoverished by the Russian Revolution of 1917. He part-

Vladimir Horowitz (Bettmann/Corbis)

nered with violinist Nathan Milstein in chamber concerts, but Horowitz's destiny lay as a solo artist, and by 1925 he was recognized as one of the most promising of young Russian pianists.

Horowitz left the Soviet Union in 1925 and built his early career in Western Europe, starting with his German debut in 1926. He arrived in the United States in 1928, making his American debut on January 12 in one of the most remarkable concerts ever heard in New York. Sir Thomas Beecham conducted the NEW YORK PHILHARMONIC with Horowitz at the piano for Tchaikovsky's Piano Concerto no. 1, a reliable warhorse that had propelled Horowitz's success in Europe. Beecham and Horowitz turned out to match poorly and disagreed on tempos. Horowitz dutifully held back through the first two movements, respecting Beecham's carefully paced baton leadership. But by the final movement Horowitz had lost patience, perhaps seeing his opportunity to impress slipping away and took charge of the tempo. Starting the third movement at a blistering pace, Horowitz left Beecham and the orchestra behind and never looked back. The result was musically chaotic but sensational in effect, and Horowitz emerged from the fiasco as a new classical superstar in New York.

Throughout the world Horowitz reigned for decades as the greatest pianist of the old romantic virtuoso school. Defying the literalism that crept into piano performance during the 1960s and 1970s, Horowitz held to the ideal of emotional effect over nitpicking technique. Nevertheless, his technical command of the keyboard was astonishing, and his risk taking was nearly always accompanied by spectacular displays of virtuosity. Nobody could generate the storms of pianistic sonority that Horowitz whipped up. More remarkable than his amazing technical mastery, though, was the tonal control and interpretive force Horowitz brought to his performances. His playing revealed the many layers of complex pieces as if each were being played by a different instrument. Although his approach to certain composers—Mozart in particular, and even romantic bellwether Chopin—was often questioned and criticized, the conviction of his interpretation was never in doubt. Horowitz had the uncanny ability to make listeners believe they were hearing a piece for the first time.

Horowitz was especially connected to composer Serge Rachmaninoff, who was himself a fantastic pianist. Horowitz's first order of business upon his arrival in the United States was to meet his idol. The two met in the basement of the Steinway headquarters in New York, and played through Rachmaninoff's Piano Concerto no. 3 together, Rachmaninoff holding down the orchestra part on a second piano. Horowitz considered that informal play through his real American debut. Later,

Rachmaninoff allowed Horowitz to combine the two existing versions of the composer's Piano Sonata no. 2 into a customized performance version.

Praise of Horowitz's playing was not universal. His intensely personal, sometimes idiosyncratic interpretations of standard repertoire drew bewilderment and ire from some critics. VIRGIL THOMSON called Horowitz "a master of distortion and exaggeration." To some extent, such criticism derived from Horowitz's throwback style of eccentric 19th-century pianism, which was much less expected and understood in the mid-20th century. In his defense, Horowitz once said, "The score is not a bible, and I am never afraid to dare. The music is behind those dots." Free spirit though he was as an interpreter, Horowitz was a demanding performer: his own concert grand piano was lifted out of his Manhattan apartment by crane for every concert or recording session (he also recorded in his home), and hotel rooms were redecorated to ease his feeling of dislocation.

Though lauded as the most exciting pianist in the world, Horowitz suffered from chronic anxiety and insecurity that was arguably neurotic. At the crux of his anxiety lay the question of his worth as a serious artist. Was he a profound musician and great pianist, or a mere entertainer with an oversized technique? The quandary is of historical proportions; Franz Liszt, inventor of modern piano virtuosity and usually regarded as the greatest pianist ever, likewise regarded his piano tours more as a circus than an artistic pursuit, and he retired from public performance while still a young man. Horowitz, taking his cue from Liszt, perhaps, also retired from the stage—several times. Each withdrawal into seclusion was met by grief and nervousness in the musical world, and his inevitable returns were greeted with relief and joy. All told, Horowitz took four major retirements: 1936–38, 1953–65 (which ended with a blockbuster concert in CARNEGIE HALL for which 1,500 people lined up 24 hours in advance at the ticket window), 1969–74 (broken with the first piano concert at the relatively new METROPOLITAN OPERA HOUSE in LINCOLN CENTER), and 1983–85 (the return from which, a concert in Moscow, was a global media event).

An extensive discography keeps Horowitz very much alive for legions of fans, old and new. Along with Arthur Rubinstein (a very different, but almost equally influential, pianist), Horowitz was the portal to classical music for untold numbers of people.

Horszowski, Mieczyslaw (1892–1993) *pianist*
He lived for 100 years and concertized for 90 of them. Polish-born American pianist Mieczyslaw Horszowski made his debut in Vienna at age 10, then played Beethoven's Piano Concerto no. 1 that same year in Warsaw. After several years of touring Europe, Horszowski made his American debut in CARNEGIE HALL in 1906 as a 14-year-old veteran of the concert stage. He taught at the CURTIS INSTITUTE for 50 years, from the early 1940s until his death. Horszowski's playing maintained strength and interpretive vigor to an extraordinarily old age.

Houston Symphony Orchestra
The Houston Symphony emerged as a fully professional orchestra during the 1930s but was founded in 1913. At that time, the orchestra put 35 players on the stage with conductor Paul Blitz, who led the group from 1913 to 1916. Paul Berge followed Blitz and remained until 1918. At that time the orchestra dissolved, then reformed in 1930 under Uriel Nespoli (1931–32), Frank St. Leger (1932–35), and Ernst Hoffmann (1935–47). Hoffmann brought the orchestra up to national standards. Efram Kurtz succeeded Hoffmann as music director from 1948 to 1954. A quick succession of directors included Thomas Beecham for one season (1954–55), LEOPOLD STOKOWSKI (1955–61), JOHN BARBIROLLI (1961–67), and ANDRÉ PREVIN (1967–69). The orchestra relied on guest conduc-

tors for two years, and hired Sergiu Comissiona as music director in 1979; Comissiona remained until CHRISTOPH ESCHENBACH took over in 1988. Eschenbach founded the Houston Symphony Chamber Players. Financial crises that plagued the orchestra repeatedly precipitated a massive influx of donated money in 1998, which stabilized the organization's operation.

Hovhaness, Alan (1911–2000) *composer*
Born Alan Vaness Chakmakjian, Alan Hovhaness was a prolific composer whose music did not gain widespread academic or institutional acclaim. Lacking parental support for his musical creativity as a child, Hovhaness composed secretly at night and hid his scores. Later, he attended Tufts University in Massachusetts and studied composition with FREDERICK CONVERSE at the NEW ENGLAND CONSERVATORY OF MUSIC. In 1942 Hovhaness won a scholarship to the Berkshire Music Center in TANGLEWOOD, Massachusetts, but the experience proved damaging to his self-esteem when his music was harshly criticized by BERNSTIEN, COPLAND, and others. This bitter experience might have played a part in Hovhaness's tendency to eliminate his own works; the composer destroyed dozens of his scores. Nevertheless, he was a productive composer, penning over 400 works, many for full orchestra. He wrote 30 symphonies after he turned 60, six of them written in 1986. Much of his music is lushly harmonized; Hovhaness was decidedly against atonal and academic music. His work was influenced by Asian music traditions, and much of it carries a mystical subtext.

Although his music is not often programmed today, Hovhaness received many commissions and his music was performed by LEOPOLD STOKOWSKI, among others. His most enduring work is probably his second symphony, entitled *Mysterious Mountain,* which brought Hovhaness some measure of fame and respect. Speaking on behalf of his own work, Hovhaness presaged many New Age artists: "My purpose is to create music not for snobs, but for all people, music which is beautiful and healing."

Hutcheson, Ernest (1871–1951) *pianist, educator, administrator, and writer*

Ernest Hutcheson moved from one musical to another but is best remembered as a longtime piano teacher at the JUILLIARD SCHOOL, and eventually its president. Hutcheson joined the Juilliard faculty in 1924, after having concertized extensively and taught at the Peabody Conservatory in Baltimore. He is the author of *The Elements of Piano Technique* (1907) and *The Literature of the Piano* (1948).

Ice Field (2002)

Scored for orchestra, *Ice Field,* by HENRY BRANT, won a Pulitzer Prize in 2002. The work was premiered by the San Francisco Symphony on December 12, 2001.

Imbrie, Andrew (b. 1921) *composer*

Andrew Imbrie is a composer of impeccable training who has won multiple awards, fulfilled high-profile commissions, and is an honored teacher. He studied piano into his 20s, working in Paris with NADIA BOULANGER and pianist Robert Casadesus, among others. He received an undergraduate degree at Princeton University and studied with ROGER SESSIONS from 1937 to 1948, part of that time at the University of California, Berkeley, where he received a graduate degree. He was set to teach at Berkeley but received a grant for overseas study, spending two years in Rome. Imbrie did join the Berkeley faculty when he returned in 1949, remaining there until 1991. He has taught since 1970 at the SAN FRANCISCO CONSERVATORY. He has touched down briefly as a visiting professor at numerous other institutions, including Harvard University, Brandeis, University of Chicago, and New York University. He was composer in residence at TANGLEWOOD in 1991.

While he was a student at Princeton, Imbrie's first string quartet won the New York Music Critics' Circle Award in 1944. He also received two Guggenheim Fellowships (1953 and 1959), the Alice M. Ditson Award from Columbia University (1947), and an award from the American Academy of Arts and Letters (1971), and he was elected to both the National Institute of Arts and Letters and the American Academy of Arts and Sciences.

Imbrie has composed for orchestra, stage, choral groups, and chamber groups. He has received commissions from the NEW YORK PHILHARMONIC, SAN FRANCISCO SYMPHONY (and that city's opera company), and the Naumburg and Ford Foundations.

In Memory of a Summer Day (1980)

Scored for soprano solo and orchestra, this work by DAVID DEL TREDICI won a Pulitzer Prize in 1980. It was commissioned and premiered by the St. Louis Symphony for its 100th anniversary; the first performance took place on February 23, 1980. This piece was Del Tredici's first non-12-tone work. The work eventually became part of an enormous performance piece, with three other commissions: *Quaint Events, Happy Voice,* and *All in the Golden Afternoon.* The entire project was completed and titled *Child Alice* in 1981.

Institute for Studies in American Music

A division of the Conservatory of Music and Brooklyn College (of the City University of New York), the Institute for Studies in American Music was founded in 1971 by H. Wiley Hitchcock. An academic organization, the institute sponsors conferences and publishes a biannual newsletter.

Institute of Musical Art   See JUILLIARD SCHOOL.

Isaac Stern Auditorium

The main concert hall of the CARNEGIE HALL complex, which consists of three stages. The hall is named for violinist ISAAC STERN, who mounted a drive to save Carnegie Hall from destruction in 1962, when it was slated for demolition. With LINCOLN CENTER set to open and Carnegie's home orchestra, the New York Philharmonic, ready to move across town, there seemed little reason for Carnegie Hall to remain open. But Carnegie's role had always been split between hosting the Philharmonic and serving as a showcase for visiting orchestras and performers. Stern convinced the city to purchase the building, which now enjoys protection as an historical landmark. Isaac Stern Auditorium is the world's most prestigious stage for the finest orchestras, chamber groups, and solo performers.

Isbin, Sharon (b. 1956) *guitarist*

A preeminent classical guitarist in the post-Segovia world, Sharon Isbin attended Yale University. She won the Toronto International Guitar Competition in 1975, the Munich International Competition in 1976, and the Queen Sofia Competition in 1979, the same year as her New York debut in ALICE TULLY HALL. Isbin taught at the MANHATTAN SCHOOL OF MUSIC from 1979 to 1989, then founded the guitar department at the JUILLIARD SCHOOL. She has toured on four continents. Like many classical stars, Isbin crosses over to other genres on some recordings, traveling as far afield musically as the folk songs of Joan Baez. In June 2004, Isbin became the first guitarist in 26 years to appear with the NEW YORK PHILHARMONIC. In 2005 the Philharmonic was scheduled to release a recording with Isbin that would be the first disc ever released by the orchestra featuring a guitarist.

Istomin, Eugene (1925–2003) *pianist*

American pianist Eugene Istomin was a "Curtis wunderkind" who entered the famed CURTIS INSTITUTE at age 12. He won a youth competition in Philadelphia, which led to a performance with the PHILADELPHIA ORCHESTRA, and the same year (1943) he won the prestigious Levintritt Award in New York, leading to a debut with the NEW YORK PHILHARMONIC during the same week as the Philadelphia concert. His connection with cellist Pablo Casals began in 1950, when Istomin was the youngest performer at the Prades Festival, directed by Casals. (Much later, Istomin married Casals's widow.) In 1988, Istomin embarked on a four-month solo piano tour of 30 American cities, carrying two concert grand Steinway pianos with him. In

Sharon Isbin (Courtesy of Sharon Isbin; Photo by J. Henry Fair)

addition to his solo career, Istomin was a noted chamber music player, and formed a famous, well-traveled trio with LEONARD ROSE and ISAAC STERN.

Ives, Charles (1874–1954) *composer*

Charles Ives was an emigmatic and progressive composer whose legacy has brought him to a revered position in American music. He is now regarded as one of the great figures in American cultural history, an artist far ahead of his time who did not enjoy the success he deserved, and at the same time, a composer whose work is still difficult to listen to. Astoundingly, Ives was a part-time composer, a corporate executive who created his scores at night and on weekends for the most part. Opinion is divided when it comes to his place in the pantheon of composers, but everyone seems to agree that Ives contributed a unique voice to classical music.

Born to a musical family in a musical town (Danbury, Connecticut), Ives was encouraged in every one of his musical impulses. His earliest and most important influence was his father, George Ives, who was a bandleader in the army during the Civil War and a music teacher afterward. George Ives notably made a career in music during an era in which such a profession was unusual. Charles studed piano and organ as a youngster. By the time of his teen years, Ives was a locally famous performer and composer who played in his father's bands and wrote marches for them. Already, Ives was weaving popular songs into original marches, a technique that would serve him well throughout his life. While his father thought Charles might develop into a concert pianist, Ives concentrated on the organ. An early work, *Variations on "America,"* was a complex and mature piece for organ. During these teen years the young Ives also excelled at sports, captaining baseball and football teams.

Ives's early life exposed him to a wide range of popular music, refined by snatches of formal education brought home by a variety of sources, thanks to his father. The juxtaposition of formal and ver-nacular music was to characterize profoundly Ives's mature compositions. The advanced and jarring compositional techniques Ives used as an adult—pieces written in two simultaneous keys, conflicting rhythms and meters—owe much to his father's unorthodox at-home training, which included such bizarre exercises as singing a popular tune while being accompanied on the piano in a different key. As much as Ives turned out to be a music visionary, well ahead of his time, so was his father a mentor of amazing open-mindedness and eagerness to experiment. One biographer described him as a "Yankee tinker in music." George Ives once set two marching bands around a park playing different tunes to gauge how the music blended as they moved toward and away from each other.

Charles became a professional organist at age 14, and continued as a working organist during his student career at Yale University. He started at Yale in 1894, and his father died that fall. The sudden, early loss of his father was a blow to Ives that affected him for the rest of his life. In the short term, though, he forged ahead at Yale. Though not a star academically, Ives was successful socially and in sports. His music studies were taken over by HORATIO PARKER, one of the most influential and rigorous academicians of the time. Their relationship was tentative at first, especially when Ives brought in examples of unhinged music, such as the *Fugue in Four Keys,* which he composed around that time. But Ives needed formal music grounding and must have known it, for he buckled down to be a good, if unspectacular music student. Ives wrote his First Symphony and First String Quartet while at Yale.

When Ives left Yale in 1898, he veered away from the professional music path and began working at a life insurance company. His later remarks made it clear that this decision was motivated by a desire to stay artistically free, even if commercially unsuccessful—and that meant making a living in a more reliable way than composition. Speaking of the composer's life and the necessity of supporting a family, Ives once said, "how can he let them starve on his dissonances?" Working in New York,

Ives accepted two church positions as organist and continued composing as he liked in spare time. In 1902 Ives "quit music," by giving up his organist positions. This release from the contraints of playing prescribed church music seemed to free Ives's creativity, and he embarked on a creative phase that moved his music beyond experimentation to mature, large-scale works using unorthodox techniques. The first sketches for Symphony no. 3 came from this period, as did the First Piano Sonata.

While Ives's music from this and later periods might sound, at first hearing, like a more advanced version of his father's "tinkering," Ives's intent was always emotional and evocative. He did not experiment for the sake of experimenting. He embodied an oddly wide spectrum of influences, and those influences served his artistic purposes. Therefore, although music written in multiple keys and conflicting rhythms is hard to get used to, it should be approached with an appreciation for the diverse palette of American life that it represents.

In 1906 Ives suffered a physical breakdown, after years of leading a demanding double life. In the wake of his recuperation, Ives courted and married (in 1908) Harmony Twitchell, who provided a profound stability to his life. Most biographers mark the marriage as the end of Ives's musical apprenticeship, advanced and pioneering though it was, and the start of his mature composition phase. Soon after marriage, Ives and a business partner started a new insurance company, which quickly became one of the country's leading underwriters. Ives was one of the first to develop a network of insurance agents, and he also invented estate planning as an insurance metric. He continued to compose, both experimentally and more traditionally in the forms of symphonies, sonatas, and quartets. Characteristically, an Ives composition developed over years of part-time effort, with multiple revisions along the way, in parallel with many other pieces.

Performance was always a problem. Being outside the music institutions, Ives was not commissioned to compose, and he rarely heard his difficult, complex works performed. He sent scores to conductors, composers, and other musicians, hoping to inspire interest, and informal readings of orchestral pieces were sometimes arranged. On the whole, though, Ives moved through his entire creative period virtually unrecognized by the musical audience at large; he was, in effect, a cult figure known only to modernist musicians.

Ives's composing career ended in 1927 in one of the mysterious cessations of creative energy that sometimes bring composers to a halt in midlife. Ives's cessation was perhaps less mysterious than that of AARON COPLAND, who was at the height of his powers and in perfect health when he laid down his pen. Ives devoted his remaining years to revising his substantial portfolio of work and trying to promote his pieces to the musical establishment. Both ventures confused his legacy. On the first count, Ives's hundreds of undated revisions make it difficult for musicologists to determine when he developed some of his harmonic innovations. On the second count, his overall failure to gain recognition muddied the composer's reputation after his death. Still, his efforts at self-promotion cannot be faulted in principle, and Ives had the resources to distribute his music fairly widely. He collected many of his art songs into a volume entitled *114 Songs* and sent it to everyone who might appreciate, perform, or publish it. In 1927 not a piece of Ives's music had been published since the 1890s.

Ives's efforts during this retirement period were not totally unrewarded. HENRY COWELL's periodical *New Music* championed Ives's work and published smaller pieces. Ives's now-famous *Three Pieces in New England* was rescored at the request of the leader of the Boston Chamber Orchestra, Nicolas Slonimsky. Pianist JOHN KIRKPATRICK premiered the *Concord* Sonata in 1939 in a concert that marked a high point for Ives—one critic called the Concord "the greatest music written by an American." Ives won a Pulitzer Prize for his Third Symphony after composer LOU HARRISON requested the score and edited it for performance. Nevertheless, despite isolated breakthroughs, Ives was perhaps the least exposed composer of his stature in history. Even today his music is hard for many to follow; a multi-concert Ives minifestival staged by the NEW YORK PHILHARMONIC in 2004 drew poorly at the ticket window. Nevertheless, Ives's reputation has built steadily since his death in 1954, assisted by his widow and a growing number of influential musicians. It is possible that Ives will always be regarded as a maverick, and certainly as a unique creative force in music.

Janis, Byron (b. 1924) *pianist*

One of the few students of VLADIMIR HOROWITZ, Byron Janis was at the height of a virtuoso career when his finger were afflicted by a severe arthritic disease. In addition to Horowitz, Janis studied with Adele Marcus, Josef Lhevinne, and Rosina Lhevinne. He made his orchestra debute in 1943, playing the Second Piano Concerto of Sergey Rachmaninoff with the NBC SYMPHONY ORCHESTRA. His CARNEGIE HALL debut, which followed his work with Horowitz and launched his career, took place in 1948. His debut in Moscow was a legendary and possibly unique tour de force in which he played three major concertos, plus one movement of yet another concerto as an encore. Psoriatic arthritis began afflicting Janis's hands in 1973, forcing the pianist to cut drastically his performance schedule. He did not publicize his condition for 12 years. During that time he rebuilt his keyboard technique to accommodate his disability and returned to the stage playing much of the same repertoire as in his younger days. Janis has long been considered a Chopin specialist, though he has also recorded Beethoven, Rachmaninoff, Schubert, and Liszt.

Jansons, Mariss (b. 1943) *conductor*

Mariss Jansons is a Latvian conductor who has been affiliated with several American orchestra, most notably as music director of the PITTSBURGH SYMPHONY ORCHESTRA. Jansons is a perfect example of the modern conductor who juggles multiple high-profile positions. At the same time that he accepted the appointment in Pittsburgh, Jansons was music director of Norway's Oslo Philharmonic Orchestra, and he conducted both groups for three years. In 2003 (still with Pittsburgh), he was named music director of the Bavarian Radio Symphony Orchestra (Germany). In 2004 he took on the Royal Concertgebouw Orchestra of Amsterdam, leaving Pittsburgh but keeping the Bavarian job. He has long been affiliated with the St. Petersburg Philharmonic Orchestra (Russia) and the London Philharmonic Orchestra, recording with both groups. He has guest-conducted many major orchestras and has been honored by the Norwegian government.

Janssen, Werner (1899–1990) *conductor*

The first native New Yorker to conduct the NEW YORK PHILHARMONIC (1934), Werner Janssen fulfilled a string of musical directorships in the mid-20th century. He led the BALTIMORE SYMPHONY ORCHESTRA from 1937 to 1939, his own orchestra (the Janssen Philharmonic, founded to promote new music) from 1940 to 1952, the UTAH SYMPHONY ORCHESTRA for the 1946–47 season, the Portland Symphony Orchestra from 1947 to 1949, and the San Diego Symphony Orchestra from 1952 to 1954. Janssen took his graduate and postgraduate degrees at Dartmouth College and studied composition at the NEW ENGLAND CONSERVATORY OF MUSIC with FREDERICK CONVERSE and others. As a recipient of the Rome Prize, Janssen lived in Rome between 1930 and 1933, studying with Italian composer

Ottorino Respighi. His conducting career was launched after performances of Jan Sibelius symphonies in Helsinki, Finland, which were praised by the composer. Janssen's own composing activities focused on stage and film music. He composed about 45 film scores.

Järvi, Neeme (b. 1937) *conductor*

Born in Estonia and father of conductor Paarvo Järvi, Neeme Järvi immigrated to the United States in 1980 and became a U.S. citizen in 1987. He won the Accademia of St. Cecilia Conducting Competition in 1971 and made his U.S. debuts (at the METROPOLITAN OPERA and with other orchestras) in 1979. He became music director of the DETROIT SYMPHONY ORCHESTRA in 1990 and planned to step down in 2005, to become conductor laureate. His tenure with Detroit will have been the second-longest in the orchestra's history; OSSIP GABRILOVICH was music director in Detroit from 1918 to 1936.

Järvi, Paarvo (b. 1963) *conductor*

Born in Estonia, Paarvo Järvi is an American conductor who currently leads the CINCINNATI SYMPHONY ORCHESTRA (since 2001). Järvi moved to the United States at age 17, in 1980, and studied at the CURTIS INSTITUTE with MAX RUDOLF. He has guest-conducted around the world, maintaining particularly strong associations with the Royal Stockholm Philharmonic (Sweden) and the City of Birmingham Symphony Orchestra (England).

Johannesen, Grant (b. 1921) *pianist*

An American who specializes in French piano music, Grant Johannesen studied with Robert Casadesus and Egon Petri (at Princeton and Cornell Universities, respectively). His 1944 debut in New York preceded by five years his victory in the Ostend International Competition. He toured with the NEW YORK PHILHARMONIC in the 1950s and the

CLEVELAND ORCHESTRA in 1968. Johannesen has recorded the complete piano music of French composer Gabriel Fauré.

Johansen, Gunnar (1906–1991) *pianist*

An American born in Europe, Johansen studied first with his father, then with Egon Petri in Germany. From the age of 18 and into his 20s, Johansen toured Europe actively, then moved to the United States, where he was noted for marathon performance and recording cycles. He made weekly broadcasts on NBC Radio and became artist in residence at the University of Wisconsin in 1939—a position he held for nearly 40 years. At Wisconsin Johansen performed the entire piano repertoire of Bach, Mozart, Beethoven, Schubert, and Chopin, an astounding intellectual, physical, and interpretive project. He

Paarvo Järvi (Courtesy of Paarvo Järvi; Photo by Sheila Rock)

wrote his own music as well, but nothing that has entered the standard repertoire.

Johns, Paul Emile (1798–1860) *pianist*

Born in Poland, Paul Emile Johns emigrated to America in his teens. He played a Beethoven piano concerto in public in 1819, and that performance is thought to be the first of a Beethoven piano concerto in the United States. Johns knew pianist Frédéric Chopin in the Paris of the 1830s, and Chopin dedicated one set of mazurkas (op. 7) to Johns. Johns himself dabbled in composition, was an organist, and later abandoned music altogether to build a cotton empire.

Johnson, Edward (1878–1959) *opera singer*

A tenor and opera administrator, Edward Johnson got his performing start in Boston, New York, and Italy. He landed roles in the Italian premieres of two Gia Como Puccini operas. He was the lead tenor of the Chicago Opera from 1919 to 1922, then moved to New York's METROPOLITAN OPERA, where he sang leading tenor roles until 1935. In that year Johnson became general manager of the Metropolitan, remaining in that position until 1950.

Johnson, Thor (1913–1975) *conductor*

Thor Johnson created two American firsts in classical music. He organized the first army symphony orchestra during his World War II military service (1942–46), and he was the first American-born musician to assume the directorship of a major American symphony orchestra—the CINCINANTI SYMPHONY ORCHESTRA, which he took over in 1947. He was the conductor of the Nashville Symphony Orchestra from 1967 to 1975. Unlike that of many other American conductors, Johnson's career did not have a European component, though he did train in Leipzig, Germany, and Prague, Czeckoslovakia, after attending the North Carolina State University and the University of Michigan.

Johnston, Ben (b. 1926) *composer*

A radical avant-garde composer, Ben Johnston used 12-tone techniques as applied to pitch and other musical elements, experimented with alternate tunings and scales (microtonality), and used charts in his notation to convey advanced and unusual concepts to organize his music. By the time he was 18, Johnston was interested in tunings different from the well-tempered system that has been the basis of Western music since before Bach. He studied at William and Mary College, the CINCINNATI CONSERVATORY, and Mills College. His teachers were JOHN CAGE, HARRY PARTCH, and French composer Darius Milhaud. He taught at the University of Illinois from 1951 until his retirement in 1983.

Jones, Sissieretta (1868–1933) *opera singer*

One of the most celebrated singers of her time, Sissieretta Jones (whose performing nickname was sometimes "Black Patti," a reference to white singer of the time Adelina Patti) lived in an era during which black singers could follow the career paths of white singers only to a certain point. So although Jones attended the NEW ENGLAND CONSERVATORY and made her debut at Steinway Hall in New York, she never joined a major opera company and spent much of her career touring with a musical vaudeville company. Jones was born in Virginia just after the Civil War, to former slaves. She sang in a church choir where her voice projected effortlessly above the other singers. As a child she took lessons at the Providence (Virginia) Academy of Music. In addition to her classical and vaudeville performances, Jones was a hit on Broadway, singing in theaters as early as 1888. She received critical praise from mainstream publications for the extraordinary range of her voice, which seemed to encompass the scope of both soprano and contralto. She was praised by composer ANTONÍN DVOŘÁK when he lived in the United States, was well paid, and toured Europe where she sang for the prince of Wales at the Covent Garden opera house in London. She performed at the White House for President William

Henry Harrison in 1892. In 1896 she formed "Black Patti's Troubadors," a traveling vaudeville troupe that presented, among other acts, compressed versions of operas. Her work with this group dominated the final phase of her career. "The flowers absorb the sunshine because it is their nature," she said. "I give out melody because God filled my soul with it."

Joplin, Scott (1867–1917) *composer*

As the greatest composer of ragtime, Scott Joplin is often regarded more as a jazz figure than a classical one. Still, he composed his syncopated, bouncy piano numbers called rags, in formal style and considered them performance pieces, not improvisatory jazz tunes. His collected rags have been issued by classical publisher G. SCHIRMER. Joplin was born in Sedalia, Missouri, and moved to Texarkana, a town on the border of Texas and Arkansas, sometime during his childhood. Though few details are known of his boyhood, he learned the rudiments of music early. He was taught basic piano skills by an outside figure sometimes identified as Julius Weiss, a German immigrant musician.

Joplin eventually made Sedalia his home base. He played lead cornet in the Queens City Comet Band and performed also with his own quartet. He worked as a pianist in Sedalia's Maple Leaf Club, later immortalized in Joplin's "Maple Leaf Rag" (1899), perhaps his most famous piece. That rag was Joplin's first fully credited work to be published; two earlier published rags were erroneously attributed to another man. The "Maple Leaf Rag" sold about 500,000 copies in its first 10 years and continued selling at that pace for the next two decades. When the publisher, music store owner John Stark, moved to St. Louis, he called his company "The House of Classic Rags," seeming to define the middle ground between classical and jazz upon which Joplin stood.

Joplin's fortunes turned downward. His wife, Freddie Alexander, died of pneumonia at age 20, a mere 10 weeks after they married, in 1904. Joplin's productivity slowed and his finances were damaged

by a failed opera, *A Guest of Honor.* Joplin never succeeded in producing his most ambitious, large-scale works. He composed a ballet, piano concerto, and symphony, but these works were not published and the scores, tragically, are lost. He tried for years to produce his opera *Treemonisha*, but despite rave notices from critics who saw the score, that dream was never realized. Joplin was sadly marginalized at the time of his death, and ragtime suffered a similar fate as new forms of jazz took center stage. A Joplin revival of sorts occurred in the 1970s, spurred considerably by the ragtime soundtrack of the movie *The Sting*. Since then, ragtime has been recognized as a semiclassical genre of substance, and Joplin its foremost individual creative force.

Jorda, Enrique (1911–1996) *conductor*

An American conductor born in Spain, Jorda had a career that transpired mostly in Europe, South America, and Australia. His one major American appointment was as music director of the SAN FRANCISCO SYMPHONY ORCHESTRA, which he led from 1954 to 1963. Between 1940 and 1984, Jorda held the podium in cities as far-flung as Madrid (Spain), Cape Town (South Africa), San Sebastián, Spain, and London.

Juilliard School

The preeminent conservatory and performing arts school in the United States, Juilliard was founded in 1905 by Frank Damrosch as the Institute of Musical Art. The school's original home was on Fifth Avenue and 12th Street in New York, but it moved to Claremont Avenue in lower Harlem in 1910. In 1924 the school received an endowment from the Juilliard Musical Foundation, a foundation for the advancement of music created by textile merchant August D. Juilliard, and changed its name to the Juilliard School of Music. Having occupied three different locations in Manhattan, Juilliard moved downtown to the newly constructed Lincoln Center Complex in 1968. At that time the school initiated a drama division and enlarged its dance department (in 1951, at the instigation of then-president WILLIAM SCHUMAN), thereby broadening its mandate and shortening its name to Juilliard School. Juilliard's drama division was founded by Schuman's replacement, PETER MENNIN, in 1967. Juilliard moved its facility again in 1968 to the newly constructed LINCOLN CENTER (the Claremont Avenue building was taken over by the MANHATTAN SCHOOL OF MUSIC).

Juilliard presidents have included John Erskine (1928–37), ERNEST HUTCHESON (1937–45), Schuman (1945–62), Mennin, (1962–83), and Joseph W. Polisi (from 1984). Polisi's tenure has seen the creation of the Institute for Jazz Studies and the emergence of the Juilliard Orchestra (a student ensemble) as an internationally touring group.

Juilliard String Quartet

A pedagogical and performing quartet, the Juilliard String Quartet was founded in 1946 by WILLIAM SCHUMAN, then president of the Juilliard School of Music (later the JUILLIARD SCHOOL). The founding members were Robert Mann (violin), Robert Koff (violin), Robert Hillyer (viola), and Arthur Winograd (cello). The quartet's current players are Joel Smirnoff (violin), Ronald Copes (violin), Joel Krosnick (violin), and Samuel Rhodes (cello). The Juilliard String Quartet is the quartet in residence at the Library of Congress, where the group plays on preserved Stradivarius instruments housed in that institution. The group is also the quartet in residence at the Juilliard School.

Kahn, Eric Itor (1905–1956) *pianist*
A German-born American, Eric Kahn specialized in chamber music and settled in the United States in 1941. He founded the ALBENERI TRIO with Benar Heifetz and ALEXANDER SCHNEIDER in 1944.

Kalichstein, Joseph (b. 1946) *pianist*
Joseph Kalichstein is an American of Israeli birth who is a popular performer in the New York classical scene. He moved to America from Israel to attend the JUILLIARD SCHOOL, and made his New York recital debut in 1967. Following that successful engagement, LEONARD BERNSTEIN invited Kalichstein to appear with the NEW YORK PHILHARMONIC. He has performed with innumerable major orchestras in the United States and around the world.

Kalish, Gilbert (b. 1935) *pianist*
Gilbert Kalish performs an unusually broad repertoire. He is celebrated for his adventurous recordings of modernists such as CHARLES IVES and GEORGE CRUMB. He helped found the Contemporary Chamber Players in New York and played in the Boston Symphony Chamber Players in 1969. He has been artist in residence at Swarthmore College and Rutgers University. He joined the faculty of SUNY Stony Brook in 1970 and is head of the performance faculty there. Kalish has recorded about 100 discs.

Kapell, William (1922–1953) *pianist*
An American whose life and career were cut short by a plane crash, William Kapell won the Naumburg Award in 1941, which led to his New York debut that year. Kapell's legacy is carried forward by his limited and valuable discography. He was a refined, original, and graceful pianist.

Katchen, Julius (1926–1969) *pianist*
An American of Russian lineage, Julius Katchen started his career in New York and eventually settled in Paris. Known as a conservative, contemplative pianist, Katchen specialized in the piano music of Brahms, all of which he recorded. Katchen gave his New York debut at age 12, and was still a child when he gave a performance with the NEW YORK PHILHARMONIC.

Kavafian, Ani (b. 1948) *violinist*
Born in Turkey, violinist Ani Kavafian emigrated to the United States when she was 10 years old and began studying at the JUILLIARD SCHOOL in 1966. Three years later she made a New York debut, and in 1976 she won the Avery Fisher Prize. A concert with the NEW YORK PHILHARMONIC followed the next year. Dedicated to chamber music as well as solo concertizing, Kafavian is associated with the Chamber Music Society of Lincoln Center.

Kay, Ulysses (1917–1995) *composer*

Ulysses Kay didn't relish the description of him as one of the leading black composers of his day, but he accepted it to emphasize the lack of black composers in the classical music industry. He studied piano, violin, and saxophone as a child and attended the University of Arizona and the EASTMAN SCHOOL OF MUSIC. At the Berkshire Music Center (later TANGLEWOOD) he studied with PAUL HINDEMITH. He taught at Herbert H. Lehman College of the City University of New York from 1968 to 1988. He was awarded a Fulbright Scholarship and a Guggenheim Fellowship, and the Prix de Rome. In 1958 he represented the United States in a cultural exchange program with the Soviet Union and was elected to the American Academy of Arts and Letters in 1979. He completed five opera, 20 orchestral works, 30 choral pieces, and 15 works for chamber groups.

Keene, Christopher (1946–1995) *conductor and opera administrator*

Christopher Keene championed new music and American music. Specializing in opera from his early career, Keene conducted Britten's *Rape of Lucretia* at the age of 19. By 1966 he was assistant conductor at the San Francisco Opera. Composer GIAN CARLO MENOTTI invited him to conduct *The Saint of Bleecker Street* at the SPOLETO FESTIVAL in 1968. His connection to Spoleto deepened after that, and between 1977 and 1980 Keene was music director of the festival. He led the Syracuse Symphony Orchestra from 1975 to 1984, and he founded and directed the Long Island Philharmonic Orchestra from 1979 to 1990. Keene is remembered for his musical directorship of the New York City Opera (1982–86) and subsequent position as general manager of the company (1989–95).

Kelley, Edgar Stillman (1857–1944) *composer*

Called the "Dean of American composers" in his *New York Times* obituary, Edgar Kelley was a pianist, organist, writer, and composer. He studied in the United States during a time when music conservatories were few and young institutions. Most serious musicians of that day went to Europe for advanced study, and Kelley spent four years in Germany. He settled in San Francisco as a 23-year-old, where he was an organist, teacher, and music critic for the *San Francisco Examiner*. He commuted between San Francisco and New York during the 1880s, then was a professor at Yale University in 1901–02. Kelley moved to Berlin, Germany, in 1902 and spent eight years there teaching piano. He returned to take a teaching post at the Cincinnati Conservatory of Music, where he taught composition from 1911 to 1934. He is the author of two books: *Chopin the Composer* (1913) and *The History of Musical Instruments* (1925). Kelley's best-remembered works are two symphonies: *Gulliver—His Voyage to Lilliput* (completed in 1900 and premiered in 1937) and *New England* (premiered in 1913).

Kellogg, Clara Louise (1842–1916) *opera singer*

One of the first American-born opera singers to establish a respected career in Europe, Clara Louise Kellogg did her most active work in London between 1867 and 1876. She also toured the United States, both during and after the Civil War, and strove to gain acceptance for operatic performances translated from their original European language (usually German or Italian) into English.

Kennedy Center for the Performing Arts

The Kennedy Center in Washington, D.C., opened in September 1971 with roots dating back to the National Cultural Center Act of 1958. Signed into law by President Dwight Eisenhower, the act authorized construction of an arts center. The city of Washington, D.C., lacking an orchestra (the Washington Symphony Orchestra had operated for just a few seasons before 1912), needed an arts center to fill a cultural void in the nation's capital.

However, the government did not provide funds for the center's completion, and years of fund-raising were required; President Kennedy took up this cause vigorously, placing the prestige of his office behind the project. In 1961 Kennedy appointed Roger L. Stevens chairman of the endeavor; Stevens brought experience in both real estate (he had brokered the sale of the Empire State Building) and theatrical production, and he remained at the helm for 30 years. Following Kennedy's assassination in 1963, Congress authorized millions of dollars to complete the center as a tribute. Other nations began contributing then, and a completed center was opened in 1971. Because of the center's status as a living presidential memorial, it enjoys the benefit of annual federal funding that covers the operation of the physical facility. The Kennedy Center's premiere concert featured a commissioned work: LEONARD BERNSTEIN's Mass.

The center embodies three main performance venues. The Kennedy Center Opera House seats an audience of 2,300 and hosts dance performances in addition to opera. The Kennedy Center Concert Hall is the largest auditorium, seating 2,442 and featuring a 4,144-pipe organ. The Eisenhower Theater is a recital hall seating 1,100. Eisenhower Hall is suitable for theatrical productions and contains an orchestra pit that holds 40 musicians. A fourth venue, the Millennium Stage, hosts small audiences for performances of all kinds of music and stage presentations.

The NATIONAL SYMPHONY ORCHESTRA is not officially an artistic component of the Kennedy Center, but the center is its home base and might easily be considered the house orchestra. Official groups housed by the center include the Washington Opera, the Washington Ballet, and the Master Chorale of Washington. The center organizes its performances into festivals, of which it presents about 10 each year. Kennedy Center awards the annual Marian Anderson Award to midcareer singers. Also annually, the center produces the Kennedy Center Honors, a televised gala of performances and awards.

Kernis, Aaron Jay (b. 1960) composer

Aaron Jay Kernis has been compared to LEONARD BERNSTEIN in the ease with which he assimilates varied styles and influences. Though strictly trained as a classical composer, Kernis sometimes incorporates jazz or rock elements in his pieces. He grew up in Philadelphia and southern California in an unmusical family. He absorbed a wide range of avant-garde music as a youngster, from JOHN CAGE to Frank Zappa. He started writing his own music at age 12. His formal studies took place at the San Francisco Conservatory, the MANHATTAN SCHOOL OF MUSIC (bachelor's degree, 1981), and Yale University. In these schools he worked with JOHN ADAMS, JACOB DRUCKMAN, MORTON SUBOTNICK, and CHARLES WUORINEN.

Kernis attained recognition in 1983 when his orchestral work *Dream of the Morning Sky* was programmed in the NEW YORK PHILHARMONIC's "Horizons" festival by Druckman, who was responsible for piece selection but was not the festival conductor. The piece was decently received, but fireworks came after the concert in a stage interview with conductor Zubin Mehta, who did not like the work. Kernis didn't favor Mehta's conducting of it, and a spirited argument set the audience aquiver and made headlines for Kernis.

Commissions did not come quickly after that, but currently Kernis is a busy and successful composer. In 1993 he was appointed composer in residence of the SAINT PAUL CHAMBER ORCHESTRA. In 1998 he won a Pulitzer Prize for his String Quartet no. 2, which was premiered in 1990 by the LARK QUARTET in New York. That same year he was named music adviser to the MINNESOTA ORCHESTRA. In 2002 Kernis received the $200,000 Grawemeyer Award given by the University of Louisville. Asked to describe Kernis's music, Carter Brey, principal cellist of the NEW YORK PHILHARMONIC, said, "He's capable of irony and wit, but won't take cover behind those qualities. There's a lot of passion to his writing, and what ties his disparate pieces together are the grand gestures, the way he'll go for a big romantic statement."

Kim, Earl (1920–1998) *composer*

A composer of vocal music primarily, Earl Kim studied with composers Arnold Shoenberg, ERNEST BLOCH, and ROGER SESSIONS. He taught composition at Princeton University between 1952 and 1967, then at Harvard University from 1967 to 1990. He received commissions from the Koussevitzky Foundation and the Naumberg Foundation, and won the Paris Prize and the National Institute of Arts and Letters Award.

Kim, Young Uck (b. 1947) *violinist*

A prodigious violinist, Young Uck Kim entered the CURTIS INSTITUTE at age 14 and made his debut with the PHILADELPHIA ORCHESTRA two years later in a nationally broadcast concert. EUGENE ORMANDY, music director of the orchestra, invited Kim to tour with the Philadelphians the following season. His New York debut came in 1966, at a Young People's Concert with LEONARD BERNSTEIN. Bernstein introduced Kim by saying, "Young Uck Kim is a genius, and I do not use that word lightly." Although Kim began performing widely after that, he remained enrolled at Curtis until 1969. Kim has recorded all the Mozart violin concertos and performs in a chamber trio with cellist YO-YO MA and pianist EMANUEL AX (Ax-Kim-Ma Trio). He has played with most major orchestras and conductors around the world.

Kimmel Center for the Performing Arts

Opened in 2001, the Kimmel Center is a multistage performance complex that serves as home for the PHILADELPHIA ORCHESTRA, the Philly Pops, the Chamber Orchestra of Philadelphia, and the Philadelphia Chamber Music Society. The orchestra plays in 2,500-seat Verizon Hall. The Kimmel Center also owns the Academy of Music, where the Opera Company of Philadelphia and the Pennsylvania Ballet perform. The Perelman Theater, a 650-seat recital hall, is part of the center. The Merck Arts Education Center provides cultural classes. One of the center's most attractive features is the Dorrance H. Hamilton Garden, a landscaped rooftop used for receptions and general enjoyment.

The Kimmel Center was conceived in 1996, after the Philadelphia Orchestra acquired the city property it sits on. The city government wished to consolidate its far-flung cultural resources, so merged its plans with the orchestra's independent plan to build a new home. The center incorporates over 429,000 square feet of performance and audience space, and cost about $265 million to build.

Kirchner, Leon (b. 1919) *conductor and pianist*

Leon Kirchner is an accomplished pianist and conductor, but his legacy will probably be based on his composition. He grew up in Los Angeles and studied with 12-tone pioneer Arnold Schoenberg. He has won the New York Music Critics Circle award twice and received the Naumberg Award for his Piano Concerto no. 1. His third quartet, the score of which includes a part for electronic tape, won a Pulitzer Prize in 1967. Kirchner is a member of the American Academy of Arts and Letters.

Kirkpatrick, John (1905–1991) *pianist and scholar*

John Kirkpatrick is strongly associated with composer CHARLES IVES. In 1939, when Ives was struggling for recognition, Kirkpatrick gave the premiere performance of the complex and difficult Second Piano Sonata (Concord Sonata). The sonata was reviewed superlatively, shining a much-needed spotlight on Ives's music. After Ives's death, Kirkpatrick catalogued the composer's manuscripts at the request of Ives's widow; the result, published by Yale University, was the first systematic organization of Ives's music. Kirkpatrick studied piano at Princeton University and with NADIA BOULANGER in Paris. He taught at Monticello College and Mount Holyoke College, and was chairman of the music department at Cornell University from 1949 to 1953 after joining the faculty in 1946.

Kirkpatrick, Ralph (1911–1984) *harpsichordist*

One of the few renowned harpsichordists of the 20th century, Ralph Kirkpatrick began his studies on the piano at age six. He graduated from Harvard University in 1931, and was awarded a Paine Travelling Scholarship for European study; he went to France where he worked with NADIA BOULANGER (the famous theorist) and Wanda Landowska (one of the few other famous harpsichordists). He made his European debut in Berlin in 1933, playing Bach's monumental *Goldberg Variations* on the harpsichord, the instrument for which the piece was originally written. One might term Kirkpatrick a general specialist, in that he performed ancient music on a variety of period instruments. He mastered the clavichord in addition to the harpsichord, and performed Mozart on the fortepiano, the precursor to the modern piano. He received a Guggenheim Fellowship in 1937. He joined the faculty of Yale University in 1940 and was associated with that institution until 1976. He taught for one year (1964) at the University of California, Berkeley, where he was the Ernest Bloch Professor of Music.

Klemperer, Otto (1885–1973) *conductor*

One of the preeminent German conductors of his time, Otto Klemperer impacted the American musical scene as conductor of the LOS ANGELES PHILHARMONIC between 1933 and 1939, and conductor of the PITTSBURGH SYMPHONY in 1937 and 1938. He guest-conducted the NEW YORK PHILHARMONIC and the PHILADELPHIA ORCHESTRA. Klemperer composed on the side, fairly prolifically, but his work was not published and is not part of the standard repertoire. The bulk of his career transpired in Europe, where he was closely associated with the New Philharmonia Orchestra in London.

Kneisel, Franz (1865–1926) *violinist*

Franz Kneisel was a violinist, born in Romania but later an American citizen, who promoted the art of chamber music performance. His early and upper-level music training transpired in Europe; Kneisel attended from the Bucharest Conservatory. In 1885, the 20-year-old Kneisel was hired as concertmaster of the BOSTON SYMPHONY ORCHESTRA, one of the most adventurous and ambitious of early American orchestras. He remained in that position for 20 years, appearing often as soloist in concerto performances. He formed the Kneisel Quartet, an ensemble that attained substantial popularity, enough to afford its members to quit the symphony and devote themselves to chamber music. When the Institute of Musical Art (later to become the JUILLIARD SCHOOL) was formed in 1905, Kneisel became the first head of the violin department. Kneisel Hall, the performance theater at a chamber music school he established in Blue Hill, Maine, is named for him. It continues to operate a summer curriculum. The Blue Hill campus has attracted later chamber music masters such as ARTUR BALSAM and MURRAY PERAHIA.

Kneisel Hall Chamber Music Festival

This summer festival was founded in 1902 by FRANZ KNEISEL, an Austrian violinist who moved to the United States when invited to become the concertmaster of the BOSTON SYMPHONY ORCHESTRA. Kneisel Hall has attracted the finest practitioners of chamber music, including ARTUR BALSAM, who taught there annually, and pianist MURRAY PERAHIA. Like the TANGLEWOOD Festival, Kneisel Hall is both a tourist attraction offering concerts and an advanced summer school (in this case, an all-scholarship school).

Kolisch, Rudolf (1896–1978) *violinist*

Born in Austria, Rudolf Kolisch became an American violinist who founded the Kolisch Quartet. It was the first string quartet to play from memory; most such ensembles, even today, play from sheet music. The group championed new music and gave important American premieres of music by Arnold Schoenberg, Anton Webern, and Alban Berg.

Korn, Clara Anna (1866–1940) *pianist and composer*

Clara Korn founded the WOMEN'S PHILHARMONIC. She studied at the NATIONAL CONSERVATORY with ANTONÍN DVOŘÁK and also worked with HORATIO PARKER. She wrote a handful of works for orchestra, piano, and voice.

Korngold, Erich (1897–1957) *composer*

Austrian Erich Korngold worked for several years in Hollywood during the 1930s and early 1940s. He broke new ground in the art of film scoring, intending his soundtracks to stand alone as concert pieces if the film were removed. Like Wagner in his operas, Korngold assigned themes to characters and developed fully wrought, organic musical productions for film. He won two Academy Awards (for *Anthony Adverse* and *The Adventures of Robin Hood*). Unlike any other film composer, Korngold was a child prodigy of nearly Mozartean scale. At age nine he had composed a full-length cantata, which caused Mahler to declare the boy a genius; similar accolades came from other quarters. As a young teenager Korngold composed a ballet and a piano sonata that legendary pianist Arthur Schnabel included on his recital programs. When Korngold died, his music fell out of fashion, in Hollywood and in concert halls, and he remained mostly forgotten until a moderate resurgence of interest in the 1990s.

Kostelanetz, André (1901–1980) *conductor*

An American of Russian birth, André Kostelanetz was one of the great music popularizers of American history. He became an American citizen in 1928 after studying at the the Petrograd Conservatory (which later became the St. Petersburg Conservatory). In 1930 Kostelanetz was hired as house conductor for the CBS radio network, using his position to introduce orchestral music to a national audience via the CBS Symphony Orchestra. Kostelanetz was the perfect individual for this position because of his populist instincts and his interest in technology; his experiments with microphones and their placement led to standard practices when recording and broadcasting orchestras. He commissioned AARON COPLAND's *A Lincoln Portrait* and William Schuman's *New England Tryptich*. In 1939 he began a long affiliation with the promenade concerts produced by the NEW YORK PHILHARMONIC; he conducted that orchestra over 400 times, though he was never its music director. Generally, the promenade concerts mixed classical with light-classical repertoire. He recorded 90 works with the Philharmonic. His obituary ran on page one of the *New York Times*.

Koussevitzky, Serge (1874–1951) *conductor*

Legendary conductor of the BOSTON SYMPHONY ORCHESTRA, Serge Koussevitzky was one of the most influential American musicians in the first half of the 20th century. His influence extended beyond his life, thanks to the many works he commissioned and the careers he enabled. The *New Grove Dictionary of Music and Musicians* likens Koussevitzky's impact on the American musical scene to that of TOSCANINI, but considering the latter's comparative lack of interest in new music, one could easily argue that Koussevitzky was far more important to the development of a rich American classical tradition.

Koussevitzky was born in Russia and received most of his training there. He was primarily a double bass player during these early years. He dabbled in composition, contributing a concerto to the sparse double bass repertoire. By the age of 31 Koussevitzky had married twice and was living with his second wife in Berlin. There, in 1908, he hired the Berlin Philharmonic to make his conducting debut in a concert that featured Russian composer Sergey Rachmaninoff playing his own Piano Concerto no. 2. Koussevitzky's dedication to modern music was apparent at this time, as well as his eagerness to help composers in any way possible. He founded a publishing company in 1909 (Éditions

Russe de Musique) and printed works of Alexander Scriabin, Igor Stravinsky, Sergey Prokofiev, and Sergey Rachmaninoff. Koussevitzky formed his own orchestra in Moscow to showcase new music as well as traditional repertoire.

Koussevitzky took over the Boston Symphony Orchestra as music director in 1924 and remained at the helm until 1949—one of the most productive collaborations in the history of conducting. Under his leadership the orchestra began performing in the summer and established a summer home, TANGLEWOOD in Massachusetts. He founded the Berkshire Music Center (later renamed Tanglewood Music Center). It was in the realm of concert programming that Koussevitzky redrew the profile of American classical music. He performed nearly 100 world premieres. The Boston Symphony had always been an adventurous orchestra—much more so than its rival NEW YORK PHILHARMONIC—and Koussevitzky was the perfect music director during a fertile time of much new music. The list of Koussevitzky premieres is an astonishing inventory of new music penned by the best composers of the day: Prokofiev, Ravel, Stravinsky, Respighi, Hindemith, Honegger, DIAMOND, GERSHWIN, FOSS, and Schoenberg. In 1942 he set up the Koussevitzky Music Foundation to commission new work. Throughout the Boston period, many composers' careers were launched by the exposure they gained from Koussevitzky. Hungarian composer Béla Bartók's Concerto for Orchestra, now a staple of the concert repertoire, was the foundation's first orchestral commission. The foundation still operates in collaboration with the Library of Congress.

At the time of his death, Koussevitzky had agreed to participate in the resurrection of the Detroit Symphony, which had collapsed in 1949. The orchestra was set to resume operation in fall 1951, and Koussevitzky might have been its conductor at that time. His death was front-page news. He had been awarded honorary doctorates from Brown and Harvard Universities, and had been made a knight of the French Legion of Honor.

Kovacevich, Stephen (b. 1940) *pianist*

One of the few American pianists to study with the Grande Dame of European pianism, Myra Hess, Kovacevich has specialized, as did Hess, in playing Beethoven. At the same time, his recorded output covers the gamut from Mozart to Stravisnky, Bartók, and the Piano Concerto no. 1 of British composer Richard Rodney Bennett, which was written for him and dedicated to him. Kovacevich made his debut at age 11; he played with the San Francisco Symphony Orchestra before embarking on his European studies.

Koyaanisqatsi (1982)

PHILIP GLASS's continuously running soundtrack to the film of the same name (directed by Godfrey Reggio), *Koyaanisqatsi* refers to a Hopi Indian concept of "life out of balance." One of Glass's most widely known works, *Koyaanisqatsi* established the composer as a popular, mainstream classicist. Incorporating Glass's signature minimalistic and restless kaleidoscope of shifting harmonies, the soundtrack accompanies a no-character, no-dialogue, no-story montage of visual images evoking the complexity, discord, and beauty of the natural and urbanized worlds. *Koyaanisqatsi* is the first installment of a film trilogy (the *Qatsi* trilogy), the later parts of which are titled *Powaqqatsi* and *Naqoyqatsi*.

Kraft, William (b. 1923) *composer*

A 12-tone composer who has experimented with electronic music, William Kraft attended Columbia University and did postgraduate work at the JUILLIARD SCHOOL. He studied with HENRY BRANT and HENRY COWELL. He worked as a percussionist and timpanist in the LOS ANGELES PHILHARMONIC between 1955 and 1981, was assistant conductor from 1969 to 1972, and was composer in residence from 1981 to 1985. Kraft won two Friedheim Awards from the KENNEDY CENTER and fellowships from the Guggenheim and Ford Foundations. His works include the Concerto for Timpani and Orchestra, other percussions works, and pieces for orchestra.

Krasner, Louis (1903–1995) *violinist*

A violinist dedicated to both new and avant-garde music, Louis Krasner attempted to introduce audiences to the music possibilities of 12-tone composition. While he himself studied composition with FREDERICK CONVERSE at the NEW ENGLAND CONSERVATORY, Krasner made his mark as a violinist. He commissioned a violin concerto from German modernist composer Alban Berg in 1934 and performed its premiere two years later. He also premiered Arnold Schoenberg's Violin Concerto in the United States (1940). He was the first to record both concertos. Krasner was the concertmaster of the Minneapolis Symphony Orchestra from 1944 to 1949 and was on the faculty of Syracuse University. He also taught briefly at the New England Conservatory.

Krazy Kat (1921)

Possibly JOHN ALDEN CARPENTER's most successful work, and certainly his first big success, *Krazy Kat* is a "jazz pantomime" based on the comic strip of that name. Predating Gershwin's seminal *Rhapsody in Blue* by four years, *Krazy Kat* pioneered the use of the jazz idiom in a classical form.

Kreisler, Fritz (1875–1962) *violinist*

Kreisler was one of the most brilliant, innovative, and unusual violinists in history. Born in Vienna, he became an American citizen in 1943. A child prodigy, Kreisler established a track record of unprecedented precocity, entering conservatories in Vienna and Paris, and winning awards. His studies ended at age 12, when he emerged as a more or less finished artist. He toured the United States as a young teen, then abandoned music for premedical training and serving in the military. By 1896, when Kreisler was

21, he resumed his music career. His debut performance in 1899 with the Berlin Philharmonic launched his international renown. He made a London debut in 1902. British composer Edward Elgar composed his Violin Concerto for Kreisler and conducted its debut in 1910.

Kreisler is credited with innovations in of fingering and bowing. His tone was described as penetratingly sweet. Unlike some performers who continue in the limelight throughout their lives, Kreisler dropped out of the concert scene after 1950.

Krips, Josef (1902–1974) *conductor*

Austrian Josef Krips was music director of the BUFFALO PHILHARMONIC from 1954 to 1963 and of the SAN FRANCISCO SYMPHONY ORCHESTRA from 1963 to 1970. Krips was a guest conductor at New York's METROPOLITAN OPERA starting in 1966.

Kroll, William (1901–1980) *violinist*

A violinist who specialized in chamber music, William Kroll was taken to Germany as a nine-year-old for study. He made a prodigious debut in New York at age 14, then continued his studies at the Institute of Musical Art (later the JUILLIARD SCHOOL), working with chamber music pioneer FRANZ KNEISEL. He was associated with three established chamber groups during his performing career: the Elshuco Trio (1922–26), the Coolidge Quartet (1936–44), and the Kroll Quartet (1944–66). He also performed violin sonatas with ARTUR BALSAM. Kroll was an active teacher whose appointments included the Institute of Musical Art from 1922 to 1938, the Peabody Conservatory (later PEABODY INSTITUTE) from 1947 to 1965, the CLEVELAND INSTITUTE OF MUSIC from 1964 to 1967, Queens College in New York (from 1969), and the MANNES COLLEGE OF MUSIC (from 1943). In addition to his chamber music work, Kroll performed concertos with the BOSTON SYMPHONY and other orchestras.

Kronos Quartet

Founded in 1973 by violinist David Harrington, who was inspired by the music of GEORGE CRUMB. One of the most imaginative and adventurous chamber ensembles, Kronos regularly solicits scores from young composers and arranges music never before heard in the quartet format. The group won a Grammy Award in 2004 for Best Chamber Music Performance and in 2003 earned Musicians of the Year from *Musical America.* Though the group performs works from sources as diverse as Jimi Hendrix and Pakistani singers, it does so without gimmickry and can be considered a crossover group only cautiously. Kronos has not lost sight of its classical roots. It has collaborated with many composers and performers, notably TERRY RILEY, the founding composer of the minimalist movement. The group tours for five months during the season and performed with the same personnel until 1998, when cellist Jennifer Culp joined.

Kubelik, Rafael (1914–1996) *director*

Rafael Kubelik was born in Czechoslovakia and eventually took Swiss citizenship (1967). His activity in the United States was limited to a stormy and, in the end, unsuccessful tenure as music director of the CHICAGO SYMPHONY ORCHESTRA (1950–53). He was slated to be music director of the METROPOLITAN OPERA but resigned immediately upon arriving because the general manager who had hired him had died.

Kubik, Gail (1914–1984) *composer*

A prolific composer, Gail Kubik gained a full scholarship to the EASTMAN SCHOOL OF MUSIC at age 15, where he studied violin and composing. He received a graduate degree in music at the American Conservatory in Chicago, then worked with WALTER PISTON and NADIA BOULANGER in the late 1930s. He composed music for the U.S. Army during World War II, writing soundtracks for documentaries. After the war he received the Prix de Rome, two Guggenheim Fellowships, and a Pulitzer Prize in 1952 for his Symphony Concertante.

Kuerti, Anton (b. 1938) *pianist*

Born in Austria and raised in the United States, pianist Anton Kuerti has lived in Canada since 1965. He is pianist in residence at the University of Toronto. Kuerti's first major appearance was with the Boston Pops Orchestra, in a concert at which he played Grieg's Piano Concerto—Kuerti was 11 years old. He attended the CLEVELAND INSTITUTE OF MUSIC and the CURTIS INSTITUTE, and won the Levintritt Award. Kuerti has performed widely in his adopted Canada, and he appears often with the Toronto Symphony.

Lachmund, Carl Valentine (1853–1928)
pianist

Carl Valentine Lachmund was one of the few American pianists to study with Franz Liszt in the master's summer teaching studio in Weimar, Germany. Lachmund's claim to fame was his diary. He kept detailed notes of the Weimar sessions, including accounts of the playing and remarks of other students who became famous pianists, including Eugene d'Albert and Artur Friedheim. Along with the notebooks of AMY FAY, Lachmund's written recollection provide the most valuable first-hand English-language accounts of Liszt as a teacher. Lachmund wrote a book called *Living with Liszt,* which was published after his death (1995). Lachmund settled in New York after his European adventures, and established the Lachmund Piano Conservatory, which remained in operation for several decades.

Laredo, Jaime (b. 1941) *violinist*

Jaime Laredo entered the CURTIS INSTITUTE as a child and studied there with IVAN GALAMIAN. Laredo debuted with the SAN FRANCISCO SYMPHONY at age 11. His CARNEGIE HALL debut, traditionally the start of an artist's international career, came in 1960. He is a member of the CHAMBER MUSIC SOCIETY OF LINCOLN CENTER and has received the Handel Medallion from the city of New York. Laredo performs on viola as well as the violin, and has recorded string quartets with ISAAC STERN, YO-YO MA, and EMANUEL AX (the Stern-Ma-Ax Trio). He is a permanent member of the Kalichstein-Laredo Robinson Trio (with his wife, Sharon Robinson, and pianist JOSEPH KALICHSTEIN). Laredo has performed

Jaime Laredo (Courtesy of Frank Salomon Associates; Photo by Christian Steiner)

133

with major orchestras and musicians too numerous to list, and occasionally serves as a conductor of chamber and full-sized orchestras.

Laredo, Ruth (b. 1937) *pianist*
Ruth Laredo is sometimes regarded as the First Lady of the Piano, though one would have to argue on behalf of Brazilian pianist Martha Argerich as well. Nonetheless, Laredo has gained acclaim on several fronts since her 1962 Carnegie Hall debut. She studied with RUDOLF SERKIN at the CURTIS INSTITUTE. Her comprehensive recordings of solo piano music by Russians Sergey Rachmaninoff and Aleksandr Scriabin did much to popularize those works, especially in the case of Scriabin. Laredo is much beloved in New York for her long-running "Concerts with Commentary" series at the Metropolitan Museum of Art. She has recorded extensively, both solo and chamber repertoire, and has been associated with the Tokyo String Quartet, Guarneri Quartet, and Shanghai Quartet. She was a founding member of the "Music from Marlboro" concerts. She has won three Grammy Award nominations.

Lark Quartet
Founded in 1985, the Lark Quartet's members are Maria Bachman (violin), Deborah Buck (violin), Kathryn Lockwood (viola), and Astrid Schween (cello). The group won the 1990 Naumburg Chamber Music Award and, in 1991, the Shostakovich Competition Gold Medal. The Lark Quartet has toured extensively and recorded about one dozen discs. It debuted the Pulitzer-winning String Quartet no. 2 of AARON JAY KERNIS. The Lark Quartet has performed music of the fictional P. D. Q. Bach in concerts of humorist PETER SCHICKELE.

Larsen, Libby (b. 1950) *composer*
One of the most successful contemporary composers, Libby Larsen received undergraduate and graduate degrees from the University of Minnesota, where she studied with DOMINICK ARGENTO and others. She has been strongly associated with the state of Minnesota, serving as composer in residence to the MINNESOTA ORCHESTRA from 1983 to 1987, and founding the Minnesota Composers Forum (now the AMERICAN COMPOSERS FORUM) in 1973. Larsen has composed in a wide range of styles and has a portfolio of over 200 works. Her music, adventurous but tonal, consistently garners enthusiastic reviews. In 2003 she was named by the Library of Congress to the Harissios Papamarkou Chair in Education and Technology at the John W. Kluge Center.

Lateiner, Jacob (b. 1928) *pianist*
An American of Cuban birth, Jacob Lateiner entered the CURTIS INSTITUTE at 12 years of age. Like many Curtis prodigies, he made his first important debut in Philadelphia with the PHILADELPHIA ORCHESTRA under the baton of EUGENE ORMANDY, in 1945. The debut came after winning the Philadelphia Youth Competition. He debuted at TANGLEWOOD in 1947, and in New York the following year. Lateiner commissioned the Piano Concerto of ELLIOTT CARTER in 1967 and premiered it with the BOSTON SYMPHONY ORCHESTRA under ERICH LEINSDORF. He also premiered the Piano Sonata no. 3 of ROGER SESSIONS (1968). He was closely associated with cellist GREGOR PIATIGORSKY and violinist JASCHA HEIFETZ, and he performed many chamber concerts with them. Lateiner is a favorite pick for juries of international piano competitions. He taught at the MANNES COLLEGE OF MUSIC from 1963 to 1970, and has been on the piano faculty of the JUILLIARD SCHOOL since 1966.

Law, Andrew (1749–1821) *music compiler*
One of many tune book compilers on the late 18th century in New England, Andrew Law was part of the musical reformation movement that attempted to raise singing standards in churches. His publication *The Art of Singing* was distributed around

Boston and in Philadelphia. Law devised a new method of music notation that dispensed with the five-line staff, and published tune books using it. He had less success with that particular innovation than with his general reformist initiatives.

League of Composers/International Society for Contemporary Music

Founded in 1923 as the League of Composers, this group is dedicated to promoting contemporary music and American music in particular. AARON COPLAND's career was considerably assisted by the League of Composers in the early 1930s. The league merged with the ISCM in 1954. MILTON BABBITT and ELLIOTT CARTER are the current cochairs.

Leinsdorf, Erich (1912–1993) conductor

Born in Vienna, conductor Erich Leinsdorf became an American citizen in 1942, and worked at several important music institutions. He studied piano, cello, and composing as a child, then began taking conducting lessons in 1930, at age 18. He made his debuts in Europe, then became assistant conductor at the METROPOLITAN OPERA in 1937, on the recommendation of ARTURO TOSCANINI. Leinsdorf briefly became music director of the CLEVELAND ORCHESTRA in 1943, leaving in 1944 to serve in the army. He led the Rochester Philharmonic from 1947 to 1956—perhaps his most amicable and successful tenure. He directed the New York City Opera for one season, then returned to the Metropolitan as a conductor, but not music director. Between 1962 and 1969 Leinsdorf held his most celebrated appointment, as music director of the BOSTON SYMPHONY ORCHESTRA. The Boston assignment was Leinsdorf's last major permanent position in America; he took over the Berlin Radio Symphony Orchestra in 1980.

Leinsdorf's undramatic stage manner and nononsense musical interpretations during an era of flashy effects contributed to his job-hopping. He was also not shy about rebuking his colleagues.

Leinsdorf was a fellow of the American Academy of Arts and Sciences.

Lentz, Daniel (b. 1942) composer

An innovative and prolific composer, Daniel Lentz received his degrees from St. Vincent College, Ohio University, and took additional work at Brandeis University and the Berkshire (later TANGLEWOOD) Music Center. He studied with ROGER SESSIONS and GEORGE ROCHBERG. In 1972 Lentz was the first American, and the youngest competitor, to win the International Composers Competition in Holland. He has formed his own performing ensembles, the San Andreas Fault and the California Time Machine; the first of these toured internationally in the 1970s. Lentz has fulfilled commissions from the LOS ANGELES PHILHARMONIC, the SAINT PAUL CHAMBER ORCHESTRA, and many other groups and institutions.

Leonora (1845 or 1846)

Although WILLIAM HENRY FRY was more influential as a music critic than as a composer, his Leonora is acknowledged to be the first large-scale opera composed by an American and staged in the United States. It was premiered in Philadelphia, either in 1845 or 1846.

Leppard, Raymond (b. 1927) conductor

English conductor Raymond Leppard was music director of the Indianapolis Symphony Orchestra from 1987 to 2001. He has guest-conducted in New York, Philadelphia, Chicago, Boston, and Detroit; the remainder of his career has transpired in Europe.

Levant, Oscar (1906–1972) pianist, composer, and actor

Oscar Levant's dour visage was made famous by his appearance in several movies, notably An American in Paris. He also appeared frequently on television, where his natural facility with facts, names, and dates made him a quiz-show star. He composed jazz and stage songs and also formal classical music, including a piano concerto that he performed with the NBC SYMPHONY ORCHESTRA. Depressed, arguably neurotic, volatile, publicly confessional, and extremely funny throughout, Levant was once described as "The Henny Youngman of the intelligentsia," referring to a comic. He seemed happiest playing classics on the piano for friends. His friendship with GEORGE GERSHWIN approached idolatry. When Gershwin died tragically in 1937, Levant devoted most of his playing repertoire to Gershwin's music. Besides his film appearances, Levant is best remembered for his reminiscences, gathered into three books: *A Smattering of Ignorance* (1940), *The Memoirs of an Amnesiac* (1965), and *The Unimportance of Being Oscar* (1965).

Levine, James (b. 1943) *conductor and pianist*

A conductor first and pianist second, Levine is best known for his long and fruitful tenure as artistic director of New York's METROPOLITAN OPERA. He studied piano as a boy and made his debut with the CINCINNATI SYMPHONY ORCHESTRA at age 10. He later studied with RUDOLF SERKIN and ROSINA LHÉVINNE. He received graduate training in conducting at the JUILLIARD SCHOOL. He met GEORGE SZELL at the American Conductors Project in Baltimore, and the older maestro immediately installed Levine as assistant conductor of the CLEVELAND ORCHESTRA, a position Levine held until 1970. He turned his baton increasingly toward the operative stage, conducting Puccini's *Tosca* with the San Francisco Opera in 1970.

His association with the Metropolitan Opera started in 1973 when Levine became principal conductor in 1973. Among his many landmarks with that company, Levine instituted the *Metropolitan Opera Presents* television series in 1977, founded the Young Artist Development Program in 1980, and reinstated a then-dormant tradition of recitals and nonoperatic concerts at the METROPOLITAN

OPERA HOUSE, featuring company musicians. He began taking the Metropolitan Opera Orchestra on tours in 1991, playing standard orchestral repertoire—the orchestra played in St. Petersburg, Russia, during that city's 300th anniversary celebration in 2003.

Levine has not held a faculty position as such but has lectured widely and received innumerable honorary doctorates. He is informally, but actively, associated with two European orchestras: the Vienna Philharmonic and the Berlin Philharmonic, each of which he leads in concerts every year. He frequently is engaged in ambitious freelance activities, such as conducting the centennial-anniversary production of Wagner's *Parsifal* at Bayreuth, the preeminent showcase stage for Wagner operas. He took the orchestra of the CURTIS INSTITUTE on tour in Switzerland in 1999. He sometimes performs as piano accompanist in vocal recitals. In addition to his continued directorship of the Metropolitan Opera, Levine took over the music director position at the BOSTON SYMPHONY ORCHESTRA, replacing the retiring SEIJI OZAWA. Even in the modern tradition of jet-setting, multitenured maestros, it is perhaps unprecedented for one individual to control two such prestigious institutions.

Levine received the Manhattan Cultural Award in 1980. He appeared on the cover of *Time* in 1983, and was the subject of a PBS documentary in its *American Masters* series. He received the Gold Medal for Service to Humanity from the National Institute of Social Sciences.

Lewenthal, Raymond (1926–1988) *pianist*

Specialty pianist Raymond Lewenthal worked to revive forgotten pieces of the 19th-century romantic piano repertoire, with a show-business flair. He studied with Olga Samaroff at the JUILLIARD SCHOOL, and with pianist Alfred Cortot. He is best remembered for his resuscitations of music by Valentin Alkan, as well as Franz Liszt, Anton Rubinstein, and others. He often performed in low lights, simulating the candlelit atmospheres of

19th-century concert halls, and he wore period costumes onstage. His playing style was grand, flamboyant, and loud, if not universally acknowledged to be technically fabulous. His career was interrupted in near-tragic fashion in 1953, when Lewenthal was mugged in Central Park, New York, suffering injuries to his hands and arms. He lived in Europe and South America until returning to the United States in 1964 and resuming his career. His last appearance was with the NATIONAL SYMPHONY at the KENNEDY CENTER in 1982.

Lhévinne, Rosina (1880–1976) *teacher*

One of the great piano teachers in American history, Rosina Lhévinne was married to legendary pianist Josef Lhévinne, both of whom served on the faculty of the JUILLIARD SCHOOL. She studied at the Moscow Conservatory, which she entered at the age of nine. There, the student body also included composers Sergey Rachmaninoff, Alexander Scriabin, and pianist Josef Lhévinne. Josef was Rosina's substitute piano teacher, and they were married just after her graduation (with the school's Gold Medal) in 1898. From that point until Josef's death in 1944, Rosina subordinated her performing career in support of her husband's, although they gained some renown as a duo-piano team. While Josef built his reputation as one of history's greatest pianists, Rosina's teaching studio became a breeding ground for several of the finest virtuosos to emerge in the middle and late 20th century, including VAN CLIBURN, GARRICK OHLSSON, JOHN BROWNING, and ADELE MARCUS (who herself became an iconic teacher at Juilliard).

Lhévinne joined the Juilliard faculty in 1924 and remained on it for 50 years. Her teaching style was extremely personal, yet she had a gift for bringing out the best in a student without changing him or her. As a living connection to the grand playing style of such 19th-century pianists as Anton Rubinstein (whom Lhévinne heard in concert), she emphasized ideals of a singing, legato melody line and interpretations of large sweep—qualities

remarkably manifested in the playing of Van Cliburn when he gained international fame in 1958. She began performing on her own shortly after the death of her husband, notably in a 1963 concert with the NEW YORK PHILHARMONIC in which Lhévinne played Chopin's Piano Concerto in E minor. Her life was active to the end; she had just moved to the West Coast from New York a few weeks before her death. PETER MENNIN, president of the Juilliard School at the time of Lhévinne's death, eulogized her with these words: "She was quite simply one of the greatest teachers of this century. With her passing, a whole concept of teaching and performing goes with her."

Liberace (1919–1987) *pianist*

One of the great showmen in musical history, and a more serious classical pianist than most people knew, Liberace was born Wladziu Valentino Liberace in Milwaukee, Wisconsin. His father played in John Philip Sousa's band, and his mother was an amateur pianist who gave the boy his first lessons. He played cocktail piano jobs and was a pianist in a silent movie theater during his youth. At age 21, in 1940, Liberace played a piano concerto by Franz Liszt with the CHICAGO SYMPHONY ORCHESTRA—an auspicious debut for any aspiring artist. Liberace's career took a popular turn when, during a piano recital, an audience member called out for a popular song as an encore. Liberace obliged, breaking tradition and delighting the audience. In another concert, Liberace wore white tails, a more garish outfit than usual, so that patrons in the back rows could see him better. Again, the audience appreciated the playful spirit of this sartorial stunt.

As Liberace's unorthodox wardrobe grew, his career path solidified and he evolved into the most flamboyant novelty pianist in history. He wore sequined outfits and long fur trains, and installed candelabras on stage. Liberace was a precursor to Elton John, classical style. His concerts were glitzy and somewhat self-mocking, but Liberace also worked hard onstage and off. He was famous for his abridged preparations of famous classical pieces, such as his version of Tchaikovsky's Piano Concerto no. 1—normally running about 45 minutes—whipped through in four minutes. Even Chopin's "Minute" waltz fell victim to Liberace's editing; he played that piece in about 30 seconds.

Liberace was an orchid grower, cook, and rabid basketball fan. He turned his Las Vegas house into a self-worshipping museum, in which his bedroom contained a replica of the Sistine Chapel's famous Michelangelo fresco. Near the end of his life, Liberace was dogged by conflicting rumors about his sexuality and assertions that he had contracted, but was hiding, AIDS. His death was reported to be caused by a heart attack brought on by pneumonia, but the coroner refused this assessment. Postmortem tests revealed that Liberace indeed did have AIDS and died of medical conditions brought on by his immune deficiency. This controversy surrounding his death clouded what could have been a pure memory of a great showman and popularizer of the classical repertoire.

Lieberson, Peter (b. 1946) *composer*

Peter Lieberson composed music influenced by his studies of Tibetan Buddhism, and his music was given exposure by PETER SERKIN and the chamber group founded by Serkin, TASHI. He received non-music degrees from New York University and Columbia University in New York and studied composition with MILTON BABBITT and CHARLES WUORINEN. He founded two new-music groups, the Composer's Ensemble and the New Structures Ensemble. His breakthrough piece was *Variations,* scored for solo flute, which was premiered in 1972 and led to commissions. He wrote his Piano Concerto no. 1 for Peter Serkin on commission from SEIJI OZAWA and the BOSTON SYMPHONY ORCHESTRA; Serkin and the BSO premiered it in 1983, bringing Lieberson to national attention. The BSO followed up the piano concerto with a commission for a symphony, and Lieberson composed

Drala, which premiered in 1986, and has been performed since in Chicago, Toronto, Los Angeles, and Cleveland.

Lieberson has enjoyed important recent commissions. His third piano concerto was commissioned by the Minnesota Orchestra and premiered by Peter Serkin in November 2003. Lieberman composed the Piano Quintet for the opening of ZANKEL HALL in New York in 2003. The Cleveland Orchestra commissioned *Ah* in 2002. In 2000, Lieberson composed the Cello Concerto for YO-YO MA and the Toronto Symphony Orchestra. Many of Lieberson's piano pieces, notably *The ocean that has no West and no East* were written for Peter Serkin, and recorded by him.

Lieberson taught at Harvard University from 1984 to 1988. He won the Rappaport Prize in 1972 and an Ives scholarship from the National Institute of Arts and Letters in 1973.

Life Is a Dream (1977)

The opera of this title was produced in the mid-1970s, but LEWIS SPRATLAN received greater recognition for some of its material when a concert version of Act II won a Pulitzer Prize for 2000. The excerpt was premiered in Amherst, Massachusetts, on January 28, 2000.

Lilacs (1995)

Scored for soprano, tenor, and orchestra, *Lilacs* won a Pulitzer Prize in 1996 for GEORGE WALKER. It was commissioned and premiered by the BOSTON SYMPHONY ORCHESTRA on February 1, 1996.

Lincer, William (1907–1997) *violinist and violist*

William Lincer was a violinist and violist who began lessons at age five, then made a New York debut two years later. As a teenager, Lincer suffered a hand injury that doctors said would end his musical career. He rehabilitated his hand while studying physiology extensively; his hard-won knowledge made him all the more effective as a teacher later in life. He attended the Institute of Musical Art (later the JUILLIARD SCHOOL), with postgraduate work at Harvard University. He formed the Lincer Quartet and toured as violist of the Jacques Gordon String Quartet. His steadiest work was with orchestras, first as principal violist of the CLEVELAND ORCHESTRA, then the same position with the NEW YORK PHILHARMONIC. He taught privately until he was 53, then joined the faculty of the MANHATTAN SCHOOL OF MUSIC (1960–69), after which he taught at Juilliard.

Lincoln Center for the Performing Arts

New York's primary classical arts complex, Lincoln Center was built during the 1960s on a plot of several blocks around West 65th Street. The neighborhood was far less developed than it became after the establishment of Lincoln Center, and more than a little controversy emerged over the decision to consolidate and relocate New York's various performance institutions to a relatively desolate site. The locale is no longer controversial, though the design of Lincoln Center is often criticized as being inhospitable to casual visitors.

Currently, Lincoln Center serves as home base for the NEW YORK PHILHARMONIC, the METROPOLITAN OPERA, the NEW YORK CITY OPERA, the New York City Ballet, the JUILLIARD SCHOOL, the CHAMBER MUSIC SOCIETY OF LINCOLN CENTER, Jazz at Lincoln Center, the Film Society of Lincoln Center, the Lincoln Center Theater, and the New York Public Library for the Performing Arts (a branch of the New York Public Library). Buildings include the METROPOLITAN OPERA HOUSE, AVERY FISHER HALL (New York Philharmonic), NEW YORK STATE THEATER (New York City Opera and New York City Ballet), Walter Reade Theater (Film Society of Lincoln Center), Vivian Beaumont Theater (Lincoln Center Theater), and ALICE TULLY HALL (Chamber Music Society of Lincoln Center and many other recitals and concerts).

Lincoln Center hosts numerous specialty concert series, including the summer MOSTLY MOZART FESTIVAL, American Songbook, Great Performers, the Lincoln Center Festival, Lincoln Center Out of Doors, Live from Lincoln Center, and Midsummer Night Swing. The opera, ballet, and orchestra companies offer multiple subscription series during the full season.

Lincoln Portrait, A (1942)

Commissioned from AARON COPLAND by conductor ANDRÉ KOSTELANETZ in 1942, *A Lincoln Portrait* is scored for narrator and orchestra, and consists of fragments from Lincoln's speeches combined with musical quotations of American popular songs.

Lind, Jenny (1820–1887) *opera singer*

A Swedish soprano, Jenny Lind's impact on the American music scene came in 1850 when she toured the United States for eight months. This gallop across the country was arranged by impresario and circus manager P. T. Barnum. During this string of concerts she broke box-office records and became a star in a culturally young country that had almost no classical tradition of its own. Besides that tour, Lind's career unfolded in Europe, and she gave her last performance in 1883.

Lipkin, Seymour (b. 1927) *conductor and pianist*

Seymour Lipkin started as a pianist, switched to conducting, and returned later to his pianistic career. He entered the CURTIS INSTITUTE at age 11, in 1938, and remained their nine years studying with DAVID SAPERTON, RUDOLF SERKIN, and MIECZYSLAW HORSZOWSKI. He received no such extensive training as a conductor, though he did gain some experience at the Berkshire Music Center (later TANGLEWOOD MUSIC CENTER). He won the Rachmaninoff Piano Competition in 1948 and made his debut with the NEW YORK PHILHARMONIC in 1949. He performed with many major orchestras, then turned his attention to conducting, as many pianists have done. Lipkin never earned a permanent position with an orchestra, but he worked on the podium for about 20 years before returning to the piano. He is on the faculties of both Curtis and the JUILLIARD SCHOOL. He is artistic director of the Kneisel Hall Chamber Music Festival in Blue Hill, Maine.

List, Eugene (1918–1985) *pianist*

Eugene List's pianistic debut was impressive: he gave the American premiere of the Piano Concerto no. 1 of Russian composer Dmitry Shostakovich. This breakthrough concert was the result of winning a PHILADELPHIA ORCHESTRA competition at the age of 16. Throughout his career, List delighted in introducing repertoire that few other pianists played. He was married to Carroll Glenn, with whom he often performed. He taught at the EASTMAN SCHOOL OF MUSIC from 1964 to 1975.

Litton, Andrew (b. 1959) *conductor*

Andrew Litton received his degrees from the JUILLIARD SCHOOL, where he was the recipient of the Bruno Walter Scholarship and studied with SIXTEN EHRLING (conducting) and NADIA REISENBERG (piano). Born and raised in New York City, he had wanted to be a conductor from the age of 12 when he heard LEONARD BERNSTEIN conduct the NEW YORK PHILHARMONIC. His godfather was Richard Horowitz, timpanist with the METROPOLITAN OPERA, and Litton spent boyhood days in the orchestra pit during rehearsals.

He won Britain's Rupert Foundation International Competition in 1982. Litton was assistant conductor of the NATIONAL SYMPHONY ORCHESTRA from 1982 to 1986, and principal conductor of the Bournemouth Symphony Orchestra in England from 1988 to 1994 (he is now conductor laureate of that orchestra). Litton made his debut at the Metropolitan Opera in 1989. In 1994 he became music director of the DALLAS SYMPHONY ORCHESTRA.

Lockhart, Keith (b. 1959) *conductor*

Conductor of the UTAH SYMPHONY, Keith Lockhart started studying piano at age seven; he later attended Furman University and Carnegie-Mellon University in Pittsburgh. In addition to his duties in Utah, Lockhart is conductor of the BOSTON POPS, having succeeded JOHN WILLIAMS in 1995.

Loeffler, Charles Martin (1861–1935) *composer and violinist*

Charles Martin Loeffler was an active and well-regarded violinist but is best remembered today as a composer, even though relatively few of his works were published. His music was performed frequent-

Keith Lockhart (Courtesy of Utah Symphony and Opera)

ly in its day, and his legacy is based on the progressive nature of his work, which featured forward-looking harmonies. Loeffler decided early in his boyhood to pursue the violin as a profession. Born in Alsace, France, he studied in Germany and Paris. He moved to the United States in 1881 and was bolstered by the opportunities (and salaries) of the culturally young country. He became an American citizen in 1887. He played in New York orchestras, then became second concertmaster of the BOSTON SYMPHONY ORCHESTRA, which developed a tradition of importing musicians from Europe to fill important positions (FRANZ KNEISEL was another). Loeffler served the orchestra for 21 years, often performing the solo part of violin concertos. Loeffler retired to a horse farm in Massachusetts, from where he kept his hand in urban music making and worked on his compositions.

London, Edwin (b. 1929) *composer, conductor, and educator*

London is currently the music director of the CLEVELAND CHAMBER SYMPHONY, which he founded in 1980. He graduated from Oberlin College, in Ohio, and started his career as a French horn player. He studied composing with GUNTHER SCHULLER at the MANHATTAN SCHOOL OF MUSIC, and with French composer Darius Milhaud. He has won fellowships from the Guggenheim Foundation and the National Endowment for the Arts.

Los Angeles Chamber Orchestra

The Los Angeles Chamber Orchestra was founded in 1969 under the directorship of Sir Neville Mariner. Mariner stayed on the podium until 1978. Four other music directors have held the position since: trumpeter and conductor Gerard Schwarz (1978–86), Iona Brown (1987–92), Christof Perick (1992–95), and current director Jeffrey Kahane. The LACO has recorded numerous discs, presents a yearly season of programs and tours, and plays in radio broadcasts. The LACO performs in two

venues: Royce Hall on the U.C.L.A. campus and the Walt Disney Concert Hall.

Los Angeles Master Chorale

A choral group of 90 voices, the Los Angeles Master Chorale was the first American organization to present an entire season of choral music. It was founded in 1964 by ROGER WAGNER and performs with the Sinfonia Orchestra. The group is the chorale in residence at the Los Angeles Performing Arts Center and the Walt Disney Concert Hall. The group has recorded several discs and has performed with symphony orchestras and on film soundtracks.

Los Angeles Philharmonic Orchestra

The LAPO grew out of the Los Angeles Philharmonic Society, founded in 1878. No concerts were presented by the Philharmonic Society until 1888, at which time the orchestra resembled a chamber ensemble, employing about 35 musicians. From this germinating organization the Los Angeles Symphony Orchestra first performed in 1913. The conductor was Harlye Hamilton, who programmed contemporary American music in addition to the standard European repertoire. Adolf Tandler took over from Hamilton and conducted until 1919.

The Los Angeles Philharmonic proper was formed in 1919 when William Andrews Clark Jr. financed the orchestra until 1934. Clark hoped to hire composer and pianist Sergey Rachmaninoff as the first music director but settled for Walter Henry Rothwell (formerly conducting the St. Paul Symphony Orchestra), who remained in the position at Los Angeles until his death in 1927. Rothwell was followed by Georg Schnéevoigt (1927–29), ARTUR RODZINSKI (1929–33), and OTTO KLEMPERER (1933–39). For a few years after Klemperer the orchestra operated without a permanent music director. ALFRED WALLENSTEIN stepped up to the podium in 1943 and remained until 1956. Succeeding music directors were Eduard van

Beinum (1956–59), ZUBIN MEHTA (1962–78), CARLO MARIA GIULINI (1978–84), ANDRÉ PREVIN (1985–89), and the current music director, ESA-PEKKA SALONEN. Salonen made his American debut conducting the LASO in 1984; he maintained a close relationship with the organization in the years preceding his appointment. His current contract runs until 2006. The Los Angeles Philharmonic played in the Dorothy Chandler Pavilion from 1964 until the fall of 2003, when it moved into a new permanent home, the Walt Disney Concert Hall.

Louisiana Story (1948)
One of seven film scores composed by VIRGIL THOMSON, *Louisiana Story* won a Pulitzer Prize in 1949.

Luca, Sergiu (b. 1943) *violinist*
Born in Romania, Sergiu Luca became an American citizen in 1966. He studied in Romania, Israel, and England, making a debut at age nine with the Haifa Symphony Orchestra in Israel. He studied at the CURTIS INSTITUTE in the United States, and was a finalist in the 1964 Levintritt Competition. Like many Curtis students, Luca made his American debut with the PHILADELPHIA ORCHESTRA in 1965. In 1971 he founded the Chamber Music Northwest Festival in Portland, Oregon. Luca has directed the Texas Chamber Orchestra and Da Camera of Houston. He is on the faculty of Rice University in Houston.

Lucier, Alvin (b. 1931) *composer*
An avant-garde composer artistically connected to JOHN CAGE, Alvin Lucier has in recent years specialized in electronically generated music. He received his degrees from Yale University (1954) and Brandeis University (1960), where his teachers included ARTHUR BERGER and IRVING FINE. He met AARON COPLAND and LUKAS FOSS at the Berkshire (later TANGLEWOOD) Music Center in 1958. He has

Sergiu Luca (Courtesy of John Gingrich Management)

taught at Brandeis and at Wesleyan University. Lucier's music experiments with sonic environments that are only somewhat under the control of the performer—hence the connection, through randomness and chance, with Cage. He has positioned snare drums closely around a piano, forcing the audience to listen for slight reverberations of the snares responding to sonic vibrations from the piano. Responsiveness is key to Lucien, especially in his work with electronics. In that realm, he has contrived to make electronic systems respond to natural motions and gestures of the performers, or even their brain waves. He has experimented extensively with controlling electronic feedback, starting a movement of "feedback composers" who regard Lucier as their mentor. He has received grants from the Rockefeller Foundation and the New York State Council of the Arts.

Luening, Otto (1900–1996) *composer and conductor*

Otto Luening, best known as a pioneer in electronic music, was born to a musical family; his mother was an amateur singer and his father a music professor at the University of Wisconsin. He began composing at age six and received his teenage training in Germany. He became an accomplished flutist, performing a debut recital on that instrument in 1916. He settled in Chicago in 1920. During his eclectic career Luening played in pit orchestras in silent film theaters, arranged gospel music, was the executive director of the opera department at the EASTMAN SCHOOL OF MUSIC, and cofounded (with VLADIMIR USSACHEVSKY) the Columbia-Princeton Electronic Music Center, one of the first laboratories of its kind. As a conductor and music director at New York's Columbia University between 1941 and 1958, Luening gave important premieres of operas by GIAN CARLO MENOTTI and VIRGIL THOMSON. His students included JOHN CORIGLIANO and CHARLES WUORINEN. He cofounded the AMERICAN MUSIC CENTER in 1940.

Luening wrote over 300 compositions and published a biography in 1980, *The Odyssey of an American Composer.* Though inevitably associated with electronic music, he wrote for acoustic instruments as well; one of his last compositions was the Divertimento for Violin, Clarinet and Piano. He composed a flute concerto, chamber music, four symphonic fantasies, and three violin sonatas.

Lyon, James (1735–1794) *music compiler*

James Lyon was one of many tune-book compilers of the 18th century. His landmark accomplishment was the psalm book *Urania* (Philadelphia, 1761), which contained a few original American tunes with the usual concentration of European hymn tunes. *Urania,* the largest tune book of its day, was reprinted five times.

Lyric Opera of Chicago

One of America's most respected opera companies, and perhaps the most successfully marketed, the Lyric Opera of Chicago was founded in 1954 (as the Lyric Theater of Chicago) by arts administrator Carol Fox and two partners. The partners withdrew from the venture after the first season, and the company's name was changed before the 1956 season. Fox remained as general manager until 1980. The company performs in the Civic Opera House, which it purchased in 1993. William Mason has been the company's general director since 1997, and Sir ANDREW DAVIS is music director (since 2000). The company's box-office success is the envy of the opera industry. Ticket sales historically exceed capacity, and even in the post-2001 economic downturn that savaged other opera and orchestra companies, and dented the Lyric Opera's attendance numbers, the company avoided deficits by replacing expensive-to-produce operas with inexpensive ones. Lyric Opera guest conductors have included a distinguished roster such as GEORG SOLTI, DIMITRI MITROPOULOS, LEONARD SLATKIN, and MICHAEL TILSON THOMAS.

Ma, Yo-Yo (b. 1955) *cellist*

The most influential cellist of his generation, Yo-Yo Ma has introduced untold audiences to artistic musicmaking through his classical and crossover projects. He studied with LEONARD ROSE at the preparatory division of the JUILLIARD SCHOOL. He appeared as a teenager with LEONARD BERNSTEIN at the KENNEDY CENTER. He studied humanities for four years at Harvard University, then won the Avery Fisher Prize in 1978. Ma has performed with most major orchestras and conductors; he has recorded numerous discs, of which the Bach Cello Suites is perhaps his most famous recording. He has won 15 Grammy Awards.

Like many contemporary classical musicians, Ma crosses over into other types of music. Unlike many such musicians, though, Ma's passion for world music traditions seems genuine, and his well-publicized and well-received projects seem motivated from within rather than by marketing considerations. The Silk Road Project—named for a series of trade routes that crisscrossed ancient China—is his most ambitious and diverse venture, incorporating the efforts of many musicians, varying cultures, festivals, museums, workshops, and recordings.

Yo-Yo Ma (William Coupon/Corbis)

Maazel, Lorin (b. 1930) *conductor*

As a boy, Lorin Maazel was that rare music breed—a conducting prodigy. He began his musical studies at age five and conducted a university orchestra at age eight. He appeared at the New York World's Fair the next year, 1939. He conducted the NBC SYMPHONY ORCHESTRA, earning ARTURO TOSCANINI's praise, at age 11. Concurrent with his active conducting career, Maazel was a violinist and made his playing debut in 1945. In 1960 Maazel was both the first American conductor and the youngest conductor to direct a performance at the Bayreuth Festival for Richard

Wagner's operas. His Metropolitan Opera debut came in 1962. During these years Maazel was engaged by orchestras in Europe, the Soviet Union, and Asia. He was music director of the Berlin Radio Symphony Orchestra from 1965 to 1975.

Maazel's first major American appointment was with the CLEVELAND ORCHESTRA, where he was music director from 1972 to 1982. During this time he was also chief conductor of the French National Orchestra, a group with which he remained affiliated until 1991. Following a four-year stint in Vienna, Maazel returned to America to assume leadership of the PITTSBURGH SYMPHONY ORCHESTRA from 1988 to 1996. In 2002 he was hired as music director of the New York Philharmonic, where his work on the podium played to mixed reviews in the critical New York press. After two years, his contract was extended through 2008.

Maazel has given over 5,000 concerts and made over 300 recordings. He has committed to disc the entire orchestral works of Beethoven, Brahms, Mahler, Debussy, Schubert, and Strauss.

Mácal, Zdenek (b. 1936) *conductor*
A Czech-born American, Zdenek Mácal took U.S. citizenship in 1986. In 1966 he won the DIMITRI MITROPOULOS conducting competition in New York and made his official American debut with the CHICAGO SYMPHONY ORCHESTRA in 1972. Mácal was music director of the Milwaukee Symphony Orchestra from 1986 to 1996, and in 1995 he became music director of the New Jersey Symphony Orchestra. He relinquished that post to NEEME JÄRVI in 2004 and moved to Europe to become principal conductor of the Czech Philharmonic.

MacDowell, Edward (1860–1908) *composer*
Edward MacDowell was the most successful American composer of the second half of the 19th century and was America's first internationally recognized composer. He studied piano informally as a child, then moved to Paris at age 16 for serious train-

ing. He entered the Hoch Conservatory in Germany in 1879. While in Europe MacDowell composed two piano suites (the Modern Suite and Second Modern Suite) and his Piano Concerto no. 1. These works impressed the director of the Hoch Conservatory, who recommended MacDowell to Franz Liszt, the composer and reigning musical figure in Europe. Through Liszt's influence, MacDowell's music was performed in Europe and published. MacDowell returned to the United States in 1884 to marry Marian Nevins; they returned to Europe, settling in Frankfurt, Germany. MacDowell was back in the United States, in Boston, by 1888, and became an active teacher. He was the first music professor of Columbia University in New York in 1896. He was president of the American Musicians and Composers association from 1899 to 1900. MacDowell left Columbia in 1904 in the wake of an acrimonious relationship with the school's new president. His last years were plagued by mental illness.

MacDowell's music was profoundly informed by European traditions, contains a romantic flair, and is easy to listen to. Many of his compositions are pastoral in both quality and title. He has influenced Celtic and Norse traditions. His *Woodland Sketches* suite for piano was extremely popular and is sometimes performed today. After his death, MacDowell's wife converted their New Hampshire farm into an artists colony, the MACDOWELL COLONY, which still operates today.

MacDowell Colony
Founded by American composer EDWARD MACDOWELL and his wife, Marian, the MacDowell Colony is an artists residency retreat located in Peterborough, New Hampshire, on the farm where the MacDowells lived. They purchased the property in 1896, and MacDowell claimed to write more and better music in its bucolic setting. In 1906 Grover Cleveland, J. P. Morgan, and Andrew Carnegie established a fund to make the MacDowells' dream of establishing an artists colony feasible. Edward MacDowell died in 1908, and Marian supervised construction of the

colony's many separate studios—32 now stand on the property, each an individual building and most situated out of sight of the others. Residents are provided room, board, and exclusive use of a studio on a full-scholarship basis. The colony is not just for musicians; composers represent one category of resident, while writers, photographers, and poets are also invited to apply.

Three residency seasons are offered, and accepted applicants stay up to eight weeks at the colony. Over 5,000 creative individuals have taken advantage of the residency program, including many winners of Pulitzer Prizes, National Book Awards, Guggenheim Fellows, and other individuals whose work is deemed worthy by the MacDowell board. Unknown artists are as eligible to apply as famous ones. The roster of American composers who have immersed themselves in the MacDowell Colony experience over many decades includes SAMUEL ADLER, MARION BAUER, AMY BEACH, LEONARD BERNSTEIN, AARON COPLAND (who composed portions of *Appalachian Spring* there), RICHARD DANIELPOUR, DAVID DEL TREDICI, DAVID DIAMOND, LUKAS FOSS, ROY HARRIS, NED ROREM, and RALPH SHAPEY.

In 1997 the MacDowell Colony was awarded a National Medal of Arts.

Mahler, Gustav (1860–1911) *composer*

Gustav Mahler was an Austrian composer best known for his songs and symphonies, the latter of which rank him among some enthusiasts as a successor to Beethoven. His impact on American music, besides the many performances of his work, occurred in New York. He left Europe for the United States in 1907 to conduct at the METROPOLITAN OPERA. His second season at the Metropolitan (1908–09) was darkened by the company's marketing ploy: Toscanini was also hired, and the two celebrities clashed over opera selection. Mahler escaped to a different part of town in fall 1909, as music director of the NEW YORK PHILHARMONIC. He held this position for two seasons, and his death came toward the end of the second.

Manhattan School of Music

One of three internationally recognized music schools in New York (along with the JUILLIARD SCHOOL and MANNES COLLEGE OF MUSIC), the Manhattan School of Music was founded in 1917 by Janet Schenk. In the late 1960s, when John Brownlee was president of the school (1966–69), the opera department expanded both its size and reputation, becoming an important training ground for singers and attracting attention to its performances. In 1969 the school took over the building previously occupied by Juilliard when that conservatory moved to LINCOLN CENTER. The school is located on the Upper West Side of Manhattan, next to Columbia University. Atypical of an urban conservatory, Manhattan School of Music provides apartment-style living quarters for most of its undergraduate students.

Mannes College of Music

One of three internationally recognized music schools in New York (along with the JUILLIARD SCHOOL and MANHATTAN SCHOOL OF MUSIC), Mannes was founded by violinist David Mannes and his wife, pianist Clara Damrosch. The school was opened in 1916 as the David Mannes Music School. The institution passed from David Mannes to his son Leopold Mannes, during a time when conductor GEORGE SZELL, composer Georges Enesco, and other celebrities taught there. The school changed its name in 1953 and became a degree-offering, accredited college. In 1984 Mannes moved to larger quarters on West 85th Street, where it remains today.

Marcus, Adele (1906–1995) *teacher*

An influential teacher on the piano faculty of the JUILLIARD SCHOOL, Adele Marcus is better remembered for minting new virtuosos than for her own performing career. Nonetheless, she was an outstanding talent who entered Juilliard as a student at age 15 (studying with Josef Lhévinne [see ROSINA LHÉVINNE]) and won the Naumburg Prize in 1929.

She became her teacher's assistant, then joined the faculty proper in 1954; she taught until 1990. Among her students were HORACIO GUTIÉRREZ and BYRON JANIS.

Mariner, Neville (b. 1924) *conductor*

British conductor Neville Mariner is primarily identified with the London orchestra Academy of St.-Martin-in-the-Fields, which he founded in 1959 and has directed ever since. He has held two significant American posts. First, Mariner became director of the LOS ANGELES CHAMBER ORCHESTRA in 1969. Second, he was music director of the MINNESOTA ORCHESTRA from 1978 to 1986. He was knighted in Britain in 1985.

Marlboro Music School and Festival

Marlboro is an advanced summer school for chamber music in Vermont, founded in 1951 by pianist RUDOLF SERKIN. It operates with the ideal that there be neither teachers nor students, but participants. Many of these participants—Serkin, cellist Pablo Casals, pianist MIECZYSLAW HORSZOWSKI, to name but a few world-famous artists who have engaged in the Marlboro experience—have played a mentoring role to the young musicians. The festival, which transpires over five weeks each summer and often sends groups on limited tours, hews to the Marlboro ideal by always trying to mix experienced performers with less experienced ones. The current artistic directors of Marlboro are American pianist RICHARD GOODE and Japanese pianist Mitsuko Uchida. Well-known artists who played at Marlboro before they became stars include YO-YO MA, JAIME LAREDO, and MURRAY PERAHIA.

Marsalis, Wynton (b. 1961) *composer and trumpet player*

One of the great crossover performers and composers of modern American history, Wynton Marsalis has done more than anyone to place jazz on an equal footing with classical music since GEORGE GERSHWIN. Though not as innovative a composer as Gershwin, nor as masterful at creating large musical structures, Marsalis is a much stronger educator and organizer than Gershwin was. Born in New Orleans, he showed an early aptitude for music. He performed locally by age eight, and at 14 Marsalis performed a Haydn trumpet concerto with the New Orleans Philharmonic. From the start, Marsalis showed enthusiasm for both classical and jazz repertoire, and never seemed to distinguish between them. In high school Marsalis played in nearly every community orchestra, band, and jazz ensemble available to him, as well as gigs with club bands on weekends.

Marsalis's advanced training began at age 17 when he became the youngest student ever admitted to the TANGLEWOOD MUSIC CENTER. He enrolled in the JUILLIARD SCHOOL in 1978 and played dates around New York City while a student. At Juilliard he joined the Jazz Messengers, directed by drummer Art Blakey. During this time Marsalis performed with innumerable modern jazz legends. He left the group in 1982, formed his own quintet, and also joined the V.S.O.P. II ensemble. On the classical side, by the age of 20, Marsalis had recorded the trumpet concertos of Haydn, Hummel, and Leopold Mozart.

Remarkably, in 1984 Marsalis became the first recording artist to win Grammy Awards for both a jazz recording and a classical recording—then repeated the feat in 1985. In 1987 he organized the concert and education program Jazz at Lincoln Center, of which he remains artistic director. (Jazz at Lincoln Center moved from LINCOLN CENTER to a 100,000-square-foot facility at Columbus Circle in the fall of 2004.) Throughout his student years and afterward, Marsalis composed in classical forms; his 1994 oratorio, *Blood on the Fields,* won a Pulitzer Prize in 1997. Marsalis has composed numerous ballet pieces for Garth Fagan, Twyla Tharp, Alvin Ailey, and the New York City Ballet. His large work for orchestra, choir, and big band, *All Rise,* was performed by the NEW YORK PHILHARMONIC under KURT MASUR.

Marsalis worked extensively to strengthen the jazz curriculum in schools, and has identified talented musicians and assisted in their education. He founded a national high-school jazz band competition and festival. His television series *Marsalis on Music,* launched in 1995, won a Peabody Award. Time magazine named him one of America's 25 most influential people in 1996, and the United Nations named Marsalis a UN Messenger of Peace.

Martino, Donald (b. 1931) *composer*

An expressive and modernist composer, Donald Martino grew up in New Jersey and received degrees from Syracuse University (1952) and Princeton University (1954); he studied composition with ROGER SESSIONS and MILTON BABBITT. A prolific composer, Martino has been no less active as a teacher, serving on the faculties of Princeton University (1957–59), Yale University (1959–69), and the NEW ENGLAND CONSERVATORY (chairman of the composition department, 1969–81). He was composer in residence at TANGLEWOOD, Irving Fine Professor of Music at Brandeis University, and Walter Bigelow Rosen Professor of Music at Harvard University (emeritus after resigning the chair in 1992).

Martino was awarded a Fulbright Scholarship for two years of study in Italy (1954–56). He was honored by the National Institute of Arts and Letters in 1967 and received three Guggenheim Fellowships in 1967, 1973, and 1982. A Naumburg Award financed Martino's composition of *Notturno* for chamber orchestra, which won a 1974 Pulitzer Prize, and was premiered on May 15, 1973, by the Speculum Musicae in ALICE TULLY HALL in New York. He won the KENNEDY CENTER Friedheim Award in 1985. He has fulfilled commissions for the BOSTON SYMPHONY ORCHESTRA and the Koussevitzky Foundation. Martino is a fellow of the American Academy of Arts and Sciences.

Martinon, Jean (1910–1976) *conductor and composer*

French conductor and composer Jean Martinon held one important post in the United States—he was music director of the CHICAGO SYMPHONY ORCHESTRA from 1963 to 1969. During that time the orchestra commissioned his Symphony no. 4 (*Altitudes*) for the CSO's 75th anniversary.

Mason, Daniel Gregory (1873–1953) *composer and writer*

Part of a musical family, Daniel Mason was both a composer and a writer on music. He studied with JOHN KNOWLES PAINE at Harvard University and also worked with GEORGE WHITEFIELD CHADWICK. A force in music appreciation, Mason's first book was *From Grieg to Brahms* (1902). He began lecturing at Columbia University in 1905 and stayed on campus until 1942; he became MacDowell Professor in 1929 and head of the music department in 1940. He received honorary degrees from several institutions including the EASTMAN SCHOOL OF MUSIC and OBERLIN COLLEGE, and was a member of the National Institute of Arts and Letters. In his musical outlook Mason was a staunch conservative, promoting the central Austro-German composers (Bach, Handel, Haydn, Mozart, Beethoven, Brahms) and barely acknowledging 20th-century music of any sort, from impressionism to 12-tone academic writing. His best-remembered composition is the orchestral overture *Chanticleer.*

Mass (1971)

Not a church work despite its name, LEONARD BERNSTEIN's *Mass* is a concert/theater piece that employs sets, costumes, choreography, multimedia presentations, and a startling variety of musical styles. The piece was commissioned for the opening of the KENNEDY CENTER FOR THE PERFORMING ARTS at the request of Jacqueline Kennedy Onassis, and was premiered there on September 8, 1971. While *Mass* is not meant to be liturgical, it does roughly follow the structure of a Roman Catholic mass, albeit with interruptions and unexpected juxtapositions and arguments. The piece is hugely scored for pit orchestra, two choruses, a boys choir, ensemble of singers and stage chorus, ballet company, marching band, and rock band. Its musical range is extraordinary, polarized by blues and folk on the one hand, and rigorous 12-tone serialism on the other.

Mass is an ambitious work that received mixed reviews and harsh words from at least one Catholic archbishop. (The text uses vulgar language, and, at one point in the drama, the cross is destroyed.) Music writer Peter G. Davis's review stated, "This is a work that stakes everything. I can think of few creative acts in recent times that take so many risks and achieve so much." HAROLD C. SCHONBERG, arguably the most influential critic of the early 1970s, respected Bernstein more as a Broadway composer than as a classical one, writing in the *New York Times,* "The serious musical content is pretentious and thin, as thin as the watery liberalism that dominates the message of the work."

Masselos, William (1920–1992) *pianist*

William Masselos was a pianist who loved modern music and attempted to introduce new performance traditions. He studied at the JUILLIARD SCHOOL with DAVID SAPERTON, and performed a debut concert in 1939. His NEW YORK PHILHARMONIC debut came in 1952, at which he played the Brahms D Minor Piano Concerto. He was regarded as a specialist in contemporary music, thanks in some part to his well-publicized premieres of the First Piano Sonata of CHARLES IVES in 1949 and AARON COPLAND's *Piano Fantasy,* that composer's most ambitious work for solo piano, in 1957. He also played romantic repertoire of Brahms and others. Masselos felt that the traditional piano recital had grown stagnant, and he attempted to rattle expectations by unusual programming and concert formats. He once presented a four-hour recital with several intermissions, inviting the audience to come and go as they pleased. Masselos joined the Juilliard faculty in 1976.

Masur, Kurt (b. 1927) *conductor*

Kurt Masur is a German conductor who made his mark on American audiences with two major appointments. He studied conducting at the Leipzig Conservatory in Germany during the 1940s. His early career transpired in Europe, culminating with his appointment as music director of the Leipzig Gewandhaus Orchestra, which he held for 26 years. When he left Leipzig, Masur gained the first of many conductor laureate designations he was to receive during a long and lauded career. He was credited with restoring luster to an organization whose reputation had fluctuated since the 18th century.

Masur moved his activities westward, making a London debut in 1973 and becoming music director of the London Philharmonic Orchestra in 1988. Before that year, in 1976, Masur became principal guest conductor of the DALLAS SYMPHONY ORCHESTRA, and in 1991 he landed the career-defining position as music director of the NEW YORK PHILHARMONIC. He was succeeded, in 2002, by LORIN MAAZEL, at which time the orchestra named Masur director emeritus, the first time since LEONARD BERNSTEIN that the Philharmonic had bestowed a lifetime designation on a departing music director. He became principal conductor of the London Philharmonic in 2000 and took the same position with the Orchestre National de France in 2002.

McNair, Sylvia (b. 1956) *opera singer*

A soprano of broad stylistic range, Sylvia McNair is at home on the opera stage, in the recital hall, and even singing cabaret in New York's Algonquin Room. She studied at the University of Indiana and made her operatic debut in Indianapolis (1980). She first performed in Europe in 1984. Her METROPOLITAN OPERA debut occurred in 1991. Her best-received recordings are of concert repertoire such as Handel's *Messiah,* and she has received raves for her distinctly unclassical styling when singing popular standards. McNair has made numerous recordings.

Mehta, Zubin (b. 1936) *conductor*

An internationally acclaimed Indian conductor, Zubin Mehta is the son of Mehli Mehta, founder of the Bombay Symphony Orchestra and past conductor of the American Youth Symphony Orchestra in Los Angeles. Zubin Mehta studied piano and violin as a boy, and entered the Vienna Academy when he turned 18. In 1958 he won a conducting competition organized by the Liverpool Philharmonic Orchestra. He guest-conducted in Vienna, Canada, and the United States until his first major appointment with the Montreal Symphony Orchestra, where he conducted from 1961 to 1967. During this tenure, Mehta also became music director of the LOS ANGELES PHILHARMONIC ORCHESTRA (starting in 1962), and made a brilliant reputation for himself by turning what was a regional ensemble into a widely recognized symphonic institution. He made his METROPOLITAN OPERA debut in 1965 with Verdi's *Aida*. In 1978 Mehta became music director of the NEW YORK PHILHARMONIC, and his tenure of 13 years (until 1991, when he was succeeded by KURT MASUR) is the longest in modern Philharmonic history.

Mengelberg, Willem (1871–1951) *conductor*

A Dutch conductor, Willem Mengelberg was principal conductor of the NEW YORK PHILHARMONIC from 1921 to 1927, then co-principal with ARTURO TOSCANINI. Mengelberg maintained close ties with leading composers of the day, especially Gustav Mahler, to whose works in progress Mengelberg had access. This closeness informed his orchestral performances, leading him to take unusual liberties with symphonic scores—even those of composers he did not know personally. He received an honorary degree from Columbia University in 1934.

Mennin, Peter (1923–1983) *composer and educator*

Though he wished to be known as a composer first, Peter Mennin left a legacy that arguably rests more solidly on his tough-minded, dextrous work as educator and administrator, at least in New York City. Nevertheless, Mennin wrote nine symphonies, and his work is often performed. He started the first of these symphonies at age 11, after Mennin had been taking piano lessons for six years. He studied at the OBERLIN CONSERVATORY OF MUSIC and the EASTMAN SCHOOL OF MUSIC; at Eastman he studied composing with HOWARD HANSON and received a Ph.D. in music in 1947. His Symphony no. 2, completed in 1945, was conducted by LEONARD BERNSTEIN and the NEW YORK PHILHARMONIC. The Philharmonic premiered his third and eighth symphonies as well. Characteristically, Mennin's work is dense, challenging to the ear without being academic or completely atonal, and rigorously complex.

Mennin's administrative career began in 1958 when he joined the faculty of the JUILLIARD SCHOOL. Then in 1958 he left Juilliard to take over the directorship of the Peabody Conservatory in Baltimore. It was back to New York in 1963 to assume the presidency of Juilliard, succeeding outgoing director WILLIAM SCHUMAN. Mennin remained at this position until his death 20 years later. During this eventful time for Juilliard, the school moved from its Upper West Side location near Columbia University to a new facility in LINCOLN CENTER (1969), and Mennin instituted various new initiatives including the Theater Center, the American Opera Center, and the Contemporary Music Festival. He enhanced and glamorized the Juilliard faculty by bringing in composers ELLIOTT CARTER and ROGER SESSIONS, and many virtuoso performers. Above all, Mennin brought the perfect attitude for the era in which Juilliard was establishing itself as the preeminent training institution for classical artists. Emphasizing performance, Mennin established a competitive tone in the school that, though perhaps uncomfortable for lesser talents, did produce most of the American winners of international competitions during the 1960s and 1970s.

Menotti, Gian Carlo (b. 1911) *composer*

Gian Carlo Menotti is an American composer of Italian birth. He is best known for his operas and who wrote his own librettos, mostly in English. His mother was an amateur musician, and Gian Carlo entered the Milan Conservatory at age 13. He had written his first opera two years before. By 1928 Menotti was in the United States, studying at the CURTIS INSTITUTE in Philadelphia, where he met composer SAMUEL BARBER, with whom he would forge a close personal relationship. He completed his first adult opera in 1937 (*Amelia Goes to the Ball*), and it was immediately accepted into the repertoire of the METROPOLITAN OPERA in New York. On the heels of this success, the NBC television network commissioned from Menotti an opera for radio, *The Old Maid and the Thief*. It was the first opera commissioned for broadcast, a working model that was to become particularly identified with Menotti. Continuing his success, Menotti wrote the Piano Concerto and the operas *The Medium* and *The Telephone*. His opera *The Consul* won a Pulitzer Prize in 1954.

His opera *Amahl and the Night Visitors*, commissioned by NBC for television broadcast, assures Menotti's renown for generations to come. The most successful short opera by an American composer, it has been translated widely and performed globally. It was first broadcast on Christmas Eve 1951 and is among the most performed operas in the 20th and 21st centuries. In 1973 Menotti and Barber sold the house they had lived in for 30 years, and Menotti moved to Scotland. He continued to compose and present his work on both sides of the Atlantic. He founded the Festival of Two Worlds in Spoleto, Italy, in 1958, and extended the festival to Charleston, South Carolina, in 1977. In 1984 Menotti received a KENNEDY CENTER award for lifetime achievement.

Menuhin, Yehudi (1916–1999) *violinist*

Both an American citizen and a British subject, violinist Yehudi Menuhin was considered a citizen of the world, a humanitarian, a violinist of astonishing communicative power, and one of the most startling child prodigies of music history. He described himself as an internationalist, and though he was born an American citizen, he also became a British subject later in life, and lived in Europe for the most part. He also accepted honorary Swiss citizenship in 1970. He was an outspoken environmentalist, health-food advocate, and promoter of a single world government, all before it became chic to promote such topics.

Menuhin began serious violin lessons at age five, studying with Sigmund Anker and Louis Persinger in San Francisco. He gave his first San Francisco concert at age seven, his New York recital debut at age nine, and his SAN FRANCISCO SYMPHONY debut the same year. His Paris debut, which followed in 1927, made a huge impression; then it was back to New York to play the Beethoven Violin Concerto with the NEW YORK PHILHARMONIC, which was reviewed by critic Olin Downes in the *New York Times* as a mature performance, broadening Menuhin's celebrity in the United States. He made his first recording in 1928. In April 1929, Menuhin performed three violin concertos with the Berlin Philharmonic in that city, prompting the famous episode in which physicist Albert Einstein rushed backstage to greet the boy, claiming that Menuhin was proof God existed. Menuhin was 13. As a boy, Menuhin manifested a natural technique, acquired without the usual courses of technical study. When he met Eugène Ysaÿe, the famous European violinist heard Menuhin play difficult pieces flawlessly, then asked him to perform a simple exercise; Menuhin did not understand the request.

More study and touring followed Menuhin's European triumphs, some of the performing in collaboration with his sister Hephzibah, a pianist. In 1935 Menuhin retired from performing for a year and a half; he was 19. When he reemerged, some listeners believed his playing had gained nobility but lost some of the spontaneity that had characterized his youthful performances. Stylistic changes notwithstanding, Menuhin embarked on a life of international concert touring. During World War II he gave over 500 performances for Allied troops. Soon after the war Menuhin outraged some critics by concertizing with the Berlin Philharmonic, conducted by Wilhelm Fürtwangler, who had remained and worked in Nazi Germany during the war. Menuhin defended his decision courageously and never flinched from his belief that the purpose of music was to heal human relations and build bridges between people of different enthnicities. In 1945 Menuhin performed in Moscow, sparking a period of cultural exchange between the Soviet Union and the United States.

Menuhin was exceptionally open-minded about music, expressing his appreciation, for example, of the Beatles. He toured India and developed an association with sitar player and guru to the hippie movement Ravi Shankar. Borrowing further from Indian tradition, Menuhin adopted yogic practice and incorporated it into his long-standing belief that sound violin technique was based on relaxation. He played jazz (but made no distinctive contributions to the genre) with legendary swing fiddler Stephane Grapelli. Menuhin conducted fairly actively, especially London's Bath Festival Orchestra, which was renamed Menuhin Festival Orchestra. He made his conducting debut in 1949 with the DALLAS SYMPHONY ORCHESTRA.

Menuhin commissioned violin works from over 40 composers around the world. From 1969 to 1975 he was president of the International Music Council, a division of UNESCO. He founded the Live Music Now! Organization, which coordinates music performances in hospitals, nursing homes, and prisons. Also in 1977 he founded the International Menuhin Academy in Europe for advanced violin training. He received honorary degrees from dozens of institutions and honors from 17 foreign governments. He was also made a British knight.

In 1990 Menuhin withdrew from violin performance for the most part, concentrating on his conducting career. Critics had regularly commented that his mature playing compared unfavorably with his childhood performances, and those comments seemed to increase as Menuhin grew older. Menuhin himself was more aware than anyone of his technical shortcomings, caused by his lack of methodical technical training during his prodigy years. His earlier withdrawal from the stage, when he was 19, was motivated by the need to come to grips with his spotty formal training. It speaks to the psychology of prodigy adulation, perhaps, that Menuhin was not criticized as a child for uneven technique. But the arc of his career is more complicated than that, and biographers have speculated that his personal troubles (two marriages and possibly overly protective parents) and political distress (his performances during and after World War II exposed Menuhin to scenes of appalling devastation) made his playing less lyrical. Whatever the dynamics of his decision, the last nine years of Menuhin's musical life were spent mostly as a conductor.

After Menuhin died, violinist Itzhak Perlman said, "He was a giant in this century, as a violinist, musician, personality within the musical world . . . and of course the most phenomenal child prodigy that ever existed, certainly in this century. Listening to his recordings, it is indescribable what he was able to communicate through his fiddle." Kofi Annan, the secretary-general of the United Nations, called Menuhin "a citizen of the world in the fullest sense—one whose vision and culture gave him a deep empathy with fellow human beings of every creed and color. He redeemed the century by rising above all resentment and showing what human beings at their best are capable of."

Merola, Gaetano (1881–1953) conductor

Born in Italy, Gaetano Merola became an American citizen whose first U.S. appointment was as assistant conductor of the METROPOLITAN OPERA starting in 1899. He conducted the San Carlo Opera in San Francisco from 1918 to 1922, during the years after the great earthquake that largely destroyed a vibrant opera community in that city. In 1923 Gaetano founded the SAN FRANCISCO OPERA, now one of the largest and most successful of U.S. opera houses. He introduced Wagner's monumental *Ring* cycle of operas to San Francisco in 1935.

Merrill, Robert (b. 1917) *opera singer*

Perhaps the most famous of all American baritones and the most enduring baritone lead in the history of the METROPOLITAN OPERA, Robert Merrill discarded his European opportunities, for the most part, and based his career in one company—the Met. He made his Metropolitan debut in 1945, singing the role of Germont in Verdi's *La Traviata*. Merrill's singing was regarded as robust, if lacking in subtlety. Frank Sinatra sought lessons from Merrill, and Merrill sang the national anthem and threw the first pitch before a New York Yankees game. In an era of international careers, Robert Merrill was content to be a New York star.

Mester, Jorge (b. 1935) *conductor*

Music director of the Pasadena Symphony since 1984, Jorge Mester has led several festivals and orchestras during his busy career. He was a conducting student at the JUILLIARD SCHOOL and the BERKSHIRE MUSIC CENTER, and counts among his greatest influences LEONARD BERNSTEIN, GREGOR PIATIGORSKY, and JEAN MOREL. He made his important orchestral and operatic conducting debuts in Mexico and Italy, respectively, and has guest-conducted the BOSTON SYMPHONY ORCHESTRA and the PHILADELPHIA ORCHESTRA. In 1967 he became music director of the Louisville (Kentucky) Orchestra, initiating a daring new-music project that included recording 72 premieres. In 1969 he was named director of the ASPEN MUSIC FESTIVAL. He taught intermittently at Juilliard between 1958 and 1988, chairing the conducting department during the 1980s. In 2004, adding to his responsibilities in Pasadena, Mester accepted the directorship of the Naples (Florida) Philharmonic Orchestra.

Metropolitan Opera

The preeminent opera company of the United States, New York's Metropolitan Opera gave its first performance on October 22, 1883. The original METROPOLITAN OPERA HOUSE was located on 39th Street and Broadway, and the entire venture—house and company—was started by a group of socialites who were dissatisfied with the small number of prestigious box seats available at the Academy of Music, where most New York opera was staged. For many years the Metropolitan Opera was really two companies: the private group of investors that funded operations, and the Metropolitan Opera Association, which produced the operas. In 1940 the house and its management responsibilities were taken over by the Association, which began relying on public fund-raising for part of its revenue. The Metropolitan Opera Association is the oldest continually operating opera production company in America.

The first season opened with Gounod's *Faust*, one of about 20 operas in the company's repertoire—an astounding number for a new organization. Most of the musicians, including conductors, orchestra players, chorus members, and lead singers, were imported from Europe. Italy, especially, was plumbed for talent, making the Metropolitan essentially an Italian company for its first season. Only the sets came from New York. Henry Abbey managed the company in the first season (the titles of general manager and artistic director, later to signify important positions at the Met, were not yet in use), and he brought the company to the end of the first season with a substantial financial loss of $300,000—a gigantic sum in 1884. Leopold Damrosch managed the second season, and he created an essentially German company, searching Germany for talent during the summer of 1884. German singers could be hired less expensively than Italian ones, and the company's second season was a success, producing mostly German operas. Admission prices ranged from 50 cents to $3, and the large German population of New York swarmed to the theater. However, Damrosch died in midseason, partly, it was thought, from overwork.

Henry Abbey returned in 1891, with the forbearance to place somebody else (Maurice Grau) in control of the production budget. Grau lightened the heavy German repertoire and hired world-class singers from all over Europe. Only 16 Americans made it to the Metropolitan stage before 1900. Heinrich Conried was the next manager, from 1903 to 1908, when Giulio Gatti-Casazza was lured from his directorship of La Scala, the famous Italian house in Milan. With Gatti-Casazza came ARTURO TOSCANINI, who conducted at the Met from 1908 to 1915. Toscanini debuted with Verdi's *Aida* in 1908. Gatti-Cosazza's tenure could be considered the start of the Metropolitan's modern era. He presented an international range of operas, all in the original language, sung and conducted by the finest artists available. The company's American representation grew. In 1931 the tradition began of radio, broadcasting the Saturday-afternoon performances. Gatti-Cosazza retired in 1935.

Rudolf Bing was general manager from 1950 to 1972, and his years were as eventful and important to the company's evolution as were Gatti-Cosazza's. Bing modernized the company both technically and socially. Rejecting complaints from many sides, Bing hired talent based on merit alone, regardless of race, and brought the company's first black singers onto the stage. He also managed the move from the old Metropolitan Opera House to a new one built in LINCOLN CENTER, which opened on September 16, 1966. The premiere opera in the new house was *Antony and Cleopatra* by SAMUEL BARBER, commissioned for the occasion. The audience loved the building; the critics hated the opera. It was the beginning of the end of Barber's career, but the start of a new era of glamour and influence for the Met. Audiences were thrilled by the elegant marble columns, grand sweeping staircase, and Austrian crystal chandeliers that rose into the gilded

ceiling as they dimmed. Performers and stagehands loved the expanded backstage areas and the gigantic stage itself.

James Levine was appointed artistic director in 1976 and continues in that role today; he has worked with a string of administrators in the general manager position. The directorship of the company is generally attributed to Levine. While the artistic quality remains superb, the Metropolitan is often criticized for its conservative repertoire. Its lack of adventurousness is reflected in the absence of new commissions at the new building until 1991, when John Corigliano wrote *The Ghosts of Versailles* for the company.

Metropolitan Opera House

Performance home of New York's METROPOLITAN OPERA, the original Metropolitan Opera House was located on 39th Street and Broadway. It was constructed by a group of New York socialites who wished to be visible attendees of the opera, and the distinctive feature of the house was the large number of boxes lining the walls. The building was opened on October 22, 1883, with a performance of Gounod's *Faust*. This building was destroyed by fire on August 27, 1892, and rebuilt in its original location. In 1966 the Metropolitan Opera moved to its present site in the newly constructed LINCOLN CENTER. The premiere performance in that building was on September 16, 1966, when *Antony and Cleopatra* by SAMUEL BARBER was presented.

Milhaud, Darius (1892–1974) *composer*

A modernist French composer whose style went far beyond the reigning impressionism of his day, Milhaud's impact on American music was as a teacher. When World War II began in Europe, Milhaud moved to the United States and accepted a teaching position at Mills College in Oakland, California. He was at Mills from 1940 to 1971, and a continual succession of young composers passed through his studio.

Milnes, Sherrill (b. 1935) *opera singer*

Baritone Sherrill Milnes played many instruments as a child but inclined toward singing by the time he was of college age. He studied at Drake University and Northwestern University, and made his debut in 1960 with the Opera Company of Boston. His first performance at the NEW YORK CITY OPERA was in 1964, and the following year he debuted at the METROPOLITAN OPERA.

Milstein, Nathan (1904–1992) *violinist*

Born in the Ukraine, Nathan Milstein became an American citizen in 1942. He studied at the St. Petersburg Conservatory in Russia and made his performing debut in Odessa in 1920. He was of the generation of young Russian virtuosos that included DAVID OISTRAKH, GREGOR PIATIGORSKY, and VLADIMIR HOROWITZ. Milstein and Horowitz emigrated from the Soviet Union together in 1925, leaving the country on a concert tour and staying abroad. Milstein first went to Brussels, then made his American debut with the NEW YORK PHILHARMONIC in 1929, settling in the United States after that. He became an American citizen in 1942.

Milstein's playing was often described as "aristocratic" and "elegant." Like all extraordinarily musical virtuosos, Milstein cared more about conveying feeling than impressing with speed or dexterity. HAROLD C. SCHONBERG wrote in the *New York Times* that Milstein "managed to imbue the music with a kind of elegance that completely transcended any hint of vulgarity." He was considered warmer than JASCHA HEIFETZ and more secure technically than JOSEPH SZIGETI. At the time of his death, Glenn Dicterow, then the concertmaster of the NEW YORK PHILHARMONIC, said this: "You heard three notes of the man and you knew who was playing. It was pure, uncluttered, honest playing free of any technical problems. He set a standard that nobody today can touch." In 1987 Milstein was awarded KENNEDY CENTER honors for lifetime achievement.

Minnesota Orchestra

The symphonic institution of Minneapolis, the Minnesota Orchestra was founded as the Minneapolis Symphony Orchestra in 1903, giving its first concert on November 5 of that year. Enjoying a friendly rivalry with its smaller cousin, the SAINT PAUL CHAMBER ORCHESTRA, the orchestra established itself as the state's preeminent full-size symphonic ensemble in 1968 by changing its name to the Minnesota Orchestra. The St. Paul Symphony Orchestra had played the first orchestral repertoire heard in Minneapolis in the last quarter of the 19th century. As early as 1907, the Minneapolis Symphony Orchestra was touring the country, reaching both coasts. The orchestra began recording in 1923 and has received six Grammy Award nominations.

The Minnesota Orchestra has been conducted by 10 music directors over its century-plus history: Emila Oberhoffer (1903–22), Henri Verbrugghen (1923–31), EUGENE ORMANDY (1931–36), DIMITRI MITROPOULOS (1937–49), ANTAL DORATI (1949–60), STANISLAW SKROWACZEWSKI (1960–79), Sir NEVILLE MARINER (1979–86), EDO DE WAART (1986–95), Eiji Oue (1995–2002), and the current music director, OSMO VÄNSKÄ. Ormandy brought the orchestra to international recognition, and Mitropoulos and Dorati both expanded its repertoire and prestige. Guest conductors have played a vital part in the orchestra's operation, introducing accomplished musicians such as Charles Dutoit, LEONARD SLATKIN, and Michael Steinberg. The Minnesota Orchestra performs 200 concerts each year, and employs 90 musicians.

Mitropoulos, Dimitri (1896–1960) *conductor and pianist*

Born in Greece, conductor and pianist Dimitri Mitropoulos became an American citizen in 1946. He attended the Athens Conservatory, then taught there for 15 years. In 1930 he appeared in a concert with the Berlin Philharmonic, filling in on short notice; he played Sergey Prokofiev's Piano Concerto

Minnesota Orchestra (Courtesy of the Minnesota Orchestra)

no. 3 and also conducted the piece from the piano. Unlike piano concertos by Mozart and Haydn, the Prokofiev Third is hardly meant to be conducted by the player, who has his hands full playing the challenging solo part. This double feat of coordination and musicianship put Mitropoulos on the map. He toured Europe after this, repeating the concerto, and in 1936 was invited by KOUSSEVITZKY to conduct some concerts with the BOSTON SYMPHONY ORCHESTRA. Immediately following his American debut, Mitropoulos was appointed music director of the Minneapolis Symphony Orchestra (later the MINNESOTA ORCHESTRA), which position he held until 1948.

In Minneapolis, Mitropoulos showed his commitment to heavy, challenging, and sometimes modern music. His audiences did not always appreciate his adventurous programming, but that did not stop Mitropoulos from showcasing Mahler symphonies (not as well recognized then as they are today), music of ROGER SESSIONS, and symphonies of Dmitry Shostakovich—all of which played to unaccustomed ears in the American Midwest during the 1940s. He guest-conducted many other leading American orchestras during this time. He became the music director of the NEW YORK PHILHARMONIC in 1950, staying until 1958. During this tenure Mitropoulos came under intermittent critical attack for his handling of the orchestra. Either as a result or by coincidence, Mitropoulos began shifting his focus to the METROPOLITAN OPERA, and in his final season with the Philharmonic he shared conducting duties with LEONARD BERNSTEIN, who became his successor the following season.

Mitropoulos is a somewhat forgotten conductor now, but reissues of his most important recordings, including the first American recording of Mahler's first symphony, keep him alive for connoisseurs of past-generation conducting.

Monk, Meredith (b. 1942) *composer and performance artist*

Meredith Monk attended Sarah Lawrence College, graduating in 1964 after studying theater, dance, and music. Hoping to make her way in the dance world, Monk experienced a personal revelation about the role of her own voice in forging a career in composition. "I suddenly had a kind of revelation," she said, "that the voice could be flexible and fluid like the body and that I could use the same process I had used to find my own movement style to find my own voice." From the start of her creative career, Monk felt no limitations of genre or medium; her first major work *16-Millimeter Earrings,* contained film of the composer dancing, matched to an electronic soundtrack. Much of her work has

concentrated on the voice, and she has developed what is known as "extended vocal technique." She has received the MacArthur Award, the Brandeis Creative Arts Award, and two Guggenheim Fellowships. Monk was awarded an honorary doctorate by Bard College.

Monteux, Pierre (1875–1964) *conductor*

French-born Pierre Monteux became an American citizen in 1942, settled in Maine, and established the Pierre Monteux School for student conductors, which still operates a six-week summer session. NEVILLE MARINER, ANDRÉ PREVIN, and LORIN MAAZEL attended the Pierre Monteux School.

Monteux started off learning the violin and entered the Paris Conservatory at age nine. He first conducted an orchestra at age 12. Through his twenties, Monteux mixed conducting with performing with violin or viola in chamber music concerts. In the 1913–14 season, he conducted at the Paris Opera. Monteux first traveled to the United States at the hire of the Metropolitan Opera. He joined that company as director of its French repertoire, a position he held until 1919. He conducted the BOSTON SYMPHONY ORCHESTRA from 1920 to 1924. At the end of that tenure, Monteux moved back to Europe for 10 years, as music director of the Amsterdam Concertgebouw Orchestra. He founded the Orchestre Symphonique de Paris, with which he premiered Prokofiev's Symphony no. 3. His École Monteux in Paris, founded in 1932, presaged his school in Maine.

From 1936 to 1952 Monteux was back in the United States as music director of the SAN FRANCISCO SYMPHONY. He resumed his association with the Boston Symphony, frequently guest-conducting it. He also sometimes took the podium at New York's Metropolitan Opera in the mid-1950s. Although his home remained in Maine, Monteux's last appointment was with the London Symphony Orchestra, an assignment he accepted in 1961, at the age of 86. It had been 74 years since he first conducted an orchestra. He was a much-respected artist who did his work in the rehearsal hall, never dramatizing the physical art of conducting for the audience's sake. His son, Claude Monteux, is a conductor, flutist, and musical adviser to the Pierre Monteux School.

Moore, Douglas (1893–1969) *composer and music administrator*

Douglas Moore attended Yale University, where he studied with Horatio Parker. He showed an inclination toward songwriting in college and later in the navy. Further studies in Europe (with composer Vincent d'Indy and Nadia Boulanger) preceded Moore's first job as curator of music and organist at the Cleveland Museum of Art. While in Cleveland he toyed with stage acting and began writing music based on American lore. His most significant orchestral work from this period was the *Pageant of P. T. Barnum,* completed in 1924; it was performed often and became popular. In 1926 Moore joined the faculty of Columbia University in New York, became the head of the music department in 1940, and remained there until his death. He composed several Americana-based operas and operettas including *The Headless Horseman* (1936), *The Devil and Daniel Webster* (1938), and *The Ballad of Baby Doe* (1956), the last of which is the only one of his works to have gained an enduring presence in the operatic repertoire. His opera *Giants of the Earth* won a 1951 Pulitzer Prize. He served as president of the American Society of Composers, Authors and Publishers (ASCAP) and president of the National Institute of Arts and Sciences.

Moran, Robert (b. 1937) *mixed-media composer*

Robert Moran studied in Vienna, then worked with Darius Milhaud at Mills College. In 1963 he joined the faculty of the San Francisco Conservatory and directed the New Music Ensemble in that city until 1972. In 1969 Moran created the first in a series of enormous mixed-media installations in San Francisco, calling for the participation of 100,000 performers, two radio stations, a television station, 30 skyscrapers, six airplanes, and dance ensembles. Called *39 Minutes for 39 Autos,* it was successful enough to encourage other cities to commission similar events. Moran produced citywide performance pieces for Bethlehem, Pennsylvania (*Hallelujah,* 1971), Graz, Austria (*Pachelbel Promenade,* 1975), and Hartford, Connecticut (*Market to Asylum,* 1982). He was composer in residence at the Buffalo Philharmonic from 1975 to 1977, and held the same position at Northwestern University in 1977–78.

Morel, Jean (1903–1975) *conductor*

Jean Morel was a French conductor who influenced numerous younger conductors at the Juilliard School, where he taught from 1949 to 1971. He also was conductor of the Juilliard Orchestra. James Levine, Jorge Mester, and Leonard Slatkin have named Morel as an influence on their conducting.

Mormon Tabernacle Choir

Founded in 1847, the Mormon Tabernacle Choir is one of the country's oldest continuously operating classical institutions. Its radio program, *Music and the Spoken Word,* is the longest-running radio broadcast in the country. The choir was formed from informal origins in the aftermath of the itinerant Mormon community settling in the Salt Lake Valley. The choir's first conductor, John Parry, arrived in 1849, the year sometimes regarded as the founding date. Other conductors have included Evan Stephens (1880–1916), Anthony C. Lund (1916–35), J. Spencer Cornwall (1935–57), Richard P. Condie (1957–74), Jay Welch (1974–75), and the two current directors, Jerold Ottley and Craig Jessop. The choir admits audiences free of charge to its weekly rehearsals. It does not present a performance season as such, but has performed extensively with orchestras and at ceremonial events.

Mostly Mozart Festival

A summer series held in New York's Lincoln Center, the Mostly Mozart concerts feature music of Bach, Haydn, Schubert, and other classical-era and pre-classical composers, in addition to Mozart. Begun in 1967, the festival is a showcase for a wide range of established and new classical artists, and the atmosphere of the concerts blends erudition (some preconcert lectures are featured) with informal fun.

Muck, Carl (1859–1940) *conductor*

Carl Muck was a German conductor who led the BOSTON SYMPHONY ORCHESTRA from 1912 to 1918. His tenure in Boston was curtailed by his internment during the height of anti-German hysteria inspired by World War I. After the war Muck resumed his career in Europe.

Munch, Charles (1891–1968) *conductor and violinist*

Charles Munch was a French conductor and violinist who was music director of the BOSTON SYMPHONY ORCHESTRA from 1949 to 1962. Like his compatriot PIERRE MONTEUX before him in that city, Munch introduced much French music into the orchestra's repertoire. As the successor to SERGE KOUSSEVITZKY, Munch could not equal his impact as a promoter of new music and composers. But he nonetheless premiered several new works by American composers ROGER SESSIONS, SAMUEL BARBER, LUKAS FOSS, WALTER PISTON, and WILLIAM SCHUMAN.

Musical America

An industry performing arts magazine, *Musical America* was founded by John C. Freund in 1898. After the first year the magazine's publication was interrupted for lack of funds; it resumed in 1905 dedicated solely to music. *Musical America* currently publishes print and online editions; most of which are accessed only by subscribers. The organization bestows annual awards to outstanding musicians.

Musical Quarterly

The preeminent scholarly music journal of the United States, *Musical Quarterly* was founded in 1915 by musicologist OSCAR SONNECK. More than a journal about musical figures, it has historically been a meeting ground for them. Contributors to its pages include AARON COPLAND, HENRY COWELL, MARC BLITZSTEIN, Arnold Schoenberg, and many others. The journal is currently published by Oxford University Press.

Muti, Riccardo (b. 1941) *conductor*

Italian conductor Riccardo Muti made his American debut in 1972, leading the PHILADELPHIA ORCHESTRA. Eight years later he became music director of that orchestra (1980–92); during his tenure he advocated construction of a new concert hall, which eventually resulted in the building of the KIMMEL CENTER. He received his training in Italy, and currently is the director of the famed Italian opera company, La Scala.

"My Days Have Been So Wondrous Free"

Composed by FRANCIS HOPKINSON (1759), this song for voice and harpsichord was the first American-composed secular piece of music. Musicians of that day were affiliated with churches and typically compiled hymn tunes from other sources for use with their congregations, occasionally contributing an original hymn to their compilations. Hopkinson was an amateur musician, and his landmark song was the earliest known example of pure art music in America, as determined by the pioneer musicologist OSCAR SONNECK.

Nagano, Kent (b. 1951) *conductor*

Kent Nagano took clarinet and piano lessons as a child in Morro Bay, California. He obtained a bachelor's degree from the University of California, Santa Cruz, and his master's from San Francisco State University, then undertook postgraduate work at the University of Toronto. He took over the Berkeley Symphony Orchestra in 1978, at the same time beginning an association with French composer Olivier Messiaen, much of whose music he introduced to California audiences. Nagano joined the faculty at the TANGLEWOOD MUSIC CENTER in 1984, and that year also made a debut appearance with the BOSTON SYMPHONY ORCHESTRA. He has held conducting positions at three European institutions: the Lyon (France) Opera (1989–98), London Symphony Orchestra (1990–98), and Hallé (Germany) Orchestra (1992–2000). He was appointed music director of the Orchestre Symphonique de Montreal, Canada, starting in 2006.

Nancarrow, Conlon (1912–1997) *composer*

One of the most bold and original of American composers, Conlon Nancarrow is best remembered for his series of studies composed for player piano. Freed from the consideration of making his music playable by human hands, Nancarrow explored astonishingly complex polyrhythms and dense textures. He attended the Cincinnati College Conservatory, then later studied privately with ROGER SESSIONS and WALTER PISTON. He moved permanently to Mexico City in 1940 when the United States refused to renew his passport because of his outspoken socialism. He started writing for traditional instruments, but after reading provocative music theories of HENRY COWELL, Nancarrow purchased a player piano and his own punch machine for making piano rolls—the hole-punched rolls of paper that determine which notes are played by the automated instrument. Nancarrow owned two player pianos, which he modified with leather and steel tips on the hammers to make their sound more metallic and their articulation clearer in his extremely rapid studies. He composed about 50 studies in this unprecedented manner. In 1982 Nancarrow won a MacArthur Foundation Award.

National Conservatory of Music

Founded by Jeannette Thurber in 1885 in New York, the National Conservatory was intended to set the standard of an emerging American classical tradition. Thurber lured the renowned central European composer ANTONÍN DVOŘÁK to the directorship of the school, and Dvořák served in that post from 1892 to 1895. During that time he was much beloved by his adopting country and composed his Symphony no. 9, the *New World* Symphony. However, Dvořák's tenure proved to be a brief high point for the National Conservatory. The school's funding suffered from an economic recession, and though Thurber applied (unsuccessfully) for federal funding, ultimately the school did not survive.

National Symphony Orchestra

Perhaps surprisingly, the nation's capital did not have a continually operating symphony orchestra until the National Symphony was founded in 1931. Before then, the Washington Symphony Orchestra performed sporadically between 1905 and 1912. The National Symphony was first conducted by Hands Kindler, who was followed by Howard Mitchell in 1949. ANTAL DORATI conducted from 1970 to 1977, succeeded by MSTISLAV ROSTROPOVICH. The current music director, appointed in 1996, is LEONARD SLATKIN. In 1971, the orchestra started its close affiliation with the newly built KENNEDY CENTER FOR THE PERFORMING ARTS, performing there and functioning as an orchestra in residence. The National Symphony has premiered about 1,000 compositions, most by American composers. The orchestra commonly performs at ceremonial occasions and for heads of state. The National Symphony employs 100 musicians and maintains a year-round season of about 175 concerts. The organization implements strong community outreach and educational programs.

NBC Symphony Orchestra

The first orchestra created by a broadcast company, the NBC Symphony was founded specifically for conductor ARTURO TOSCANINI, who directed the group from 1937 to 1954. The NBC Symphony was hugely important to the musical life of the country and the average citizen's awareness and appreciation of classical music. Most of the orchestra's concerts were broadcast nationally on the radio during an era when radio was a reigning entertainment medium (to an extent difficult to comprehend today). A generation of listeners listened to near-weekly broadcasts of live classics and became a society far more abreast of new composers and the immortals than today's audiences. While Toscanini was not the most adventurous programmer and did not seek out new composers as did SERGE KOUSSEVITZKY in Boston or LEOPOLD STOKOWSKI in Philadelphia, he might nonetheless be considered

the most influential force for music appreciation in the United States in the first half of the 20th century, thanks to the NBC Symphony. It is not too much to say that Toscanini made SAMUEL BARBER an instant star when he broadcast two of that composer's orchestral works in the 1940s.

Though Toscanini had total artistic control of the NBC Symphony—it was *his* orchestra to a greater extent than enjoyed by permanent music directors of civic orchestras—the maestro was not beyond sharing the responsibilities and benefits of the job. Toscanini suggested extending the NBC Symphony season to a year-round 52 weeks and creating secondary conductorships to direct the full slate of performances. ARTUR RODZINSKI, who helped organize the orchestra before Toscanini took it over, was the first permanent guest conductor to be assigned; he handled 10 concerts a year while engaged as music director of the CLEVELAND ORCHESTRA. Other guest conductors were invited to lead the orchestra as needed, providing a high-profile platform in New York (and nationally, through the broadcasts) upon which conductors could gain exposure.

New England Conservatory of Music

Founded in 1867 by Eben Tourjee, the New England Conservatory is America's oldest continually operating independent music school. (The PEABODY INSTITUTE and OBERLIN CONSERVATORY were founded earlier, but both lost their independence when they merged with larger institutions.) A leading training ground for classical and jazz musicians, the conservatory feeds strongly into the BOSTON SYMPHONY ORCHESTRA, nearly half of whose members come from the conservatory's graduates and faculty.

New England Psalm-Singer, The

Published in 1770 by WILLIAM BILLINGS, a singing instructor, *The New England Psalm-Singer* remarkably contained 127 original hymn tunes in an era when other tune books merely compiled European melodies. For this unprecedented creative accomplishment, Billings is sometimes considered America's first composer, notwithstanding the original art song published by FRANCIS HOPKINSON published in 1759. Regardless of that debate, *The New England Psalm-Singer* was a landmark event in the early history of American classical music.

New Jersey Symphony Orchestra

In the early 1920s, groups of musicians performed at the Montclair (New Jersey) Art Museum. One such group was the Llewellyn Ensemble. On November 27, 1922, the Llewellyn was joined by other musicians in a concert considered to represent the seed that grew into the New Jersey Symphony Orchestra. In 1923 the various museum performing groups consolidated as the Montclair Orchestra. This ensemble changed names depending on which county it was performing in over the next few years. In 1927, the name changed to the New Jersey Orchestra. The group expanded partly by acquisition of smaller groups, and in 1937 it became the New Jersey Symphony Orchestra. In 1940 Frieder Weissman became music director; at that time, the orchestra presented four programs in its season. Samuel Antek succeeded Weissman in 1947, after a difficult period during World War II in which most of the orchestra's members left for military service. Star performers appearing with the NJSO during these early years included cellist Pablo Casals and singer BEVERLY SILLS.

When Antek died in 1958, the orchestra hired Matyas Abas as music director but his tenure was short-lived, and the organization relied on guest conductors for two years. That instability did not stop the orchestra's growing reputation, though, as the American Symphony Orchestra League upgraded the group's status to one of the 25 top orchestras in America. In 1966, the orchestra performed the world premiere of ROGER SESSIONS's Symphony no. 6. Music directors from the 1960s included Kenneth Schermerhorn (1962–68), Henry Lewis (1968–76), MAX RUDOLF (1976–77), and Thomas Michalak

(1977–83, including the canceled 1980–81 season). Guest conductors again filled the gap from 1983 to 1985. Highlights during these years include the orchestra's debut at CARNEGIE HALL in 1970, tenor Luciano Pavarotti's first appearance in 1972, and the introduction, in 1979, of the orchestra's method of presenting its season in multiple locations around the state.

In 1985, HUGH WOLFF was appointed music director. Wolff resigned in 1991 and was replaced by ZDENEK MACAL. In 1997 the orchestra moved into the New Jersey Performing Arts Center in Newark, but continues dividing its season among other venues. In 2001, the NJSO's recording of ANTONÍN DVOŘÁK's Requiem and Symphony no. 9 *From the New World* received a Grammy Award. In 2002 Macal was named music director emeritus, and NEEME JÄRVI became music director designate. Järvi takes the podium as Music Director in 2005.

New York City Opera

Second in New York to the METROPOLITAN OPERA in prestige, the New York City Opera is an institution of international importance that has enjoyed its share of glamour over the years. It was founded on February 21, 1944, with a performance of Puccini's *Tosca*. The mayor of New York christened the new company "The people's opera company." Music critic Olin Downes, reviewing the premiere performance for the *New York Times,* wrote: "The performance was of the most refreshing sincerity, competence, and dramatic impact," comparing it explicitly and insultingly to the Metropolitan's rival production of that opera. Ticket prices started at 85 cents. The entire first season consisted of nine performances of three operas over seven days.

The New York City Opera was founded on the ideals of affordable prices, innovative repertoire, and furnishing a showcase for American voices. The first season took steps toward those ideals, even if the company's initial roster was mostly of European origin. The company moved to the NEW YORK STATE THEATER OF LINCOLN CENTER in 1966, which sits directly next to the METROPOLITAN OPERA HOUSE. Ten years earlier, BEVERLY SILLS made her debut with the company, and her breakthrough performance of Cleopatra in Handel's *Julius Caesar* took New York by storm and established Sills as an international star. She never forsook the New York City Opera, keeping the company as her home base and lending it substantial star wattage next to the Metropolitan. The company formed its repertoire around Sills's strengths, and the singer eventually became general director of the NYCO. In 1993, the New York City Opera became the first company in the world to use supertitles to translate operas during performance, setting off a trend that reached into far corners of the operatic world and further fulfilling the company's mission to make opera meaningful to the common person. Paul Kellogg is the current general director.

New York Philharmonic Orchestra

The NYPO is the oldest orchestra in the United States, and one of the world's oldest and most venerated ensembles. Begun modestly in 1842 as the PHILHARMONIC SYMPHONY SOCIETY OF NEW YORK, the orchestra has operated continuously since then. Starting with 63 musicians, the group was increased to 100 players in 1867, and currently fills the stage with about 115 musicians. The Philharmonic Society played in a variety of venues until 1867, when it moved into the Academy of Music; it took residence in the METROPOLITAN OPERA HOUSE in 1886, and from 1892 the Philharmonic gave its concerts in CARNEGIE HALL. Seventy years later, in 1962, the orchestra moved to Philharmonic Hall (later named AVERY FISHER HALL) in the newly constructed LINCOLN CENTER FOR THE PERFORMING ARTS. In 2003 the boards of the New York Philharmonic and Carnegie Hall discussed a merger that would have created an enormous cultural institution and moved the Philharmonic back to Carnegie. Amid criticism that Carnegie Hall was betraying its role as a showcase for the world's greatest orchestras by committing its schedule to an in-house ensemble,

and that the Philharmonic was attempting to break its lease with Lincoln Center, the talks were discontinued and the merger scrapped.

The idea for a new orchestra in New York had been brewing since 1839, fomented by a group of musicians who had played at a memorial service. The Philharmonic Society of New York was called to business in 1842 by URELI CORELLI HILL, a 40-year-old conductor who had led the New York Musical Fund Society since its founding in 1828. Hill conducted the Philharmonic's first concert and many of its subsequent concerts during the first five years, though the orchestra did not employ a formal music director until 1848 (Theodore Eisfeld). In its first quarter century, the Philharmonic Society produced six concerts or fewer each season. Throughout its long history, the Philharmonic has rarely been known as an adventurous programming orchestra (the exception being when PIERRE BOULEZ was music director from 1971 to 1977), but the first 70 years saw several U.S. premieres of important European pieces, including Beethoven's Symphony no. 9 (1846), Berlioz's *Symphonie Fantastique* (1866), Brahms's Symphony no. 4 (1886), Tchaikovsky's Symphony no. 6 (1894), Mahler's second and fourth symphonies (1908 and 1904, respectively), and Rachmaninoff's Piano Concerto no. 3 (1909), the last of which featured the composer as soloist, and was a world premiere.

The Philharmonic has never been the only orchestra in New York. Over three dozen other orchestras currently perform in the city. In the 19th century the Philharmonic Society competed with a number of shorter-lived groups, most notably the NEW YORK SYMPHONY SOCIETY, founded in 1878 by LEOPOLD DAMROSCH. The two organizations merged in March 1928, becoming the New York Philharmonic-Symphony, gradually thereafter known as the New York Philharmonic Orchestra. Contrary to other accounts, including the Philharmonic's own historical narrative on its Web site, Leopold Damrosch did not lead the Philharmonic on a U.S. tour in 1882, nor did anybody else. That tour, led by Damrosch, was performed by the New York Symphony Society, 46 years before the merger. The New York Philharmonic's historical lineage is clearly attached to the Philharmonic Society, not the Symphony Society, despite the complicating fact of Damrosch's having conducted the Philharmonic Society for a single season (1876–77). The New York Philharmonic did not mount a large-scale tour until ARTURO TOSCANINI took it through Europe in 1930.

The historical roster of music directors appointed by the Philharmonic Society is an impressive list:

URELI CORELLI HILL (1842–47)
Theodore Eisfeld (1848–65)
Carl Bergmann (1855–76)
LEOPOLD DAMROSCH (1876–77)
THEODORE THOMAS (1877–91)
Anton Seidl (1891–98)
Emil Paur (1898–1902)
WALTER DAMROSCH (1902–03)
Wassily Safonoff (1906–09)
Gustav Mahler (1909–11)
Josef Stransky (1911–23)
WILLEM MENGELBERG (1922–30)
ARTURO TOSCANINI (1928–36)
JOHN BARBIROLLI (1936–41)
ARTUR RODZINSKI (1943–47)
BRUNO WALTER (1947–49)
LEOPOLD STOKOWSKI (1949–50)
DIMITRI MITROPOULOS (1949–58)
LEONARD BERNSTEIN (1958–69)
GEORGE SZELL (1969–70)
PIERRE BOULEZ (1971–77)
ZUBIN MEHTA (1978–91)
KURT MASUR (1991–2002)
LORIN MAAZEL (2002–present; under contract
    through 2006)

Toscanini and Bernstein are the most celebrated of this celebrity list. Toscanini's regime was famous for its glamour and disciplined music making, and he internationalized the orchestra. Bernstein was the Philharmonic's greatest populist and also a dra-

matic performer; he made the orchestra a media-friendly organization and instituted the legendary Young People's Concerts.

The New York Philharmonic has performed on five continents and has recorded about 2,000 albums.

New York Pro Musica Antiqua
Operating from 1954 to 1974, the New York Pro Musica Antiqua was dedicated to historically authentic performances of music from the Middle Ages and Renaissance. The groups was formed by NOAH GREENBERG, who died in 1966. Subsequent directors included John White (1966–70), Paul Maynard (1970–72), and George Houle (1972–74).

New York State Theater
Located in New York's LINCOLN CENTER, the New York State Theater is home to the NEW YORK CITY OPERA and the New York City Ballet. The theater seats an audience of 2,755.

New York Symphony Society
The New York Symphony Society was one of two major symphonic institutions in New York between 1878 and 1928. (The competing orchestra was the PHILHARMONIC SYMPHONY SOCIETY OF NEW YORK, precursor of the NEW YORK PHILHARMONIC ORCHESTRA.) The NYSS was founded in 1878 by LEOPOLD DAMROSCH, and the musical directorship of the orchestra remained in the Damrosch family for its entire existence. After Leopold died, his son Walter took over. The orchestra became a member-owned body in 1903, with musicians and some outside investors assuming financial risk, but that arrangement lasted only until 1907, when a reorganization along modern lines put a board of directors in place and gave the musicians salaries. During this period, H. H. Flagler was an important financier of the NYSS, funding general operations and—historically—the orchestra's tour of Europe in 1920, which was the first

overseas venture by an American orchestra. To some extent, the NYSS operated in the shadow of the Philharmonic, but it was a strong-minded organization that programmed more adventurously than its older, more conservative competitor. In March, 1928, the sibling rivalry came to an end as the two symphonies merged. The resulting orchestra was called the Philharmonic-Symphony Society Orchestra for several years, gradually assuming the name New York Philharmonic Orchestra. The modern orchestra's lineage is associated with the Philharmonic Society, not the Symphony Society, so the NYSS came to an end with the 1928 merger.

Notturno (1973)

Composed by DONALD MARTINO, *Notturno,* scored for a small chamber orchestra, won a 1974 Pulitzer Prize. It was premiered on May 15, 1973, in New York by Speculum Musicae.

Oberlin Conservatory of Music

Now part of Oberlin College, the Oberlin Conservatory was founded in Oberlin, Ohio as an independent musical academy in 1865, making it one of the oldest continually operating music conservatories in the United States (though not the oldest, as claimed). Oberlin College had been founded in 1833, and the Conservatory merged with it in its second year, 1866. Music students benefit from access to the broader liberal arts resources of the college—though, again, claims notwithstanding, Oberlin is not the only conservatory so linked to a larger institution (see PEABODY INSTITUTE). Nor did the Conservatory establish the first electronic music studio, as advertised, but it did join that movement relatively early, in 1969. Oberlin can legitimately lay claim to important breakthroughs: in 1892 it established the first full-time professorship in music history, and in 1921 it established the first four-year college degree program in music education. The Conservatory enrolls about 595 students and employs a faculty of 75.

Of Reminiscences and Reflections (1993)

Composed by GUNTHER SCHULLER after a period of inactivity following his wife's death, this orchestral piece is partly inspired by her memory. It was premiered on December 2, 1993, by the Louisville (Kentucky) Orchestra, which had commissioned it, and received a Pulitzer Prize in 1994.

Ohlsson, Garrick (b. 1948) *pianist*

The first American pianist to win the Chopin Competition in Warsaw, Garrick Ohlsson has been identified with the music of Chopin despite his

Garrick Ohlsson (Courtesy of Garrick Ohlsson and ICM Talent; Photo by P. J. Griffiths)

wide-ranging repertoire. He grew up in White Plains, New York, where he attended the Westchester School of Music, leaving there at age 13 to study at the JUILLIARD SCHOOL. At Juilliard Ohlsson worked with SASCHA GORODNITZKY and ROSINA LHÉVINNE. He won the Busoni Competition in Italy in 1966 and the Montreal Piano Competition in 1968 before triumphing at Warsaw in 1970. His extroverted, uncomplicated playing style was considered a breath of fresh air in the midst of dreamy, introverted Chopin interpretations, and he was lauded for bringing a muscular American style to romantic music. He remains a hero in Poland and has toured around the world. Ohlsson has introduced the piano music of Carl Maria von Weber and Federico Busoni to audiences, and he has recorded the complete piano music of Brahms and Chopin.

Oliveira, Elmar (b. 1950) *violinist*

Elmar Oliveira is one of the most prolific, adventurous, and prize-winning violinists of his generation. One of the wave of young virtuosos who stormed the world's music competitions in the 1970s, Oliveira studied at the MANHATTAN SCHOOL OF MUSIC before becoming the first American violinist to win the Tchaikovsky Competition in 1978; only two other violinists have taken the gold medal in that contest since, and they were cowinners in 1982. He was also the first violinist to win the Avery Fisher Prize. Oliveira won first prize in the Naumburg International Competition. He has toured around the world, performing a diverse repertoire of standard and contemporary works. Frustrated with the typical artist-label relations when recording, Oliveira founded his own label, Artek, in 1998.

114 Songs (1922)

114 Songs is a self-published and self-distributed body of work by CHARLES IVES. Ives was an important American composer whose startling originality left much of his work unrecognized during his lifetime. Hoping to raise his profile and gain a larger audience for his music, Ives collected, revised, and added to a group of songs that represented the full spectrum of his career to that point. (Ives stopped composing in 1927, so as it turned out, the *114 Songs* represented his entire stylistic variety.) Ives published this collection in 1922 and distributed the book to influential musicians and critics. This tactic might have seemed desperate, and indeed, it was received unfavorably in some quarters. One music journal referred to Ives as a "joker." The venture was partially successful, though, as many of the songs received performances around the world. The *114 Songs* gave Ives a claim to the reputation of being a serious composer. After retiring from his corporate career as an insurance executive in 1930 (Ives had always been a part-time composer), and with original compositions behind him, Ives spent his retirement revising his work and continually questing for acceptance. He attracted powerful advocates (notably HENRY COWELL), but in the end he was embittered by the success of less original composers. The *114 Songs* remains as a stylistic survey, though it is not regarded as a single work and was never intended to be performed as such.

On the Transmigration of Souls (2002)

This dramatic work by JOHN ADAMS is scored for full orchestra, chorus, children's chorus, two pianos tuned a quarter-tone apart, and amplified sound design. The piece won a 2003 Pulitzer Prize. It was commissioned and premiered by the NEW YORK PHILHARMONIC and conceived as a tribute to the survivors of the September 11, 2001, terrorist attacks on the United States. The first performance was on September 19, 2002, at AVERY FISHER HALL in New York. The premiere included 252 performers. The text quotes from missing persons posters and newspaper obituaries. The piece, although explicitly inspired by the terrorist event, is unprogrammatic. Adams said of it: "I didn't want to turn it into some kind of musical documentary. My piece is really a piece of remembrance and reflection."

Audience response to the premiere performance was muted, not as a reflection of the piece's quality but in respect to its dramatic force. Beethoven's Symphony no. 9, also a dramatic work scored for orchestra and chorus, followed Adams's work on the program.

Oppens, Ursula (b. 1944) *pianist*

Ursula Oppens studied piano first with her mother, then at the JUILLIARD SCHOOL. She won first prize in the Busoni International Piano Competition in 1969, then took the Avery Fisher Prize in 1976. In 1972 she helped found the chamber group SPECULUM MUSICAE. She currently holds the post of John Evans Distinguished Professor of Music at Northwestern University in Evanston, Illinois.

Ormandy, Eugene (1899–1985) *conductor*

Legendary conductor of the PHILADELPHIA ORCHESTRA for 42 years, Eugene Ormandy was born in Budapest, Hungary, and became an American citizen in 1927. Named Jenő Blau, after a Hungarian violinist with whom the boy eventually studied, he attended the Royal Academy of Music in Budapest, studying violin and composition (with Zoltán Kodály). He graduated as a teenager and toured Hungary as a violinist by age 18. He arrived in New York in 1921 on the promise of a lucrative concert tour. The promoter went bankrupt, and Ormandy, in dire financial straits, quickly took a job in the house orchestra of New York's Capitol Theater (legend says that Ormandy was down to his last nickel when he first walked into the Capitol), playing in the second violin section at first but quickly progressing to concertmaster. In 1924 he conducted the orchestra—Ormandy's podium debut—when the regular leader fell ill. Soon after he was appointed associate director.

Ormandy remained with the Capitol Theater orchestra until 1929, conducting a performance schedule in which every programmed piece was played 28 times a week—invaluable experience for a young conductor. An acquaintance of Ormandy who worked with manager Arthur Judson gradually moved him toward bigger and better opportunities. (When Judson first saw Ormandy conduct, in a dance concert, he famously remarked, "I came to see a dancer and instead I heard a conductor.") Ormandy's break came in 1931, when legendary conductor ARTURO TOSCANINI withdrew from a guest-conducting engagement with the PHILADELPHIA ORCHESTRA. Many established conductors refused to fill in for the maestro, fearing unflattering comparisons, and Ormandy, with less to lose, stepped up to the podium. His success resulted in a quick escalation of his career: a week later Ormandy was headed to Minneapolis to take over the Minneapolis Symphony Orchestra, whose music director had been forced by illness to retire. Ormandy remained at this position for five years. The Minneapolis Orchestra improved in quality and stature under Ormandy's direction, and RCA signed the group to its first major recording contract.

Ormandy's influence in Philadelphia actually began several years before his official 42-year reign. There was his first, daring appearances in place of Toscanini. Then, Philadelphia's regular conductor, LEOPOLD STOKOWSKI, announced his semiretirement, a period during which he would scale back about half his engagements with the orchestra. Ormandy was an important part of the fill-in conducting staff and, gradually, came to assume all the missing half of Stokowski's leadership. In 1938 Ormandy was named music director of the Philadelphia Orchestra by a governing board that was most likely somewhat impatient with the lingering instability of the situation, even as Stokowski continued to hang on to his share of the directorship. In 1941 Stokowski stepped down for good, and Ormandy started his long, near-exclusive collaboration with the Philadelphia Orchestra.

Ormandy's influence on the Philadelphia Orchestra's sound cannot be overestimated, but it would be a mistake to think that he instantly elevated a provincial ensemble as he did in Minneapolis. Stokowski had handed Ormandy a virtuoso instrument. The gradual change wrought by Ormandy led to the development of the "Philadelphia sound," which was largely a function of warming and enriching the tone of the string sections. Ormandy was quick to take credit for the orchestra's sound, noting that the "Philadelphia sound" disappeared when other conductors led the orchestra. Ormandy's experience as a violinist helped enormously. He taught the string players to bow in a uniform fashion, rather than allowing each player to determine individual bow strokes, reversing the free-bowing tradition instituted by Stokowski. His characteristic emphasis on a full and passionate string sound was displayed in his physical conducting style, as Ormandy often curved his left hand into the violinist's playing position and shook his wrist as if creating a vibrato tone. That gesture, more than any other outward manifestation of Ormandy's style, represented his way of communicating with the orchestra. At the same time, Ormandy was a quiet, undramatic conductor who did not gesture unnecessarily.

The Philadelphia Orchestra made its first overseas tour in 1949 under Ormandy and subsequently traveled around the world. In 1973 they undertook an historic tour of China. He recorded constantly, producing hundreds of discs for Columbia Records and, starting in 1968, RCA. (Later the orchestra moved to the Angel record label.) The Philadelphia Orchestra still promotes the "Philadelphia sound," which is directly attributable to Ormandy; preserving and showcasing that sound was part of the rationale for building the KIMMEL CENTER in 2001. Ormandy's last concert was in New York, conducting the Philadelphia Orchestra as its conductor laureate. His obituary ran on page one of the *New York Times*.

Ornstein, Leo (1893–2002) *composer and pianist*

Leo Ornstein was an exceptionally long-lived pianist and composer who enjoyed an exceptionally short period in the limelight. He has been described as the

Leo Ornstein (Courtesy of Severo Ornstein)

most important American musical figure in the 1920s, when he stormed through concert halls with dynamic programs that included his own challenging music. In the 1920s he withdrew from the concert stage, preferring to compose in solitude and teach privately. Ornstein was born in Russia and attended the Petrograd University as a child. He emigrated to the United States (New York) at age 14, entered the Institute of Musical Art (later JUILLIARD SCHOOL) and performed his piano debut at age 18. He started composing his first piano works in 1913, shortly after which he embarked on European tours. Ornstein's pieces were savagely percussive, more so even than the mechanistic formulas of composer GEORGE ANTHEIL that scandalized Paris or the earthy stompings of Béla Bartók. One critic wrote that Ornstein's hammering of the piano might break apart the instrument and shatter the windows. Much of his work was atonal to boot; the combination of raw power and disregard of tonality stunned audiences. Renowned music critic James Huneker wrote, "I never thought I should live to hear Arnold Schoenberg sound tame, yet tame he sounds, almost timid and halting, after Ornstein, who is, most emphatically, the only true-blue, genuine, futurist composer alive."

Ornstein first garnered attention as an avant-gardist in 1914 with a London recital featuring works by 12-tone composer Arnold Schoenberg, his own music, and Busoni's transcriptions of Bach, of which the last group was a startling novelty at the time. Following up with the same type of concert in New York in 1915, Ornstein became an underground favorite of the avant-garde, which abandoned him when he composed less futuristic works. Ornstein became disenchanted with what he perceived as a trend toward novelty, not musical substance, and increasingly resented the constraints of his own success. He and his wife founded a music school in Philadelphia. His music was rediscovered by Vivian Perlis, a music researcher at Yale University, in the 1970s. An early biography of Ornstein was published in 1918. A modern biography was published in 2004 by Indiana University Press.

Orpheus

A chamber orchestra with the distinguishing characteristic of rehearsing and performing without a conductor, Orpheus was founded in 1972 by cellist Julian Fifer. The chamber orchestra consists of 26 players, and its mission is to approach the orchestral repertoire with the principles of shared interpretation standard in chamber music. Demonstrating an unprecedented level of democracy in a symphonic performing group, Orpheus members have complete control over programming and interpretation. Section leaders rotate in avoidance of the usual orchestral hierarchy. Every aspect of rehearsing, recording, scheduling, and performing is subject to a unique and evolving group process. Orpheus has toured extensively, recorded over 60 discs, been the subject of a documentary film, and been studied by business schools.

Ozawa, Seiji (b. 1935) *conductor*

Born in China of Japanese descent, Seiji Ozawa has made most of his career as a headlining conductor in America. He studied piano as a child and teenager, and switched to conducting while enrolled at the Toho School of Music in Tokyo. He first conducted the Japan Philharmonic Orchestra in 1954. He moved to Paris and won an international conducting contest there, bringing him to the attention of CHARLES MUNCH, who invited him to the TANGLEWOOD MUSIC CENTER. There, he studied with the two great French conductors Munch and PIERRE MONTEUX, both of whom enjoyed tenures as music director of the BOSTON SYMPHONY ORCHESTRA, which would play importantly in Ozawa's future. Ozawa won the Koussevitzky Prize at Tanglewood. He traveled to Berlin for studies with legendary German conductor Herbert von Karajan. After this, LEONARD BERNSTEIN made Ozawa assistant conductor of the NEW YORK PHILHARMONIC, a position he held from 1961 to 1965.

Opportunities and appointments came quickly. Ozawa guest-conducted the CHICAGO SYMPHONY ORCHESTRA during the early 1960s. He was artistic director of the RAVINIA FESTIVAL (summer home of the Chicago Symphony) from 1965 to 1969, and music director of the Toronto Symphony Orchestra during the same period. He took over the SAN FRANCISCO SYMPHONY between 1970 and 1976. In 1970 he became artistic director of Tanglewood. While still conducting in San Franscisco, Ozawa accepted his most important appointment, music director of the BOSTON SYMPHONY ORCHESTRA. He led that orchestra for an unprecedented 29 years (only SERGE KOUSSEVITZKY approached that record, with a 25-year tenure), until his resignation in 2002.

Ozawa and the city of Boston enjoyed a mutually felt love affair. His dancelike podium style has been popular wherever he worked, and Ozawa's commitment to new music fit in well with Boston's long history of adventurous programming. He took the orchestra on continent-spanning tours. He shepherded the orchestra through its 100th-anniversary gala and Tanglewood's 50th-anniversary celebrations, with new commissions ordered for both milestones. He recorded almost 150 discs on ten record labels. His television productions with the orchestra won two Emmy Awards. Ozawa received honorary doctorates from Harvard University, the NEW ENGLAND CONSERVATORY, and other institutions.

In 2002 Ozawa became music director of the Vienna Philharmonic.

Paine, John Knowles (1839–1906) *composer and educator*

Although John Knowles Paine is not a household name, his career influenced the course of American music and music education for decades. Paine was the country's first music professor at the college level, as well as the first American composer to write a symphony. Born to a musical family in Maine, Paine was tutored in music by Hermann Kotzschmar, a German immigrant. He studied music and organ playing in Europe for three years (1858–61). He concertized on that instrument upon his return to America, and won a teaching position at Harvard University. He became a full professor of music in 1875 and created a music curriculum for his new department that was widely copied at other colleges. Paine's was a conservative voice in music, and his grounding was deep and traditional. His concerts and classes emphasized Bach. Perhaps his greatest influence was wrought in the teaching studio; his student list reads like a Who's Who of early 20th-century American composition: JOHN ALDEN CARPENTER, FREDERICK S. CONVERSE, ARTHUR FOOTE, EDWARD BURLINGHAME HILL, CARL RUGGLES, and others. His own composing received many performances and overwhelming praise in its time but is mostly unplayed today.

Parker, Horatio (1863–1919) *composer, organist, and educator*

Horatio Parker's music is not much heard on modern stages, but his influence on 20th-century composers will always be recognized. He studied organ and piano as a boy, and landed his first church organist job at age 17 in Needham, Massachusetts. He studied composition in Germany from 1882 to 1885. Returning to the United States, Parker taught in New York and served as organist in several churches. Parker's music became recognized and often performed in the decades preceding and following the turn of the century. He was also active as a conductor and continued to do church work. His opera *Mona* won the METROPOLITAN OPERA prize and was performed several times by that company in 1912. His Concerto for Organ and Orchestra was performed in several American cities during the early 1900s.

Parker's lasting contributions to music were made as a faculty member at Yale University, where he started teaching in 1894, and later as dean of the music department, to which position he was named in 1904. He remained at Yale until his death.

Partch, Harry (1901–1974) *composer and inventor*

Called "one of the great unsung musical geniuses of the 20th century," Harry Partch was a composer, inventor of instruments, and theorist. He also invented a new system of music with which to play them. In his fascination with new scales, Partch rebelled against the fundamental underpinning of Western music: the 12-tone chromatic scale. In its place, Partch developed a 43-tone microtonal scale.

Partch played piano in his early years, accompanying silent movies. He spent the 1920s as a piano teacher and part-time violist. By that time he was interested in new systems of tuning and scales. His first new instrument was an "adapted viola," which incorporated the larger fingerboard of the cello, enabling the performer to play microtones between the traditional notes of the scale. In 1928 he completed *Exposition of Monophony,* a theoretical paper explaining his new system. In 1932 Partch presented his first concerts of original music. He won a grant for overseas study, living in England during 1934–35. He made an "adapted guitar" and a new keyboard instrument called the ptolemy. He returned to the United States in 1935, during the Great Depression, and spent at least nine months as a hobo, traveling through the Western states. This experience found its way into his later work, both atmospherically in the music and explicitly in accompanying texts.

During the 1940s Partch invented new instruments and started writing for larger groups. He taught at the University of Illinois from 1956 to 1962. Partch's final collection of new instruments included guitars, bowed string instruments, many types of struck percussion devices, and various reed organs and types of bellows instruments. His greatest acolyte was probably BEN JOHNSTON, who worked to preserve Partch's extremely difficult portfolio of music and instruments, while expanding his systems and adding his own innovations to microtonality (Johnston never invented instruments).

Peabody Institute

The oldest musical academy in the United States, Peabody was founded in 1857 as the Peabody Conservatory in Baltimore, Maryland, by philanthropist George Peabody. In 1977 the conservatory became part of Johns Hopkins University and changed its name to Peabody Institute. A synergy resulted from this merger: Peabody musicians enjoy access to a broader liberal arts program than at most conservatories, and musical university students benefit from a world-class music division. The school

finished a $26.8 million renovation in April 2004. Peabody alumni include pianist ANDRÉ WATTS and composer DOMINICK ARGENTO; faculty members have included pianists LEON FLEISHER and HAROLD BAUER. Robert Sirota is the school's current director.

Pennario, Leonard (b. 1924) *pianist*

Leonard Pennario is an active pianist who made his debut at age 12 with the DALLAS SYMPHONY ORCHESTRA. He played the Liszt Piano Concerto no. 1 in Carnegie Hall at age 19. He has toured extensively in the United States, both as a soloist and as a chamber musician.

Perahia, Murray (b. 1947) *pianist*

A pianist known for taste and integrity, Murray Perahia graduated from the MANNES COLLEGE OF MUSIC in New York, then studied with ARTUR BALSAM. He took a strong interest in chamber music, working with Balsam at KNEISEL HALL and Rudolf Serkin at MARLBORO. A studious artist, Perahia did not rush into an early debut, making his with the NEW YORK PHILHARMONIC when he was 25—rather on the old side for a rising piano star. Just after his debut Perahia won first prize in the Leeds International Piano Competition.

Perahia was always a lyrical pianist, especially in the early years of his career. He is a dedicated Bach and Mozart player, and as the other stars of his generation (GARRICK OHLSSON, EMANUEL AX, and others) were exhibiting their virtuosity, Perahia displayed a more modest, self-contained style of musicianship. His fields of study at Mannes were composing and conducting, and he approaches music with a purity of thought separate from the typical pianistic ambitions. In the 1990s, though, Perahia developed a sharper edge to his keyboard style and expanded his repertoire, claiming his stake to showpieces by Liszt and Chopin. He won the 2002 Grammy Award for solo instrumental recording with his reading of the complete Chopin Études—a formidable challenge that many great pianists never attempted. He has recorded all the Mozart piano concertos in the dual role of pianist and conductor. He is the principal guest conductor of the Academy of St. Martin in the Fields in London.

Perle, George (b. 1915) *composer and writer*

George Perle is associated with 12-tone music but has differentiated himself by refusing to approach music academically or with overt intellectualism. He studied at DePaul University (Indiana) and New York University. He has sat on the faculties of the University of Louisville (Kentucky, 1949–57), the University of California, Davis (1957–61), and Queens College (New York, 1961–84). He has been engaged in visiting professorships at numerous universities and was the Ernest Bloch Professor at the University of California, Berkeley, in 1989. His Wind Quintet IV was awarded a 1986 Pulitzer Prize.

Perle is as renowned for his writings and work as a theorist as for his music. He was one of the first American composers to recognize the importance of composers Arnold Schoenberg, Anton Webern, and Alban Berg and the atonal school of composition they represented. His book *The Operas of Alban Berg* was awarded the Otto Kinkelday Award of the American Musicological Society and the ASCAP Deems Taylor Award. His *Serial Composition and Atonality* is a classic in the field. Two other books, *Twelve-Tone Tonality* (1977) and *The Listening Composer* (1990) are important statements of Perle's musical philosophy.

Perle was composer in residence at the TANGLEWOOD MUSIC CENTER in 1967, 1980, and 1987, and at the MARLBORO MUSIC FESTIVAL in 1993. He held the same position with the SAN FRANCISCO SYMPHONY ORCHESTRA from 1989 to 1991. Perle has been a member of the American Academy and Institute of Arts and Letters since 1978.

Persichetti, Vincent (1915–1987) *composer*

Vincent Persichetti was one of the most prolific and respected American composers of the 20th century. A prodigy, he entered the Combs Conservatory in Philadelphia at age five and graduated 15 years later. During that time Persichetti supported himself (from the age of 11) as a piano accompanist and church organist. Upon graduation he was immediately installed on the Combs faculty, heading the composition department while receiving his postgraduate education at the Philadelphia Conservatory (master's in 1941, doctorate of music in 1945). There, again, Persichetti was appointed head of the composition department after graduation. He joined the faculty of the JUILLIARD SCHOOL (then the Juilliard School of Music) in 1947 and ascended to the head of that composition department in 1963.

Persichetti is not identified with a single style to the same extent as many other composers, thanks to his belief that the explosion of stylistic possibilities afforded by the 20th century should be utilized fully. Accordingly, his works span the gamut from childlike to complex, harmonically simple to abstruse. He was ferociously creative, leaving a portfolio of nine symphonies, several concertos, a good deal of large-scale choral work, 25 "Parables" for chamber ensembles, and a substantial collection of piano music that includes 12 sonatas. In 1973 Persichetti was commissioned to compose a piece for President Richard M. Nixon's inauguration, to be performed by the PHILADELPHIA ORCHESTRA. The composer fulfilled the commission with *A Lincoln Address,* with a text part taken from Lincoln's second inaugural speech. Some of the text was deemed too politically sensitive at the time; the performance was eliminated from the inaugural program and its premiere took place about a month later, performed by the St. Louis Symphony.

Persichetti was awarded numerous honorary doctorates in addition to the one he earned in Philadelphia. He received three Guggenheim Fellowship awards, two grants from the National Foundation on the Arts and Humanities, a Kennedy Center Friedheim Award (the first one bestowed), and innumerable other honors. He fulfilled commissions from the PHILADELPHIA ORCHESTRA, the NEW YORK PHILHARMONIC, the Koussevitsky Foundation, and many other institutions.

Persinger, Louis (1887–1966) *conductor, pianist, and violinist*

A versatile musician, Louis Persinger played violin and piano with nearly equal excellence and also conducted, though he was known primarily as a violinist. He studied in Germany as a teenager at the Leipzig Conservatory, then lived in Brussels, Belgium, for three years for work with famed violinist and composer Eugène Ysaÿe. He returned to the United States in 1912 and debuted with the PHILADELPHIA ORCHESTRA. His first American conducting appointment was with the SAN FRANCISCO SYMPHONY ORCHESTRA in 1915. He directed the Chamber Music Society of San Francisco from 1916 to 1928. He taught at the CLEVELAND INSTITUTE OF MUSIC until 1930, then moved to the JUILLIARD SCHOOL. Among Persinger's students were ISAAC STERN, RUGGIERO RICCI, and YEHUDI MENUHIN (whom Persinger accompanied on the piano in many recitals between 1926 and 1929).

Peterson, Wayne (b. 1927) *composer*

Wayne Peterson won 1992 Pulitzer Prize for his orchestral piece *The Face of the Night, the Heart of the Dark,* which was commissioned by the SAN FRANCISCO SYMPHONY. He received all his higher education at the University of Minnesota and he won a Fulbright Scholarship while there. He is professor emeritus at the School of Music and Dance at San Francisco State University. Peterson also taught at Indiana University and Stanford University. He has composed over 60 works and has received numerous commissions and grants.

Petri, Egon (1881–1962) *pianist*

A German-born pianist who became a naturalized American citizen in the 1930s, Petri made his United States debut in 1932 and taught at both Cornell University and the San Francisco Conservatory. EARL WILD and GRANT JOHANNESEN were among his students.

Philadelphia Orchestra

The Philadelphia Orchestra was founded for a single concert in 1900, and has continued for over a century. The concert, on November 16, was organized as a benefit for families of soldiers killed in the Spanish-American War, and 85 musicians were hired for the event. Fritz Scheel conducted and continued to direct the orchestra's progress until his death in 1907; he was succeeded by Karl Pohlig (1907–12). LEOPOLD STOKOWSKI was appointed music director in 1912, and his high profile, artistic influence, and determination to use recording technology to its fullest extent made the Philadelphia Orchestra one of the country's most important classical institutions. Stokowski remained in Philadelphia until 1938, retaining his title until 1941. During its early years, the orchestra was visited by numerous guest stars. Rachmaninoff premiered many of his new works with the orchestra.

In 1938 EUGENE ORMANDY took the podium in Philadelphia, beginning one of the great musical associations in orchestral history. Ormandy directed the orchestra for 42 years, creating an identification rivaled only by GEORG SOLTI in Chicago and GEORGE SZELL in Cleveland. Ormandy is generally credited with developing the characteristically warm, full sound of the Philadelphia Orchestra. He toured the orchestra globally. RICCARDO MUTI succeeded Ormandy in 1980 and stayed until 1992. WOLFGANG SAWALLISCH followed (1993–2003), and the current music director is CHRISTOPH ESCHENBACH. Sawallisch remains conductor laureate. Only six conductors led the orchestra during its first hundred years, a remarkable record of stability.

The Philadelphia Orchestra moved from the Academy of Music, whose acoustics were the subject of ongoing complaints, to the KIMMEL CENTER FOR THE PERFORMING ARTS in December, 2001.

Philharmonia Baroque Orchestra

Founded in 1981, the Philharmonia Baroque Orchestra is based in San Francisco and concentrates on baroque, classical, and early romantic repertoire. The group presents a subscription series on multiple venues and has recorded over two dozen discs. The music director since 1985 has been Nicholas McGegan.

Philharmonia Virtuosi

Based in Purchase, New York, the Philharmonia Virtuosi is a chamber orchestra with a wide-ranging repertoire. The group was founded in 1974 by conductor Richard Kapp, who remains its conductor. The Philharmonia Virtuosi has performed in CARNEGIE HALL, LINCOLN CENTER, the KENNEDY CENTER, and the Library of Congress. The group has toured the United States, Japan, Canada, and Spain. The 2004–05 season was cancelled, and at this writing the future of the Philharmonia Virtuosi is unknown.

Philharmonic Hall

The home of the NEW YORK PHILHARMONIC in LINCOLN CENTER, Philharmonic Hall opened in September, 1962. It was renamed AVERY FISHER HALL in 1973 after receiving an endowment from philanthropist Avery Fisher.

Philharmonic Symphony Society of New York

Precursor of the NEW YORK PHILHARMONIC ORCHESTRA, the Philharmonic Society was founded in 1842 by URELI CORELLI HILL, conductor who had been working in the city since 1828. Hill conducted most of the Philharmonic's concerts during its first five years but was not named music director—a title that did not appear until bestowed on Theodore Eisfeld in 1848. During those years the orchestra played no more than six concerts annually. The Philharmonic Symphony Society competed in New York with the NEW YORK SYMPHONY SOCIETY, which had been founded in 1878. In March 1928 the Philharmonic absorbed the Symphony Society, and the combined organization (New York Philharmonic Symphony) eventually became the New York Philharmonic.

Philip Glass Ensemble

A performing group that gradually coalesced in the 1960s, the Philip Glass Ensemble performs the works of PHILIP GLASS exclusively. From its inception through the 1970s, Glass composed exclusively for the ensemble. Comprising wind instruments, keyboards, and amplification equipment, the group is occasionally supplemented by singers or string players. As a dedicated means of expressing the music of a single composer, the Philip Glass Ensemble is one of the only—and certainly the most famous—minimalist performing group.

Piatigorsky, Gregor (1903–1976) *cellist*

An American cellist born in the Ukraine, Gregor Piatigorsky was a child star who entered the Moscow Conservatory at age nine. He joined the Lenin Quartet when he was 16, and that same year took a chair in the Bolshoi Theater Orchestra. He became first cellist of the Berlin Philharmonic under Wilhelm Furtwängler in 1924. After running afoul of the Soviet authorities for refusing to name his own string quartet after Lenin (he chose Beethoven instead), Piatigorsky escaped the Soviet Union to the safety of Poland. One of the many stories of this escape has Piatigorsky swimming across the Zbruch river holding his cello above the water. Throughout his career Piatigorsky entered concert halls for concerto performances by wending through the orchestra, his cello held above his head.

Drawn to chamber music throughout his career, in these early years Piatigorsky performed with German pianist and Beethoven specialist Arthur Schnabel, with whom he gave the world premiere of Arnold Schonberg's *Pierrot Lunaire*. Piatigorsky left the Berlin Philharmonic to devote himself to a solo career, and he began an extensive touring itinerary. His mission was not only to play music or build a career, but to elevate the cello as a viable and accepted solo instrument, on an equal footing with the piano and the violin. He was successful, partly through expanding the instrument's repertoire by modifying and arranging music written for other instruments. He emerged as the greatest cellist of his generation, and the career of modern classical idol Yo-Yo Ma probably would not have been possible without the popularizing efforts of Piatigorsky.

Piatigorsky's playing was of the old school—he was a thoroughly romantic musician who indulged in grand gestures, dramatic tempo fluctuations, and long, singing lines. Though some affectations began to seem out of date in the later stages of Piatigorsky's career, his stage charisma, musical authority, and command of the instrument never flagged. His cello tone was described in the *New York Times* like this: "The tone had every sonority and shading—an organ fullness and virility; lyrical beauty and intensity in passages of sustained song; or fine spun as silk in pianissimo measures." His name became synonymous with cello virtuosity in much the same was as Jascha Heifetz on the violin or Vladimir Horowitz on the piano. Piatigorsky once told a student, "Forget about modesty. Be a show-off. There has never been written a modest symphony."

He made his American debut with the New York Philharmonic in 1929, the same year as Nathan Milstein, who also emigrated from Russia. Piatigorsky's frequent chamber music partner in America was Heifetz, with whom he founded the Heifetz-Piatigorsky concert series in Los Angeles. He also performed with Horowitz and Milstein in trio works. Piatigorsky directed the chamber music curriculum at the Tanglewood Music Center (then called Berkshire Music Center). He taught at the University of Southern California, Los Angeles, where a chair was established in his honor after his death.

Pinkham, Daniel (b. 1923) *composer*

Daniel Pinkham started out with piano lessons, then studied organ, harpsichord, and composition. He attended a private secondary school, Phillips Academy, then attended at Harvard University (1940–44), where he encountered Walter Piston and Aaron Copland. He worked with Paul Hindemith and Samuel Barber at the Tanglewood Music Center (then called Berkshire Music Center). Like many 20th-century American composers, Pinkham studied with Nadia Boulanger, spending several years in her studio (1941–47). He won a Fulbright Scholarship in 1952 and a Ford Foundation Grant in 1960. He was a visiting lecturer at Harvard during the 1957–58 year. He has been awarded several honorary degrees and is currently senior professor of musicology at the New England Conservatory. Pinkham has composed four symphonies, three concertos for organ and orchestra, many other orchestral scores, cantatas, and oratorios. He has created the soundtracks to 20 documentary films. The London Symphony Orchestra has recorded two of his symphonies and other works.

Piston, Walter (1894–1976) *composer*

One of the most respected composers in American music history, Walter Piston studied engineering and art in his teen years before entering Harvard University, where he studied composition with Edward Burlingame Hill. He was at Harvard from 1920 to 1924, during which time he conducted a student orchestra and after which he left for Paris for studies with Nadia Boulanger. Piston was back in the United States in 1926, and he joined the Harvard faculty, remaining there until his retirement in 1960. As a teacher, Piston influenced numerous younger composers, including Leonard Bernstein and Elliott Carter.

Piston was one of many composers whose careers were furthered by the generosity of Serge Koussevitsky during his years as conductor of the Boston Symphony Orchestra; Koussevitsky commissioned 11 major works from Piston, who

Walter Piston (Courtesy of G. Schirmer)

generally conducted his own premieres. Piston also fulfilled commissions from several other leading orchestras. Piston's engineering talent shone through his music through expert and meticulous craftsmanship and a taste for classical structures. His notation writing was so neat that some of his works were published without additional typesetting. He did not produce a huge portfolio of music; Piston was a slow and thoughtful worker. He assimilated the latest trends in music, incorporating academic techniques such as 12-tone writing into some of his works. He was perhaps more respected by other composers than loved by concert audiences, but some of his orchestral music was received well. He finished eight symphonies, five string quartets, seven concertos, and other works.

Piston received Pulitzer Prizes for his Symphony no. 3 (1947) and Symphony no. 7 (1960). He received a New York Music Critics Circle Award, a Guggenheim Fellowship, several honorary doctorates, and was elected to the American Institute and Academy of Arts and Letters.

Pittsburgh Symphony Orchestra

Founded in 1895 as the Pittsburgh Orchestra, the Pittsburgh Symphony owes its birth to George Westinghouse, who corralled 25 investors to guarantee the group's early financing. That inner circle of investors grew more than fivefold during the following 15 years, as the city's iron, coal, and steel industrialists pitched into the cultural endeavor. Frederick Archer was the orchestra's first conductor. Victor Herbert, a theater conductor of flamboyant style, was chosen as conductor in 1898. Herbert was criticized in one musical journal as a "clever bandmaster." Thanks partly to Herbert's reputation as a showman on the podium, the orchestra was invited to play in CARNEGIE HALL in New York, and the concerts were a decided success at the box office. Herbert left the Pittsburgh Symphony in 1904 and was succeeded by Emil Paur. He had already led both the BOSTON SYMPHONY ORCHESTRA (the country's preeminent symphonic institution at the time) and the PHILHARMONIC SYMPHONY SOCIETY OF NEW YORK (forerunner of the NEW YORK PHILHARMONIC ORCHESTRA and likewise an elite institution). Paur was a stern antidote to Herbert's wanton popularizing, as he kept the repertoire strictly classical and held the instrumental quality to the highest standards. Although the orchestra's improvement was undeniable, some observers believed that Paur's aloof perfectionism and challenging programs alienated audiences of the Herbert era. Nonetheless, Paur stayed for several years, until disaster struck the orchestra in 1910.

Economic conditions and rebellious musicians protesting the hiring of European players led to investor panic and loss of subscribers. With the orchestra's benefactors unable to establish an ongoing endowment and audiences on the wane, the 1910 season was canceled. Not until 1926 did Pittsburgh regain its orchestra, and then only as an experiment. The musicians, most of whom worked steadily in theater pits, rehearsed without pay under the baton of Elias Briskin, a violinist. After playing a single successful concert, a weekly series was established, and this new-found momentum grew

Pittsburgh Symphony Orchestra
(Courtesy of Pittsburgh
Symphony Orchestra)

into a revived, ongoing orchestra—now called the Pittsburgh Symphony Orchestra. Antonio Modarelli was named music director, and he remained until 1937. In 1936 the orchestra began broadcasting syndicated radio concerts.

In 1937 famed conductor OTTO KLEMPERER was hired as music director, and he was widely credited with bringing the orchestra up to a high cultural standard in less than one season. His work done, Klemperer left after one year and was replaced by the equally renowned FRITZ REINER, who was music director from 1938 to 1948. Reiner was notoriously dictatorial, even cruel to his musicians at times, but he raised the orchestra's international profile and gained it an important recording contract. Reiner left for the METROPOLITAN OPERA (and later the CHICAGO SYMPHONY), and Pittsburgh relied on guest conductors until WILLIAM STEINBERG was hired in 1952. Steinberg remained for 23 years, during which time the orchestra thrived artistically and in its back office; in the late 1950s, the Pittsburgh Symphony was the only major American orchestra to sell every seat as a season-long subscription. In 1964 the orchestra toured Europe extensively at the behest of the U.S. State Department. For three years of his contract (1969–72), the much-sought Steinberg held dual directorships, the other with the Boston Symphony. In 1971 the orchestra moved its

home from the Syria Mosque (sole venue since the 1926 reorganization) to the newly constructed HEINZ HALL. Steinberg retired in 1976, and no subsequent director has been as closely identified with the Pittsburgh Symphony as he was.

ANDRÉ PREVIN, who was simultaneously directing the London Symphony Orchestra, was appointed music director in 1979. Previn conducted in Pittsburgh until 1984. At that time LORIN MAAZEL was brought in—not as music director but as music consultant, with the job of organizing the search for a new music director. While on the scene he dazzled audiences with his conducting and took the orchestra on tour. Inevitably, the search ended with Maazel himself, who officially became music director in 1988; he remained until 1996. MARISS JANSONS succeeded Maazel, and worked in Pittsburgh until the start of the 2004 season. The orchestra performs a 20-week season, and spins off a Pops ensemble and a chamber orchestra. During summers, free concerts and other community outreach events are staged.

Ponselle, Rosa (1897–1981) *opera singer*

Considered one of the great sopranos of the 20th century, Rosa Ponselle made a remarkable debut at the METROPOLITAN OPERA: it was her first operatic performance anywhere. She had studied singing with her mother, and Ponselle's sister Carmela was a mezzo-soprano who sang at the Metropolitan. Rosa's professional experience before the 1918 debut at the Metropolitan consisted of appearing in movie theaters and vaudeville houses. She came to the attention of opera star Enrique Caruso, who played opposite her in her debut. Ponselle continued singing at the Metropolitan until 1937. Critic Allen Hughes, writing her obituary in the *New York Times,* called Ponselle "indisputably one of the greatest operatic talents this country has ever produced." Her voice was lauded for its range and flexibility.

Rosa Ponselle (Corbis)

Ponti, Michael (b. 1937) *pianist*

Michael Ponti made his concert tour at age 17 and was a persistent competition warrior. He entered the Busoni Competition in Italy four times before winning first prize. He has specialized in unusual repertoire by forgotten romantic composers and has made several such recordings. He has also recorded the complete piano music of Tchaikovsky and Scriabin.

Porgy and Bess (1935)

GEORGE GERSHWIN composed this stage work as a so-called folk opera. The composer explained the unfamiliar term like this in a 1935 *New York Times* article he wrote about the work: "The explanation is a simple one. 'Porgy and Bess' is a folk tale. Its people naturally would sing folk music." The cross-genre properties of *Porgy and Bess* have been confusing from the start, reflecting Gershwin's seamless crossover among the classical, folk, and jazz realms. Familiar songs from the musical, especially "Summertime" and "It Ain't Necessarily So" have become jazz standards sung by every lounge act in America. But Gershwin was, among many things, a serious and highly trained classical composer who produced a fully-scored work of stage art. Yet it opened and ran on Broadway, not in an opera house. (Such openings were neither unprecedented nor have they been unequalled since; THE SAINT OF BLEECKER STREET, a full-fledged opera by GIAN CARLO MENOTTI that won a 1955 Pulitzer Prize, opened in the Broadway Theater in New York.) Gershwin argued that if he had created a new form combining opera and popular theater, it arose naturally from the material at hand.

Porgy and Bess is derived from DuBose Heyward's 1925 novel, *Porgy.* Ironically, in the mixed reviews after the musical opened in New York's Alvin Theater in 1935, it turned out that music critics liked the dramatic portions of the work, and theater critics liked the musical portions of the work. Over time, critics generally have lashed into *Porgy and Bess* as a flawed work whose popularity is due to its parts (the enduring songs) rather than to its whole. Gershwin and his producers made stringent cuts to the score before opening night, however, and in recent years the full score has come to light and been recorded, returning a measure of respect to Gershwin, posthumously, for the scope and effectiveness of the work. Gershwin spent most of two years on the project, challenged by its mix of orchestral composition and songwriting.

As a modern fixture in the musical repertoire, *Porgy and Bess* has migrated to the opera stage and enjoyed productions at the NEW YORK CITY OPERA and many other houses around the world. Recordings are reviewed in classical publications next to Bach and Prokofiev, for example.

Porter, Quincy (1897–1966) *composer and viola player*

Quincy Porter is best known for his works scored for strings—especially string quartets. He received a bachelor of arts degree in 1919 and bachelor of music in 1921 from Yale University, and also studied composition with Vincent d'Indy and ERNEST BLOCH. He was an enthusiastic educator, joining the faculty of Vassar College in 1932, then becoming dean of the NEW ENGLAND CONSERVATORY in 1938. He became director of the Conservatory in 1942. In 1946 he joined the Yale music faculty, remaining there until 1965. Porter's *Concerto Concertate* won a 1954 Pulitzer Prize. His music twice won awards from the Society for the Publication of American Music.

Posselt, Ruth (b. 1914) *violinist*

As a child prodigy, Ruth Posselt made debuts in CARNEGIE HALL and SYMPHONY HALL in Boston at age 10. She performed with the NEW YORK PHILHARMONIC when she was 14. She studied with Jacques Thibaud and was the first American violinist to tour the Soviet Union. She formed an enduring association with the BOSTON SYMPHONY ORCHESTRA, with which she premiered violin concertos of WALTER PISTON, SAMUEL BARBER, and

EDWARD BURLINGAME HILL. She taught at Florida State University starting in 1962.

Powell, Maud (1867–1920) *violinist*

Maud Powell was the first woman to form a professional American string quartet. Besides this claim to fame, Powell was a successful concert violinist who toured aggressively and premiered many violin concertos that are now standard repertoire to audiences throughout the United States. She also championed American composers and was a popular touring artist in Europe. Powell studied violin as a child in the United States and later in Europe (in Germany at the Leipzig Conservatory and in Paris at the Paris Conservatory). She made debuts in Berlin and Paris before coming home to the United States for an 1885 debut with the Philharmonic Society of New York (later the NEW YORK PHILHARMONIC) under THEODORE THOMAS, who hired Powell after she strode into a Philharmonic rehearsal and requested an audition. Thomas continued to promote Powell's career, arranging for her to perform at the World's Columbian Exposition in Chicago in 1893. Of an entrepreneurial spirit, Powell founded a trio in addition to the quartet, and a slightly larger chamber group called the Maud Powell Concert Company, with which she visited South Africa in 1905. She was the first concert artist to record with the Vicktor Company, on a label that would later become RCA Red Seal. Those early discs became international best-sellers.

In a survey of Powell's recordings, record critic Joseph Magil wrote: "Not as dreamily romantic as Joachim, not as facile as Sarasate, not as breathlessly exciting as Ysaÿe, not as tonally opulent or stylistically modern as Kreisler, Powell was an intelligent, tasteful interpreter who conveyed a strong involvement with the music she played."

Powell, Mel (1923–1998) *arranger and composer*

In the tradition of GEORGE GERSHWIN and WYNTON MARSALIS, Mel Powell was a dual musician, operating with great skill in both the jazz and the classical worlds. Unlike Marsalis, though, Powell divided the two strains of his career rather than integrating them. He was a composer and arranger in the big-band jazz era, then turned his attention primarily to classical forms. He received a bachelor of music degree from Yale University (1952), where he encountered PAUL HINDEMITH, who was to exert a strong influence on Powell's compositions. He later returned to Yale as a faculty member from 1957 to 1969, chairing the music department and running the new electronic music studio (1960–69)—one of the first such studios in the country. He left Yale in 1969 to found the music school at the California Institute of the Arts. His earliest teaching jobs were at the MANNES COLLEGE OF MUSIC and Queens College in New York.

Powell was a restless, inquisitive composer, and his music transformed from relatively conservative techniques influenced by Hindemith to academic serialism. He was an award-winning composer. He took a 1990 Pulitzer Prize for his orchestral piece *Duplicates,* which was commissioned by the Koussevitzky Foundation. He received awards from the Guggenheim Foundation and the American Academy of Arts and Letters.

André Previn (Courtesy of G. Schirmer)

Previn, André (b. 1929) *pianist*

Born in Germany as Andreas Ludwig Priwin, André Previn received early training in Germany and Paris, then immigrated with his family to the United States in 1939. He became an American citizen in 1943. Living in Los Angeles, Previn worked as a piano accompanist to silent films and as an orchestrator for MGM Studios. He composed film music and conducted, self-taught for the most part. In these early years Previn followed his interests in both classical music and jazz with equal enthusiasm—the start of a career in which he was unusually skilled in both fields. He took composition lessons in Los Angeles and conducting lessons from PIERRE MONTEUX while in the army.

While establishing himself as a jazz and concert pianist, Previn made his conducting debut with the St. Louis Symphony Orchestra in 1962. In 1967 he became the music director of the HOUSTON SYMPHONY ORCHESTRA. This appointment started a chain of music directorships with major orchestras, some of which overlapped: London Symphony Orchestra (1969–79, and conductor laureate since 1993), PITTSBURGH SYMPHONY ORCHESTRA (1976–84), Royal Philharmonic Orchestra (1985–91), and LOS ANGELES PHILHARMONIC (1985–89). He has guest-conducted innumerable leading orchestras around the world, maintaining a special relationship with the Vienna Philharmonic.

Previn's composing career equaled his stellar pianistic and conducting accomplishments. His first opera, *A Streetcar Named Desire,* was premiered in 1998 in San Francisco. In 2002, he conducted the Boston Symphony Orchestra in his own Violin Concerto, written for violinist Anne-Sophie Mutter, who played the solo part. In 2003, the

Emerson String Quartet premiered Previn's String Quartet at Carnegie Hall. He has written numerous large-scale works for individual performers, including a piano concerto for Vladimir Ashkenazy, a cello sonata for YO-YO MA, and songs for Janet Baker and SYLVIA MCNAIR.

Previn was knighted in 1996 by Britain's Queen Elizabeth II. His career might be compared to that of LEONARD BERNSTEIN, insofar as Previn has refused to categorize himself or be limited by specialization.

Price, Leontyne (b. 1927) *opera singer*

One of the best-known American sopranos of the 20th century, Leontyne Price grew up in the Deep South and attended the Juilliard School of Music (later the JUILLIARD SCHOOL) on scholarship. She was chosen as a lead by Virgil Thomson in his opera *Four Saints in Three Acts* and soon after starred as Bess in GEORGE GERSHWIN's *PORGY AND BESS*. Other notable appearances were as Tosca in Puccini's opera in a televised production in 1955, and Cleopatra in the premiere of SAMUEL BARBER's *ANTONY AND CLEOPATRA,* which opened the new METROPOLITAN OPERA HOUSE in LINCOLN CENTER. Price was renowned as a Verdi heroine; her signature role was Aida. She increased her recital concertizing in the 1970s, and retired from operatic singing with a farewell televised performance of *Aida* in 1985, viewed by millions.

Queler, Eve (b. 1936) *conductor*
Eve Queler studied conducting at the MANNES COLLEGE OF MUSIC and with LEONARD SLATKIN. She was the first woman conductor to lead the CLEVELAND ORCHESTRA and the PHILADELPHIA ORCHESTRA. In 1968 Queler founded the Opera Orchestra of New York, which she continues to lead; the group performs concert versions of operas in CARNEGIE HALL, concentrating on operas rarely heard.

Rabin, Michael (1936–1972) *violinist*
Born to a musical family, violinist Michael Rabin received early lessons from his pianist mother and violinist father (who played in the NEW YORK PHILHARMONIC). Rabin made his concerto debuts in 1950—one in Cuba, and one in New York's CARNEGIE HALL with the Philharmonic under DIMITRI MITROPOULOS. He toured internationally.

Ramey, Samuel (b. 1942) *opera singer*
One music critic wrote that Samuel Ramey's voice "speaks with God." Hyperbole aside, bass Samuel Ramey is a preeminent opera star and one of the most recorded basses in history, with over 80 discs to his credit. His fame rests not only on the quality of his voice, but on the flexibility of his style; Ramey crosses easily and effectively from the speed and range necessary in Handel and Mozart to the dramatic projection required in Wagner and Verdi. His voice reaches into the range of baritone,

and he sings with unusual expressive power and scope. Accordingly, he is in extraordinary demand internationally. In 1985 the Paris Opera built an entire production of Meyerbeer's *Robert le Diable* for him. A typical season for Ramey was 2003, when he appeared in starring or solo roles with the Los Angeles Opera, the NEW YORK PHILHARMONIC, SAN FRANCISCO SYMPHONY, SAN FRANCISCO OPERA, SEATTLE SYMPHONY, CHICAGO LYRIC OPERA, METROPOLITAN OPERA, Paris Opera, Royal Opera, and Covent Garden. Any one of these engagements would represent breakthrough exposure for most singers.

Ramey made his debut with the NEW YORK CITY OPERA in 1973 and concentrated much of his early career with that company. Like many City Opera singers, he was snubbed by the neighboring Metropolitan for years. Ramey turned to Europe, Chicago, and San Francisco for new stages. He appeared in Chicago and San Francisco in 1979 and began building his European reputation in the early 1980s. His Metropolitan Opera debut finally came in 1984. He began giving solo recitals in 1987, at CARNEGIE HALL. He has appeared with virtually every major opera house and orchestra, under virtually every major conductor.

Ran, Shulamit (b. 1949) *composer and pianist*
Born in Israel, Shulamit Ran is now an American composer and pianist. She studied at the MANNES COLLEGE OF MUSIC and worked with NORMAN DELLO JOIO and RALPH SHAPEY (composition) and NADIA

REISENBERG (composition). In 1967, at age 18, she toured with the NEW YORK PHILHARMONIC and LEONARD BERNSTEIN, performing her *Cappricio* for piano and orchestra. In 1991 Ran became composer in residence at the CHICAGO SYMPHONY ORCHESTRA (until 1997, the first woman to hold that position) and won a Pulitzer Prize for her Symphony no. 1. She has received fellowships from the Rockefeller (1968), Ford (1972), and Guggenheim (1977, 1990) Foundations. Ran is a member of the American Academy of Arts and Sciences. She has fulfilled commissions from the PHILADELPHIA ORCHESTRA, CHAMBER MUSIC SOCIETY OF LINCOLN CENTER, BALTIMORE SYMPHONY, Koussevitzky Music Foundation, and other institutions.

Rands, Bernard (b. 1934) *composer and teacher*

Bernard Rands was born in England, educated in Wales, and emigrated to the United States in 1975. He moved to America to accept a professorship at the University of California, San Diego, where he stayed until 1985. After San Diego Rands joined the faculty of Boston University and also taught at the JUILLIARD SCHOOL. In 1988 Rands became the Walter Bigelow Rosen Professor of Music at Harvard University. While at Harvard, he was composer in residence at the PHILADELPHIA ORCHESTRA from 1989 to 1996. His *Canit del Sole* won a 1984 Pulitzer Prize, and *Le Tambourin* won the 1986 KENNEDY CENTER Freidheim Award.

Ravinia Festival

Summer home of the CHICAGO SYMPHONY ORCHESTRA, Ravinia is promoted as America's oldest outdoor music festival, but it has not operated continuously since its founding and did not start as a music festival, as such. Located north of Chicago in Highland Park, Illinois, Ravinia was founded in 1904 by a railroad company. It began to dedicate its summer programs to music in 1911, after the then-bankrupt railroad company sold the property to a group of Chicago residents. Opera was a big part of Ravinia's programming from 1911 through about 1930, when stars from around the world performed there. During the Great Depression (early 1930s), Ravinia ceased operating for five years. In 1936 it reopened as the official summer residence of the Chicago Symphony. The performance pavilion burned in 1949 and was rebuilt. SEIJI OZAWA was the first music director, appointed in 1961; he was succeeded by JAMES LEVINE in 1971. CHRISTOPH ESCHENBACH replaced Levine in 1994; JAMES CONLON accepted the job to begin in 2005.

Ravinia attracts 600,000 visitors each summer. As many as 150 concert events are presented, in all genres of music. The 2004 lineup included storyteller and radio personality Garrison Keillor, folk singer John Prine, pop singer Neil Sedaka, as well as Chicago Symphony performances.

Reich, Steve (b. 1936) *composer*

Steve Reich is often called a minimalist composer and sometimes joined with Philip Glass as one of its two leading exponents. But such a constraining category does not do justice to Reich's breadth of ambition and scientific approach to music, nor to the multimedia aspects of his work. He has been called "America's greatest living composer," and his music has created an emotional impact in concerts that goes beyond what is possible with the simple drones of less questing minimalism.

Reich graduated from Cornell University in 1957, then did postgraduate work at the JUILLIARD SCHOOL, where he studied composing with WILLIAM BERGSMA and VINCENT PERSICHETTI. The famously open-minded Persichetti was a perfect mentor for the young Reich, who had rebelled against traditional music education. Reich took a master's of music degree from Mills College in 1963. He created his own performance ensemble in 1966. In the early 1970s Reich traveled abroad to study drumming in Africa and Balinese gamelan playing.

These world-music influences had profound effect on his later compositions, but Reich is primarily interested in pure music elements of melody and rhythm, as opposed to specific national traditions and genres. In his early work, especially his first piece, *It's Gonna Rain,* Reich explored the possibilities of speech as melody, and asynchronicity as rhythm. These principles reached mature expression in his 1988 piece *Different Trains,* in which instruments take their notes from loops of speech on tape, and the phasing of two tapes out of sync creates a rhythmic impulse. Reich has incorporated tape and video into his music. The debut performance of *Different Trains* received spectacular reviews, and the recording of the piece won a Grammy Award in 1990.

As both a respected classical figure and an underground cult favorite, Reich and his ensemble have performed in venues as different as CARNEGIE HALL and the Bottom Line jazz club in New York. In 1997, a 10-disc retrospective of his works was issued by the Nonesuch record label. In 2000, Reich received a Schuman Prize from Columbia University and a Montgomery Fellowship from Dartmouth College. He was awarded an honorary doctorate from the California Institute of the Arts. He has received commissions from many leading orchestras and festivals; his work has been conducted by MICHAEL TILSON THOMAS, ZUBIN MEHTA, and others. In 1994 he was elected to the American Academy of Arts and Letters.

Reinagle, Alexander (1756–1809) *composer*

Alexander Reinagle was an early American composer and theatrical entrepreneur who operated theater companies in Philadelphia and Baltimore. His mark on history was made by composing four piano sonatas in the early 1790s, which by some evaluations are the best surviving piano pieces from the 18th century in America. Whether true or not, their historical importance lies in being the first piano sonatas composed by an American. The piano (then called the fortepiano) was a new instrument at the time, invented in Italy, and Reinagle's use of it in compositions and in his theaters' orchestra pits was amazingly progressive.

Reiner, Fritz (1888–1963) *conductor*

Born in Hungary, Fritz Reiner was an American conductor made famous by a succession of high-powered orchestral appointments. He knew Richard Strauss and worked in Europe until coming to America in 1922. Reiner was music director of the CINCINNATI SYMPHONY ORCHESTRA from 1922 to 1931, the PITTSBURGH SYMPHONY ORCHESTRA from 1938 to 1948, and the CHICAGO SYMPHONY ORCHESTRA from 1953 to 1963. He became an American citizen in 1928. In Chicago, his most important tenure, Reiner remains legendary as the director who brought that orchestra to the top level of international standards. In Chicago and in his other cities, Reiner became famous as an orchestra builder. Between and during appointments, Reiner guest-conducted all over the world. He was a regular conductor at New York's Metropolitan Opera from 1948 to 1953. Reiner taught at the CURTIS INSTITUTE from 1931 to 1941, where his students included LEONARD BERNSTEIN.

Reiner was a master of economical movement on the podium. The stylistic antithesis of his student Bernstein, Reiner could conduct an entire symphonic movement while remaining nearly motionless, making tiny movements with his baton that were meaningful to the musicians and nearly invisible to the audience. His work was done in rehearsal, and as a perfectionist he could be compared to ARTURO TOSCANINI. Feared by students and orchestra players, Reiner could be tyrannical, but, if anything, demanded more of himself than of his associates. He died on the eve of returning to the Metropolitan Opera for a performance of Wagner's *Götterdämmerung* after an absence of 10 years.

Reisenberg, Nadia (1904–1983) *pianist*

Born in Russia, Nadia Reisenberg made her American debut in 1922, playing among other works a piece by pianist Ignacy Paderewski with the composer in the audience, and settled in the United States after that. Her active teaching career gave her more renown than her performance work; Reisenberg held positions on the faculties of the CURTIS INSTITUTE (at the invitation of pianist and then-director Josef Hofmann), MANNES COLLEGE OF MUSIC, and JUILLIARD SCHOOL. RICHARD GOODE was one of her students.

Reynolds, Roger (b. 1934) *composer*

Roger Reynolds was a science student at the University of Michigan, where he also studied composing through two degree courses. He graduated with a master of music in 1961, and lived in Europe and Japan for the next eight years. He returned to the United States in 1969 and joined the music faculty of the University of California, San Diego. There, he founded the Center for Music Experiment in 1972. In 1988 Reynolds composed *Whispers Out of Time*, which won a 1989 Pulitzer Prize. Reynolds has completed a substantial portfolio of orchestral, instrumental, vocal, chamber, and electro-acoustical pieces. He has successfully carried the experimental idealism of the 1960s into the present day.

Rhapsody in Blue (1924)

A seminal work of American music, and arguably GEORGE GERSHWIN's most important composition, *Rhapsody in Blue* is a piece for piano and orchestra that was premiered in New York's Aeolian Hall on February 12, 1924, to critical and popular acclaim. More than just a new successful piece of music *Rhapsody* installed Gershwin as an historical figure who placed the jazz idiom in a classical context, elevating a native expression of American music to concert status and blending it with European tradition. To that point, Gershwin had been known primarily as a song composer. As *Rhapsody in Blue* was immediately incorporated into the standard repertoire, Gershwin became an instant star. As a music property, *Rhapsody in Blue* generated over $250,000 for Gershwin in performance and publishing fees during the first ten years of its existence. As a career event, it changed Gershwin's life, enabling him to concentrate more on classical forms and less on

theater pieces, and brought him in contact with the day's leading classical composers including Sergey Prokofiev, Darius Milhaud, Alban Berg, Francis Poulenc, and Maurice Ravel.

Ricci, Ruggiero (b. 1918) *violinist*

Ruggiero Ricci was one of six children, each of whom received family support for their early music studies; three of the children became accomplished musicians, and Ricci became the star of the family. He gave his debut at age 10 in San Francisco, and the next year he performed a New York debut in CARNEGIE HALL. He embarked on a European tour in 1932 at age 14. The pressures of being a child prodigy sometimes do not encourage a stable adult career, but Ricci seems to have experienced a seamless transition to maturity. His personal repertoire was enormous, and he specialized in works of violinist and composer Niccolò Paganini—the most challenging body of violin compositions. He edited an early Paganini concerto, the manuscript of which was lately discovered, and gave its first performance in 1977. He premiered the violin concerto of Alberto Ginastera. Ricci taught at Indiana University from 1970 to 1973, at the JUILLIARD SCHOOL from 1975 to 1978, and at the University of Michigan at Ann Arbor from 1982 to 1988. He authored the book *Left-Hand Violin Technique* (1988).

Riegger, Wallingford (1885–1961) *composer*

A modernist, Wallingford Riegger was born in Albany, Georgia and grew up in New York City. He was a member of the first graduating class of the Institute of Musical Art (later the JUILLIARD SCHOOL). Upon graduation in 1907, Riegger left for three years of study in Berlin. He made a conducting debut in Germany in 1910. He also played cello, and his first professional job in the United States was as principal conducting work. He hoped to become a conductor in America but could not gain momentum in that direction. He taught during the

1920s (at the Institute of Musical Art and Ithaca College), and began to compose during those years. Of all the prominent American composers in the 20th century, Riegger approached the profession in the most roundabout way. He met with some success from the start: his 1922 Piano Trio won the Paderewski Prize. His modernist music was hard to swallow from the beginning; the 1927 work *Study in Sonority* was received poorly, sometimes with booing. However, the piece was programmed by LEOPOLD STOKOWSKI and the PHILADELPHIA ORCHESTRA in 1929. Other important premieres included the *Rhapsody* for orchestra in New York (1931) and the *Dichotomy* in Berlin (1932).

In 1928 Riegger settled in New York and became personally acquainted with CHARLES IVES, CARL RUGGLES, and HENRY COWELL—leading avant-garde composers each, though Ives worked in seclusion and anonymity for the most part. In the 1930s Riegger was a full-time composer, and created modern dance scores for several leading dance companies including Martha Graham. He also wrote pure, unprogrammatic music: symphonies, chamber music, and concertos. His Symphony no. 3 was commissioned by Columbia University, and received a New York Music Critics Circle Award in 1948; its recording won the Naumburg Foundation Recording Award. Riegger became one of the most successful of the modernist composers in the mid-20th century, enjoying a fairly continual stream of commissions, awards, and important performances. His work garnered respect in Europe as well as in the United States.

Riley, Terry (b. 1935) *composer*

Terry Riley is generally considered the father of minimalism, whose compositions influenced STEVE REICH, PHILIP GLASS, and JOHN ADAMS. Between 1957 and 1961 he studied at San Francisco State University, the SAN FRANCISCO CONSERVATORY, and the University of California, Berkeley. His early work was atonal, but Riley quickly became enamored of long tones and repeated phrases—hall-

marks of minimalist writing. His 1961 String Trio can be regarded as the first notated piece in minimalist style, with its reoccurring short phrases. But his most famous work, and the one usually hailed as the minimalist starting point, is *In C* (1964), which allows performers to repeat phrases at their discretion, then move on to other phrases. Riley has a long-standing collaboration with the Kronos Quartet, for which he has written 12 string quartets. Riley's work set the stage for minimalism; his study of music from other countries created an early form of world music; and his exploration of long tones and arrhythmic composition can be viewed as the forerunner of New Age music.

Robert Shaw Chorale

Formed by the renowned choral conductor ROBERT SHAW, the Chorale operated from 1949 to 1965. It was the preeminent touring and recording chorale of its time. The U.S. State Department sent the group on extensive tours through Europe, the Soviet Union, the Middle East, and Latin America. Recordings of the Robert Shaw Chorale ranged from popular and theatrical material to the foundation stones of choral classical repertoire, and they garnered four Grammy Awards (of Robert Shaw's 14 Grammys).

Rochberg, George (b. 1918) *composer*

Through a long composing career, George Rochberg has not been afraid to reassess his work and evolve with the times. He adopted the academic stylings of the 12-tone school from about 1950 to 1965, then shifted to a more tonal style in his later career. He attended the MANNES COLLEGE OF MUSIC from 1939 to 1942, studying with Leopold Mannes and GEORGE SZELL. After World War II Rochberg entered the CURTIS INSTITUTE, where he worked with GIAN CARLO MENOTTI. He joined the faculty of Curtis and remained there until 1954. He has been an active teacher, sitting on the faculties of the University of Pennsylvania (1960–79; head of the music department until 1968, then Annenberg Professor of Humanities); State University of New York at Buffalo; and the Temple University Institute of Music.

Rochberg became involved with atonal music and 12-tone theory when on a Fulbright Scholarship in Rome. He authored *The Hexachord and Its Relation to the Twelve-Tone Row* in 1955, and contributed theoretical articles to music journals. Rochberg has received numerous awards, including a George Gershwin Memorial Award (1952 for his *Night Music*), the Society for the Publication of American Music Award (1956 for String Quartet no. 1), two Guggenheim Fellowships (1956 and 1966), Naumburg Recording Award (1961, for Symphony no. 2), the Naumburg Chamber Composition Award (1972, String Quartet no. 3), Kennedy Center Friedheim Award (1979, String Quartet no. 4), the Brandeis Creative Arts Award (1985), appointment to the American Academy of Arts and Letters (1985), and election to the American Academy of Arts and Sciences (1986). He has been awarded honorary doctorates from the Curtis Institute and several universities.

Rodzinski, Artur (1892–1958) *conductor*

One of the great American conductors in the first half of the 20th century, Artur Rodzinski had a career marked by brilliance and controversy. He was born in Poland and made his career there until he was 33. In 1925 LEOPOLD STOKOWSKI invited Rodzinski to Philadelphia as an assistant conductor. While in Philadelphia Rodzinski became associated with the CURTIS INSTITUTE, taking over the orchestral department there. He got his own orchestra in 1929, when he assumed the conductorship of the LOS ANGELES PHILHARMONIC. In 1933 Rodzinski took over the CLEVELAND ORCHESTRA, his first groundbreaking job. Rodzinski was one of the great orchestra builders who migrated to America from Europe in the early and middle of the 20th century, and he elevated the Cleveland Orchestra to the top rank, where it has (largely) remained since. While

working in Cleveland he guest-conducted in New York and European cities, creating excitement wherever he took the podium.

In 1937, when the NBC broadcasting company was starting to create an orchestra for ARTURO TOSCANINI (the NBC SYMPHONY ORCHESTRA), Toscanini requested that Rodzinski be in charge of assembling and preparing the ensemble. Toscanini had just left his position as music director of the NEW YORK PHILHARMONIC, and it was widely presumed that Rodzinski would inherit that position. However, JOHN BARBIROLLI got the Philharmonic job, holding it in a controversial and largely unsuccessful tenure until 1942. Rodzinski took over the Philharmonic in 1942 (controversially firing several of the musicians immediately), and restored the orchestra to a greatness it had not experienced since Toscanini left. The drama of Rodzinski's delayed appointment caused some bad blood between the conductor and Arthur Judson, manager of the Philharmonic. Their uneasy relationship exploded in 1947, when Rodzinski issued an ultimatum to the Philharmonic board, demanding that they choose Judson or himself to continue their association with the orchestra. Rodzinski lost that showdown, and it was later revealed that he had already been negotiating with the CHICAGO SYMPHONY ORCHESTRA.

Rodzinski moved to Chicago and worked his magic with that orchestra during the 1947–48 season, but his success there was brought down by more controversy. The orchestra fired him for unprofessional behavior that included last-minute program changes and (according to the *Grove Dictionary of Music and Musicians*) for attempting to negotiate a longer contract. Rodzinski was gone by the fall of 1948, and he settled in Italy, guest-conducting occasionally in the United States and more frequently in Europe.

Rorem, Ned (b. 1923) *composer*

More than a famous American composer, Ned Rorem is a master of American arts and letters whose books and essays contribute to his renown nearly as much as his symphonies, operas, and other compositions. He studied piano and theory as a child, and was tremendously influenced by his introduction of French impressionists Claude Debussy and Maurice Ravel. His college years were spent at Northwestern University and the CURTIS INSTITUTE. He worked as a music copyist for VIRGIL THOMSON in exchange for lessons in orchestration. Finally, he received bachelors and masters degrees at the JUILLIARD SCHOOL. His first composition to gain attention was the art song "The Lordly Hudson," and indeed, Rorem has always been best known as a song composer. He has written over 500 songs.

Rorem lived in Paris for several years in the 1950s, and his book *The Paris Diary* (along with a later companion volume, *The New York Diary*) established him as a compelling observer of society and culture. During these years he accepted a Fulbright Scholarship (1951) and a Guggenheim Fellowship (1957). In 1959 he became composer in residence at the University of Buffalo, and his Symphony no. 3 was performed by LEONARD BERNSTEIN and the NEW YORK PHILHARMONIC in a nationwide broadcast. Moving on from Buffalo, Rorem took a similar position at the University of Utah. Many commissions and miscellaneous awards followed, and in 1976 Rorem won a Pulitzer Prize for *Air Music*. He joined the faculty at Curtis in 1980.

Rose, Leonard (1918–1984) *cellist*

The foremost American-born cellist of the mid-20th century, Leonard Rose studied in Miami, New York, and Philadelphia (at the CURTIS INSTITUTE), and enjoyed a career first as a leading orchestral cellist, then as a concert soloist. His first orchestra job was with the NBC SYMPHONY ORCHESTRA under ARTURO TOSCANINI, where he was assistant principal cellist. In 1939 he moved to the CLEVELAND ORCHESTRA, where he was principal cellist under ARTUR RODZINSKI; Rose stayed in Cleveland until 1943. While there, he taught at the CLEVELAND INSTITUTE OF MUSIC and OBERLIN CONSERVATORY.

When Rodzinski moved to New York and took over the NEW YORK PHILHARMONIC, he took Rose with him and installed him as the principal cellist. In New York he taught at the JUILLIARD SCHOOL and performed nearly 20 times as a soloist with the Philharmonic. He joined the Curtis faculty in 1951, remaining there until 1962. Teaching at the leading institutions put Rose in a position to influence the emerging generation of cellists; LYNN HARRELL and YO-YO MA studied with him. As noted in Rose's *New York Times* obituary, at one point four of the PHILADELPHIA ORCHESTRA cellists, five in the New York Philharmonic, six in the Cleveland Orchestra, and seven in the BOSTON SYMPHONY ORCHESTRA were students of Rose.

Rose made a deliberate career change in 1951, quitting his orchestra job and devoting himself to a solo career. He performed concertos, and also chamber music with EUGENE ISTOMIN and ISAAC STERN (the Istomin-Stern-Rose trio) starting in 1962. Rose commissioned a cello concerto from WILLIAM SCHUMAN (*A Song of Orpheus*).

Rosen, Charles (b. 1927) *pianist and writer*

A pianist and provocative writer on music, Charles Rosen first played the piano at age four and entered the JUILLIARD SCHOOL preparatory division at age seven. During his teen years he studied with Moriz Rosenthal, who had been a pupil of Franz Liszt. His higher education transpired at Princeton University, where Rosen marched through a three-degree curriculum and ended up with a Ph.D. in 1951—having specialized in Romance languages. He also studied mathematics and philosophy, demonstrating his wide-ranging interests and fluency in arts and letters that was to inform his later writing. He made his New York debut as a pianist in 1951, and that same year made the first complete recording of Debussy's *Études* for piano.

Rosen's writing includes books and articles. His first book, *The Classic Style: Haydn, Mozart, Beethoven*, won the National Book Award for Arts and Letters in 1972. He often contributes articles to the *New York Review of Books*. His most recent popular title is *Piano Notes: the World of the Pianist*, in which he holds forth on the decline of classical music and the unimportance of pianistic lineage, among many other topics. Rosen is a merciless critic of sacred traditions, and his piano playing reflects that objectivity and lack of sentimentality. His performances have been criticized for lack of warmth, and just as often praised for their intellectual rigor.

Rosenstock, Joseph (1895–1985) *conductor*

Born in Poland, Joseph Rosenstock had a conducting career that transpired mostly in Europe. However, he maintained close ties with both the METROPOLITAN OPERA and the NEW YORK CITY OPERA. He first conducted at the Metropolitan in 1929, then worked in Germany and Japan until 1948, when he made his debut at the New York City Opera. He stayed there for four years, and became general manager of the company from 1952 to 1956. It was back to Europe after that; then Rosenstock returned to the Metropolitan for seven seasons between 1961 and 1968. During that time he conducted in both the old opera house and the new one in LINCOLN CENTER.

Rostropovich, Mstislav (b. 1927) *cellist and composer*

A Russian/Swiss cellist and composer, Rostropovich has traveled the globe as an ambassador of peace, freedom, and great music, and might be considered a global citizen. Fortunate to be born to musical parents—his mother was a pianist and his father a cellist—Rostropovich got an early start and attended the Gnesis Institute in Moscow, then the Moscow Conservatory. He received the Stalin Prize in 1951, but his relations with his homeland soured. Although he traveled widely in the West during the 1950s and made his American debut in Carnegie Hall in 1956, his freedom was restricted in 1970, and he was eventually condemned by the Soviet government for his sympathies with Aleksandr

Solzhenitsyn, and was stripped of his citizenship. He left the country in 1974 and did not return for 16 years. A tireless advocate of freedom and human rights, Rostropovich played his cello at the site of the Berlin Wall as it was being torn down in 1989.

Rostropovich's career is fairly evenly divided between the cello and conducting. His artistry as a cellist inspired many composers to write new cello works, including Benajamin Britten, ARTHUR BLISS, Aram Katchaturian, Witold Lutoslawski, Dmitri Shostakovich, and especially Sergey Prokofiev, with whom Rostropovich enjoyed a close friendship. On the podium, Rostropovich has guest-conducted most of the world's leading orchestras. He was the music director of the NATIONAL SYMPHONY ORCHESTRA in Washington, D.C., from 1977 to 1996, when he was succeeded by LEONARD SLATKIN. It was with the National Symphony that Rostropovich finally returned triumphantly to Russia in 1990.

As a cellist and conductor, Rostropovich has been a champion of new music, displaying an uncanny intuition of the composer's intentions. His interpretations are famous for their sympathy and care.

Rothwell, Walter Henry (1872–1927) *conductor*

Walter Rothwell was born in London and spent his formative years in Vienna and Germany. He worked with composers Anton Bruckner and GUSTAV MAHLER. In the United States, Rothwell is credited with a few "firsts." He was the first conductor to perform English versions of Wagner's opera *Parsifal* (1904) and Puccini's *Madama Butterfly* (1906). He was the first and only principal conductor of the short-lived Saint Paul Symphony Orchestra (1908–15). And Rothwell was the first conductor of the LOS ANGELES PHILHARMONIC in 1919, remaining in that position until his death in 1927.

Rouse, Christopher (b. 1949) *composer*

One of the most successful contemporary composers, Christopher Rouse studied at the OBERLIN CONSERVATORY and Cornell University, and took private lessons with GEORGE CRUMB. He finished his education by 1977, and had already received a fellowship from the National Endowment for the Arts (1976). He taught at the University of Michigan, Ann Arbor, from 1978 to 1981, then at the EASTMAN SCHOOL OF MUSIC starting in 1981. In 1986 Rouse became the first composer in residence in the history of the BALTIMORE SYMPHONY ORCHESTRA, which commissioned his Symphony no. 1 in 1988. That work won a Kennedy Center Friedheim Award, and in the same year the Cleveland Quartet commissioned his String Quartet no. 2. He has received commissions from the NEW YORK PHILHARMONIC, the ASPEN MUSIC FESTIVAL, YO-YO MA, the CHAMBER MUSIC SOCIETY OF LINCOLN CENTER, and several other institutions and foundations. Rouse won a 1993 Pulitzer Prize for his Trombone Concerto. Influenced by rock and roll of the 1960s and 1970s, Rouse in his early career composed in fast, sustained tempos with a great deal of dissonance, creating violent soundscapes. From the mid-1980s, Rouse has sought to blend his naturally advanced harmonies with a clearer and more accessible tonality. The result is emotionally compelling music with a broad and compelling range of influences.

Rubinstein, Arthur (1887–1982) *pianist*

Born in Poland, American pianist Arthur Rubinstein is sometimes regarded as one of the great performers of the 20th century, and nearly always regarded as one of the great musical personalities. His famous joy of life and stage charisma were legendary. These natural gifts were seen by some as substituting for disciplined study, depth of interpretation, and technical command. If VLADIMIR HOROWITZ and Rubinstein were the most celebrated pianists of their era, they were also opposites in ways: Horowitz was the superb technician with absolute tonal control of the instrument, and Rubinstein was the warm communicator who placed more emphasis on musical meaning and the live-concert experience than on technical mastery.

Rubinstein himself asserted that Horowitz was the better pianist, but not the better musician.

Rubinstein was a child prodigy who seemed born with an innate grasp of the musical language. He absorbed his lessons of his older sister at the piano, and played for the great violinist Joseph Joachim in Berlin when he was three years old. Joachim took an enduring interest in the boy and managed his music education when the Rubinsteins returned to Berlin in 1897. At that time, Heinrich Barth became his teacher, and while the two got along well for a time, Rubinstein eventually bridled against the disciplines of sustained piano study. The young man had success with public performances in Europe, and built toward his Paris debut in 1904. By this time he had left Barth and discontinued all further supervised study.

Rubinstein made his American debut in 1906, performing with the PHILADELPHIA ORCHESTRA in CARNEGIE HALL. He was not well received; at 19 years of age, he could no longer be considered a prodigy, and his technical and musical maturity were questioned. Rubinstein shone in American society, though, thanks to his facility with language (he was fluent in eight languages) and tremendous personal charm. He learned music quickly—perhaps too quickly—as a side benefit of his excellence in sight-reading. Later in life Rubinstein confessed that his early performances were underprepared. Nevertheless, he undertook an active touring schedule from 1906, through the United States and Europe. His travels took him to Spain and South America, as his exposure to the music there started a lifelong romance with Spanish composers.

Rubinstein's watershed moment occurred in 1932, when he married and withdrew from the concert stage. Many great pianists have taken sabbaticals or longer retirements, including Horowitz, who withdrew for extended periods four times during his career. Unlike Horowitz, though, Rubinstein suffered not a bit from insecurity or touches of neurosis. During his disappearance from public life he came to grips with his lack of training and thoughtfulness, essentially re-creating his repertoire to a higher standard. He reemerged a new pianist in an American tour in 1937. He became an American citizen in 1946.

As a newly respected and deservedly famous pianist, Rubinstein was an insatiable and spontaneous performer. He said, "At every concert, I leave a lot to the moment. I must have the unexpected, the unforeseen. I want to risk, to dare. I want to be surprised by what comes out." He would sometimes play two or three piano concertos in one night. He recorded with the same unslaked passion, putting to disc all the music of Chopin and much of the Beethoven repertoire. Interpretively, the mature Rubinstein belied his extroverted personality. His Chopin was restrained to the point of chilliness, and his Beethoven was strict in its classicism. Rubinstein never displayed the rhythmic idiosyncrasies favored by many European pianists of his generation.

Rubinstein was a bon vivant for whom the pleasures of life were far more important than its disciplines. Noting that some people accused him of dividing his attention equally among music, wine, and women, Rubinstein denied the characterization vehemently; women occupied most of his thoughts, he said. He seemed to know everybody and have stories about most people. His teasing humor was legendary; once, during a casual duet with Albert Einstein, who was an amateur violinist, Einstein repeatedly entered four beats late. After the third attempt, Rubinstein turned to the scientist with mock exasperation and said, "For God's sake, Professor, can't you count to four?"

Rubinstein retired from concertizing in 1976, and was awarded the United States Medal of Freedom. HAROLD C. SCHONBERG wrote of him, "No pianist has put everything together the way Rubinstein has. Others may be superior in specific things, but Rubinstein is the complete pianist." The Arthur Rubinstein International Piano Master Competition was inaugurated in Israel in 1974 in his honor. He was honored with awards and medals from innumerable countries. Rubinstein died in his sleep at the age of 95, having performed for 85 years.

Rudel, Julius (b. 1921) conductor

Long associated with the New York City Opera, Julius Rudel was born in Vienna and became an American citizen in 1944. He studied at the MANNES COLLEGE OF MUSIC. He first joined the New York City Opera as a rehearsal pianist and quickly made a conducting debut the next year. He directed the company from 1957 to 1979. He also directed the CARAMOOR FESTIVAL and was music adviser at WOLF TRAP.

Rudolf, Max (1902–1995) conductor

A German-born conductor who took American citizenship in 1946, Max Rudolf made his early career in Europe, conducting the Berlin Philharmonic and the Göteborg Symphony Orchestra in Sweden. He moved to the United States in 1945, landing in Chicago and quickly moving to New York, where he made his METROPOLITAN OPERA debut in 1946. He remained on the conducting staff of the Metropolitan until 1958, serving also as assistant manager from 1950. He became music director of the CINCINNATI SYMPHONY ORCHESTRA from 1958 to 1970. He was head of the conducting department at the CURTIS INSTITUTE in the early 1970s and again in the 1980s. Rudolf was music director of the DALLAS SYMPHONY ORCHESTRA for the single season of 1973–74. He wrote a textbook of conducting called *The Grammar of Conducting* (1950).

Ruggles, Carl (1876–1971) composer

Carl Ruggles was an important American composer whose music requires a tolerance for dissonant harmonies. He has been associated with 12-tone composer Arnold Schoenberg and CHARLES IVES but is independent of both in style and musical intent. Though he composed dissonant music, Ruggles did not follow the serial school represented by Schoenberg, and though his music conveys a similar sense of American ruggedness as Ives's scores, he did not depend on the same deliberate musical collisions as Ives. VIRGIL THOMSON wrote of Ruggles:

"Wry, salty, disrespectful, and splendidly profane, he recalls the old hero of comic strips, Popeye the Sailor, never doubtful of his relation to sea or soil."

Ruggles grew up on a farm in Massachusetts, born into a prominent family whose history of patriotism and creative achievement stretched back to 15th-century England. He showed an inclination for the violin as a child and became proficient enough to play chamber music with members of the BOSTON SYMPHONY ORCHESTRA as a teenager. A plan developed to send Ruggles to Prague for composition lessons with ANTONÍN DVOŘÁK, but the adventure fell through at the last minute when his financial sponsor died.

Throughout his life, Ruggles manifested a preference for rural living. In 1907 he moved to Winona, Minnesota, and founded an orchestra there; for the next ten years he occupied himself conducting the Winona Symphony. During those years he also started painting—an avocation he continued that reduced his time for composition. Ruggles wrote music slowly and carefully, and left the world with relatively few, but highly polished, works.

He moved to New York in 1917 and acquainted himself with avant-garde composers of the day, including Ives and HENRY COWELL. He hoped to interest the METROPOLITAN OPERA in his opera *The Sunken Bell.* Unsuccessful on that count, Ruggles started up an orchestra at the Rand School of Social Science, and published his first work—the song "Toys," composed for his four-year-old son. He was in the city for 20 years, during which period he at least started, and occasionally completed, many of his major pieces. One of them was the large orchestral work *Sun-Treader,* which received its premieres in Paris and Berlin, neither performance attended by Ruggles. Ruggles did not hear the piece played until a 1965 recording was issued; its American premiere took place the following year.

From 1938 to 1943, Ruggles taught at the University of Miami. After that brief tenure he settled in Vermont. During his final 28 years, Ruggles concentrated mostly on revising his music—in this regard he was much like Charles Ives. But whereas Ives found himself unable to compose new music, Ruggles seemed to embark on his revision projects by choice. He also concentrated increasingly on his abstract painting. He started a few new music pieces but finished only one: the hymn "Exaltation," composed in memory of his wife.

Ruggles was not an award winner. The organizations and institutions so eager to celebrate the establishment of an American classical tradition in the mid-20th century ignored his work for the most part, and his relative lack of productivity probably detracted from his celebrity. Ruggles did not benefit from glamorous premieres by major orchestras, and he did not pump out a massive portfolio of symphonies and concertos. One opera, nine pieces for orchestra, a handful of chamber music works, and some songs are the result of his life's efforts. However, the music is undeniably worthwhile: challenging, craggy, fierce and passionate, and thoroughly American in spirit, texture, and harmony.

Saint of Bleecker Street, The (1954)

An opera by GIAN CARLO MENOTTI that won a Pulitzer Prize in 1955, *The Saint of Bleecker Street* premiered on Broadway (the Broadway Theater on December 27, 1954), not in an opera house. In addition to the Pulitzer, the work won the Drama Critics' Circle Award and the New York Music Critics' Circle Award.

Saint Paul Chamber Orchestra

Founded in 1959, the Saint Paul Chamber Orchestra is a 35-member ensemble that performs music of all periods. Founder Leopold Sipe conducted the orchestra from 1959 to 1971. DENNIS RUSSELL DAVIES, who held the SPCO's podium from 1972 to 1980, took the group on its first international tour. Pinchas Zukerman followed Davies, remaining in St. Paul until 1987. Zukerman's tenure saw a tremendous rise in the orchestra's profile and subscription sales. Following a brief period of uncertainty, in which Stanislaw Skrowaczewski advised and conducted the ensemble, famed early-music specialist Christopher Hogwood was brought in as director of music (1988–92). During this time, artistic responsibility was diversified. HUGH WOLFF was principal conductor, and composer JOHN ADAMS held the creative chair. The three principals formed the SPCO's Artistic Commission. Andreas Delfs, also music director of the Milwaukee Symphony Orchestra, is the current conductor. The orchestra's close collaboration with Minnesota Public Radio, begun in 1969, brings performances from St. Paul to 120 Public Radio stations around the country. The Saint Paul Chamber Orchestra has won 11 ASCAP Awards for adventurous programming. The organization has commissioned nearly 100 new works.

Salonen, Esa-Pekka (b. 1958) *conductor*

Esa-Pekka Salonen is a Finnish conductor who became music director of the LOS ANGELES PHILHARMONIC in 1992. He took a yearlong break from that position in 2000 to compose. Before going to the United States, Salonen built his career in Europe, where he was associated with the Swedish Royal Opera, the Philharmonia Orchestra in London, the Oslo Philharmonic, the New Stockholm Chamber Orchestra, and the London Sinfonietta.

Salzman, Eric (b. 1933) *composer, music writer, and record producer*

Eric Salzman composed his best-known work, *Civilization and Its Discontents* (1977), a musical for the theater, in collaboration with composer Michael Sahl. He studied composing in high school, then at Columbia and Princeton Universities. He studied with MILTON BABBITT and ROGER SESSIONS, and he received a Fulbright Scholarship for study in Italy. When he returned to the United States in 1958, he began a career as music critic, writing for the *New York Times*, *Herald Tribune*, and *Stereo Review*. He produced several classical discs for Nonesuch

Records between 1975 and 1990. Salzman has taught at Queens College of the City University of New York and at New York University.

Sándor, György (b. 1912) pianist

György Sándor was born in Budapest, Hungary, and settled in the United States after his piano debut at Carnegie Hall in 1939. Notably, Sándor has recorded the complete piano music of Zoltán Kodály and Sergey Prokofiev, and most of the music of fellow Hungarian Béla Bartók, with whom Sándor is especially associated. Sándor's recording of Bartók's piano music won the Grand Prix du Disque in 1965. He premiered Bartók's Piano Concerto no. 3 with the Philadelphia Orchestra in 1946. He taught at the University of Michigan from 1961 to 1981, then joined the faculty of the JUILLIARD SCHOOL in 1982, where he remains today. Sándor is the author of *On Piano Playing: Motion, Sound and Expression*, published in 1981.

San Francisco Chamber Orchestra

Founded in 1953 and comprising players from the SAN FRANCISCO SYMPHONY, the orchestra was an informal venture until 1957, when the current name was adopted. Edgar Braun was guest conductor from 1955 and became music director after Adrian Sunshine, the previous director, left the position. Braun led the orchestra until just before his death in 2002. Benjamin Simon is the current music director.

San Francisco Conservatory of Music

The San Francisco Conservatory of Music was founded in 1917 by Ada Clement as the Ada Clement Piano School, and began in a remodeled private home. The first class contained 40 students, and the student body grew quickly from there. Recognizing the need for school of music in San Francisco, the Clement Piano School reincorporated in 1923 as the San Francisco Conservatory of Music. Instruction

was extended to other instruments besides the piano. Composer ERNEST BLOCH was appointed director of the school in 1925. Chamber music has long been valued at the school, which has invited a series of trios and quartets to the faculty and artist-in-residence positions. In 1956 the conservatory moved to Oak Street and is currently planning its next move to a custom-built structure whose doors are scheduled to open in the fall of 2006.

Perhaps the period of greatest growth for the San Francisco Conservatory came during Milton Salkind's tenure as director. Salkind was appointed in 1967, and during his 24-year term the school expanded to 250 students, instituted more stringent performance requirements, and induced visits from international stars such as Alfred Brendel, LEON FLEISHER, Placido Domingo, BEVERLY SILLS, and YO-YO MA. Salkind hired JOHN ADAMS to the composition department. Colin Murdoch has been the school's director since 1992. The San Francisco Conservatory currently hosts about 270 students each year.

San Francisco Opera

The San Francisco Opera has been revered since the city's first operatic production, in 1851, of Vincenzo Bellini's *La Somnambula*. During the next 55 years, until San Francisco was devastated by the 1906 earthquake, opera was performed nearly 5,000 times by 20 companies in 26 different venues. The Tivoli Theater, operating between 1879 and 1906, produced an opera every night but 40 during that period, for a total of over 4,000 performances. On that foundation of opera appreciation, the San Francisco Opera was founded in 1923, and is now the second-largest opera company in North America after New York's METROPOLITAN OPERA. It was first housed in the Civic Auditorium, and moved to the War Memorial Opera House in 1932. Operas by Italian composer Giacomo Puccini premiered both houses; *La Bohème* first, then *Tosca*. KURT ADLER conducted the opera company from 1953, when Merola died, to 1981. Pamela Rosenberg is the current director, under a contract that runs through 2006. Rosenberg faced difficult financial challenges during her administration, and was forced to cut back company operations by about 25 percent, canceling new productions and eliminating some staff.

San Francisco Symphony Orchestra
Founded in 1911, the San Francisco Symphony's first conductor was Henry Hadley, who directed the orchestra until the 1915 appointment of Alfred Hertz as music director. When Hertz left the orchestra, the podium was shared by Basil Cameron and Issay Dubroven until 1936, when PIERRE MONTEUX was brought in as music director. Monteux stayed until 1952, touring the orchestra domestically and making the SFSO's first recordings. ENRIQUE JORDA succeeded Monteux, following two years of guest conductors between 1952 and 1954. Jorda's tenure was not entirely successful in the minds of subscribers, who were put off by his unusual programming. JOSEF KRIPS took the podium from 1963 to 1970, programming conservatively during his reign. Krips took the orchestra to Europe for the first time. The charismatic SEIJI OZAWA took over in 1970 and stayed in San Francisco until 1976. Ozawa was succeeded by EDO DE WAART (1977–85); during his tenure the orchestra moved to the newly opened Louise M. Davies Symphony Hall (1980). Herbert Blomstedt conducted the orchestra from 1985 to 1995, and his period is regarded as one of the most successful directorships in the company's history. He remains conductor laureate in San Francisco, even as he leads the Gewandhaus Orchestra in Leipzig, Germany. MICHAEL TILSON THOMAS is the current music director in San Francisco, and his years have been marked by a popular blend of standard and unusual repertoire, and heightened stature for the orchestra.

Saperton, David (1889–1970) *pianist*
A virtuoso, David Saperton received his first lessons from his father, and made his Pittsburgh debut at age 10. He played Chopin's Piano Concerto in E-minor at the METROPOLITAN OPERA HOUSE when he was 15. Steaming ahead, he made a European debut when he was 19, and toured the Continent. He was known for marathon performance stunts, such as six recitals in six days in New York, without repeating any pieces, and including some of the most virtuoso showpieces ever written. Saperton married a daughter of legendary pianist and composer LEOPOLD GODOWSKY, after which Saperton became interested in Godowsky's compositions and arrangements. Saperton recorded Chopin's *Études* for piano with Godowsky's famous, nearly unplayable studies on the *Études*. Saperton taught at the CURTIS INSTITUTE and had private students, including JORGE BOLET, GARY GRAFFMAN, WILLIAM MASSELOS, and ABBEY SIMON.

Sawallisch, Wolfgang (b. 1923) *conductor*
A German conductor, Wolfgang Sawallisch was music director of the Philadelphia Orchestra from 1993 to 2003, when he was succeeded by CHRISTOPH ESCHENBACH. He was first heard in America as leader of the Vienna Symphony Orchestra during a tour. While in Philadelphia, Sawallisch navigated the move to the KIMMEL CENTER, the orchestra's new performing space, in 2001. Sawallisch has made concert appearances as a chamber music pianist.

Schickele, Peter (b. 1935) *music humorist*
The preeminent classical music humorist, Schickele follows in the tradition of VICTOR BORGE, but with a stronger inclination toward composition and more elaborate stage productions. Schickele often appears with small orchestras that play his fractured arrangements of classical music. His alter ego is P. D. Q. Bach, the fictional son of Johann Sebastian Bach.

Schickele began as a serious composer, receiving a bachelor's degree from Swarthmore College, and studying with ROY HARRIS and DARIUS MILHAUD. Schickele obtained a master's degree from the JUILLIARD SCHOOL, where he studied with WILLIAM

BERGSMA and VINCENT PERSICHETTI. He received a Ford Foundation grant to work with high school students in Los Angeles, and was on the Juilliard faculty from 1961 to 1965. He continued in a serious vein through the 1960s, but his comic presentations were appearing as early as 1957. He composed farcical works that satirized the classics, and he invented instruments on which to play them. At first such fabrications found their audience at Juilliard while Schickele was a student, but by 1965 he had gained enough renown to give a P. D. Q. Bach concert in New York's TOWN HALL.

Schickele is best known for his lampooning of classical pretensions—indeed, in most circles that is all he is known for. Nevertheless, he has scored music for television and Broadway, and hosts a Public Radio program called *Schickele Mix,* "dedicated to the proposition that all musics are created equal." In the eclectic survey of music featured on the program, Schickele might juxtapose Ravel, the Beach Boys, and Cole Porter. The program won the ASCAP Deems Taylor Award in 1993. Of his many satirical recordings, four P. D. Q. Bach discs have won Grammy Awards.

Schippers, Thomas (1930–1977) *conductor*

A conductor who specialized in opera, Schippers studied at the CURTIS INSTITUTE. He made his conducting debut after winning a contest sponsored by the PHILADELPHIA ORCHESTRA. In 1950 he began a fruitful association with composer GIAN CARLO MENOTTI, which led to his being appointed as music director of the FESTIVAL OF TWO WORLDS in Spoleto, Italy, which Menotti founded. His association with Menotti was one of the strongest influences on Schippers's career; he conducted more than one premiere of Menotti operas, and was the conductor of the historic first television broadcast of *AMAHL AND THE NIGHT VISITORS.* The two had a falling out in 1976.

Schippers was on the conducting staff of the New York City Opera in the 1950s and also guest-conducted at the METROPOLITAN OPERA and the NEW YORK PHILHARMONIC. During a Philharmonic

tour of the Soviet Union, Schippers alternated concerts with LEONARD BERNSTEIN. Schippers was on the podium at the gala opening of the new METROPOLITAN OPERA HOUSE in LINCOLN CENTER in 1966, leading the orchestra for SAMUEL BARBER's newly commissioned opera, *Antony and Cleopatra.* The performance was a disaster but it did not reflect on Schippers, who was the first American conductor to lead the Metropolitan on opening night of any season. Schippers was music director of the CINCINNATI SYMPHONY from 1970 until his death (succeeding MAX RUDOLF), and joined the faculty of the Cincinnati Conservatory of Music in 1972. He had been a front-runner to succeed Bernstein as music director of the New York Philharmonic in 1969, but the appointment went to PIERRE BOULEZ.

Schippers was modest about his many triumphs, attributing his success to "unbelievable luck and an incredible series of accidents." But he died at age 47, still considered one of America's most respected young conductors.

Schirmer   See G. SCHIRMER.

Schneider, Alexander (1908–1993) *conductor and violinist*

An American violinist and conductor, Schneider was born in Vilnius, Germany and built his early career there. He first traveled to the United States in 1932 as a member of the Budapest String Quartet, and settled in the United States in 1938. He continued performing with the Budapest String Quartet until 1944. An enthusiastic chamber musician, Schneider found new partners in the United States, including Benar Heifetz, MIECZYSLAW HORSZOWSKI, RALPH KIRKPATRICK, and EUGENE ISTOMIN. He played with the ALBENERI TRIO and the New York Quartet. He was awarded the Elizabeth Sprague Coolidge Medal for his chamber music work. He became associated with cellist Pablo Casals in 1950, when he persuaded the great cellist to come out of retirement, and he organized the Festival Casals in 1957.

Schneider rejoined the Budapest String Quartet in 1955, remaining with the group until it disbanded in 1967. He founded the New York String Orchestra in 1968; he formed the BRANDENBURG ENSEMBLE, an orchestra of young musicians, in 1972. Both ensembles were used as teaching institutions, and Schneider gained renown for his selfless dedication to education.

Schonberg, Harold C. (1915–2003) *music critic*

Harold Schonberg was the most important popularizer of classical music through the written word in the United States from the late 1950s through the early 1990s. He took piano lessons as a boy, and though he turned into a competent pianist, his larger talent was a prodigious musical memory by which, even as a child, he remembered music in detail after only one hearing. He wanted to be a music critic from the age of 12. Aiming for a career centered in New York, he received degrees from Brooklyn College (B.A., 1937) and New York University (M.A., 1938). He was music critic of the *New York Sun* from 1946 to 1950 but was primarily associated with the *New York Times,* for which he started writing in 1950. He became senior music critic there in 1960 and remained in control until 1980. Schonberg's readership was vast and his influence astounding. He once received a called-out rebuke from a singer taking his bows on the stage of the METROPOLITAN OPERA. He received a Pulitzer Prize for music criticism, the first such award bestowed. He continued placing articles in the *Times* after his formal retirement.

In addition to his topical criticism, and just as important to his legacy, Schonberg wrote several books that remain popular—40 years after their first publication in some cases—for their readability. His five most enduring books are *The Great Pianists* (1963), *The Great Conductors* (1967), *The Lives of the Great Composers* (1970), *The Glorious Ones: Classical Music's Legendary Performers* (1985), and *Horowitz: His Life and Music* (1992).

Schonberg defended his famously direct and unapologetic style of criticism as follows: "Criticism is only informed opinion. I write a piece that is a personal reaction based, hopefully, on a lot of years of study, background, scholarship and whatever intuition I have. It's not a critic's job to be right or wrong; it's his job to express an opinion in readable English." An educated musician, Schonberg carried music scores to concerts to verify accuracy and determine which edition was used by the performers. He excelled particularly in reviews of pianists; his favorite was JOSEF HOFMANN, and he lauded Russian giants Emil Gilels, Svindoseau Richter, Lazar Berman, and Evseny Kissin. He saved his most scathing commentary for the academic composing styles of the mid-20th century founded on 12-tone serialism. "Certain it is that the decades of serialism did nothing but alienate the public, creating a chasm between composer and audience," he wrote after his retirement.

Schuller, Gunther (b. 1925) *composer*

A more skilled composer than generally given credit for, Gunther Schuller leaves a legacy that will probably rest more on his work as an educator. He was born to a musical family; his father played violin in the NEW YORK PHILHARMONIC for over 30 years. Schuller became an accomplished french horn player at an early age; he became the principal horn player for the CINCINNATI SYMPHONY at age 17, and joined the orchestra of the METROPOLITAN OPERA two years later (1945–59). While in Cincinnati, Schuller composed a Concerto for Horn, which the orchestra premiered with the composer as soloist.

In New York, Schuller was exposed to a tremendous amount of jazz and followed his interest in that direction. He listened to historical recordings and took to notating improvised solos on paper. This absorption in jazz was to influence Schuller's career both as an educator and as a composer. He wrote two historical books about jazz: *Early Jazz: Its Roots and Development* (1968) and *The Swing Era* (1989). In 1985 Schuller became music director of the Spokane Symphony Orchestra, where he was known as a highly adventurous programmer, always seeking to enlighten audiences with unusual juxta-positions of music.

His teaching began early, with a tenure at the MANHATTAN SCHOOL OF MUSIC from 1950 to 1963, and at Yale University from 1964 to 1967. He forged a long-running association with the TANGLEWOOD MUSIC CENTER (then the Berkshire Music Center), with which he was associated from 1963 to 1984. He was president of the NEW ENGLAND CONSERVATORY from 1967 to 1977. He started his own publishing companies—Margun Music and Gun-Mar—and a record label, GM Recordings.

Schuller's love of all kinds of music is reflected in his substantial creative output. He has completed over 160 works in many genres of music. His advocacy of wind instruments, unrepresented as they are in the standard solo repertoire, is demonstrated in his many concertos for horn, bassoon, saxophone, and other instruments. He won a 1994 Pulitzer Prize for *Of Reminiscences and Reflections*, inspired by memory of his wife, who died in 1993. He won the Gold Medal from the American Academy of Arts and Letters (1997), a BMI Lifetime Achievement Award (1994), a MacArthur Foundation Award (1991), and the William Schuman Award from Columbia University (1988).

Schuman, William (1910–1992) *administrator and composer*

An important American composer and administrator, William Schuman grew up in New York City and took violin lessons. He began writing songs as a boy, possibly completing about 100. This avocation continued after he enrolled in New York University to earn a business degree, during which time he collaborated with songwriter Frank Loesser. The two of them wrote much material for radio and vaudeville, but in Schuman's mind this musical activity was a hobby. He turned a corner while still at NYU, realized that his profession lay in classical music, and withdrew from the university. He studied privately with faculty members of the Juilliard School and obtained a bachelor of science degree in music

education from Teacher's College of Columbia University in 1935. That year he accepted his first teaching position, at Sarah Lawrence College in Bronxville, New York. While teaching at Sarah Lawrence he earned a master of arts degree from Columbia in 1937.

In 1938 Schuman won a composition contest with his Symphony no. 2. On the competition jury was AARON COPLAND, who recommended the work and the composer to SERGE KOUSSEVITSKY, the renowned conductor of the BOSTON SYMPHONY ORCHESTRA and supporter of new music. Koussevitsky premiered the prize-winning symphony, as well as Schuman's *American Festival Overture* in 1939, and the Symphony no. 3 in 1941. The third symphony won the New York Music Critics Circle Award. Schuman accepted the first Pulitzer Prize in music for *A Free Song*, in 1943.

Schuman accepted a job as director of publications at music publisher G. SCHIRMER in 1944. The next year, he started his signature position as president of the JUILLIARD SCHOOL (then known as the

William Schuman (Courtesy of G. Schirmer)

Institute of Musical Art and the Juilliard Graduate School). His reign at Juilliard was monumental, and Schuman proved to be as talented at arts administration as he was at music composition. He reorganized the institution, merging the Institute and the Graduate School into the unified Juilliard School of Music. Later, after adding a dance division, the school changed its name again to the Juilliard School. He revived the Juilliard Opera Theater and invited an impressive roster of distinguished composers to the faculty, including William Bergsma, Peter Mennin, and Vincent Persichetti. Schuman helped found the Juilliard String Quartet, which served as a model of an institutionally supported chamber group.

One of Schuman's most significant initiatives at Juilliard was convincing the board of LINCOLN CENTER, while that performing arts center was still in the planning stage, that Juilliard should be part of the plan. His arguments were so persuasive that he was named president of Lincoln Center concurrent with his presidency of Juilliard. Schuman guided the school through its transition from its building at the southern edge of Harlem to a new facility on the northern edge of the Lincoln Center campus. Schuman founded the Lincoln Center Student Program, cofounded the CHAMBER MUSIC SOCIETY OF LINCOLN CENTER, and started the MOSTLY MOZART FESTIVAL. A heart attack in 1968 convinced him to retire from his various administrative positions, though he remained available for guidance via boards and committees. In 1969 he was named president emeritus of Juilliard.

Schuman's composing style was robust, lyrical, and well crafted. He finished 10 symphonies, five ballet scores, concertos for piano, violin, viola, and cello, four string quartets, and many other works. About his composing style, Schuman himself said, "the music is always melodic and has a sense of line. My music can always be sung. And I have never written a note in my life that was not deeply felt." He was a famously effective orchestrator and made a hit with his arrangement of Charles Ives's *Variations on "America."* He was intermittently chairman of the MACDOWELL COLONY, and received the National Medal of Arts in 1987 and Kennedy Center Honors in 1989.

Schwantner, Joseph (b. 1943) *composer*

A Pulitzer Prize winner (in 1979 for *Aftertones of Infinity*), Joseph Schwantner studied at the Chicago Conservatory and Northwestern University. He taught at the EASTMAN SCHOOL OF MUSIC from 1970 to 1982, when he became composer in residence at the Saint Louis Symphony Orchestra. He was elected to the American Academy of Arts and Letters in 2002. Schwantner has fulfilled commissions from dozens of institutions around the world, and his work has been performed extensively by leading orchestras. He has written a great deal of chamber music, and also composed for larger groups. Schwantner has experimented with atonal music without committing to it. A long list of awards includes the Bearns Prize from Columbia University (1967), a Rockefeller Foundation Grant (1978), a Guggenheim Fellowship (1978), and a KENNEDY CENTER Friedheim Award (1981).

Schwarz, Gerard (b. 1947) *trumpeter and conductor*

Gerard Schwarz's career moved progressively from orchestra chairs to orchestra podiums. He studied trumpet with William Vacchiano, principal trumpeter of the NEW YORK PHILHARMONIC, but is mostly self-taught as a conductor. In 1965 he joined the AMERICAN BRASS QUINTET and stayed with that group until 1973, touring extensively. His first orchestral job in 1966 was as third-chair trumpeter with the AMERICAN SYMPHONY ORCHESTRA; after three years he moved to the first chair. He also played with the Aspen Festival Orchestra and the Casals Festival Orchestra. In 1971 he became the only wind player to receive a Ford Foundation Grant, which he used to commission a trumpet concerto from composer of concertos for wind instruments GUNTHER SCHULLER. In 1973 Schwarz was invited to become co-principal trumpeter of the New York Philharmonic; Schwarz performed with the Philharmonic until 1977, when he left orchestra playing entirely and committed himself to a conducting career.

Schwarz had made his podium debut in 1966 with the Eric Hawkins Dance Company, of which he became music director; he held the same position with the Eliot Feld Dance Company. He founded the New York Chamber Orchestra in 1977, and from 1978 to 1985 he was music director of the Los Angeles Chamber Orchestra. His association with the SEATTLE SYMPHONY ORCHESTRA began in 1983, and he became principal conductor there the following year. Also in 1984, Schwarz was appointed music director of the MOSTLY MOZART FESTIVAL summer series in New York. In 2001 he took on the musical directorship of the Royal Liverpool Symphony Orchestra. Schwarz has received the Ditson Conductor's Award from Columbia University and an honorary doctorate from the JUILLIARD SCHOOL.

Seattle Symphony

The first performance of the Seattle Symphony was in December 1903, when violinist Henry West assembled 24 musicians to give a single concert. Most of the players were professionals working in Seattle's musical theaters. Michael Kegrize took over leadership of the orchestra between 1907 and 1909, and by the end of his tenure Seattle was attracting musical stars of substantial standing; FRITZ KREISLER and JOSEF HOFMANN performed with the orchestra in 1909. John Spargur succeeded Kegrize until 1920, when the orchestra ceased operating for six years. From 1921 to 1926 an ensemble called the Seattle Civic Orchestra was conducted by Davenport Engberg; some historical accounts regard the Civic Orchestra as a continuation of the Seattle Symphony. The Seattle Symphony proper was reformed in 1927 under Karl Krueger. Basil Cameron (1932–38) and Nicolai Sokoloff (1938–40) followed Krueger, and conductor Sir Thomas Beecham came

to Seattle in 1940. Beecham's tenure was not long (he left during the 1942–43 season) but is considered significant for the improvement he brought to the orchestra. Carl Bricken, Eugene Linden, and Milton Katims conducted the orchestra through 1976, with Katims conducting for 22 years. Rainer Miedél was music director after Katims, until his death in 1983, during which period the orchestra was never more popular in Seattle. GERARD SCHWARZ, the Seattle Symphony's current music director, entered the scene as music adviser in 1983. Schwarz has continued the orchestra's tradition of performing contemporary music. Starting in the mid-1980s, the Seattle Symphony has had a succession of composers in residence, including RICHARD DANIELPOUR and STEPHEN ALBERT. The orchestra won the ASCAP Edwards Award for adventurous programming. Schwarz has recorded 85 discs with the orchestra, which have garnered 10 Grammy Award nominations. Those recordings include the Great American Composers series on the Delos label, started in 1989.

Serkin, Peter (b. 1947) *pianist*

Peter Serkin comes from an illustrious line of musicians. His grandfather was Adolf Busch, violinist and composer. Busch's daughter, Serkin's mother, was an amateur musician who gave Peter his first piano lessons. RUDOLF SERKIN, Peter's father, was one of the great American pianists, and one of the finest Mozart and Beethoven interpreters in the history of piano playing. It was in this milieu that Peter Serkin grew up. He was 11 years old when he entered the CURTIS INSTITUTE, where his father was a celebrated teacher. At Curtis, he studied with MIECZYSLAW HORSZOWSKI and Rudolf Serkin. In 1959 Serkin made debuts at the MARLBORO MUSIC FESTIVAL and in New York. In his early teens he performed double concertos with his father under GEORGE SZELL and the CLEVELAND ORCHESTRA.

As an adult performer, Serkin has been strongly attracted to modern repertoire and daring recital choices. In the late 1960s and through the 1970s, when piano recitalists were mostly bound to the central (and fairly antique) repertoire, Serkin was programming Schoenberg, Webern, and Messiaen. He dressed informally on stage and gained a loyal, partly underground following among music students. In 1973 Serkin founded Tashi, a quartet comprising piano, clarinet (RICHARD STOLTZMAN), violin (IDA KAVAFIAN), and cello (Fred Sherry). In 1983 he joined the faculty of the MANNES COLLEGE OF MUSIC, and he has also taught at Curtis and the JUILLIARD SCHOOL.

In the 2003–04 season, Serkin concertized in the United States and Japan. He continued a longstanding association with composer Peter Lieberson by premiering his Piano Concerto no. 3 with the MINNESOTA ORCHESTRA; Lieberson had composed his first concerto for Serkin in 1982, and Serkin premiered it with the BOSTON SYMPHONY ORCHESTRA. Serkin appeared in LINCOLN CENTER's Great Performers series. For the second consecutive year, Serkin performed the complete keyboard concertos of Bach with JAIME LAREDO and the BRANDENBURG ENSEMBLE. Serkin performed in the opening festival of ZANKEL HALL. He received an honorary doctorate from the NEW ENGLAND CONSERVATORY in 2001.

Serkin, Rudolf (1903–1991) *pianist*

Rudolf Serkin famously said that the music he played was more important to him than the piano. Nonetheless, his legacy installs him firmly as one of the great 20th-century pianists. Serkin was not of flamboyant style; he did not scorch his audiences as did VLADIMIR HOROWITZ, nor did he drive them to their feet in an emotional frenzy as did ARTHUR RUBINSTEIN. Serkin's repertoire was conservative, extending from Bach through Brahms for the most part, and his style was that of a classicist. Transparency and penetration were his hallmarks, and listeners could easily detect depth of thought behind the music. He did not own the naturally fluent technique of a born virtuoso, and Serkin had to practice hard for his keyboard triumphs. Music writer Donal Henahan attributed Serkin's technique to a "lifetime of monastic labor." Serkin

claimed that he needed five hours to warm up sufficiently at the piano. In the end he was an excellent technician whose interpretive gifts were held in awe by colleagues and piano connoisseurs. His approach to music was intellectual, but not without lightness of touch and feeling in some pieces. Perhaps no pianist since Artur Schnabel was as respected an interpreter of Beethoven.

Serkin was born in Austria, and he studied piano as a boy in Vienna. He encountered composer Arnold Schoenberg as a teenager, and was swept up in the emerging modernist school. Later, Serkin faded away from Schoenberg and academic music generally. His next great influence was a more lasting one, coming in the person of Adolf Busch, the great German violinist. He lived with Busch and his family in Berlin as a sort of apprentice, and the two formed a chamber duo that lasted for 32 years. Serkin made his American debut in 1936 with the NEW YORK PHILHARMONIC under ARTURO TOSCANINI and settled in the United States. Busch, though he became a Swiss citizen, spent a great deal of time after that in the United States performing with Serkin. The two essentially co-founded the Marlboro Music Festival, though the official founding was credited to Busch. Serkin took over directorship of the festival when Busch died in 1952.

Serkin taught at the CURTIS INSTITUTE starting in 1938 and directed the school from 1968 to 1975. His students included his son PETER SERKIN, EUGENE ISTOMIN, and RICHARD GOODE. He played twice at the White House, in 1966 and 1970. President John F. Kennedy awarded him the Presidential Medal of Freedom. He was a member of the American Academy of Arts and Sciences, and the National Council on the Arts. He received honorary doctorates from numerous schools, including Harvard University and the NEW ENGLAND CONSERVATORY.

Sessions, Roger (1896–1985) *composer*

One of the giants of American composition, Roger Sessions seemed destined to be remembered primarily as an educator until the second half-century of his life. As a composer, he was respected by colleagues more than loved by audiences; a fellow composer once remarked that "everybody loves Roger Sessions except the public." Most of his works were composed between the ages of 50 and 75. No matter when they were written, Sessions sometimes had to wait a long time to hear them; his Violin Concerto languished for 25 years before LEONARD BERNSTEIN had it performed in his first season as music director of the NEW YORK PHILHARMONIC; the Symphony no. 6 waited 11 years (from 1966 to 1977) before getting a public reading from the Juilliard School Orchestra.

Sessions was a precocious youth who entered Harvard University at 14 and graduated in 1915. He later obtained a second degree from Yale University (1917). He studied composing with Horatio Parker and ERNEST BLOCH. Sessions started his institutional teaching career immediately upon leaving Yale, when he landed a job at Smith College. He remained at Smith for four years, then followed Bloch to Cleveland and worked for him at the CLEVELAND INSTITUTE OF MUSIC, where he remained until 1925. With the support of grants and fellowships from the Guggenheim Foundation, the Carnegie Foundation, and a Rome Prize, Sessions and his wife lived in Europe from 1925 to 1933. His work from this period includes the first piano sonata and first symphony. After his return Sessions gained a faculty position at Princeton University, starting in 1936. He moved to the University of California, Berkeley, from 1945 to 1953, then returned to Princeton until 1965. From 1966 to 1983 Sessions taught at the JUILLIARD SCHOOL. He lectured at Harvard in 1968–69.

Sessions shifted to high compositional gear during his years in California, and continuing until about 1970. From that period date six of his nine symphonies, the second and third piano sonatas, and his opera *Montezuma*. His work grew increasingly modernistic, and by the 1950s most of his output was completely atonal. However, there is a distinct lack of any academic or theoretical quality to his writing; Sessions's harmonic vocabulary

evolved naturally, through his urge to express human experience in new ways—he always felt that was the purpose of music.

Sessions continued composing to the end of his life. His Concerto for Orchestra dates from that period; it was commissioned by the BOSTON SYMPHONY ORCHESTRA and won a 1981 Pulitzer Prize. (Sessions had won a previous Pulitzer, in 1974, as a career award.) He was elected to the American Academy of Arts and Letters and the American Academy of Arts and Sciences. He won a Brandeis Creative Arts Award in 1958 and the MacDowell Medal in 1968.

Severance Hall

The performance venue of the CLEVELAND ORCHESTRA, Severance Hall opened in 1931 and was renovated between 1998 and 2000. The Cleveland Orchestra, founded in 1918, had led a somewhat itinerant life, moving from one home to another. The Severance Hall project was started by John Long Severance, president of the orchestra's Board of Trustees, and was intended as a gift to his wife. Elisabeth Severance died shortly after her husband's initial pledge, and the gift turned into a memorial

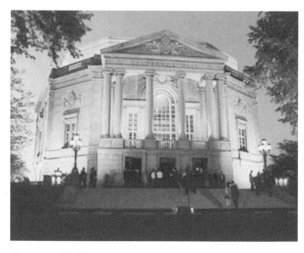

Severance Hall (Courtesy of the Cleveland Orchestra)

effort. The original hall cost $7 million. From the start, and continuing today, Severance Hall is widely regarded as one of the most beautiful of the old-style American concert halls. The much-needed renovation, which modernized all stage facilities, cost over $36 million.

Shaham, Gil (b. 1971) *violinist*

Gil Shaham was born in Champaign-Urbana, Illinois, but took his early studies in Jerusalem, Israel, appearing with the Jerusalem Philharmonic at age 10, then performed with ZUBIN MEHTA and the Israel Philharmonic the following year. He won the Claremont Competition, also in Israel, and was awarded a scholarship to the JUILLIARD SCHOOL, where he studied with DOROTHY DELAY. In 1989 he replaced violinist Itzhak Perlman on short notice at a concert with the London Symphony Orchestra, an appearance that made his career. Shaham toured with the PHILADELPHIA ORCHESTRA and CHRISTOPH ESCHENBACH in the 2003–4 season. He won a Grammy Award for his 1998 album *American Scenes* with ANDRÉ PREVIN.

Shapero, Harold (b. 1920) *composer*

A member of the informal "Stravinsky School," Harold Shapero studied piano in his early years, then composition with WALTER PISTON, PAUL HINDEMITH, and NADIA BOULANGER. Curiously, Shapero was more of a modernist in his early, Piston-influenced works than later, after he had studied with theoretical fundamentalist Boulanger. Shapero seemed particularly malleable during his formative periods, following one model after another before finding his own voice. Shapero was a friend and creative associate of two other Piston students, Arthur Berger and Irving Fine, and it was AARON COPLAND who christened the trio the "Stravinsky School." Shapero's most productive period was 1940–50; LEONARD BERNSTEIN conducted the premiere of his Symphony in 1948. In 1951 Brandeis University hired Shapero to start its music depart-

ment; he hired his friend Berger soon after getting started and remained at the school for 37 years.

Shapey, Ralph (1921–2002) *composer*

An original and fiercely independent composer, Ralph Shapey received no formal education beyond high school. He studied composition privately with STEFAN WOLPE. During high school he was conductor of the Philadelphia Youth Orchestra. He guest-conducted leading American orchestras from time to time, including the PHILADELPHIA ORCHESTRA and the CHICAGO SYMPHONY. Shapey's compositions incorporated modern harmonies within traditional formal structures. He considered himself a romanticist in spirit. A critic once wrote of him, "Shapey is not to be fit into any fashion, but be remembered as one of the best—and greatest—of the romantic radicals. Perhaps only Beethoven stormed the heavens with such ferocity." His *Concerto Fantastique* was chosen by the Pulitzer committee to receive a 1992 Pulitzer Prize, but in an unusual development the Pulitzer board overturned that decision and gave the prize to a work by WAYNE PETERSON instead. Shapey taught at the University of Chicago from 1964 to 1992. While there he founded the university's Contemporary Chamber Players, a group that still presents a four-concert season. Shapey left a large portfolio of compositions, most of which are scored for chamber groups of various sizes. He also wrote piano music, one symphony and other orchestral pieces, and works for solo instruments besides the piano.

Shaw, Robert (1916–1999) *conductor*

Renowned as America's greatest choral conductor, Robert Shaw also maintained a career on the orchestral podium. Shaw came from a family of evangelical preachers—his mother sang in the church choir and the family often sang hymns around the piano. Shaw's first job was organizer and conductor of the Fred Waring Glee Club, a choral group bearing the name of a radio personality in the 1930s; the ensemble was formed in 1938 and Shaw directed it until 1945. In 1943 the National Association of Composers and Conductors named Shaw "America's greatest choral conductor." He won a Guggenheim Fellowship in 1944. In 1941 he founded the Collegiate Chorale in New York, which he directed until 1954. He made his symphonic debut in 1946, conducting the Naumburg Orchestra, but remained primarily a choral conductor for many years afterward. That same year Shaw came to the attention of ARTURO TOSCANINI, conductor of the NBC SYMPHONY ORCHESTRA, who made Shaw his chorus manager. In 1948 he founded the 40-voice Robert Shaw Chorale, with which he toured until 1965, and with which he made several historic and popular recordings. The Chorale commissioned choral music from Benjamin Britten, AARON COPLAND, and SAMUEL BARBER.

As late as 1950, Shaw studied symphonic conducting with PIERRE MONTEUX and ARTUR RODZINSKI. He became associate conductor under GEORGE SZELL at the CLEVELAND ORCHESTRA from 1956 to 1967, in which position he organized the orchestra's chorus. He took over an orchestra of his own—the ATLANTA SYMPHONY ORCHESTRA—in 1967 and stayed there until 1988, when he was named music director emeritus and conductor laureate. He created the Atlanta Symphony Orchestra Chorus. Upon retiring from the orchestra, he founded the Robert Shaw Institute at Emory University, also in Atlanta.

Shaw's numerous contributions to choral singing and choral directing cannot be overestimated. He was made a member of the National Council on the Arts in 1979, and received the National Medal of Arts in 1992.

Sheng, Bright (b. 1955) composer

Sheng is a Chinese-American composer closely tied to Chinese musical traditions and deeply involved with American music institutions. He received his training in China and moved to New York in 1982, where he received graduate degrees at Queens College (1984) and Columbia University (1993). He

was composer in residence at the LYRIC OPERA OF CHICAGO from 1989 to 1992, and filled the same position for the SEATTLE SYMPHONY ORCHESTRA from 1992 to 1995. He serves on the faculty of the University of Michigan, Ann Arbor (since 1995). Sheng received a MacArthur Award in 2001. He earned fellowships from the Guggenheim, Rockefeller, and Naumburg Foundations in the early 1990s. He won a Kennedy Center Award in 1995. In 1999 Sheng was commissioned by President Bill Clinton to compose a piece of music to honor Chinese Premiere at a state dinner. YO-YO MA commissioned a cello concerto from Sheng, to be scored for traditional Chinese orchestra. He has guest-conducted a handful of leading American orchestras and is artistic adviser to YO-YO MA's Silk Road Project.

Shifrin, Seymour (1926–1979) composer

Seymour Shifrin attended the High School of Music and Art in New York, and as a teenager was given a private scholarship by WILLIAM SCHUMAN for composition lessons. He received degrees from Columbia University in 1947 and 1949. He then lectured at Columbia for a year before traveling to France on a Fulbright Scholarship to study with DARIUS MILHAUD. His two major university appointments were at the University of California, Berkeley, from 1952 to 1966, and Brandeis University from 1966 to 1979. Shifrin received two Guggenheim Fellowship awards (1956 and 1960), the Bearns Prize in 1949, and grants from the National Institute of Arts and Letters (1957) and the Koussevitsky Foundation (1965). His best-known pieces are the chamber work *Satires of Circumstance* and *Three Pieces for Orchestra*.

Shumsky, Oscar (1917–2000) violinist

A violin prodigy, Oscar Shumsky made his debut at age eight with the PHILADELPHIA ORCHESTRA and LEOPOLD STOKOWSKI. He entered the CURTIS INSTITUTE at age 11 and studied there for eight years.

He made an adult debut (aged 17) in New York in 1934. Shumsky joined the NBC Symphony Orchestra in 1939. As a conductor, Shumsky started with the Canadian National Festival Orchestra in 1959, and conducted the Westchester Symphony Orchestra. He taught at Curtis and the Peabody Conservatory, and joined the faculty of the JUILLIARD SCHOOL in 1953.

Sills, Beverly (b. 1929) *opera singer*

Born and raised in Brooklyn, New York, Beverly Sills grew up to be an opera diva despite her father's early resistance to her talent and ambition. She left home to join a touring opera company at age 15, only later receiving her father's blessing and financial support after he heard her perform. She made an official professional debut with the Philadelphia Civic Grand Opera Company in 1947. She joined the New York City Opera, the company with which she would be closely associated for 25 years, in 1955. Sills became the New York City Opera's star soprano, her successes and preferences influencing the company's repertoire. She had a terrific theatrical presence and a skilled, technically solid voice, if one not as beautiful as those of competing divas. Sills did not make her Metropolitan Opera debut, across the courtyard of Lincoln Center, until 1975, just five years before her retirement. She ascended to the general directorship of the New York City Opera in 1979, holding that position until 1989. She became chairman of the board at Lincoln Center in 1993.

Simon, Abbey (b. 1922) *pianist*

Abbey Simon entered the CURTIS INSTITUTE as a 10-year-old pianist, and studied with DAVID SAPERTON and HAROLD BAUER. He left Curtis in 1941, the same year he won a Naumburg Award, and made his New York debut at TOWN HALL that year. He has toured the world extensively, garnering spectacular reviews. Simon is known as a keyboard colorist, thoroughly in command of the piano's tonal possi-

bilities. He has recorded the complete piano music of Ravel and Chopin, as well as other solo and concerto repertoire. He taught at Indiana University from 1960 to 1974, and has also taught at the JUILLIARD SCHOOL and the University of Houston.

Skrowaczewski, Stanislaw (b. 1923) *conductor*

Stanislaw Skrowaczewski is an American conductor born in Poland who made his name conducting Polish orchestras. A prodigy of the piano and the podium, he conducted Beethoven's Piano Concerto no. 3 from the piano at age 13. He made his American conducting debut with the CLEVELAND ORCHESTRA in 1958. He conducted the NEW YORK PHILHARMONIC in 1960, filling in for DIMITRI MITROPOULOS. He was music director of the Minneapolis Symphony Orchestra (now the MINNESOTA Orchestra) from 1960 to 1979. He has composed four symphonies and other works.

Skyscrapers (1924)

Following the success of his "jazz pantomime" *Krazy Kat*, JOHN ALDEN CARPENTER continued his quest for a new American classical idiom with this ballet. It was premiered at the Metropolitan Opera, then enjoyed success in Europe. During the 1920s, in both America and Europe, modernism in music evoked urban qualities of industrialization and impersonalization. *Skyscrapers* fits into a program aesthetic along the same lines as music by Stravinsky and GEORGE ANTHEIL.

Slatkin, Felix (1915–1963) *violinist and conductor*

Husband of ELEANOR ALLER and father of LEONARD SLATKIN, Felix Slatkin attended the CURTIS INSTITUTE for studies with EFREM ZIMBALIST (violin) and FRITZ REINER (conducting). Interestingly, he played in the violin section of the St. Louis Symphony, the same orchestra later (and currently) directed by his son. He moved to Los Angeles in 1937, and, with his wife, played in the Hollywood studio orchestras. He founded the HOLLYWOOD STRING QUARTET in 1947 (with Aller in the cello chair).

Slatkin, Leonard (b. 1944) conductor

Born to musical parents (FELIX SLATKIN and ELEANOR ALLER), Leonard Slatkin became the conductor best known as the longtime leader of the St. Louis Symphony Orchestra and, later, of the NATIONAL SYMPHONY ORCHESTRA. He studied with JEAN MOREL at the JUILLIARD SCHOOL and made his debut conducting the Youth Symphony Orchestra of New York at CARNEGIE HALL. He became assistant conductor of the St. Louis Symphony in 1968, and Slatkin climbed the bureaucratic ladder of that organization, becoming in turn associate conductor, associate principal conductor, and principal guest conductor. For two years (1977–79) he was music director of the New Orleans Symphony Orchestra, then finally claimed the top job at St. Louis in 1979, where he remains today. Slatkin's dedication to the orchestra has created an ensemble remarkably responsive to his musical directives. He guest-conducts all over the world.

Society for American Music

Founded in 1975 as the Sonneck Society, after pioneering American musicologist Oscar Sonneck, the mission of the Society for American Music is "To stimulate the appreciation, performance, creation and study of American music in all its diversity, and the full range of activities and institutions associated with that music." The society understands American music to encompass all of North America, not only the United States. The group was spawned at an annual meeting of the Society for Ethnomusicology at Wesleyan College. Its own annual meetings have taken a broad selection of themes, from American instrument building to jazz. The society produces the quarterly journal *American Music,* published by the University of Illinois Press.

Solti, Georg (Sir) (1912–1997) conductor and pianist

Georg Solti's legacy as a conductor is so overwhelming that many people do not realize, or forget, that he was also a first-rank pianist. Solti himself might have preferred to forget, since he turned to the piano as a career track out of desperation, when he could not find conducting appointments. As a child, the piano was his first instrument, and Solti gave a recital at age 12. He entered the Liszt Academy in Budapest, Hungary, his homeland, while still a boy; he studied piano with Ernő Dohnányi and Béla Bartók, and studied composition with Zoltán Kodály. He graduated in 1930, still with little conducting experience, and he did not get much opportunity to stand on a podium until his debut in 1938, when he conducted Mozart's opera *The Marriage of Figaro* in Budapest. Until then he had worked as an assistant to other conductors, and in the percussion section of ARTURO TOSCANINI's orchestra at the Salzburg Festival.

Solti left Hungary when World War II broke out and he moved to Switzerland, where conducting jobs were even scarcer. At loose ends, he turned to the piano again, practiced assiduously, and won first prize in the Geneva International Competition in 1942. The prize money plus the five students allowed by the government kept him going for a few years. He gradually worked back into conducting in other European countries, gaining his first permanent appointment as music director of the Bavarian State Opera. In 1947 Solti signed a recording contract with Decca Records that was to last for 50 years, the longest exclusive recording agreement in history. In those early years, Solti recorded both as a conductor and a pianist.

His career rolling now, Solti built his reputation in Europe. He conducted at Richard Strauss's funeral. He made a British debut in 1949. He became music director of the Frankfurt Opera in 1952. In 1953 Solti conducted in the United States for the first time, at the SAN FRANCISCO OPERA. In 1961 Solti became music director of Covent Garden in London, with the intention of turning it into the world's foremost opera house. He remained at that position for 10 years.

In 1969 Solti moved to America and accepted the directorship of the CHICAGO SYMPHONY ORCHESTRA. Already an internationally respected institution, under Solti's 22-year reign the Chicago Symphony became the superstar of American orchestras, universally lauded as one of the world's great ensembles. Solti recorded nearly the entire standard orchestral repertoire in Chicago. The relationships between Solti, the orchestra, and the city were love affairs; he proclaimed himself a fulfilled man, and the city built statues in his honor. Solti was a busy conductor during his Chicago years, holding positions simultaneously with several European institutions.

The Solti sound, both in the Chicago years and throughout his conducting career, is characterized by relentless energy, thrilling rhythmic propulsion, astonishing accuracy within the huge ensemble, and massive sonic force when needed. His tempos tended to be quick. Even short excerpts of Solti's recordings are marked with his dynamism and exuberance. Music writer James R. Oestrich wrote of his Chicago work in the *New York Times,* "There suddenly seemed something new under the sun: an orchestra that could grasp those huge, complex works whole and, with remarkable sustained virtuosity and power, render them as gleaming monolithic unities, seemingly perfect in every detail and cumulatively overwhelming." By the mid-1970s, the Chicago Symphony sold out entire seasons before opening night.

Solti's physical style of conducting was called graceless, but it was undeniably energetic. He stuck to the standard repertoire for the most part, happy to explore the first half of the 20th century, but, in his words, "I leave it to the next generation to explore after 1950." In his life, Solti recorded over 250 discs and 40 operas, and received 32 Grammy Awards, more than any other musician of any genre.

Sonneck, Oscar (1873–1928) *musicologist*

The first great American musicologist, Oscar Sonneck trained as a musician in Germany from a young age, then returned to the United States in 1899. He was determined to publish "a correct and adequate historical presentation" of the performing arts in America, a daunting task in a still-young country that had not kept methodical records. Very few biographies had been published; church records were sparse; music journals did not exist for the most part. Sonneck turned to newspapers as the most reliable historical records, and he spent two years examining back issues of every American newspaper he could get his hands on, plucking bits of information from concert notices and advertisements. Three major books resulted from this exhaustive process: *A Bibliography of Early Secular American Music* (1905), *Early Concert-Life in America* (1907), and *Early Opera in America* (1915). These works, and many of Sonneck's other scholarly innovations, were greeted with indifference by society at large (which might be expected), and even by the musical establishment.

In 1902 Sonneck became head of the music division of the Library of Congress, where he curated a tremendous collection of books and music manuscripts. He resigned from the Library in 1917, becoming director of publications at music publisher G. SCHIRMER. Schirmer was at that time publisher of the MUSICAL QUARTERLY (now published by Oxford University Press), which Sonneck had founded and edited since 1915. Sonneck became vice president of Schirmer in 1921.

Sonneck's musicological work was unique and groundbreaking. No organized effort had been made before him to present an historical reference of American music, nor had the American musical society even conceived of such a thing. Sonneck was an entirely original force in American research at the turn of the 20th century, and his work remained an unequaled (and largely unappreciated) body of scholarship for decades. As late as the 1960s, musicology research in America was still directed toward Europe, and young scholars wishing to take up the threads laid down by Oscar Sonneck risked their academic careers. The Sonneck Society (now called SOCIETY FOR AMERICAN MUSIC) was formed in

1975 to honor and continue the type of research he initiated.

Sousa, John Philip (1854–1932) *composer and conductor*

Born of immigrant parents, John Philip Sousa became the foremost promoter of patriotic band music in American history. He learned to play violin, flute, and several brass instruments as a child, and his unruly temperament nearly led him to the life of a traveling circus musician when his father enrolled him as an apprentice member of the U.S. Marine Band. Sousa was 13 then, and although he was discharged in 1875, Sousa returned to the marines as leader of the band in 1880. In 1892 he left the service and formed his own civilian band. Sousa was a composer of brassy and stirring marches. His best-known work is undoubtedly "Stars and Stripes Forever," which he composed in 1896. He led his band on four international tours before joining the U.S. Naval Reserve during World War I. He resumed touring with his own band in 1919, and continued conducting up to his death in 1932.

Sousa is not generally considered a classical composer, and his patriotic marches certainly do not derive from the European symphonic tradition. Yet he was an accomplished composer in a strictly formal sense and unquestionably a skilled conductor. Of his 300 works, about a third are marches. He also composed 10 operas, several orchestral suites, and *The Last Crusade* scored for orchestra, choir, and organ, his most ambitious work. He wrote novels as well. Sousa received several honorary degrees.

Sowerby, Leo (1895–1968) *composer and organist*

Leo Sowerby was a composer and organist who won a 1946 Pulitzer Prize for his cantata *Canticle in the Sun.* He studied piano as a child and studied at the American Conservatory in Chicago. He was awarded the first Rome Prize, which led to three years' study in Italy. He served a long tenure on the faculty of the American Conservatory (1925–62), working as organist and choirmaster at an Episcopal cathedral during most of that time as well. Sowerby was elected to the National institute of Arts and Letters.

Spalding, Albert (1888–1953) *violinist*

Born in Chicago, Albert Spalding received violin training in Italy, and made his debut in Paris at age 14. His U.S. debut came at CARNEGIE HALL in 1908. One of the first American violinists to gain an international following, Spalding met Camille Saint-Saëns, Eugène Ysaÿe, and Joseph Joachim— legendary European violinists each.

Spano, Robert (b. 1961) *conductor*

Born in Ohio, conductor Robert Spano grew up in a musical family and played piano, violin, and flute as a boy. He studied at the OBERLIN CONSERVATORY, where he now is professor of conducting. Spano also studied with MAX RUDOLF at the CURTIS INSTITUTE. He has directed the conducting fellowship program at the TANGLEWOOD MUSIC CENTER since 1998. Spano is currently director of the BROOKLYN PHILHARMONIC ORCHESTRA (since 1996) and the ATLANTA SYMPHONY ORCHESTRA (since 2001). He was assistant conductor of the BOSTON SYMPHONY ORCHESTRA from 1990 to 1993, and has guest-conducted in Cleveland, Philadelphia, Chicago, and Los Angeles.

Speculum Musicae

This chamber group was founded in 1972 by pianist URSULA OPPENS to promote modern music. The name means "a mirror of music," revealing the group's intent to discover and faithfully reproduce the composer's wishes. Seven to 10 performers make up the ensemble, which does not use a music director or conductor.

Spoleto Festival

Founded in 1958 in Spoleto, Italy, the Spoleto Festival is formally titled the FESTIVAL OF TWO WORLDS. It was started by composer GIAN CARLO MENOTTI. Two versions of this festival exist, the original, which still operates in Spoleto, and a U.S. spin-off located in Charleston, South Carolina. Perhaps incongruously, the U.S. festival is almost always called the Spoleto Festival, while the festival in Spoleto is almost always called the Festival of Two Worlds. The original intent of the festival was to present musical dramas, but the programming has expanded to include chamber music and recitals in both locations, while still maintaining some emphasis on theater pieces. THOMAS SCHIPPERS was an artistic director and music director in Italy until 1975; Menotti was involved until about 1965. The Charleston festival has several artistic managers, including CHARLES WADSWORTH, who directs the chamber music programming.

Lewis Spratlan (Courtesy of Lewis Spratlan; Photo by Frank Ward)

Spratlan, Lewis (b. 1940) *composer*

Lewis Spratlan is a composer who has drawn on an unusual range of influences, from academic classical to jazz, from world music to minimalists. He studied at Yale University and Tanglewood, and won a 2000 Pulitzer Prize for his opera *Life Is a Dream*. He was awarded a Guggenheim Fellowship in 1981. He teaches at Amherst College.

Starker, Janos (b. 1924) *cellist*

Born in Hungary, cellist Janos Starker was principal cellist of the Budapest Philharmonic Orchestra before settling in the United States in 1948. In America, like so many other cellists, he gained renown as an orchestra player before devoting more time to a solo career. He held the principal cello chair in the DALLAS SYMPHONY ORCHESTRA, the orchestra of the METROPOLITAN OPERA, and the CHICAGO SYMPHONY ORCHESTRA under FRITZ REINER, with whom Starker had worked at the Metropolitan. Starker stayed in Chicago for longer than he had intended, in order to finance his family's escape from Hungary during its revolution of 1956. In 1958 he finally escaped the constraints and relative anonymity of orchestra playing, beginning to teach at Indiana University, Bloomington, while veering musically toward chamber music and the solo repertoire. He has played with several leading chamber ensembles, and in 1968 he performed the premiere of the Cello Concerto of Miklos Rosza. He also commissioned the Cello Concerto of ROY HARRIS. Starker has a strong attack, and plays with a musical style that might be called more severe than lyrical.

Steinberg, William (1899–1978) *conductor*

Born in Germany, William Steinberg immigrated to the United States in 1936. His training and early appointments were in Europe, where he conducted new music more enthusiastically than he would later in his career. He was lured to the United States partly by ARTURO TOSCANINI, who installed him as associate conductor of the NBC SYMPHONY ORCHESTRA, and partly by diminishing career opportunities in Germany during the emergence of Nazism. While working with the NBC orchestra under Toscanini, Steinberg guest-conducted other orchestras. He led the SAN FRANCISCO OPERA from 1944 to 1948. Not shy about taking on multiple responsibilities, even when they were separated by great distances, Steinberg assumed the directorship of the BUFFALO PHILHARMONIC from 1945 to 1953. In Buffalo, he raised the orchestra's level partly by importing European musicians.

His next appointment was the one for which Steinberg is best remembered: he was music director of the PITTSBURGH SYMPHONY ORCHESTRA from 1952 to 1976. During these years, characteristically, Steinberg filled his plate with other work, notably as music director of the London Philharmonic, senior guest conductor of the NEW YORK PHILHARMONIC, and music director of the BOSTON SYMPHONY ORCHESTRA. Each of these three additional jobs occurred while Steinberg was leading the Pittsburgh orchestra.

Steinberg was a solid, staid, undemonstrative conductor who drew attention to the music, not to himself. Music writer HAROLD C. SCHONBERG wrote of him, "His is a calm, logical beat, and he makes music in a calm, logical well-proportioned manner." He had an impish sense of humor, though, and was not beyond surprising his players and audiences. During one outdoor concert threatened by poor weather he played Beethoven's Symphony no. 9 in reverse order, starting with the fourth movement, so that the audience might hear that glorious choral movement, at least, before the rain started.

Steinberg retired to California and donated his books and scores to the University of Pittsburgh.

Stern, Isaac (1920–2001) violinist

Born in the Ukraine, Isaac Stern was brought to the United States when he was one year old, and became one of history's great violinists. He made his debut with the SAN FRANCISCO SYMPHONY when he was 15, and studied at the SAN FRANCISCO CONSERVATORY. That year he performed with the LOS ANGELES PHILHARMONIC. He gave two important New York performances, in 1937 and 1939, with further study in San Francisco between them. The first New York concert drew mixed reviews, and some negative comments unsettled the young Stern. He considered becoming a concertmaster, for which position he had offers, but he decided to follow his instinct and persevere. Later in life, Stern related that the second New York concert garnered rave reviews, but he probably had not played as well. Nonetheless, after the second New York concert, Stern had completed his formal training and launched his touring career.

Sol Hurok, the leading impresario for classical artists at that time, began representing Stern, and the violinist became one of the busiest touring musicians of the era. In one seven-month tour, Stern played 120 concerts—more than one every second day. He played for Allied troops during World War II and made his European debut (outside the U.S.O. stages) in 1948. By the late 1950s Stern had toured the Soviet Union (the first American violinist to do so), South America, Japan, Israel, Australia, and most European countries. Stern's passion for playing outran Hurok's passion for booking him, and the manager futilely begged the violinist to ease his schedule. Stern formed a trio with Eugene Istomin (piano) and Leonard Rose (cello); the three performed together from 1961 to 1984. Stern's other great chamber music collaboration was in the quartet format, with EMANUEL AX (piano), JAIME LAREDO (violin and viola), and YO-YO MA (cello).

Stern made his first recordings in 1945, and left a huge discography that represents a wide-ranging artistic legacy. In 1984 the record label CBS Masterworks named Stern its artist laureate, the first time such a designation had been created for a recording musician. Stern also worked in Hollywood, playing the soundtracks for movies featuring famous violinists as characters, including *Humoresque* (1946), *Tonight We Sing* (1953), and *Fiddler on the Roof* (1971).

Stern could play anything he wanted on the violin, but his instrumental technique remained always at the service of the music. He was a warm interpreter, and off the stage he was a humanitarian and cultural ambassador. He recorded actively, exclusively for the Sony Classical (formerly CBS Masterworks) label, which issued a 44-disc retrospective in 1995. Stern was largely responsible for saving CARNEGIE HALL in 1960, when the historic building was slated for destruction. He helped convince New York City to purchase the hall, which then came under protection as an historical landmark. In 1997 the main concert hall of Carnegie's three performance spaces was renamed ISAAC STERN AUDITORIUM. Over the course of his career, Stern himself performed over 200 times in Carnegie. Following his leadership role in saving the building, Stern became president of the Carnegie Hall Corporation; as president, he played an important role in Carnegie's restoration in 1986, and he helped produce the centenary celebration of 1991. It is not too much to say that Stern is remembered as much by some for saving Carnegie Hall as he is for his concertizing.

Stern was an important part of the formation of the National Endowment for the Arts, and was on its advisory board after its creation in 1964. Unsurprisingly, Stern's obituary was carried on page one of the *New York Times*.

Still, William Grant (1895–1978) *composer and conductor*

A groundbreaking African-American composer and conductor, William Grant Still studied with GEORGE CHADWICK and EDGARD VARÈSE. In 1931 his *Afro-American Symphony* was premiered by the Rochester Philharmonic, becoming the first orchestral work by a black composer to be played by a leading orchestra. Still composed for film but was primarily interested in pure classical music. He was the first African American to conduct a major orchestra, the LOS ANGELES PHILHARMONIC, in 1936.

Stock, Frederick (1872–1942) *conductor*

Frederick Stock had his brightest moments in Chicago. He was affiliated with the Theodore Thomas Orchestra (later the CHICAGO SYMPHONY ORCHESTRA), starting as assistant conductor in 1899. By 1903 he was conducting all out-of-town performances, and when Thomas died in 1905, Stock took over the musical directorship of the orchestra, remaining in charge until his death in 1942. During that exceptionally long tenure Stock continued Thomas's work of creating a virtuoso ensemble, and he was adventurous in programming modern works. Russian composer Sergey Prokofiev gave the American premiere of his Piano Concerto no. 3 in Chicago with Stock conducting.

Stokowski, Leopold (1882–1977) *conductor*

Leopold Stokowski was born in London to parents of uncertain lineage, despite confident assertions in some references that they were Polish and Irish. Even Stokowski's name is believed by some to be a status-seeking Europeanization of the simpler Leo Stokes. If true, the name change would be characteristic of Stokowski's sense of drama and stage effectiveness, which shone through his American career. Stokowski is remembered as a superstar—indeed, classical music's first conducting superstar. He dominated the stage and his audiences, actually walking off if listeners made too much noise in the hall. His experiments with lighting, in which house lights were turned off entirely and the concert hall was illuminated by a giant spotlight positioned beneath the conducting podium, seemed designed both to enhance the music's atmosphere and to enlarge his own persona. (Concerning audience noise, Stokowski once tactfully stated: "A painter paints his pictures on canvas. But musicians paint their pictures on silence. We provide the music, and you provide the silence.")

He made his early career in England, primarily as an organist and choirmaster, after being the youngest student ever to enroll in the Royal Academy of Music, at age 13. He first came to the United States in 1905 to work at St. Bartholomew's Church in New York. After three years Stokowski returned to Europe hoping to launch a conducting career, and made his Paris conducting debut in 1908. He parlayed this scant experience into an appointment as music director of the CINCINNATI SYMPHONY ORCHESTRA, which lasted from 1909 to 1912. In 1912 he accepted his signature appointment as music director of the PHILADELPHIA ORCHESTRA. (He demanded, and received, a large salary in Philadelphia; along with the money he received criticism for his hard-nosed negotiating.) It was Stokowski who first defined and created the "Philadelphia sound," characterized by lushness and sensuality. He was a pioneer in several ways, not least in rearranging orchestra seating and encouraging the string players to bow out of unison, creating a seamless, full sound. He applied the same asynchronous technique to the breathing of the wind players. Stokowski's interest in acoustics and the concert hall's contribution to the orchestra sound was unusual for his day. "Every hall is different," he said. "One must adapt oneself to the conditions: how it sounds when it is empty, how it sounds when it's full of people. A concert hall is a musical instrument."

Stokowski is uniformly regarded as the conductor who made the Philadelphia Orchestra into a leading international institution. The Russian composer Sergey Rachmaninoff, who used the orchestra for some of his important premieres, asserted that it was the best of orchestras. Stokowski resigned from the Philadelphia Orchestra in 1936, in the prime of his career, partly because of disagreements with the orchestra board over programming. Stokowski was an enthusiastic, even insistent supporter of contemporary music, often planning more modern music than his audiences or bosses wanted to hear. He gave hundreds of world premieres—more even than the legendary SERGE KOUSSEVITZKY while leading the BOSTON SYMPHONY ORCHESTRA, though Koussevitzky was more personally involved with unknown composers, so he more directly influenced their careers. Stokowski tended toward new music of established composers.

As a showman, Stokowski was more flamboyant than LEONARD BERNSTEIN. Many conductors work without a score, conducting from memory; Stokowski turned the skill into a gimmick by loading up the music stand with scores before the concert, then sweeping them to the floor before beginning the performance. He led without a baton, further tossing tradition to the wind. Stokowski wasn't above altering scores on stage and in the recording studio to make them, in his mind, better—and he accepted harsh criticism for this practice. He would add or remove parts, changing the character of the orchestration. He once said, "You must realize that Beethoven and Brahms did not understand instruments. Composers like Ravel, Debussy, and Mozart did." He himself dabbled in nearly every instrument, and claimed that his broad knowledge helped him communicate with his players.

Stokowski recorded actively over a period of 60 years, being fascinated with the medium. (Optimistically, he signed a six-year recording contract on his 94th birthday.) Stokowski became a national figure when he acted the part of the conductor in the Walt Disney animated film *Fantasia*.

Stokowski's relationship with the Philadelphia Orchestra did not end amicably; he walked off the stage after the final performance of his final year without taking any bows, and it was 19 years before he returned as a guest conductor. Immediately after Philadelphia, Stokowski's energy was undimmed, onstage and off. In 1945, at the age of 63, he married the 21-year-old American heiress Gloria Vanderbilt, with whom he had two sons; the couple was later divorced. He created and conducted the All-American Youth Orchestra and engaged in short stints in the 1940s with the New York City Symphony (created by him), the Hollywood Bowl Symphony Orchestra (also created by him), and the NBC SYMPHONY ORCHESTRA (with ARTURO TOSCANINI). He performed with the New York Philharmonic, though never assumed directorship of the orchestra. His next permanent position was as music director of the HOUSTON SYMPHONY ORCHESTRA (1955–60). In 1961 he made his METROPOLITAN OPERA debut on crutches, having recently broken his hip. More orchestra creation followed, as Stokowski founded the AMERICAN SYMPHONY ORCHESTRA, and conducted it from 1962 to 1972. He returned to London in 1972, elderly but active, and continued to work until just before his death.

Stokowski leaves a mixed legacy. His showmanship in a conservative and tradition-bound field such as classical music was disliked by many. He not only scolded audiences for their noisy behavior, but harangued them about issues unrelated to the concert at hand; such boorish behavior created antagonism. Furthermore, his directorship of major American orchestras on the basis of relatively little experience made him appear as a charlatan to his detractors. But his elevating effect on the Philadelphia Orchestra cannot be denied, and his relentless advocacy of new music provided exposure to huge and important portions of the orchestral repertoire. He profoundly impacted the musical life of America during the 1920s and 1930s.

Stoltzman, Richard (b. 1942) clarinettist

Richard Stoltzman is the preeminent clarinettist in America. He grew up in Omaha, San Francisco, and Cincinnati. His first instrument, the saxophone, he learned from early lessons with his father. He attended Ohio State University, studying both music and mathematics, then at Yale University. Stoltzman attended the MARLBORO MUSIC FESTIVAL for 10 years (1966–76), making contacts that would mold his career. Stoltzman made his debut in 1973, and in 1976 he won an Avery Fisher Award. In 1973 he became a founding member of the chamber group Tashi, led by PETER SERKIN, whom Stoltzman met at Marlboro.

Stoltzman's relationship to his instrument goes beyond mastery; he is an innovator of the clarinet's possibilities as a solo instrument. His positioning of the clarinet at the center of the concert stage can be likened to GREGOR PIATIGORSKY's elevation of the cello as a headlining instrument. Stoltzman presented the first clarinet recital in the history of Carnegie Hall. In 1986 he became the first clarinettist to win all Avery Fisher Prize (as distinct from his earlier Avery Fisher Award). The clarinet has been a lead jazz instrument since Benny Goodman, and Stoltzman does perform jazz, but he is not a crossover artist with the same multigenre commitment as, say, YO-YO MA or WYNTON MARSALIS. Stoltzman founded an alliance of performing arts institutions to commission new clarinet works.

Stringmusic

Composed by MORTON GOULD for the NATIONAL SYMPHONY ORCHESTRA, and dedicated to conductor MSTISLAV ROSTROPOVICH on his departure from that orchestra, Stringmusic won a 1995 Pulitzer Prize. The previous year, Gould had been awarded a Kennedy Center Honor for his contributions to American culture. Stringmusic was premiered by the National Symphony Orchestra on March 10, 1994, at the KENNEDY CENTER.

Strube, Gustav (1867–1953) conductor

Born in Germany, Gustav Strube became the first conductor of the BALTIMORE SYMPHONY ORCHESTRA in 1916, remaining at that post until 1930. He taught at the Peabody Conservatory, and also in Baltimore. Earlier, he conducted the BOSTON POPS intermittently between 1898 and 1912.

Stucky, Steven (b. 1949) composer

Steven Stucky was appointed composer in residence at the LOS ANGELES PHILHARMONIC in 1988, and his tenure represents the longest composer residency in the history of American orchestras. He is an expert on the Polish composer Witold Lutosławski, and wrote the book *Lutoslawski and His Music* in 1981. Stucky's music has been performed by innumerable leading American orchestras, and the recording of his *Cradle Songs* won a Grammy Award in 2000.

Subotnick, Morton (b. 1933) *composer*

Morton Subotnick is a pioneer composer of music created for electronics. Most of Subotnick's compositions call for a digital instrument of some kind in combination with an acoustic instrument, or a computer part, or innovative processing that determines the order of musical events. He is part electrical engineer, part inventor, and part musician. Subotnick received a master's degree from the University of Denver in 1958, and a master's in 1960 from Mills College. He was a fellow at the Institute for Advanced Studies in Princeton (the same institution at which Albert Einstein worked) from 1959 to 1960. He taught at Mills College (1959–66) and New York University (1966–69) before moving to the California Institute of the Arts in 1969, where he currently holds the MEL POWELL Chair in the Composition, Theory, and New Music department.

Subotnick's most popular work to date has been *Silver Apples of the Moon,* composed in 1967 for synthesizer and commissioned by Nonesuch Records—the first classical work commissioned by a recording company. Subotnick wrote the work specifically for home listening, and crafted its two movements to fit on the two sides of a vinyl LP. Many of Subotnick's subsequent works involved the use of his own innovations in altering voltage and recording it. However, since 1985 he has been working with commercially available synthesizer equipment.

Switched-On Bach

A 1968 hit record produced by composer WENDY CARLOS, *Switched-On Bach* was a rendering of pieces by Johann Sebastian Bach using synthesizers, which were new, relatively primitive, and difficult to program at the time. Carlos followed up the success of the LP with *The Well-Tempered Synthesizer,* which featured other baroque composers, and *Switched-On Bach II* and *Switched-On Brandenburgs* in the late 1970s. All four albums were released as a box set in 1999. In 1992 the original *Switched-On Bach* was reworked with modern digital instruments and released as *Switched-On Bach 2000.*

Carlos did not merely exploit new technology; she helped develop it as an assistant to Robert Moog, who developed the pioneering electronic instrument, the Moog Synthesizer. The album represented the first popular application of synthesizer technology in an era in which academic music (both acoustic and electronic) had alienated classical music audiences and driven them from the concert hall. *Switched-On Bach* not only boosted society's understanding of synthesizers, but increased its awareness and appreciation of Bach.

Symphony Hall

The performance home of the BOSTON SYMPHONY ORCHESTRA, Symphony Hall was inaugurated as the New Boston Music Hall in 1893, funded by Henry Lee Higginson, founder of the Boston Symphony. (The name changed in 1900.) The hall is rectangular and severe in appearance, appropriate to an upstanding New England institution, and its strict design is belied by a warm, responsive sound. Wallace Savine, a Harvard physicist, designed the hall's acoustics, and in so doing created the first performance space designed scientifically. Savine became a founder of the science of acoustics. Revolutionary in its time, today Symphony Hall is still regarded as one of the world's great concert halls.

Szell, George (1897–1970) *conductor*

One of the great American conductors, George Szell was born in Budapest, Hungary, and grew up in Vienna, Austria. A prodigy of prodigies, Szell corrected his mother's mistakes on the piano at age two, started playing the piano and composing very early, and completed his formal study of music at age 12. In Vienna he came under the wing of Richard Robert, who had taught RUDOLF SERKIN. Robert gave him concert opportunities as a child without overexposing or exploiting him. Szell made a concert tour of Europe at age 11 and was called "the new Mozart." While it was often speculated that Szell was ultimately headed for the conductor's podium, as a child and young man he was a pianist and composer. At the age of 14 he signed an exclusive 10-year agreement with a music publisher. He was 16 when he finally got a chance to conduct, filling in for the ailing director of a resort orchestra where Szell's family spent summers. Following that modest but successful debut, Szell climbed quickly up the institutional hierarchy until he was conducting the German Opera in Prague.

In the 1930s Szell's career became international. He made his U.S. debut with the St. Louis Symphony Orchestra in 1930. In 1936 he first conducted the Concertgebouw Orchestra of Amsterdam, with which he was to continue a lifelong association. From 1936 to 1938 he led the Scottish Orchestra, following SIR JOHN BARBIROLLI, who departed that orchestra for the NEW YORK PHILHARMONIC. In 1939 Szell and his wife settled in New York, and he lived for the rest of his life in the United States. In New York, Szell taught at the MANNES COLLEGE OF MUSIC and made his New York conducting debut with the NBC SYMPHONY ORCHESTRA—four concerts at the invitation of ARTURO TOSCANINI. Between 1942 and 1946 he became one of the most important conductors at the METROPOLITAN OPERA.

In 1946 Szell accepted his most important (and final) permanent appointment, music director of the CLEVELAND ORCHESTRA. Szell extended an already illustrious line of music directors in Cleveland, the fourth since the orchestra's founding in 1918. Three others have followed him, and in that group of seven most people regard Szell as having "made" the orchestra into the world-class institution it is. He expanded the player roster (after firing 12 of the 94 musicians he inherited) and

began touring the orchestra internationally. He combined solid European tradition with the dazzling technical capacity of an American-trained orchestra to create an unequaled transparency of sound and depth of interpretation. Szell was not associated with new music, but he did program some 20th-century repertoire. His strong areas were within the standard orchestral repertoire from Haydn to Strauss, but he also conducted the music of Americans MORTON GOULD, LUKAS FOSS, PETER MENNIN, AARON COPLAND, HOWARD HANSON, SAMUEL BARBER, and others.

Szell was a notoriously old-school tyrant on the podium. He idolized Toscanini, and emulated the Italian conductor's perfectionism and mercilessness. Szell was famous for sharpening his batons—to make them light and better balanced, it must be said, but the image conveys his antagonistic and humorless relationship with his orchestra. He believed in total immersion in the musical score, from which egoless realm truth and beauty might emerge. He said that a conductor must "think with the heart and feel with the brain," an image that conveys his ideal synergy of thought and feeling. Szell was a fastidious conductor who honed the Cleveland sound into a model of transparency. He seemed to assign precise values to every element of music and reveal those values with perfect clarity to the listener. In pursuit of this perfection Szell was more than willing to sacrifice niceties in the rehearsal hall; he did not know many of his players' names and habitually delivered caustic and profane instructions. Even at home, Szell was said to correct his wife's casual whistling.

Szell was a chevalier in the French Legion of Honor, and was awarded honorary doctorates from Case Western Reserve University and Oberlin College, both in Cleveland.

Szigeti, Joseph (1892–1973) violinist

Born in Budapest, Hungary, Joseph Szigeti became an American citizen in 1951. Trained in Europe, Szigeti was performing in public by the age of 10 and made his debut in Berlin in 1905 at age 13. A London debut followed two years later, and Szigeti settled in that city for a period. He made his American debut at New York's CARNEGIE HALL in 1925. He toured internationally after that and settled in the United States in 1940. He became an American citizen in 1951; keeping his American citizenship, Szigeti settled in Switzerland after 1960, where he became a semiretired writer who emerged occasionally to serve on competition juries.

Szigeti was rarely credited with producing a beautiful or sensuous violin tone, and his best work occurred when playing the classicists (Beethoven and Brahms, for example), and modern music of his time. Several 20th-century composers, including Béla Bartók, Sergey Prokofiev, and ERNEST BLOCH, wrote works for Szigeti.

Tanglewood Music Center

Formerly the Berkshire Music Center, Tanglewood is the summer home of the BOSTON SYMPHONY ORCHESTRA. The summer season features concerts for the public and an advanced music curriculum for budding artists. A reported 20 percent of American orchestra musicians are Tanglewood alumni. The BSO began performing in the Berkshires in 1936 and gave its first concert in Tanglewood in 1937. The Berkshire Music Center began formal operation in 1940. In 1986 the Boston Symphony acquired land surrounding the center, nearly doubling the size of the campus. Currently four performing spaces are maintained: a small theater, the Koussevitzky Music Shed, a small chamber music hall, and the Seiji Ozawa Hall. While musicians regard Tanglewood as a kind of postgraduate learning experience, regular music lovers and tourists are attracted to Tanglewood for its superb concerts featuring the greatest classical artists of the day.

Tashi

Tashi is a clarinet quintet founded as a quartet in 1973 by PETER SERKIN. Its members are RICHARD STOLTZMAN (clarinet), IDA KAVAFIAN (violin), Theodore Arm (violin), Steve Tenenbom (viola), and Fred Sherry (cello).

Taub, Robert (b. 1955) *pianist*

Robert Taub, who began playing as a child, studied with Jacob Lateiner from the JUILLIARD SCHOOL faculty. Taub attended Princeton University, where he graduated in 1977. He did graduate work at the Juilliard School. He won the International New Music Competition in 1978, the Peabody-Mason Award in 1981, and a Martha Baird Rockefeller Grant in 1981. Taub is more an intellectual pianist than a virtuoso, but he possesses top-flight technical resources. His specialties lie far from the thundering romantic literature favored by virtuosos. Taub focused on the Beethoven piano sonatas early in his career, performing the complete cycle in Princeton between 1994 and 1997. At that time Taub was artist in residence at Princeton's Institute for Advanced Study, the first musician to hold that position. He has recorded the Beethoven Sonatas and continues to perform them. Additionally, Taub is committed to modern music. He has premiered many of MILTON BABBITT's works, and he also premiered the Two Piano Concerto by MEL POWELL. He made the first recording of the Piano Concerto of ROGER SESSIONS.

Taub is currently visiting professor at Kingston University in London.

Taylor, Deems (1885–1966) *composer*

One of the most successful American composers during his time, Deems Taylor had no trouble getting his music published and performed. However, his works have not endured in the standard repertoire. He studied piano in his early years and attended New York University, from which he graduated in 1906. His first profession was music criticism Taylor was the music critic for *New York World* in the early 1920s, and he edited *Musical America* in the late 1920s. His voice gained fame when he was the intermission commentator at NEW YORK PHILHARMONIC radio broadcasts between 1936 and 1943. His writing was respected from the start, and Taylor was elected to both the National Institute of Arts and Letters and the American Academy of Arts and Letters (1924 and 1935, respectively).

Taylor wrote seven operas, a film score, and choral and orchestral music. His style derived from European traditions of the 19th century, and he was firmly opposed to 12-tone theory and any sort of academic music. His resistance to modernism made his music accessible, and his skills made it popular, but its lack of defining style made it transient. The METROPOLITAN OPERA, which often produced Taylor's stage works in the late 1920s and early 1930s, never does today, and modern concert audiences have no exposure to Taylor.

Temirkanov, Yuri (b. 1938) *conductor*
A Russian, Yuri Temirkanov built his early career after winning the Soviet All-Union Conductors' Competition in 1968. He served as music director of the Leningrad (now St. Petersburg) Philharmonic and chief conductor of the Kirov Opera and Ballet Theater. He began conducting the Royal Philharmonic Orchestra in London in 1980, becoming its music director in 1992. Temirkanov is music director of the BALTIMORE SYMPHONY ORCHESTRA, which he joined in 1999. The Baltimore Symphony was the first American orchestra to perform in the Soviet Union (1987).

Thalberg, Sigismond (1812–1871) *composer and pianist*
Sigismond Thalberg was a German pianist and composer who was generally regarded as one of the two greatest piano virtuosos in Europe during the mid-19th century, the other being Franz Liszt. Thalberg and Liszt dueled in a famous concert con-

frontation to determine who was the better, the diplomatic verdict being that Thalberg was the best pianist and Liszt the *only* one. Liszt never visited the United States, despite his historically intrepid tours to the far corners of Europe, but Thalberg brought his act to America and lived in the United States for a few years. He gave his first U.S. concerts in the 1850s, to general acclaim. As such, he can be regarded as the first of the many European virtuosos to dazzle audiences in American concert halls until American music schools began turning out homegrown artists. Thalberg's playing was a bit gimmicky: he famously created transcriptions of operas in which the two thumbs carried the melody while the outer fingers rippled elaborate ornaments above and below it, creating a three-handed effect. Thalberg's reputation was not damaged when this trick was uncovered, though, as his general technique and tone production were at the top level in all music. A review from an 1856 recital in New York lauded "the wonderful ease and smoothness with which the ceaseless shower of notes dropped from his almost motionless wrists." In all, Thalberg gave 56 concerts in New York between 1856 and 1858.

Thomas, Augusta Read (b. 1964) *composer*
Currently the composer in residence of the CHICAGO SYMPHONY ORCHESTRA (through 2006), Augusta Thomas also teaches at Northwestern University. Her chamber opera *Ligeia* won the International Orpheus Prize. Her 1999 work *Aurora* was commissioned by the Berlin Philharmonic Orchestra.

Thomas, Michael Tilson (b. 1944) *conductor*
One of the most accomplished American conductors in the prime of his career, Michael Tilson Thomas was born in Los Angeles and attended the University of Southern California. He studied piano, conducting, and composing. At age 19 he became conductor of the Young Musicians Foundation Debut Orchestra. He won the Koussevitzky Prize for

conducting at the TANGLEWOOD MUSIC CENTER in 1969, and soon after was appointed assistant conductor of the BOSTON SYMPHONY ORCHESTRA. He once replaced music director William Steinberg on the podium in midconcert—that was, in fact, Thomas's New York debut. He was elevated to associate conductor in 1970 and in 1971 accepted an appointment as music director of the BUFFALO PHILHARMONIC, where he stayed until 1979. During this period he led the NEW YORK PHILHARMONIC Young People's Concerts (founded by LEONARD BERNSTEIN) on television. From 1981 to 1985 he was principal guest conductor of the LOS ANGELES PHILHARMONIC. In 1988 he founded the New World Symphony Orchestra, a training orchestra for conservatory graduates. Also in 1988, Thomas became principal conductor of the London Symphony Orchestra.

Thomas was offered the directorship of the SAN FRANCISCO SYMPHONY ORCHESTRA in 1995, and he accepted a contract that runs through 2005. (He had made his debut with the orchestra in 1974.) Thomas has become closely identified with this orchestra and is highly regarded for the innovative programming and high musicianship he has brought to the group. His commitment to American music is pronounced; in his inaugural season at San Francisco, Thomas programmed at least one American work in every concert, ending the season with a two-week festival of American music. He presented a similar festival, *American Mavericks,* in 2000. His and the orchestra's 15-disc recording contract had won five Grammy Awards at the time of this writing. Thomas and the orchestra launched a private record label in 2001, the first project for which will be the complete cycle of Mahler symphonies; the first disc (Mahler's Symphony no. Eight) won a Grammy. Thomas has taken the orchestra around the world, and he received the Chevalier des Arts et des Lettres award after their first visit to France in 1996. He has received the President's Award from the National Academy of Recording Arts and Sciences and the Ditson Award from Columbia University.

Thomas, Theodore (1835–1905) *conductor and violinist*

First and inaugural music director of the CHICAGO SYMPHONY ORCHESTRA, Theodore Thomas came to America from East Friesland at the age of 10, after a prodigious childhood in Europe performing on the violin. As a youngster in New York, Thomas quickly established himself as a player in orchestra pits, and he embarked on a brief concert tour when he was 15 years old.

Thomas returned to New York in 1850 and studied conducting. He formed the Mason-Thomas duo with American pianist William Mason, and the two played together until 1862, when Thomas founded the Theodore Thomas Orchestra (1862). With his own orchestra, Thomas's entrepreneurial talent flowered and he produced a series of summer concerts in New York, Philadelphia, Cincinnati, and other cities. The orchestra was popular but suffered the usual financial difficulties. It was disbanded in 1888. The next year one of its supporters, Chicago businessman Charles Norman Fay, asked Thomas if he would relocate to Chicago if he were given his own orchestra. Famously, Thomas replied, "I would go to hell if they gave me a permanent orchestra." The result was the Chicago Orchestra (called the Chicago Symphony Orchestra after 1913).

During his 13-year tenure as music director of the CSO, Thomas introduced American audiences to the music of Anton Bruckner, ANTONÍN DVOŘÁK, Edward Elgar, Edvard Grieg, Bedřich Smetena, Piotr Ilyich Tchaikovsky, and—most notably—American premieres of the work of Thomas's friend Richard Strauss. Strauss himself conducted the Chicago Symphony Orchestra at Thomas's invitation. Thomas worked diligently to move the CSO out of its first home—the Auditorium Theater—which Thomas regarded as too cavernous for satisfactory listening. In 1904 the orchestra moved to ORCHESTRA HALL, less than a month before Thomas died of pneumonia. He worked to the end, conducting his last concert 10 days before his death.

Thompson, Randall (1899–1984) composer

Randall Thompson was one of the most popular composers in American history, and his published works also enjoyed unprecedented success, yet his work is not universally respected. This seeming conflict is not uncommon with classical music of great popularity; many academicians and musicologists (not to mention competing composers) believe that music must challenge audiences and develop a new musical vocabulary to be deemed "good." Thompson wrote mostly choral music, often on commission, and some of his works were beloved by the entire nation. His *The Testament of Freedom* was perform in a Carnegie Hall memorial service in 1945 after the death of President Franklin D. Roosevelt. In his *New York Times* obituary Thompson was characterized as "music's Norman Rockwell."

Thompson received his Bachelors and Masters degrees from Harvard University (1920 and 1922), where he studied with EDWARD BURLINGAME HILL; he also studied with ERNEST BLOCH in New York. He was awarded the Rome Prize in 1922, and studied in Italy. He lectured at Wellesley College in the late 1920s and received a Guggenheim Fellowship in 1929.

Thompson was a busy educator. He became professor at the University of California, Berkeley, starting in 1937. He directed the CURTIS INSTITUTE from 1939 to 1941, and he directed the music department of the School of Fine Arts at the University of Virginia. He taught at Princeton University's fledgling music department from 1946 to 1948, and in 1948 joined the faculty at Harvard, where in 1951 he was appointed to the Walter Bigelow Rosen chair. Thompson was elected to the National Institute of Arts and Letters.

Thomson, Virgil (1896–1989) composer and writer

Virgil Thomson was a composer and writer who divided his energies fairly evenly between these two pursuits, but it is his music criticism for which he is better remembered than his compositions most of which were scored for piano or organ. He took piano lessons as a child, and later studied composing with EDWARD BURLINGAME HILL at Harvard University. As an adult, Thomson took a greater interest in the organ than the piano. He studied with NADIA BOULANGER in Paris and found himself agreeably matched to that city. He lived in Paris, for the most part, until 1940. There, he met writer and poet Gertrude Stein and the two planned opera collaborations. They ended up writing two operas together: *Four Saints in Three Acts (1927–1928)* and *The Mother of Us All* (1947).

When Thomson returned to the United States in 1940, he was appointed music critic of the *New York Herald Tribune.* His reviews made him famous. Concise instead of airy, direct instead of circumspect, flagrantly opinionated instead of cautious, his articles fearlessly targeted many of the day's revered performers and composers. Four compilation books of his criticism were published. His composed soundtrack for the 1948 film *Louisiana Story* won a 1948 Pulitzer Prize—the only one awarded for a film score. He won a National Book Critics Circle Award, a Kennedy Center Honor (1983), and was elected to the National Institute of Arts and Letters.

Thomson was one of the greatest men of letters of his time, a socially active individual who seemed to know everyone important. When he died, LEONARD BERNSTEIN said, "The death of Virgil T. is like the death of an American City: it is intolerable."

Thorne, Francis (b. 1922) composer

Francis Thorne was born to a musical lineage. His father was a ragtime pianist and his grandfather a music writer. He studied at Yale University with PAUL HINDEMITH but emerged from that experience playing jazz. He returned to classical studies with DAVID DIAMOND, and his Elegy for Orchestra (1962) was premiered by EUGENE ORMANDY and the PHILADELPHIA ORCHESTRA. He founded the AMERICAN COMPOSERS ORCHESTRA in 1977 and the

Thorne Music Fund, which operated between 1964 and 1974 to commission new work from contemporary composers.

Tibbett, Lawrence (1896–1960) *opera singer*

A baritone, Lawrence Tibbett starred at the METROPOLITAN OPERA for almost three decades. He broke through in dramatic fashion while replacing a scheduled singer, who had become ill, in a production of *Falstaff.* At the end of one scene, immediately following a dramatic solo by Tibbett, the audience ovation grew noisier and refused to abate, despite many curtain calls by the bewildered ensemble. It eventually became clear that the house wished to see Tibbett take a bow alone and would not let the production continue, despite the conductor's attempts, until he did. After a sustained 15-minute ovation, Tibbett finally took his solo bows, and the opera continued. He made his final Metropolitan appearance in 1950. He enjoyed success away from the opera stage as well, particularly in films and light theater.

Time's Encomium (1969)

With this electronic piece, composed at the Columbia-Princeton Electronic Music Center, CHARLES WUORINEN became the youngest composer to win a Pulitzer Prize for music. The Pulitzer came in 1970; the piece was premiered at the Berkshire Music Festival (later TANGLEWOOD MUSIC FESTIVAL) on August 16, 1969.

Toscanini, Arturo (1867–1957) *conductor*

Perhaps the most famous conductor in history, Arturo Toscanini was a patriotic Italian who never renounced his citizenship despite his vehement and often demonstrated opposition to fascism in the early part of the 20th century. His impact on American music appreciation was incalculable from 1908, when he first arrived to conduct at the METROPOLITAN OPERA, until 1950. During this era in which America struggled to forge its own cultural identity, Toscanini represented the fiercest, most passionate sort of European traditionalism and perfectionism. Through his many live performances with three major New York institutions, and innumerable broadcast performances, Toscanini was the American standard bearer for pure excellence in music.

He was the son of a tailor, and he showed musical gifts as a child. He studied cello at the Parma Conservatory from age nine and began his professional career as a cellist—ironically, playing second cello at La Scala, the famous Milan opera house with which Toscanini would become closely identified during his early conducting career. He was a born conductor, though, and the opportunity suddenly arose at one performance, while on tour in Brazil, for Toscanini to take over the orchestra during *Aida* when the regular conductor was indisposed. (Many conductors, including LEONARD BERNSTEIN, got their big break in this fashion.) Demonstrating his uncanny musical memory, the young cellist conducted the opera without a score, made a hit, and was a conductor from that moment.

From the start of his baton career, Toscanini's temperament was fully formed: he was exacting, disciplined, perfectionistic, tyrannical, and driven by musical ideals he never thought he attained. He eventually advanced to the directorship of La Scala, at which he was given an unusual degree of control over operatic productions. He championed German composer Richard Wagner to Italian audiences, who were largely unfamiliar with German opera. He left La Scala in 1908, along with Guilio Gatti-Casazza, the general manager, to take over the Metropolitan Opera in New York. Toscanini stayed at that position until 1915. The two celebrities attracted one of the greatest collection of star opera singers ever to perform regularly at the Metropolitan.

Toscanini turned away from his operatic idealism over the years, veering toward pure orchestral conducting. After returning to Europe (he was the first Italian conductor to perform at the Bayreuth

Festival, which showcases the operas of Wagner), Toscanini made his U.S. return to lead the NEW YORK PHILHARMONIC from 1928 to 1936. He shared the podium with Willem Mengelberg at first, then took sole control. He took the Philharmonic to Europe for the first time in its history and lifted the orchestra to the first rank of international orchestras.

After leaving the Philharmonic Toscanini conducted the Vienna Philharmonic and other orchestras in Europe, but his work in New York was not finished. He returned in 1937 to take control of the NBC SYMPHONY ORCHESTRA, which had been created expressly for him. This position was Toscanini's most important, at least as regards his modern legacy, because he made most of his recordings with the NBC Orchestra. He also toured widely with the group, and, perhaps most important, his NBC concerts were broadcast nationally on the radio during an era in which classical music radiocasts were prime-time, mainstream entertainment in America. Toscanini and NBC did as much to popularize classical music in the 1940s as any other institutional force in America.

In addition to the colossal amount of music Toscanini introduced to audiences in New York, America, and the rest of the world, he is remembered as the archetype of a dictatorial conductor. His legacy in this regard is almost cartoonish, but there was nothing imaginary about his podium rages or dominating behavior. To his credit, though, as brutal as he could be to his orchestra players, Toscanini was even more demanding and unforgiving of himself. Self-critical in the extreme, he never realized his conception of perfection in his own mind. But he brought beauty into the lives of uncounted millions and raised the musical standard of an entire nation.

Arturo Toscanini (Bettmann/Corbis)

Tower, Joan (b. 1938) *composer*

Joan Tower is an instrumental composer exclusively—she has never written an opera or songs. She received graduate degrees at Columbia University after attending Bennington College. She received a Guggenheim Award in 1973, and was composer in residence at the SAINT LOUIS SYMPHONY ORCHESTRA from 1985 to 1987. She has taught at Bard College and is a member of the American Academy and Institute of Arts and Letters.

Town Hall

A concert hall in New York, Town Hall opened in 1921. It was built by suffragists who needed a place to meet. During the 1940s it was commonly used to present jazz concerts. The hall was purchased by New York University in 1958. Renowned for its excellent sight lines and fine acoustics, Town Hall is one of the most desirable places to hear jazz and classical music in New York.

Treemonisha (1911)

A three-act opera by ragtime composer SCOTT JOPLIN, *Treemonisha* was never produced in Joplin's lifetime, though he spent years promoting it. The work was completed in 1911 and reviewed favorably by critics who saw the score. But Joplin was not regarded seriously as a classical composer of substance, and he was never able to make headway with his orchestral work, which included a ballet, a piano concerto, and a symphony. *Treemonisha* was his biggest heartbreak in the second half of his life, which saw the composer become increasingly marginalized and forgotten. During the American ragtime revival of the 1970s, *Treemonisha* was rediscovered and produced, and Joplin was posthumously awarded a Pulitzer Prize in 1976—not for the opera specifically, but for Joplin's contributions to American music.

Since then *Treemonisha* has enjoyed sporadic attention from opera and light opera houses. Alterations have been introduced periodically. Joplin's original orchestration has unfortunately been lost (also lost are his other orchestral works), and at least three composers have stepped up with competing orchestrations in its stead. (Two of those composers are WILLIAM BOLCOM and GUNTHER SCHULLER.) When the opera was produced by the Opera Theatre of St. Louis in 2000, its three rather short acts were condensed to one act. *Treemonisha* tells the story of a highly educated daughter of former slaves in Arkansas, the title character, who is kidnapped then rescued, and refuses to punish her abductors. She is proclaimed leader of her community after this adventure, and the opera culminates in an ensemble ragtime piece that elevates the genre to new heights.

Trimble, Lester (1923–1986) *composer and music critic*

Lester Trimble studied with DARIUS MILHAUD, AARON COPLAND, and NADIA BOULANGER. He edited *Musical America* from 1960 to 1961, then was the director of the AMERICAN MUSIC CENTER until 1963. In the 1967–68 season, Trimble was composer in residence at the NEW YORK PHILHARMONIC under LEONARD BERNSTEIN. He taught at the JUILLIARD SCHOOL.

Tucker, Richard (1913–1975) *opera singer*

One of America's most famous tenors, Richard Tucker was primarily identified with the METROPOLITAN OPERA, where his robust singing style and astounding projection overcame any lack of subtlety in his acting. (The *New York Times* once commented that his acting skill "never went much beyond the standard tenor's device of raising one arm to express mild emotion and two arms to suggest deeper matters.") He gave his debut at the Salmaggi Opera in New York in 1943. He was invited to sing in ARTURO TOSCANINI's broadcast production of *Aida* in 1949. His Metropolitan debut came in 1945, and in his 30-year Metropolitan career Tucker sang over 600 performances.

His career was something of an accident; Tucker had no thought of becoming a professional musician until he married his wife, whose brother was tenor Jan Peerce. Tucker and Peerce engaged in a friendly rivalry; Tucker began taking voice lessons; and he was auditioning at opera companies within a few years. His career was primarily American; although Tucker sang in Europe he didn't care for the experience. He once withdrew from curtain calls following an opera in Italy when he heard the impassioned audience calling for an encore with the expression "Bis! Bis!" Tucker thought they were yelling "Beast! Beast!"

Tucker died unexpectedly at the peak of his career, and Schuyler Chapin, the general manager of the Metropolitan Opera, announced the news to a shocked full hall on January 8, 1975.

Tudor, David (1926–1996) *pianist and composer*

David Tudor attained fame among the avant-garde as a pianist, and eventually gave himself over to composition. In his early years Tudor played the organ and held positions as organist at the Trinity Church in Swarthmore and at Swarthmore College in Pennsylvania. But it was on the piano that his performance career flourished. Tudor was the main exponent of JOHN CAGE's controversial music, and he premiered many of Cage's works including the infamous *4'33"*. Tudor gained his first success as a modernist pianist in 1950 when he premiered the difficult Second Piano Sonata of PIERRE BOULEZ. Tudor was unique among pianists in his ability to understand and negotiate the peculiar difficulties of modern piano scores, and he was much appreciated by avant-garde composers for this skill. Cage said that nearly everything he composed between 1950 and 1970 was written explicitly for Tudor, or with the pianist in mind. Tudor succeeded Cage as music director of the Merce Cunningham Dance Company in 1992.

Tudor lost interest in performing in the late 1960s and gradually eliminated his concert schedule to concentrate on composing. Here, he experimented with electronic music but always preferred to integrate electronics with acoustic instruments. His innovations were often deeply original, and he sometimes invented and built novel instruments to realize the electronic portions of his scores.

Tudor taught at the University of California, Davis, and at Mills College.

Tully, Alice (1902–1993) *opera singer*

A mezzo-soprano and soprano, Alice Tully began her singing career with a debut in 1927, and continued until her stage retirement in 1950. She made her opera debut with the Salmaggi Opera Company in New York, in 1933. In 1958 Tully inherited a fortune from her grandfather, William Houghton, who founded the famous Corning Glass Works. On that financial basis, combined with an enduring love for music, Tully became one of the country's great musical philanthropists. She donated millions of dollars to cultural institutions in the second half of her life, the most famous recipient of which was ALICE TULLY HALL, the recital hall of LINCOLN CENTER.

Tully originally bestowed her gift anonymously to the soon-to-be-built hall, and allowed her name to be attached only when convinced that the acoustics would be superb. Tully also required that the seating rows leave more leg room than standard in concert halls, reportedly to accommodate a tall friend of hers.

Related to the Alice Tully Hall project, Tully cofounded the CHAMBER MUSIC SOCIETY OF LINCOLN CENTER (with WILLIAM SCHUMAN and CHARLES WADSWORTH), an organization that commissions new chamber music and performs both new and standard chamber repertoire. The society spawned similar organizations in other cities and is responsible in part for the popularity of chamber music in the United States.

Tureck, Rosalyn (1914–2003) *pianist*

One of history's great Bach interpreters on the piano, Rosalyn Tureck was born in Chicago and was performing from an early age. She studied with Olga Samaroff at the Juilliard School of Music (later the JUILLIARD SCHOOL). She made her debut with the PHILADELPHIA ORCHESTRA playing the massive Brahms Piano Concerto no. 2. In 1937 she played a series of all-Bach recitals in New York's TOWN HALL, which helped focus her career. She founded the International Bach Society in 1968 and the Tureck Bach Institute in 1981. She occasionally conducted, and infrequently performed on the harpsichord or clavicord. Tureck lectured widely and wrote scholarly articles. She received honorary degrees from Roosevelt University (1968) and Oxford University (1977). She was honored with awards from numerous countries. Tureck's playing was smoothly contoured, finely articulated, and scholarly.

12 New Etudes for Piano (1977–1986)

This set a piano études (musical studies) won the Pulitzer Prize in 1988 for composer WILLIAM BOLCOM. Bolcom began work on the set in 1977 and was composing the études for pianist Paul Jacobs. Working on the project intermittently, Bolcom had finished nine pieces when Jacobs died in 1983. Bolcom stopped work on the *12 New Etudes* until hearing the first nine played by Canadian pianist Marc-André Hamelin. The experience revived Bolcom's inspiration for the project, and he quickly completed the set. *12 New Etudes for Piano* is dedicated to both Jacobs and Hamelin. The extremely varied pieces express a good deal of dissonance along with some atonality. Bolcom wrote an earlier set of 12 piano études, completed in 1966.

Upshaw, Dawn (b. 1960) *opera singer*

Soprano Dawn Upshaw has met success both on the opera stage and in recital; she spends several months of the year concertizing when not singing at the METROPOLITAN OPERA. Her light, firm voice is ideal for Mozart and Handel. She has also recorded Broadway material. Upshaw studied at the MANHATTAN SCHOOL OF MUSIC.

Ussachevsky, Vladimir (1911–1990) *composer*

A pioneer electronic music composer, Vladimir Ussachevsky studied at the EASTMAN SCHOOL OF MUSIC (Master of Music in 1936 and Ph.D. in 1939). He was a professor of music at Columbia University, and he frequently collaborated with OTTO LUENING, who also worked at Columbia. The two of them, with MILTON BABBITT and ROGER SESSIONS, founded the COLUMBIA-PRINCETON ELECTRONIC MUSIC CENTER, which Ussachevsky directed from 1958 to 1980.

Utah Symphony

A full-time professional orchestra founded in 1940, the Utah Symphony employs 83 members and performs over 200 concerts a year. The orchestra's major influence and mentor was MAURICE ABRAVANEL, music director between 1947 and 1979.

Abravanel took a local ensemble of about 50 part-time players, presenting five to 10 concerts a year, and built one of America's most respected symphony orchestras. Perhaps because of the orchestra's remote location, its reputation has depended on an aggressive recording schedule: 138 recorded discs were in the orchestra's portfolio in the fall of 2003, representing over two releases per year over the ensemble's lifetime. From the arrival of Abravanel, the Utah Symphony has employed only three full-time music directors: Abravanel himself (1947–79), Joseph Silverstein (1983–88), and Keith Lockhart (since 1988). The orchestra performs in ABRAVANEL HALL, which was constructed in 1979 and renamed in 1993, the year of Abravanel's death.

In 2002 the Utah Symphony merged with the Utah Opera to become the Utah Symphony and Opera. Previous to the merger the orchestra accompanied the opera in five performances a year; since the merger the Utah Symphony has maintained its own schedule of symphonic concerts in addition to an expanded performance schedule of operas. The merged resources of the two organizations benefited the orchestra, which expanded its personnel and enhanced its performance space. In the first two seasons of the merged company, during a time when many American orchestras cut back or stopped operating entirely, the Utah Symphony & Opera improved its ticket sales.

𝓋

Vanessa (1957)

A four-act opera by SAMUEL BARBER, with libretto by fellow composer and personal partner GIAN CARLO MENOTTI, *Vanessa* won a 1958 Pulitzer Prize. It was first produced on January 15, 1958, at the METROPOLITAN OPERA. The opera is inspired by writer Isak Dinesen's *Seven Gothic Tales.*

Vänskä, Osmo (b. 1953) *conductor*

A Finnish conductor, Osmo Vänskä is currently music director of the MINNESOTA ORCHESTRA (since 2003). Before the Minnesota appointment Vänskä was chief conductor of the BBC Scottish Symphony Orchestra. He has guest-conducted extensively in the United States, and recorded extensively, notably the orchestral works of Sibelius. Vänskä began his career as a clarinettist in Finland.

Varèse, Edgard (1883–1965) *composer*

Called the Father of Electronic Music, Varèse wrote the first major works with sounds on tape. More than these innovations, though, he was a composer of startling originality who refused to affiliate with any compositional school, resisted serialism while composing atonally, and broke new ground as an American original. He grew up in Paris and first arrived in the United States in 1917 to conduct the Requiem of Hector Berlioz. The following year he was a guest conductor of the CINCINNATI SYMPHONY ORCHESTRA. He settled in the United States then and became an American citizen in 1926. As a conductor, Varèse introduced modern music to his audiences, presenting composers Arnold Schoenberg and Anton Webern to Cincinnati listeners for the first time.

His own music was controversial and sometimes cacophanous. He founded his own orchestra,

Osmo Vänskä (Courtesy of the Minnesota Orchestra)

233

the New Symphony Orchestra, in 1919. He was a cofounder (with Carlos Salzedo) of the International Composers' Guild in 1921; the guild, which lasted for six years, presented a great deal of contemporary music. In 1928 Varèse founded the Pan American Association of Composers. He was interested in ancient music as well, and in 1943 founded the Greater New York Chorus, which specialized in baroque and Renaissance music.

In 1953 Varèse received a tape recorder, then a new piece of technology, and began his electronic experiments. His two pioneering works, which included tape, were *Déserts* (1954) and *Poème électronique* (1957). The latter work was scored for tape alone.

Varèse was elected to the National Institute of Arts and Letters; he received a Brandeis Award in 1962 and the first Koussevitzky International Recording Award in 1963.

Visions of Terror and Wonder (1976)

Scored for mezzo-soprano and orchestra, this work by American composer RICHARD WERNICK received a 1977 Pulitzer Prize. It was commissioned by the Aspen Music Festival's Conference on Contemporary Music and the National Endowment for the Arts. It was premiered at the Aspen Music Festival on July 19, 1976.

Voigt, Deborah (b. 1960) *opera singer*

Deborah Voight was praised by *MUSICAL AMERICA* as "the greatest living interpreter of the dramatic heroines of Wagner and Richard Strauss." She studied at California State University and in the development program of the SAN FRANCISCO OPERA, where she made her debut in 1986. A string of competition victories between 1988 and 1990 (the Pavarotti Voice Competition, the Rosa Ponselle Gold Medal, and the Verdi Competition) led to a London debut, then her first performance at the METROPOLITAN OPERA in 1992. In 2004 Voigt sang at the Vienna Opera and the Metropolitan; her future plans involved more recital performance. She gave her CARNEGIE HALL recital debut in April 2004, with JAMES LEVINE at the piano.

Vonk, Hans (b. 1942) *conductor*

A Dutch conductor, Hans Vonk was music director of the SAINT LOUIS SYMPHONY ORCHESTRA from 1996 to 2002. He was a spectacularly popular conductor in Saint Louis among both listeners and orchestra players. After his St. Louis debut in 1994, there was a public outcry to halt the search for a new music director to replace the outgoing LEONARD SLATKIN. During those 1994 concerts, orchestra players stamped their feet, hit their music stands, and refused to take bows until Vonk had received three curtain calls, all in a display of support rarely seen from a symphony orchestra.

In 1998 Vonk was paralyzed by Guillain-Barré syndrome, a temporary form of polio, and was paralyzed for the duration of the disease. He recovered and continued his work in St. Louis but stepped down in 2002 to deal with continuing health concerns. He has guest-conducted in New York, Philadelphia, Cleveland, Boston, and Los Angeles.

Wadsworth, Charles (b. 1929) *pianist*
One of America's most noteworthy accompanists, Charles Wadsworth studied piano with Rosalyn Tureck and was a favored collaborator of Beverly Sills. In 1960, Wadsworth created the Chamber Music Series at the Festival of Two Worlds in Spoleto, Italy, at the invitation of the festival's founder, Gian Carlo Menotti. (See Spoleto Festival.) In 1965 Wadsworth began discussions with William Schuman, then president of the new Lincoln Center in New York, about a chamber music foundation at Lincoln Center, a more ambitious and continuously operating version of what Wadsworth had created at Spoleto. The two of them, along with former singer and philanthropist Alice Tully, founded the Chamber Music Society of Lincoln Center, which operates today. With Wadsworth at the helm, the society commissioned more than 60 new works and gave over 1,000 performances. The society now performs an annual series of Wadsworth Concerts (founded in 1995) featuring vocal chamber music. In 1989 Wadsworth received the Handel Medallion from New York's mayor, Ed Koch. Wadsworth performed for five presidents and has been honored by several countries.

Wagner, Roger (1914–1992) *conductor*
A choral conductor, Roger Wagner was born in France and moved to California at age seven, where he prepared for the priesthood. Along the way he studied organ, then conducting (with Bruno Walter), and became an American citizen in the 1940s. In 1946 he founded the Roger Wagner Chorale, which later became the Los Angeles Master Chorale.

Walker, George (b. 1922) *pianist and composer*
George Walker received most of his training at the keyboard, studying with French pianist Robert Casadesus, British pianist Clifford Curzon, and Rudolf Serkin. He toured in the United States and abroad, composing as a sideline. His compositions gained quiet renown, and Walker received awards from the MacArthur Foundation and the American Academy and Institute of Arts and Letters. His 1995 piece *Lilacs* won a Pulitzer Prize the following year.

Wallenstein, Alfred (1898–1983) *cellist and conductor*
Alfred Wallenstein began his orchestral career when he joined the cello section of the San Francisco Symphony at age 17. He held jobs with the Los Angeles Philharmonic, Chicago Symphony Orchestra, and New York Philharmonic under Arturo Toscanini. In 1943 he became music director of the Los Angeles Philharmonic, remaining on the podium until 1956. He taught at the Juilliard School and was head of the orchestral department from 1971.

Walter, Bruno (1876–1962) *conductor*
A foremost conductor of his time, Bruno Walter belied the stereotype of the conductor as tyrant. He was amiable, happy in his profession, and lacking in

idiosyncracies both personally and musically. He was born in Berlin and raised in Germany; he left at the start of Jewish persecution under the Nazi regime. Before emigrating, Walter worked extensively with GUSTAV MAHLER, who helped build his early conducting career in Europe. Walter settled in the United States after 1939 and became an American citizen in 1946. His first U.S. appearance was in CARNEGIE HALL in 1923, when he conducted the New York Symphony Orchestra. New York remained the center of Walter's American career; he was music adviser to the NEW YORK PHILHARMONIC from 1947 to 1949, and conducted that orchestra frequently into the 1950s. His debut at the METROPOLITAN OPERA in 1941 was greeted with 13 curtain calls; it installed Walter as an important conductor there during the same period. It was for Walter that LEONARD BERNSTEIN dramatically substituted on short notice in a New York Philharmonic concert, launching his career.

In addition to his technical accomplishments and wide range of experience conducting on two continents, Walter was a moral force in music. He frequently referred to music's spiritual values, and was strongly opinionated about the roles of musicians and listeners. He wrote that "the vast, transcendental realm of the soul harbors the spring from which music flows," and he conducted with an unusual (and, in its time, unfashionable) commitment and sentiment. He shaped his performances with an ear for singing lines and conveying beauty, rather than with excessive attention to details of execution and ensemble precision. His conducting was spacious, unhurried, and gentle. Many observers noted that his performances, even of the standard repertoire pieces, sounded like premieres. His obituary was carried on page one of the *New York Times*.

Ward, Robert (b. 1917) *composer*

Robert Ward composed the opera *The Crucible,* his best-known work. Based on Arthur Miller's play about the Salem witch trials, it was commissioned by the NEW YORK CITY OPERA and completed in 1961. He studied with Howard Hanson at the EASTMAN SCHOOL of MUSIC and did postgraduate work at the JUILLIARD SCHOOL. He held faculty and administrative positions at the North Carolina School of the Arts from 1967 to 1975, and taught at Duke University from 1978 to 1987.

Watts, André (b. 1946) *pianist*

André Watts is a preeminent pianist whose career was launched in dramatic fashion, making him a classical box-office draw second only to VAN CLIBURN in the 1960s. He studied at the Philadelphia Music Academy and also attended the Peabody Conservatory. He performed a Haydn piano concerto with the PHILADELPHIA ORCHESTRA at age nine. In 1963 Watts was chosen by LEONARD BERNSTEIN to perform Franz Liszt's Piano Concerto no. 1 at a Young People's Concert, broadcast nationally. Then, when Canadian pianist Glenn Gould canceled his appearance with the New York Philharmonic a few weeks later, Bernstein selected Watts to perform the Liszt concerto again, this time in a regular-season concert at PHILHARMONIC HALL. These back-to-back successes galvanized Watts's career, making his a household name overnight among music lovers. He embarked on a world tour sponsored by the U.S. State Department in 1967. Showing unusual maturity and desire to refine his musicianship, Watts continued studying (with LEON FLEISHER) while touring. In 1973 he began teaching at the Berkshire (later TANGLEWOOD) Music Center. In 1988 Watts and the New York Philharmonic celebrated the 25th anniversary of his spectacular debut with a performance in which he played three piano concertos.

Watts plays in the grand romantic style, with a monumental technique, great fluidity, and a muscular American-trained style. He received an Avery Fisher Prize in 1988. He was the youngest person (26 years old) ever to receive an honorary doctorate from Yale University; many other institutions have followed suit. In the fall of 2004 Watts began an appointment to the Jack I. and Dora B. Hamlin Endowed Chair in Music at Indiana University.

Wa-Wan Press

Founded by composer and music historian ARTHUR FARWELL in 1901, the Wa-Wan Press was a subscription publication dedicated to releasing newly composed music. The name "Wa-Wan" was taken from a tribal peace ceremony performed by Omaha Indians. The company's mandate included finding and publishing music influenced by Native American ("Amerindian") sources, but its larger mission was to expose and promote new American music of all sorts. Accordingly, Wa-Wan Press was the first publisher of many pieces by 37 different composers. The press was an extraordinary accomplishment; a PBS biography of Farwell called Wa-Wan "one of the most significant and idealistic efforts of our cultural history." The near-monthly issues contained two volumes each—one of vocal and the other of instrumental music. They were handsomely produced and included elaborate, scholarly introductions by Farwell. After initial success, Wa-Wan Press suffered a loss of subscribers and was sold to the large music publishing house G. SCHIRMER in 1912. Schirmer, while offering the catalogue of previously published pieces for sale, did not continue publishing new pieces. A reprint of the entire Wa-Wan Press output was published by Arno Press in collaboration with the *New York Times* in 1970.

Weill Recital Hall

Formally known as the Joan and Sanford I. Weill Recital Hall, but commonly called Weill Recital Hall or Weill Hall, this is the smallest of the three stage venues in CARNEGIE HALL. Weill is located on Carnegie's third floor, and seats 268 at full capacity. Formerly called the Chamber Music Hall (it is ideal for chamber music and solo recitals), Weill was renamed in 1986 after the chairman of Carnegie's board and his wife.

Weisgall, Hugo (1912–1997) *composer*

One of the most important American opera composers, Hugo Weisgall was born to a family with a long musical history. He was born in Poland and became an American citizen in 1926 after moving to the United States with his family in 1921. He studied at the Peabody Conservatory and the CURTIS INSTITUTE. Although he composed in other genres, Weisgall's operatic output made him famous. His breakthrough came with his opera *Six Characters in Search of an Author*, first produced by the NEW YORK CITY OPERA in 1959. His most frequently performed opera is *The Stronger*. He taught at the JUILLIARD SCHOOL (1957–70) and Queens College (1961–83). He was president of the AMERICAN MUSIC CENTER from 1963 to 1973. He received three Guggenheim Fellowships and a Gold Medal from the American Academy and Institute of Arts and Letters.

Welser-Möst, Franz (b. 1960) *conductor*

Currently the music director of the CLEVELAND ORCHESTRA under a contract running through 2012, Franz Welser-Möst is an Austrian conductor. He aspired to be a pianist but suffered injuries in an

Franz Welser-Möst (Courtesy of the Cleveland Orchestra)

auto accident that ended his pianistic hopes. He made his American debut with the SAINT LOUIS SYMPHONY ORCHESTRA in 1989, and guest-conducted in many cities following that. He was music director of the Zürich Opera from 1995 to 2000. Previously, he was music director of the London Philharmonic. He received an honorary doctorate from Case Western Reserve University.

Wernick, Richard (b. 1934) *composer*

Richard Wernick is a modernist composer whose *Visions of Terror and Wonder,* scored for mezzo-soprano and orchestra, won a 1977 Pulitzer Prize. He studied at Brandeis University, Mills College, and the TANGLEWOOD MUSIC CENTER, working at one time or another with a succession of high-profile teachers including IRVING FINE, HAROLD SHAPERO, ARTHUR BERGER, and AARON COPLAND. Composing in an academic style that incorporates serialism and 12-tone dissonances, Wernick has garnered many awards from the Ford Foundation, the Guggenheim Foundation, and the National Institute of Arts and Letters. He is the only composer to have been awarded the Kennedy Center Friedheim Prize three times (1986, 1991, 1992). He was given two national Endowment for the Arts composition grants (1979 and 1982). In 2000 he won the Alfred I. DuPont Award. From 1983 to 1989 Wernick was the consultant for contemporary music to the PHILADELPHIA ORCHESTRA. He taught at the University of Chicago before his signature teaching assignment at the University of Pennsylvania, where he was Magnin Professor of Humanities from 1968 to 1996.

Wild, Earl (b. 1915) *pianist*

Earl Wild is a pianistic throwback to the 19th-century tradition of transcription playing. He is famous for his many virtuoso piano arrangements of orchestra works and even jazz songs, which form an important basis of his repertoire. At the same time, Wild has played a standard selection of

Earl Wild (Courtesy of Michael Rolland Davis)

piano music extending from Mozart to modern composers.

Demonstrating a strong inclination toward music at an early age, Wild eventually attended a program for gifted children at Pittsburgh's Carnegie Mellon University, remaining there through college. Two talents determined the shape of his early career. First, his propensity for musical arrangement, which led him to compose piano transcriptions while a teenager, some of which were featured on local radio stations. Second, an uncanny sight-reading fluency made him an ideal ensemble pianist. It was therefore the case, rather unusually for a concert pianist of Wild's stature, that he spent many years as a staff orchestra pianist and in-house pianist for broadcast networks. Being an orchestra pianist involves playing occasional piano parts scored in orchestra pieces, not playing solo parts of concertos for piano and orchestra. As a teenager he was the pianist of the PITTSBURGH SYMPHONY ORCHESTRA under Otto Klemperer. In 1937 he became the staff pianist at NBC, which meant playing piano parts in the NBC SYMPHONY ORCHESTRA under ARTURO TOSCANINI. In 1942 Toscanini and the orchestra performed GEORGE GERSHWIN's *RHAPSODY IN BLUE* with Wild as piano soloist. The spectacularly successful broadcast concert was a watershed for both Gershwin and Wild; in the latter case it made Earl Wild a household name and, oddly, gave him a reputation as a Gershwin specialist, even though he had never performed a Gershwin piece before. Wild took advantage of this association by making concert transcriptions of many Gershwin songs.

Wild was a musician in the U.S. Navy during World War II, after which he became house pianist and composer at the ABC network, where he remained until 1968. During all this staff work, Wild was simultaneously engaging in a concert career. During the war, he performed as a concerto soloist with the U.S. Navy Symphony Orchestra, and was invited to play at the White House. Wild has the unequaled distinction of having played for six consecutive presidents, starting with Herbert Hoover. During his NBC and ABC affiliations, Wild played concerts all over the world. In 1949 he performed the premier of the Piano Concerto of PAUL CRESTON. ABC commissioned Wild's most ambitious original composition, the Easter Oratorio, which was broadcast in 1962 with Wild at the podium. In 1982 Wild won the Liszt Medal awarded by the government of Hungary; that same year, the 100th Anniversary of Franz Liszt's death, Wild gave three all-Liszt-themed recitals in CARNEGIE HALL: Liszt the Poet, Liszt the Transcriber, and Liszt the Virtuoso.

Wild spent time on the faculties of the EASTMAN SCHOOL OF MUSIC, the MANHATTAN SCHOOL OF MUSIC, and the JUILLIARD SCHOOL. He is currently the distinguished visiting artist at Carnegie Mellon University. On his 80th birthday, Wild performed a solo recital in Carnegie Hall in which he played a virtuoso program of Liszt and Chopin; he repeated the performance on his 85th birthday in a concert described by one critic as "a weirdly uneven recital." Wild has an extensive discography; he began recording in 1939 and has been associated with 20 different labels. He received a Grammy Award in 1997 for an 80th-birthday disc entitled *Earl Wild: The Romantic Master.*

Williams, John (b. 1932) *composer*

The preeminent film composer of the present day, John Williams has dominated the field for 30 years. His encompassing Hollywood career hides Williams's pure-music composing. However, his classical training and orchestration skills shine through his soundtracks and revived the art of symphonic film scoring. He has written a symphony, several concertos, and other works that have received modest exposure; additionally, Williams sometimes creates concert versions of his film scores for orchestral performance.

Williams began playing the piano at eight years of age, and studied with ROSINA LHÉVINNE at the JUILLIARD SCHOOL. In 1956 he began taking jobs as a studio pianist in Hollywood, graduating to arranging and composing. His first scores were for television shows, for which he won two Emmy Awards, and in the early 1960s he began scoring movies. He is perhaps most identified with the movies of Steven Spielberg, of whose films Williams has scored all but one. Williams has also enjoyed fruitful collaborations with directors George Lucas, Robert Altman, and Oliver Stone. His affinity for action and science-fiction movies was established in the 1970s with *Star Wars* (Lucas) and *Close Encounters of the Third Kind* (Spielberg).

One need only listen to a Williams score as pure music, separated from its film, to appreciate Williams as a classical composer. His style in film work owes much to 19th-century and early 20th-century European and American classical traditions and harmonies, that is, his music is generally tonal and accessible. At his best, Williams evokes uncanny characterizations and atmospheres; his work in the *Harry Potter* movies is masterful on both points.

As a pure-music composer, Williams is more adventurous and occasionally more rigorously dissonant than in his film music. From 1980 to 1993 he was director of the BOSTON POPS ORCHESTRA, succeeding the legendary ARTHUR FIEDLER; it is difficult to imagine another figure who could accept such a daunting role. The job gave Williams opportunities to compose and program his own music. He was named Boston Pops laureate conductor in 1993.

Williams has received multiple Grammy Awards and nominations; he has received five Academy Awards and more than 36 nominations. He has guest-conducted several leading orchestras, in London, Cleveland, Pittsburgh, Philadelphia, Chicago, Dallas, San Francisco, and Los Angeles, and is currently artist in residence at the TANGLEWOOD MUSIC CENTER. Williams has been awarded honorary doctorates from 14 colleges and universities, including the NEW ENGLAND CONSERVATORY.

Windows (1972)

Composed by JACOB DRUCKMAN, the orchestral piece *Windows* was awarded Pulitzer Prize in 1972. It was premiered by the CHICAGO SYMPHONY ORCHESTRA on March 16, 1972.

Wittgenstein, Paul (1887–1961) *pianist*

Paul Wittgenstein was an accomplished pianist who lost his right arm during World War I, barely a month after his piano debut in his home city of Vienna, Austria. He built a career as a left-handed pianist. Twenty-six years old and a prisoner of war, Wittgenstein practiced with his left hand on a wooden crate that he used as a makeshift keyboard, developing his new technique to music playing in his head. He developed a superlative facility with his left hand, inspiring several composers to write music for him, some of which has entered the standard repertoire, including Sergey Prokofiev's Piano Concerto no. 4, Maurice Ravel's *Concerto for the Left Hand,* and *Diversions* by Benjamin Britten. The Ravel concerto was Wittgenstein's debut piece, which he introduced in Montreal (1934), Boston, and New York. Audiences and critics were astonished at the seemingly 10-fingered sounds produced by Wittgenstein. Ravel said of his concerto, "The listener must never feel that more could have been accomplished with two hands." That was clearly Wittgenstein's mandate as well. A French review of Wittgenstein's first performance of the Ravel work in Paris stated, "It was a miracle. His left hand had become two hands." The piece would not have been written if not for Wittgenstein's disability, and it is now part of the established concerto repertoire. Wittgenstein settled in New York, taught, and became an American citizen in 1946.

Wolff, Hugh (b. 1953) *conductor*

Hugh Wolff studied at Harvard University, the Peabody Conservatory, and the Paris Conservatory. He received advanced training in piano, conducting, and composition. He made his debut in CARNEGIE HALL (1979) with the NATIONAL SYMPHONY ORCHESTRA. Wolff was music director of the Northeastern Pennsylvania Orchestra (1981–86), associate conductor of the National Symphony Orchestra (1982–85), and music director of the New Jersey Symphony Orchestra (1985–93). He became principal conductor of the SAINT PAUL CHAMBER ORCHESTRA in 1988, ascending to music director in 1992. During his tenure in St. Louis Wolff twice won the ASCAP award for adventurous programming. Appointment as conductor of the Frankfurt Radio Symphony Orchestra came in 1997; his twice-expanded contract runs through 2006. With the Frankfurt orchestra, Wolff made a rare recording of the Symphony no. 1 of GEORGE ANTHEIL.

Wolf Trap

Wolf Trap is a national park in Virginia dedicated to performing arts, operated by the Wolf Trap Foundation. It was founded by Catherine Filene Shouse, who donated 100 acres of farmland to the U.S. government in 1966. Wolf Trap maintains two performing spaces, the larger of which is Filene Center, which opened in 1971. In 1981, Shouse donated more land and moved two historic barns from New York State to Virginia, and The Barns at Wolf Trap opened as a second stage venue. Wolf Trap presents year-round performances at The Barns and a summer schedule in the unwalled Filene Center. During the summer, The Barns is occupied by the Wolf Trap Opera Company. All kinds of music is featured at Wolf Trap, including classical, folk, and pop.

Wolpe, Stefan (1902–1972) *composer*

Born in Germany, composer Stefan Wolpe emigrated to the United States in 1938. Wolpe lived in Europe and Israel, after which his music revealed both traditional classical and Middle Eastern influences when he discovered serialism and atonal writing. He resisted the academic nature of serialism and its repetitiveness, seeking to create what he considered a more genuine modernism. In America he became a well-known teacher at the Settlement Music School in Philadelphia (1939–42), the Brooklyn Free Music Society (1945–48), the Contemporary Music School (1948–52, which Wolpe cofounded), and the Philadelphia Academy of Music (1949–52). He chaired the music department at C.W. Post College of Long Island University from 1957 to 1968. His students included MORTON FELDMAN, RALPH SHAPEY, and DAVID TUDOR.

Wolpe's life was plagued by bad fortune. He received a Guggenheim Fellowship in 1961, but not until he had applied 10 times. In 1963 he was diagnosed with Parkinson's disease, making it at first difficult, then impossible to continue working. In 1970 a fire in an apartment into which he had recently moved damaged his music manuscripts and destroyed his art collection. One consequence of Wolpe's disease was less density to his late works; the composer claimed he could not work out complex rhythmic relationships in his mind, and he was often unable to notate music fluently enough to

work out such complications on paper. In February 1972, shortly before his death, Wolpe was the subject of a retrospective at a Columbia University concert, and in 2002, the centenary of his birth, many retrospectives were held.

Women's Philharmonic

Founded in 1981 by Elizabeth Seja Min, Miriam Abrams, and Nan Washburn, the Women's Philharmonic is based in San Francisco. The orchestra's entire repertoire consists of works composed by women, and all the players are women. The orchestra's start-up funding came entirely from private donations. It has commissioned nearly 50 works and given well over 100 premieres. The Women's Philharmonic has received the ASCAP Award 17 times for adventurous programming.

Wuorinen, Charles (b. 1938) *composer*

A relentlessly serious composer who discards sentimentality and has no use for popular influences, Charles Wuorinen has been called "the poster child for unlikable music." He began composing at age five, even before receiving piano lessons, and by the age of 12 had decided to be a composer, against his parents' wishes. In 1954, the 16-year-old Wuorinen received the Young Composers Award, sponsored by the NEW YORK PHILHARMONIC. He received his degrees from Columbia University (B.A. in 1961; M.A. in 1963), from which he graduated in 1963. A prolific composer in his student days, Wuorinen received no fewer than three Bearns Prizes from Columbia and four BMI Student Composer Awards—in both cases records that have not since been matched. He founded the Group for Contemporary Music in 1962. In 1964 he joined the Columbia faculty.

Wuorinen is somewhat associated with electronic music; his first major venture in that area was TIME'S ENCOMIUM, composed in 1968 on commission by Nonesuch Records; the piece won a 1970 Pulitzer Prize. With that, Wuorinen became the youngest composer ever to receive a Pulitzer. Other awards have included an American Academy of Arts and Letters Award (1967), two Guggenheim Fellowships (1968, 1972), a MacArthur Fellowship (1986), three Rockefeller Foundation Fellowships (1979, 1981, 1982), the Koussevitzky International Recording Award (1970), and many others. Controversially, Wuorinen was denied tenure at Columbia University and has since taught at the MANHATTAN SCHOOL OF MUSIC and Rutgers University in New Jersey, where he is currently professor of music. He has fulfilled dozens of commissions from institutions and individuals, including the TANGLEWOOD MUSIC CENTER, BALTIMORE SYMPHONY, CLEVELAND ORCHESTRA, Ford Foundation, MINNESOTA ORCHESTRA, NEW WORLD SYMPHONY, ST. PAUL CHAMBER ORCHESTRA, TASHI, SAN FRANCISCO SYMPHONY, and Russian composer Igor Stravinsky's widow. He has conducted his music in major U.S. cities and lectured widely. Wuorinen is the author of *Simple Composition* (1979).

Wuorinen is not a strict serialist, but his music is harshy atonal and difficult to listen to for many audiences. Wuorinen enjoys the respect and success needed to maintain the integrity of his work, and does not chase popularity. As a result, musicians and musicologists consider him a giant of American composers, while most concertgoers have not heard of him. He has composed more than 200 works.

Young, La Monte (b. 1935) *composer*

An early minimalist composer, La Monte Young is sometimes regarded as the father of the genre. Those who assert that TERRY RILEY invented minimalist composing point to Riley's *In C* from 1964. Loyalists of Young point to his 1960 work, *arabic numeral (any integer)*. Like Riley, Young was fascinated by long tones and developed that spacious style through the 1960s with works such as *The Tortoise, His Dreams and Journeys* (1964). He wrote *The Well-Tuned Piano* (1964), a rejection of equal temperament as exemplified in Bach's *Well-Tempered Klavier*.

Ysaÿe, Eugène (1858–1931) *composer, conductor, and violinist*

Eugène Ysaÿe was a Belgian violinist, composer, and conductor who achieved legendary status in the first two occupations and resorted to the third in failing health. He first toured the United States as a performer in 1894 until the outbreak of World War I in 1914, by which time neuritis and diabetes had combined to debilitate him. Turning to conducting, Ysaÿe accepted the post of music director of the CINCINNATI SYMPHONY ORCHESTRA, succeeding Ernst Kunwald. He remained in Cincinnati until 1922.

Zankel Hall

Formally known as Judy and Arthur Zankel Hall, this newest addition to the performance venues within CARNEGIE HALL was opened in September 2003. Located directly beneath the main concert hall (ISAAC STERN AUDITORIUM), the space was originally called Carnegie Recital Hall. Then, in 1960, it was turned into a film theater. The process of reclaiming the hall for music started in 1997.

Zimbalist, Efrem (1890–1985) *violinist*

Born in Russia, violinist Efrem Zimbalist settled in the United States after his American debut in 1911. He was 11 years old when he began studying with Leopold Auer at the St. Petersburg Conservatory. Zimbalist was one of the four major graduates of Auer's studio and proponents of the "Auer school" of violin playing; the others were JASCHA HEIFETZ, NATHAN MILSTEIN, and MISCHA ELMAN. He graduated with honors in 1907 and made his debuts in Berlin and London. In his American debut, with the BOSTON SYMPHONY ORCHESTRA, he premiered the violin concerto by Aleksandr Glazunov. In 1914 he married singer Alma Gluck. Zimbalist taught at the CURTIS INSTITUTE starting in 1929, and was school director from 1941 to 1968. In 1943, his first marriage having ended, Zimbalist married Mary Louis Curtis Bok, founder of Curtis. He stopped performing for the most part in 1949, dedicating himself to teaching and administrative work. Reviewing his farewell concert, music critic Olin Downes wrote in the *New York Times*, "He touched nothing that he did not give distinction and high dignity." Zimbalist did, however perform the Violin Concerto of Gian Carlo Menotti, which was dedicated to him, in 1952. Like many performers, Zimbalist also dabbled in composition; he received good notices for his musical comedy, *Honeydew*, which was produced on Broadway in 1920. In his retirement, Zimbalist served on the jury of the Tchaikovsky music competition in Moscow in 1962 and 1966. The actor Efrem Zimbalist Jr. is his son.

Zukofsky, Paul (b. 1943) *violinist*

Paul Zukofsky started playing at age four, performed in public at age six, and began advanced studies at age seven. He made his concerto debut at age 10 with the New Haven Symphony Orchestra. His formal debut in CARNEGIE HALL followed three years later. HAROLD C. SCHONBERG, then music critic of the *New York Times*, reviewed the Carnegie Hall concert with mixed impressions; he said that the young Zukofsky played with superb technique but little emotion. Since then Zukofsky has specialized in 20th-century music, and has performed the premieres of concertos by ROGER SESSIONS and CHARLES WUORINEN. Zukofsky has taught at the NEW ENGLAND CONSERVATORY and at the State University of New York at Stony Brook. He is the program coordinator of the American Composers Series at the KENNEDY CENTER.

Zwilich, Ellen Taaffe (b. 1939) *composer*

Ellen Zwilich is one of America's most frequently performed composers, and has become more popular in the more recent phases of her career as her music has become more tonal and easily understood. She received her degrees from Florida State University (B.M. in 1956; M.M. in 1962), then studied composition in New York with Elliott Carter and Roger Sessions. She played in the American Symphony Orchestra, an ensemble for young instrumentalists conducted by LEOPOLD STOKOWSKI. Zwilich enrolled in the JUILLIARD SCHOOL and studied composition with ELLIOTT CARTER and ROGER SESSIONS. In 1975 her Symposium for Orchestra was performed by the Juilliard Orchestra conducted by PIERRE BOULEZ. In 1983 Zwilich became the first woman to win a Pulitzer Prize for music with her Symphony no. 1. Commissions, major performances, and awards followed. She received the Elizabeth Sprague Coolidge Chamber Music Prize, the Arturo Toscanini Music Critics Award, an award from the American Academy of Arts and Letters, a key to the city of Cincinnati, and a Guggenheim Fellowship. Her Symphony no. 3 was commissioned for the 150th anniversary celebration of the NEW YORK PHILHARMONIC. Zwilich has written four symphonies, two string quartets, many concertos for various instruments, and choral and other music. She is currently the Francis Eppes Distinguished Professor at Florida State University.

Appendixes

Appendix I

Recommended Listening

This listening guide is provided with the assumption that the reader is capable of purchasing CDs as well finding and purchasing music online. As such, this guide is less a discography than a recommendation of important composers, performers, record labels, and online listening services that best serve the newcomer to American classical music. Certainly, no comprehensive discography could be attempted in this space. Furthermore, it lies beyond the purpose of a reference book to endorse one recording over another. But certain composers may be suggested before others, and specific recordings are invoked for early American music that is difficult to locate.

Two Important Record Labels

Anyone interested in American classical music should be aware of two record labels that, in at least a portion of their catalogs, are dedicated to American composers.

The first is Naxos, widely known as a budget classical label. The low CD prices are attractive, and the breadth of the Naxos catalog is impressive. In American music, Naxos offers the Naxos American Series, featuring recordings of a broad range of composers. More than 150 CDs are available in this series, representing composers from Sowerby to Sousa, and dozens of others represented by entries in this book. The Naxos Web site (www.naxos.com) details these recordings.

Second, the New World Records label is devoted mostly to American music. New World Records recently absorbed CRI (Composers Recordings, Inc.), a label founded by Otto Luening, which represents many dozens of little-known American composers. As with Naxos, many of the New World CDs are budget-priced. Although not as interactive as the Naxos site, the New World Records site (www.newworldrecords.org) itemizes the label's catalog.

Early American Composers

American composers of the 18th and 19th centuries are among the least-recorded composers in the world. If you are interested in hearing the work of the hymnists and other pioneers of American national style, these recordings might be of interest:

America Sings, Volume I: The Founding Years (Vox Classical).
William Billings, Francis Hopkinson, anonymously composed hymns from 18th-century tunebooks

American Classics Sampler (Naxos)
William Henry Fry, Arthur Foote, in addition to later composers Samuel Barber, John Cage, and Walter Piston

Music for all Seasons (Crystal Records)
John Antes

The Dawning of Music in Kentucky (Vanguard Classics)
Anthony Philip Heinrich

The Wind Demon (New World Records)
George Frederick Bristow, William Henry Fry, Anthony Philip Heinrich

John Knowles Paine: Symphony No. 2 (New World Records)
The symphony is conducted by Zubin Mehta, a Paine champion

MacDowell: Piano Music Volume I (Naxos)
James Barbagallo is the pianist. This recording includes the entire *Woodland Sketches* collection of piano pieces, perhaps MacDowell's most enduring and characteristic work.

Mainstream American Composers

Of the many composers listed in this book, some are considered essential. Such generalization is superficial, yet it provides starting points for new listeners unaccustomed to the unique harmonies of American music in the 20th and 21st centuries.

Aaron Copland: Copland is much beloved by all classical audiences, and his music contains much variety. Listeners who adore *Appalachian Spring* might be repelled by the Piano Variations. Nonadventurous listeners should stick to the orchestral works, and, in particular, the ballet music such as *Appalachian Spring, Rodeo,* and *Billy the Kid.* Copland's symphony entitled *Quiet City* also employs the distinctively open harmonies that mark Copland as peculiarly American.

Samuel Barber: Barber was the most popular American composer of the mid-20th century. His Adagio for Strings is probably recognizable to thousands of people who would not have believed that they were acquainted with American music. Barber's two "Essays" for orchestra are also infused with post-romantic spirit and easy-to-take drama. The only solo piano music from Barber's pen recommended here is the Piano Sonata, and it requires

greater stamina than the orchestra work. If the entire sonata is too challenging at first, try just the last movement, a thrilling fugue.

Leonard Bernstein: Bernstein penned *West Side Story,* a musical with classical overtones. He also wrote symphonies, the Concerto for Orchestra, the *Chichester Psalms,* and the ambitious, sprawling Mass. One can never be sure what a Bernstein piece will deliver. The composer drew upon numerous influences and musical experience. Nothing he wrote is harsh for the sake of harshness.

Walter Piston: Within Piston's modestly sized portfolio, the two violin concertos are unhesitatingly recommended, as well as the *Three New England Sketches.* Piston also composed several symphonies, two of which won Pulitzer Prizes. All his music is richly textured, meticulously structured, and possesses romantic threads within a finely engineered tapestry.

Charles Ives: Ives simply cannot be ignored, though many listeners would like to disregard him. His music is no less despised by those wrongly to it than it is respected by everyone who understands his amazingly progressive work. One short orchestral work that makes a good introduction is the atmospheric and beautiful *From the Steeples and the Mountains.* Somewhat more adventurous is *Three Places in New England.* Approach the Second Piano Sonata—the so-called *Concord* Sonata—with the utmost caution, but remember also that it is a landmark creation of American music.

William Schuman: Though revered by musicologists, Schuman does not get the popular attention that his work deserves; perhaps his many administrative duties prevented him from the requisite self-promotion. Schuman's music is evocative, robust, and well paced. The Violin Concerto and *New England Tryptich* are conveniently packaged together on some discs, including one from the Naxos American Series. His *American Festival Overture* launched his career, and his Symphony no. 3 was an early award winner.

John Adams: Both challenging and moving, *On the Transmigration of Souls,* which was premiered one year after the September 11 terrorist attacks, and which won a Pulitzer Prize, is recommended listening. For more traditional forms, his Violin Concerto is worthwhile. Also, *Shaker Loops,* possibly Adams's most recognized work, is on the must-listen list of American music.

Online Listening

Classical music is not represented in online listening and downloading services with the same vigor as other genres. Three services are recommended:

Rhapsody: A division of RealNetworks (www.real. com), Rhapsody is a monthly subscription service that allows unlimited, high-quality listening as well as per-track downloading. Since classical tracks are much longer than those of popular music, substantial bargains are available. At the time of this writing, Rhapsody charged 89 cents per downloaded track, so a major symphony or concerto could be owned for as little as $2.67. Tracks are downloaded directly to a burned CD, from which they can be copied to the format of choice, so portability is not a problem as with some competing services. Rhapsody carries the entire Naxos catalog, which would be reason enough to consider a subscription; it also carries other classical labels.

Naxos: The Naxos label has recently inaugurated an online listening service directly from its Web site (www.naxos.com). At this writing pricing is $19.99 per year for unlimited listening to every track of every Naxos album. Downloading and burning are currently not options. Notwithstanding that limitation, the low price makes the Naxos service an attractive option for anyone interested exclusively in classical music.

Andante: The classical service Andante (www. andante.com) does not particularly specialize in American classical music, but it does feature an ongoing schedule of recent concerts by one of America's great orchestras—the Philadelphia Orchestra. Of course, American music is included in its many recordings and archived streams for subscribers.

Appendix II

Chronology

This chronology of American classical music highlights important events, birth and death years, music premieres, and other milestones. Although not comprehensive, the chronology conveys music's evolution in America by charting milestones in the country's classical music culture. Every name and title in this time line is represented by an individual entry in the book.

Late 17th century

The *Bay Psalm Book*, generally regarded as the first American-printed book to contain music, is published.

1740

John Antes, the first American-born composer to write chamber music, is born.

1759

Francis Hopkinson publishes the song "My Days Have Been So Wondrous Free," usually regarded as the first piece of wholly original American-composed music.

1770

William Billings, a church hymn compiler, publishes the first collection of hymns to contain original compositions.

1778

William Billings publishes a compilation of his original hymns, the first of which are brought out in 1770.

1781

Anthony Philip Heinrich, "the Beethoven of America," is born.

1788

Francis Hopkinson publishes a collection of seven original songs, *Seven Songs*, with a dedication that indicated his awareness of being America's first native-born composer of secular music.

1791

Francis Hopkinson, generally regarded as America's first composer, dies.

1794

Supply Belcher, one of America's earliest composers, publishes a collection of 75 songs, most likely representing his entire output, in a book called *The Harmony of Maine*.

1798

Paul Emile Johns, a Polish-born American pianist who is probably the first to perform a Beethoven piano concerto in America, is born.

1800

William Billings, one of America's earliest composers, dies.

1802

Ureli Corelli Hill, founder of the Philharmonic Society of New York, which later becomes the New York Philharmonic Orchestra, is born.

1811

John Antes, the first American composer of chamber music, dies.

1812

Sigismond Thalberg, the German pianist whose European fame was second only to that of Franz Liszt and who stunned New York with dozens of concerts between 1856 and 1858, is born.

1813

John Sullivan Dwight, the first American-born music critic, is born.

William Henry Fry, "the father of American opera" and the first U.S.-born composer to have a full-scale opera produced in America, is born.

1815

The Handel and Haydn Society, the oldest continually operating classical performing group in America, is founded in Boston.

1816

Anthony Philip Heinrich, the first American composer to create large-scale orchestral scores, emigrates to America from his native Germany.

1819

Paul Emile Johns, Polish-born American pianist, performs a Beethoven concerto in the United States for the first time.

1820

Jenny Lind, the Swedish soprano who took America by storm in an 1850 tour arranged by P. T. Barnum, is born.

1821

Carl Bergmann, German-born American composer who introduced Richard Wagner operas to American audiences, is born.

1825

George Frederick Bristow, composer of operas, orchestral pieces, and piano music, is born.

1829

Louis Moreau Gottschalk, America's first piano virtuoso, is born.

1832

Leopold Damrosch, European conductor who founded the New York Symphony Society, which later merged with another orchestra to form the New York Philharmonic, is born.

1835

Theodore Thomas, founding music director of the Chicago Symphony Orchestra (then the Chicago Orchestra), is born.

1836

Supply Belcher, an early American composer, dies.

1839

John Knowles Paine, composer who created the music curriculum at Harvard University, is born.

1841

Antonín Dvořák, Czech composer whose three-year stay in America was meant to jump-start American classical music, is born.

1842

This year is usually regarded as the founding date of the New York Philharmonic, America's oldest orchestra. It was begun as the Philharmonic Symphony Society of New York.

1844

Amy Fay, American pianist who traveled to Europe and was one of the few American pianists to study with Franz Liszt (she later published a diary of the experience), is born.

1845

William Henry Fry's *Leonora*, the first full-scale opera composed by an American to be staged, is premiered in Philadelphia.

1846

The New York Philharmonic (then the Philharmonic Symphony Society of New York) performs the American premiere of Beethoven's Symphony no. 9.

1847

The Mormon Tabernacle Choir is founded.

Ureli Corelli Hill, founded of the Philharmonic Symphony Society of New York (later to become the New York Philharmonic), ends his presidency of the orchestra.

1849

Blind Tom (Thomas Bethune), an autistic musical prodigy who was exhibited widely and who performed in the White House, is born.

1851

Minnie Hauk, one of the first American opera singers to gain international recognition, is born.

1853

Composer Arthur Foote is born.

Louis Moreau Gottschalk, America's first great piano virtuoso, returns to the United States after studying piano in Europe, and immediately begins a breathtaking touring schedule.

1854

George Whitefield Chadwick, one of the most important American composers of his generation, is born.

John Philip Sousa, legendary bandmaster and composer of patriotic marches, is born.

1856

German pianist Sigismond Thalberg arrives in New York and dazzles audiences for two years with piano concerts. Thalberg is one of the first European musicians to tour in the New World.

1857

The Peabody Conservatory, the oldest music academy in the United States, is founded in Baltimore.

1859

A Richard Wagner opera, *Tannhäuser,* is performed for the first time in America, in New York, conducted by Carl Bergmann.

1860

Paul Emile Johns, the Polish-born American pianist, dies.

Edward MacDowell, the most successful American composer of the late 19th century and founder of the MacDowell Colony, is born.

1861

The music publisher G. Schirmer is started when Gustav Schirmer takes over another publisher in New York.

Anthony Philip Heinrich, "the Beethoven of America," dies.

Composer Charles Martin Loeffler is born.

The Brooklyn Academy of Music is inaugurated.

1862

Walter Damrosch, son of Leopold Damrosch, a prominent New York conductor, is born.

1863

Horatio Parker, composer and educator who developed the music department at Yale University, is born.

1864

Composer William Henry Fry, sometimes called "the father of American opera," dies.

1865

Piano virtuoso Louis Moreau Gottschalk, who had concertized in America for 12 wildly successful years, is forced to leave the country in the wake of charges of sexual impropriety with a teenage student.

Chamber music violinist and educator Franz Kneisel is born.

The Oberlin Conservatory is founded.

1866

Henry Burleigh, one of the first African-American composers, is born.

1867

Composer, Amy Beach, one of the most prominent women in American musical history, was born.

Scott Joplin, preeminent ragtime composer, is born.

The New England Conservatory, America's oldest continually operating independent music school, is founded.

Italian Conductor Arturo Toscanini, who became one of the greatest forces in American classical music, is born.

1868

Composer Henry F. B. Gilbert is born.

Sissieretta Jones, a celebrated singer and the first African-American singer who attempted (mostly unsuccessfully) an opera career, is born.

1869

Lawrence Freeman, the first African-American composer to conduct his own works (mostly operas), is born.

Louis Moreau Gottschalk, America's first piano virtuoso, dies.

1870

Composer Henry Eichheim is born.

1871

Frederick Converse, one of the most important composers of early 20th-century America, is born.

Sigismond Thalberg, the German pianist who electrified New York audiences in the 1850s, dies.

1872

Composer, musicologist, and publisher Arthur Farwell is born.

Edward Burlingame Hill, the composer who followed in John Knowles Paine's footsteps at Harvard University, is born.

1873

Oscar Sonneck, the first American musicologist, is born.

1874

Composer Charles Ives is born.

Conductor Serge Koussevitzky is born.

1875

Conductor Ureli Corelli Hill, founder of the Philharmonic Symphony Society of New York (later to become the New York Philharmonic), dies.

Composer John Knowles Paine becomes a music professor at Harvard University, ultimately creating a curriculum that is copied by other Ivy League universities.

1876

Composer John Alden Carpenter is born.

Composer Carl Ruggles is born.

Conductor Bruno Walter is born.

Theodore Thomas begins his musical directorship of the Philharmonic Symphony Society of New York (later to become the New York Philharmonic), before becoming founding conductor of the Chicago Symphony.

1878

Leopold Damrosch founds the New York Symphony Society.

The Los Angeles Philharmonic Society (later to become the Los Angeles Philharmonic Orchestra) is founded.

1880

Composer Ernest Bloch is born.

1881

The Boston Symphony Orchestra is founded.

1882

Composer Marion Bauer is born.

Pianist and composer Percy Grainger is born.

Conductor Leopold Stokowski is born.

1883

The Metroplitan Opera is founded, giving its first performance on October 22.

Composer Edgard Varèse, the so-called father of electronic music, is born.

1884

Composer Charles Griffes is born.

Composer Louis Gruenberg is born.

1885

The Boston Pops Orchestra is founded.

Conductor and founder of the New York Symphony Society Leopold Damrosch dies.

The National Conservatory of Music is founded.

Composer Wallingford Riegger is born.

Composer Deems Taylor is born.

1886

Composer John J. Becker is born.

The New York Philharmonic moves to the Metropolitan Opera House, where it performs until 1892.

1887

Legendary French teacher of American composers Nadia Boulanger is born.

Eleven-year-old pianist Josef Hoffman makes his dazzling New York debut at the Metropolitan Opera House.

Soprano Jenny Lind dies.

Violinist and teacher (of Isaac Stern, Yehudi Menuhin, and others) Louis Persinger is born.

Pianist Arthur Rubinstein is born.

Pianist Paul Wittgenstein is born. He loses his right arm in World War I and inspires many composers to create works for the left hand.

1888

Conductor Fritz Reiner is born.

The Theodore Thomas Orchestra is disbanded in New York, leading the way for Thomas to become founding conductor of the Chicago Symphony Orchestra.

1889

Carnegie Hall is built in New York by Andrew Carnegie.

Virtuoso pianist David Saperton is born.

Violinist Efrem Zimbalist is born.

Polish-born pianist Leopold Godowsky moves to the United States.

1891

Carnegie Hall opens its doors for its first concert on May 5, featuring Russian composer Pyotr Tchaikovsky as conductor.

The Chicago Symphony Orchestra is founded (as the Chicago Orchestra), with Theodore Thomas as conductor.

Violinist Mischa Elman is born.

Publisher G. Schirmer installs its own engraving and printing facility, establishing itself as America's preeminent music publisher.

1892

British music publisher Boosey & Hawkes opens a New York office and becomes an important publisher of American composers.

Czech composer Antonín Dvořák begins his three-year tenure as director of the National Conservatory in New York, attempting to inspire a generation of American composers and writing the *From the New World* symphony.

Composer and arranger Ferde Grofé is born.

Pianist Mieczyslaw Horszowski is born.

Sissieretta Jones performs at the White House at the apex of a singing career limited by her skin color.

1893

John Sullivan Dwight, the first American-born music critic, dies.

The symphony *From the New World* by Antonín Dvořák, inspired by America while the composer was living in New York, is premiered in Carnegie Hall to great acclaim.

Horatio Parker's *Hora Novissima* is premiered, launching Parker's national reputation.

Composer and pianist Leo Ornstein is born.

New Boston Music Hall (later Symphony Hall) is inaugurated.

1894

Composer and arranger Robert Russell Bennett is born.

Arthur Fiedler, who becomes the beloved conductor of the Boston Pops for nearly 50 years, is born.

Horatio Parker joins the faculty of Yale University, where he later becomes dean of the music department.

Composer Walter Piston is born.

1895

The Cincinnati Symphony Orchestra gives its first concert.

Frederick Stock becomes music director of the Chicago Symphony Orchestra, remaining at the post for 37 years.

Composer Paul Hindemith is born.

The Pittsburgh Symphony Orchestra is founded (as the Pittsburgh Orchestra).

Composer Leo Sowerby is born.

Composer and conductor William Grant Still is born.

1896

Pianist Simon Barere is born.

Composer Howard Hanson is born.

Edward MacDowell purchases the farm that later becomes the MacDowell Colony.

Conductor Dimitri Mitropoulos is born.

Composer Roger Sessions is born.

John Philip Sousa composes "Stars and Stripes Forever."

Composer Virgil Thomson is born.

1897

Contralto and groundbreaking civil rights ambassador Marian Anderson is born.

George Whitefield Chadwick takes over the directorship of the New England Conservatory, to transform it from a local music school to an internationally recognized training academy.

Composer Henry Cowell is born.

Soprano Rosa Ponselle is born.

Conductor George Szell is born.

1898

Composer Ernst Bacon is born.

Composer George Gershwin is born.

Composer Roy Harris is born.

The performing arts magazine *Musical America* is founded.

1899

Conductor and producer Peter Herman Adler is born.

Conductor Eugene Ormandy is born.

Conductor William Steinberg, who leads the Pittsburgh Symphony Orchestra for 25 years, is born.

Composer Randall Thompson is born.

1900

Pianist and composer George Antheil is born.

Conductor Leon Barzin, who would found the New York City Ballet, is born.

Pianist Harold Bauer makes his American debut with the Boston Symphony Orchestra.

Composer Aaron Copland is born.

The Dallas Symphony Orchestra is founded (as the Dallas Symphony Club).

Violinist Joseph Fuchs is born.

Composer and pioneer of electronic music Otto Luening is born.

The Philadelphia Orchestra is founded, performing its first concert on November 16.

1901

Composer Ruth Crawford is born.

Composer Arthur Farwell founds the Wa-Wan Press, which publishes Amerindian-inspired classical music until its discontinuation in 1912.

Violinist Jascha Heifetz is born.

Conductor André Kostelanetz is born.

Violinist William Kroll is born.

Composer Harry Partch is born.

1902

Rudolf Bing, later to become a famed general manager of the Metropolitan Opera, is born.

The Kneisel Hall Chamber Music Festival is founded in Maine.

Daniel Gregory Mason's book *From Grieg to Brahms* is published, one of the first American works of music appreciation.

Conductor Max Rudolf is born.

Musicologist Oscar Sonneck takes over the music division of the Library of Congress, where he amasses America's first large collection of books and music manuscripts.

Alice Tully, singer and music philanthropist, is born.

Composer Stefan Wolpe is born.

1903

Conductor Maurice Abravanel is born.

The Brooklyn Academy of Music is destroyed by fire; a rebuilt Academy opens in 1908.

Amy Fay takes over the New York Women's Philharmonic Society, presiding over it until 1914.

Violinist and teacher Ivan Galamian is born.

Pianist Vladimir Horowitz is born.

Violinist Louis Krasner is born.

The Minneapolis Symphony Orchestra is founded, later to become the Minnesota Orchestra.

Cellist Gregor Piatigorsky is born.

The Seattle Symphony, then an impromptu group of 24 musicians, gives its first performance.

Pianist Rudolf Serkin is born.

1904

The Chicago Symphony Orchestra moves to its permanent home, Symphony Hall.

Antonín Dvořák, the Czech composer who influenced the course of American music, dies.

Operetta composer Victor Herbert ends his controversial directorship of the Pittsburgh Symphony Orchestra and forms his own orchestra.

Composer Edward MacDowell ends his close association with Columbia University, resigning in protest of the school's new president.

Violinist Nathan Milstein is born.

Composer Horatio Parker is named dean of the music department of Yale University, with which institution he is associated until his death in 1919.

1905

Composer Marc Blitzstein is born.

Conductor Theodore Thomas dies.

Louis Coerne's opera *Zenobia* becomes the first American opera produced in Europe (Bremen, Germany).

The Institute of Musical Art (later the Juilliard School) is founded in New York.

Pianist John Kirkpatrick is born.

1906

Pianist Artur Balsam is born.

German conductor Carl Muck takes over directorship of the Boston Symphony Orchestra; he is later driven out of the country by anti-German war propaganda.

Composer Paul Creston is born.

Conductor Antal Dorati is born.

Composer Ross Lee Finney is born.

Pianist Mieczyslaw Horszowski gives his American debut at Carnegie Hall.

Pianist, actor, composer, and humorist Oscar Levant is born.

Pianist and teacher Adele Marcus is born.

Composer John Knowles Paine dies.

Pianist Arthur Rubinstein makes his American debut with the Philadelphia Orchestra in Carnegie Hall.

The San Francisco earthquake devastates cultural life in that city, destroying many of its opera halls.

1907

Oscar Sonneck's groundbreaking musicological work, *Early Concert-Life in America,* is published.

1908

Autistic savant and pianist Blind Tom Bethune dies.

The Brooklyn Academy of Music reopens after its original building burned down in 1903.

The Buffalo Philharmonic Orchestra is founded as the Philharmonic Society of Buffalo.

Composer Elliott Carter is born.

Italian Impresario and administrator Giulio Gatti-Casazza begins his legendary directorship of the Metropolitan Opera.

The Cleveland Chamber Symphony is founded by Edwin London.

Composer Edward MacDowell dies; the MacDowell Colony is founded.

Conductor Arturo Toscanini begins a seven-year conductorship of the Metropolitan Opera.

Violinist Alexander Schneider is born.

Violinist Albert Spalding makes his American debut at Carnegie Hall.

Pianist and humorist Victor Borge is born.

Leopold Stokowski becomes music director of the Cincinnati Symphony Orchestra.

1910

Composer Samuel Barber is born.

The Pittsburgh Symphony Orchestra ceases operation because of financial troubles. It resumes performances in 1926.

Composer William Schuman is born.

1911

Composer Alan Hovhaness is born.

Harpsichordist Ralph Kirkpatrick is born.

Austrian composer Gustav Mahler, who conducts the Metropolitan Opera and the New York Philharmonic, dies.

Composer Gian Carlo Menotti is born.

The San Francisco Symphony Orchestra is founded.

1912

Composer and scholar Arthur Berger is born.

Composer John Cage is born.

The Eastman School of Music is founded.

Pianist Rudolf Firkusny is born.

Conductor Erich Leinsdorf is born.

Composer Conlon Nancarrow is born.

Leopold Stokowski becomes music director of the Philadelphia Orchestra, where he remains until 1938.

Conductor Georg Solti is born.

Composer Hugo Weisgall is born.

1913

Composer Henry Brant is born.

Composer Norman Dello Joio is born.

Composer Vivian Fine is born.

Composer, pianist, and conductor Morton Gould is born.

The Houston Symphony Orchestra is founded.

The Los Angeles Symphony Orchestra, which grew out of a symphonic society founded in 1878, gives its first performance.

Tenor Richard Tucker is born.

1914

Pianist Jorge Bolet is born.

The Detroit Symphony Orchestra is founded.

Composer Irving Fine is born.

Violinist Ruth Posselt is born.

Pianist Rosalyn Tureck is born.

1915

Composer David Diamond is born.

Conductor Dean Dixon is born.

Conductor Arturo Toscanini completes his conductorship of the Metropolitan Opera, where he made his U.S. opera debut in 1908.

Musical Quarterly is founded.

Composer George Perle is born.

Composer Vincent Persichetti is born.

Music critic Harold C. Schonberg is born.

Oscar Sonneck's grounbreaking musicological book *Early Opera in America* is published.

Pianist Earl Wild is born.

1916

Composer Milton Babbitt is born.

The Baltimore Symphony Orchestra is founded.

Composer William W. Gilchrist dies.

Cellist Bernard Greenhouse is born.

The Mannes College of Music opens in New York as the David Mannes Music School.

Violinist Yehudi Menuhin is born.

Choral conductor Robert Shaw is born.

1917

The Cincinnati Symphony Orchestra makes its first recording.

Charles Griffes's *The Pleasure-Dome of Kublah Kahn* is premiered in New York, making Griffes a classical celebrity.

Composer Lou Harrison is born.

Ragtime composer Scott Joplin dies.

The Manhattan School of Music is founded.

Baritone Robert Merrill is born.

The San Francisco Conservatory of Music is founded.

Violinist Oscar Shumsky is born.

1918

Conductor and composer Leonard Bernstein is born.

The Cleveland Orchestra is founded as the Cleveland Symphony Orchestra.

Ossip Gabrilovich becomes music director of the Detroit Symphony Orchestra.

Pianist Eugene List is born.

Soprano Rosa Ponselle makes her debut at the Metropolitan Opera, her first operatic performance.

Violinist Riggiero Ricci is born.

Composer George Rochberg is born.

Cellist Leonard Rose is born.

1919

Pianist Leon Kirchner is born.

Pianist and showman Liberace is born.

The Los Angeles Philharmonic is founded as an outgrowth of the Los Angeles Symphony Orchestra.

Composer and educator Horatio Parker dies.

Edgard Varèse founds the New Symphony Orchestra.

1920

The Cincinnati Opera is founded.

The Cleveland Institute of Music is founded.

Composer Charles Griffes dies.

Pianist William Masselos is born.

Pierre Monteux begins his musical directorship of the Boston Symphony Orchestra.

Violinist Isaac Stern is born.

1921

Composer William Bergsma is born.

Composer Andrew Imbrie is born.

John Alden Carpenter's *Krazy Kat* is premiered, pioneering the use of jazz in a classical work.

Willem Mengelberg begins his conductorship of the New York Philharmonic, remaining in the position until 1927.

Composer Ralph Shapey is born.

1922

Charles Ives publishes *114 Songs*, a compilation of his own work.

Fritz Reiner becomes music director of the Cincinnati Symphony Orchestra.

Composer Lukas Foss is born.

Pianist Abbey Simon is born.

1923

Composer Leslie Bassett is born.

Soprano Maria Callas is born.

The League of Composers is founded.

Composer William Kraft is born.

Composer and educator Peter Mennin is born.

The San Francisco Opera is founded.

Composer Daniel Pinkham is born.

Composer Ned Rorem is born.

Conductor Bruno Walter makes his first U.S. appearance in Carnegie Hall, leading the New York Symphony Orchestra.

1924

Conductor Serge Koussevitsky begins his legendary directorship of the Boston Symphony Orchestra.

Composer Henry Cowell makes his New York debut in Carnegie Hall to savage reviews.

The Curtis Institute of Music is founded.

George Gershwin premieres *Rhapsody in Blue* in New York and instantly becomes an international classical superstar, installed as an historic musical figure.

Operetta composer and conductor Victor Herbert dies.

Pianist Byron Janis is born.

The Institute of Musical Art in New York changes its name to the Juilliard School of Music.

Pianist Rosina Lhévinne joins the faculty of the Juilliard School of Music, remaining there for 50 years as one of the country's most influential piano teachers.

John Alden Carpenter's ballet *Skycrapers* is premiered at the Metropolitan Opera.

Contralto Marian Anderson gives her debut at New York's Town Hall.

1925

Conductor Pierre Boulez is born.

Pianist Eugene Istomin is born.

Composer and administrator Gunther Schuller is born.

American composer George Antheil's *Ballet mécanique* is premiered in Europe, installing Antheil as the most important avant-garde composer of the day.

Composer Earle Brown is born.

Composer Morton Feldman is born.

Composer Carlisle Floyd is born.

Pianist Josef Hofmann becomes director of the Curtis Institute.

Violinist and chamber music specialist Franz Kneisel dies.

The Pittsburgh Symphony Orchestra, out of operation since 1910, resumes its performances.

Composer David Tudor is born.

1927

The American premiere of George Antheil's *Ballet mécanique* is performed in Carnegie Hall. One of the great disasters in concert history, the chaotic performance ruins Antheil's career.

Composer Dominick Argento is born.

Charles Ives stops composing, in one of the most mysterious cessations of creativity to strike a composer.

Soprano Leontyne Price is born.

Pianist and writer Charles Rosen is born.

1928

Composer Samuel Adler is born.

George Gershwin's *An American in Paris* is premiered at Carnegie Hall by the New York Symphony Orchestra.

The New York Symphony Society merges with the Philharmonic Society of New York to form the New York Philharmonic.

Composer Jacob Druckman is born.

Pianist and diarist Amy Fay dies.

Pianist Leon Fleisher is born.

Pianist Gary Graffman is born.

Pianist Vladimir Horowitz arrives in America and makes his U.S. debut on January 12.

Pianist Jacob Lateiner is born.

Violinist Yehudi Menuhin makes his first recording.

Conductor Arturo Toscanini becomes music director of the New York Philharmonic, remaining at that position until 1936.

Oscar Sonneck, America's first musicologist, dies.

1929

Composer George Crumb is born.

Minnie Hauk, one of the first American singers to gain international renown, dies.

Mezzo-soprano Marilyn Horne is born.

Violinist Nathan Milstein makes his American debut with the New York Philharmonic.

Cellist Gregor Piatigorsky makes his American debut with the New York Philharmonic.

Composer and conductor André Previn is born.

Artur Rodzinsky becomes music director of the Los Angeles Philharmonic.

Soprano Beverly Sills is born.

1930

Groundbreaking opera composer Robert Ashley is born.

Arthur Fiedler is named conductor of the Boston Pops, starting one of the most enduring collaborations of orchestra and conductor in history.

The Boston Symphony Orchestra celebrates its 50th season (1930–31), during which music director Serge Koussevitsky commissions dozens of new works.

Conductor Lorin Maazel is born.

The New York Philharmonic undertakes its first European tour, led by music director Arturo Toscanini.

Conductor Thomas Schippers is born.

1931

Composer George Whitefield Chadwick dies.

Severence Hall is built in Cleveland as the home of the Cleveland Orchestra.

Ferde Grofé composes *Grand Canyon Suite,* which helps popularize orchestral music to American audiences.

Composer Donald Martino is born.

Eugene Ormandy becomes conductor of the Minnesota Orchestra, where he remains until 1936.

The National Symphony Orchestra is founded.

1932

Pianist Arthur Rubinstein retires from public performing, a break that lasts five years.

Composer and bandleader John Philip Sousa dies.

Film composer and conductor John Williams is born.

1933

Pianist John Browning is born.

Artur Rodzinski becomes conductor of the Cleveland Orchestra, holding the position until 1943.

Celebrated singer Sissieretta Jones, whose classical career was largely thwarted because of her skin color, dies.

Otto Klemperer becomes music director of the Los Angeles Philharmonic in a tenure that lasts until 1939.

Composer Morton Subotnick is born.

1934

Pianist Van Cliburn is born.

Composer Mario Davidovsky is born.

Werner Janssen becomes the first native New Yorker to conduct the New York Philharmonic.

Composer Bernard Rands is born.

Composer Roger Reynolds is born.

Composer Richard Wernick is born.

1935

Contralto Marian Anderson gives a seminal concert in New York's Town Hall after several years' study in Europe. The concert establishes her as one of the great singers of the day.

The Buffalo Philharmonic is founded as the Buffalo Philharmonic Orchestra Society.

The Cleveland Women's Orchestra is founded.

George Gershwin's "folk opera" *Porgy and Bess* opens on Broadway.

Edward Johnson becomes general manager of the Metropolitan Opera, remaining there until 1950.

Pianist Gilbert Kalish is born.

Composer and violinist Charles Martin Loeffler dies.

Conductor Jorge Mester is born.

Baritone Sherrill Milnes is born.

Conductor Seiji Ozawa is born.

Composer Terry Riley is born.

Humorist Peter Schickele, creator of P.D.Q. Bach, is born.

1936

Conductor Maurice Abravanel makes his debut at the Metropolitan Opera, five years before taking over the Utah Symphony Orchestra.

Samuel Barber composes Adagio for Strings (an adaptation of the second movement of his earlier String Quartet), one of the most popular and enduring of all American compositions.

Conductor James DePreist is born.

Composer Rubin Goldmark dies.

Pianist Vladimir Horowitz begins the first of his four retirements from the concert stage, this one lasting until 1938.

Conductor Zubin Mehta is born.

Conductor Pierre Monteux assumes the conductorship of the San Francisco Symphony, holding the position until 1952.

John Barbirolli becomes music director of the New York Philharmonic, succeeding Arturo Toscanini in a relatively short (until 1941) and arguably unsuccessful tenure.

Ravinia becomes the official summer home of the Chicago Symphony Orchestra.

Composer Steve Reich is born.

William Grant Still becomes the first African-American conductor to lead a major American orchestra, the Los Angeles Philharmonic.

Conductor Leopold Stokowski resigns his directorship of the Philadelphia Orchestra, in conflict with orchestra management over Stokowski's programming of modern music.

1937

Pianist Jorge Bolet wins the Naumberg International Piano Competition.

The Boston Symphony Orchestra begins its summer residency at Tanglewood.

Composer John Cage meets choreographer Merce Cunningham; this leads to an enduring artistic collaboration.

Pianist John Kirkpatrick performs the premiere of Charles Ives's *Concord* Sonata.

Composer David Del Tredici is born.

Conductor Antal Dorati makes his American debut with the National Symphony Orchestra.

Composer Arthur Foote dies.

Composer George Gershwin dies suddenly at age 38 of a brain tumor.

Composer Philip Glass is born.

Conductor Neeme Järvi is born.

Pianist Ruth Laredo is born.

Conductor Dimitri Mitropoulos becomes conductor of the Minnesota Orchestra, remaining there until 1949.

Conductor Arturo Toscanini takes over the NBC Symphony Orchestra, which had been created expressly for him. Toscanini leads the orchestra until 1954, during which time the orchestra's concerts are frequently broadcast.

Conductor Otto Klemperer becomes music director of the Pittsburgh Symphony Orchestra for a single season, after which he is credited with bringing the orchestra up to high artistic standards.

Pianist Arthur Rubinstein emerges from a five-year concert retirement, having solved his technical difficulties, and begins a blazing career as one of America's most beloved pianists.

Pianist Rosalyn Tureck gives a series of all-Bach concerts in Carnegie Hall, focusing her reputation as a preeminent Bach specialist.

1938

Composer Samuel Barber wins his first Pulitzer Prize for the opera *Vanessa*.

Composer William Bolcom is born.

Composer John Corigliano is born.

Pianist Leopold Godowsky dies.

Composer John Harbison is born.

Conductor Eugene Ormandy begins an historic directorship with the Philadelphia Orchestra, succeeding Leopold Stokowski. Ormandy is credited with first creating the famed "Philadelphia sound." Ormandy conducts the orchestra for 42 years.

Conductor Fritz Reiner becomes music director of the Pittsburgh Symphony Orchestra, holding that position until 1948.

Pianist Rudolf Serkin begins a famous association with the Curtis Institute of Music, joining the faculty in this year and eventually becoming the school's director (in 1968).

Composer Charles Wuorinen is born.

1939

Composer William Schuman completes his *American Festival Overture*, which establishes him as a major American composer.

The American Music Center is founded.

In a legendary concert that unites music and civil rights, contralto Marian Anderson performs in front of the Lincoln Memorial in Washington, D.C., before an audience of 75,000 and millions of radio listeners. The concert was organized by First Lady Eleanor Roosevelt, in response to Anderson's rejection at Constitution Hall, run by the Daughters of the American Revolution.

Composer and synthesist Wendy Carlos is born (as Walter Carlos).

Composer Ellen Taaffe Zwilich is born.

1940

The Utah Symphony Orchestra is founded.

Composer Aaron Copland's ballet music *Billy the Kid* is premiered.

Composer Frederick Converse dies.

Conductor Christoph Eschenbach is born.

Sidney Foster becomes the first pianist to win the prestigious Leventritt Award.

Italian director of the Metropolitan Opera (1908–35) Guilio Gatti-Casazza dies.

Pianist Stephen Kovacevich is born.

Conductor Carl Muck, whose career in Boston was curtailed by anti-German hysteria at the start of World War I, dies.

Arturo Toscanini conducts the NBC Symphony Orchestra in radio-broadcast performances of Samuel Barber's Adagio for Strings, making Barber an instant classical star.

Composer Lewis Spratlan is born.

1941

Composer Stephen Albert is born.

Dean Dixon becomes the first African-American conductor to lead the NBC Symphony Orchestra.

Pianist William Kapell wins the Naumburg Award.

Violinist Jaime Laredo is born.

Conductor Riccardo Muti is born.

Conductor Bruno Walter makes his Metropolitan Opera debut, receiving 13 curtain calls.

Violinist Efrem Zimbalist becomes director of the Curtis Institute, a position he holds until 1968.

1942

The American Symphony Orchestra League is founded.

The Baltimore Symphony Orchestra is reorganized as a private institution after its initial founding, in 1916, as a municipally funded group.

Pianist and conductor Daniel Barenboim is born.

Antal Dorati becomes conductor of the Dallas Symphony Orchestra.

Dean Dixon becomes the first African-American conductor to conduct the New York Philharmonic.

Composer Charles Dodge is born.

Composer Henry Eichheim dies.

Aaron Copland's *Fanfare for the Common Man* is premiered; the three-minute piece becomes one of the most recognized American-composed works.

The Koussevitsky Music Foundation is formed to commission new works.

Bass Samuel Ramey is born.

Conductor Frederick Stock dies.

Clarinettest Richard Stoltzman is born.

Pianist Earl Wild makes his broadcast debut with Arturo Toscanini conducting the NBC Symphony Orchestra, playing George Gershwin's *Rhapsody in Blue*. The performance establishes Wild as a piano soloist and Gershwin specialist, though he had never before performed Gershwin.

1943

The Daughters of the American Revolution, a group that had in 1939 forbidden a performance by African-American contralto Marian Anderson in Constitution Hall, invites Anderson to perform in that hall.

Composers and partners Samuel Barber and Gian Carlo Menotti purchase the Capricorn estate in Mt. Kisco, New York, which becomes an informal artistic colony.

Conductor Leonard Bernstein is named assistant conductor of the New York Philharmonic under Artur Rodzinski.

John Cage stages a performance of his music in New York, hoping to launch his career. The concert is a devastating failure, setting off a period of impoverishment for Cage.

Conductor Erich Leinsdorf becomes music director of the Cleveland Orchestra, staying until 1946.

The first Pulitzer Prize for music is awarded, to composer William Schuman for *Free Song*.

Pianist Richard Goode is born.

Pianist Eugene Istomin wins the Levintritt Award.

Conductor James Levine is born.

Conductor Alfred Wallenstein becomes music director of the Los Angeles Philharmonic Orchestra, remaining until 1956.

Violinist Sergio Luca is born.

Conductor Artur Rodzinsky is named music director of the New York Philharmonic, remaining until 1947.

Composer Joseph Schwantner is born.

1944

George Antheil's Symphony no. 4 is premiered by the NBC Symphony Orchestra under Leopold

Stokowski, bringing Antheil back into the public eye after a career slump of 17 years following the disastrous American premiere of his *Ballet mécanique*.

The Atlanta Symphony Orchestra is founded as the Atlanta Youth Symphony Orchestra.

Composer Amy Beach dies.

Conductor Dennis Russell Davies is born.

Conductor Dean Dixon founds the American Youth Orchestra.

Cellist Lynn Harrell is born.

The Albeneri Trio is founded.

Composer Edgar Stillman Kelley dies.

Conductor Leonard Slatkin is born.

Conductor Michael Tilson Thomas is born.

1945

Composer Aaron Copland's *Appalachian Spring* wins Pulitzer Prize.

Conductor Antal Dorati is named music director of the Dallas Symphony, remaining until 1949.

Baritone Robert Merrill makes his Metropolitan Opera debut in *La Traviata*.

Violinist Isaac Stern makes his first recording.

Tenor Richard Tucker makes his Metropolitan Opera debut.

1946

Composer Charles Wakefield Cadman dies.

George Szell begins his monumental association with the Cleveland Orchestra, remaining as music director until 1970.

The Juilliard String Quartet is founded.

Conductor Max Rudolf makes his Metropolitan Opera debut.

Pianist André Watts is born.

1947

Conductor Maurice Abravanel is named music director of the Utah Symphony Orchestra, holding the position until 1979 and single-handedly turning a small local ensemble into a world-class music institution.

Composer John Adams is born.

Composer and multimedia performing artist Laurie Anderson is born.

Soprano Maria Callas makes her American debut.

Conductor Artur Rodzinski is named music director of the Chicago Symphony Orchestra, remaining for a single season.

Conductor Bruno Walter becomes music director of the New York Philharmonic, remaining for two seasons.

Pianist Murray Perahia is born.

Trumpeter Gerard Schwarz is born.

Pianist Peter Serkin is born.

1948

Soprano Kathleen Battle is born.

Pianist Garrick Ohlsson is born.

Choral conductor Robert Shaw founds the Robert Shaw Chorale.

Composer Virgil Thomson's soundtrack score to the film *Louisiana Story* wins a Pulitzer Prize—the only Pulitzer awarded to a film soundtrack.

1949

The Aspen Music Festival and School is founded.

Pianist Emanuel Ax is born.

Conductor Charles Munch becomes music director of the Boston Symphony Orchestra, succeeding the legendary Serge Koussevitzky.

Composer Henry Burleigh is born.

Conductor Antal Dorati becomes music director of the Minnesota Orchestra, remaining until 1960.

Conductor Leopold Stokowski becomes music director of the New York Philharmonic for a single season.

The Philadelphia Orchestra makes its first overseas tour under music director Eugene Ormandy.

Composer Christopher Rouse is born.

1950

Rudolf Bing becomes General Manager of the Metropolitan Opera, starting an administrative reign that sees the company's modernization and its first racial integrations.

Conductor Rafael Kubelik becomes music director of the Chicago Symphony Orchestra, remaining until 1953.

Conductor Walter Damrosch dies.

Composer Libby Larsen is born.

Conductor Dimitri Mitropoulos becomes music director of the New York Philharmonic, remaining until 1958.

Violinist Elmar Oliveira is born.

Music critic Harold C. Schonberg begins his long and influential association with the *New York Times*.

1951

Composer Gian Carlo Menotti's one-act opera *Amahl and the Night Visitors* is broadcast by the NBC television network, which had commissioned the piece. *Amahl* becomes one of the most-performed short operas in world music history.

Pianist Simon Barere dies.

Pianist Harold Bauer dies.

Composer Ross Bauer is born.

Composer John Alden Carpenter dies.

After a two-year period of inactivity, the Detroit Symphony Orchestra resumes performances.

Conductor Arthur Fiedler, famous as the leader of the Boston Pops, is hired to direct simultaneously the San Francisco Pops Orchestra.

Conductor Serge Koussevitzky dies.

The Marlboro Music School and Festival is founded.

1952

Composer John Cage writes his most famous and controversial piece, *4' 33"*, which contains no notation whatsoever; the performer is instructed to remain silent.

Soprano June Anderson is born.

Composer Arthur Farwell dies.

Conductor William Steinberg is named music director of the Pittsburgh Symphony Orchestra. He remains for 23 years, reigning over one of the most artistically and financially successful orchestral operations in American history.

1953

Pianist and humorist Victor Borge begins a run of 849 performances of a one-man show at the Golden Theater on Broadway.

Fritz Reiner is named music director of the Chicago Symphony Orchestra, remaining until 1963.

Pianist Vladimir Horowitz begins his second retirement period, this one lasting until 1965.

The San Francisco Chamber Orchestra is founded.

Conductor Georg Solti appears on an American podium for the first time, leading the San Francisco Opera.

Conductor Hugh Wolff is born.

1954

The Boston Camerata is founded.

The Brooklyn Philharmonic Orchestra is founded.

Soprano Maria Callas makes her Lyric Theatre of Chicago debut.

Conductor Georg Solti first guest-conducts the Chicago Symphony Orchestra, which he later directs for 22 years.

Pianist Van Cliburn wins the Levintritt Award.

Conductor JoAnne Falletta is born.

Conductor Thomas Beecham leads the Houston Symphony Orchestra for a single season.

Composer Charles Ives dies.

The Lyric Opera of Chicago is founded.

1955

Composer Marion Bauer dies.

The Beaux Arts Trio is founded.

Pianist John Browning wins the Levintritt Award.

Leopold Stokowski becomes the music director of the Houston Symphony Orchestra, remaining until 1960.

Cellist Yo-Yo Ma is born.

Soprano Beverly Sills joins the New York City Opera, the company with which she would be associated throughout her career.

Pianist Robert Taub is born.

1956

Coductor Marin Alsop is born.

Conductor Leonard Bernstein is named co-music director of the New York Philharmonic, sharing the post with Dimitri Mitropoulos.

Composer Richard Danielpour is born.

Guitarist Sharon Isbin is born.

Soprano Sylvia McNair is born.

Cellist Mstislav Rostropovich makes his American debut in Carnegie Hall.

1957

Leonard Bernstein's *West Side Story* is premiered at the Winter Garden Theater on Broadway.

Pianist Josef Hofmann dies.

Conductor Arturo Toscanini dies.

1958

Leonard Bernstein becomes sole music director of the New York Philharmonic, after sharing the position for two years with Dimitri Mitropoulos. Bernstein is the Philharmonic's most glamorous director and its most popular figurehead since the departure of Arturo Toscanini in 1936. Bernstein's 11-year tenure at the Philharmonic makes him the most iconic figure in American classical music history.

Van Cliburn wins the Tchaikovsky International Piano Competition in Moscow, at the height of the cold war, becoming an American classical star of unprecedented magnitude.

Conductor Artur Rodzinski dies.

Max Rudolf becomes music director of the Cincinnati Symphony Orchestra, remaining until 1970.

1959

Composer George Antheil dies.

Composer Milton Babbitt becomes director of the Columbia-Princeton Electronic Music Center.

Composer Ernest Bloch dies.

Soprano Renée Fleming is born.

Conductor Andrew Litton is born.

Conductor Keith Lockhart is born.

The Saint Paul Chamber Orchestra is founded.

Pianist Peter Serkin, Rudolf Serkin's son, makes his debut at the Marlboro Music Festival.

1960

The American Brass Quintet is founded.

Composer Edward Burlingame Hill dies.

Composer Aaron Jay Kernis is born.

Stanislaw Skrowaczewski is named music director of the Minnesota Orchestra, remaining until 1979.

Conductor Dimitri Mitropoulos dies.

Carnegie Hall is saved from demolition, largely through the political and fund-raising efforts of violinist Isaac Stern.

Soprano Dawn Upsahw is born.

Opera singer Deborah Voigt is born.

1961

The Cabrillo Festival of Contemporary Music is founded.

Pianist and composer Percy Grainger dies.

John Barbirolli is named music director of the Houston Symphony Orchestra, remaining until 1967.

Classical-jazz trumpeter Wynton Marsalis is born.

Seiji Ozawa becomes assistant conductor of the New York Philharmonic under Leonard Bernstein.

Composer Wallingford Riegger dies.

Conductor Robert Spano is born.

Conductor Leopold Stokowski makes his Metropolitan Opera debut on crutches, having broken his hip.

Pianist Paul Wittgenstein dies.

1962

The American Symphony Orchestra is founded.

Philharmonic Hall opens in Lincoln Center as the new home of the New York Philharmonic.

Samuel Barber's Piano Concerto, the premiere composition at the opening of Philharmonic Hall, wins Barber a second Pulitzer Prize.

Conductor Erich Leinsdorf becomes music director of the Boston Symphony Orchestra, remaining until 1973.

The quadrennial Van Cliburn International Piano Competition is founded.

Composer Irving Fine dies.

Violinist Fritz Kreisler dies.

Pianist Ruth Laredo makes her Carnegie Hall debut.

Conductor Zubin Mehta is named music director of the Los Angeles Philharmonic, remaining until 1978.

Conductor Lorin Maazel makes his Metropolitan Opera debut.

Conductor and composer André Previn makes his conducting debut with the St. Louis Symphony Orchestra.

Conductor Bruno Walter dies.

1963

Conductor Jean Martinon becomes music director of the Chicago Symphony Orchestra, remaining until 1968.

Conductor Sixten Ehrling becomes music director of the Detroit Symphony Orchestra, remaining until 1973.

Conductor and composer Lukas Foss is named conductor of the Buffalo Philharmonic Orchestra, remaining until 1970.

Composer Paul Hindemith dies. Hindemith, who remained a German citizen, was influential as an American teacher.

Conductor Josef Krips becomes music director of the San Francisco Symphony Orchestra, remaining until 1970.

Peter Mennin assumes the presidency of the Juilliard School.

Conductor Fritz Reiner dies.

Writer Harold C. Schonberg's landmark book *The Great Pianists* is published.

André Watts performs with the New York Philharmonic under Leonard Bernstein, launching his career.

1964

Composer Marc Blitzstein dies.

Conductor Pierre Monteux dies.

Conductor Seiji Ozawa becomes the first music director of the Ravinia Festival.

1965

Singer and civil rights ambassador Marian Anderson gives her last performance, in Carnegie Hall.

Soprano Maria Callas makes her final operatic performance at the Metropolitan Opera.

The Chamber Music Society of Lincoln Center is founded.

Composer Henry Cowell dies.

Pianist Leon Fleisher suffers a disability of his right hand, forcing him into a career as left-handed pianist and teacher. In 1995, Fleisher resumes two-handed performing.

Pianist Vladimir Horowitz emerges from his second retirement period with a spectacular concert in New York.

Composer Edgard Varèse dies.

1966

The Metropolitan Opera House in New York's Lincoln Center is inaugurated.

Composer Samuel Barber's opera *Antony and Cleopatra* is premiered at the gala opening of the Metropolitan Opera House in Lincoln Center, New York. The opera is disastrously reviewed, sending Barber's career and mental health into a spiral from which he never recovers.

The New York City Opera moves to the New York State Theater in Lincoln Center, New York.

Pianist Rudolf Serkin makes the first of two appearances at the White House.

Composer Deems Taylor dies.

1967

Violinist Joshua Bell is born.

Opera singer Mary Garden dies.

André Previn is named music director of the Houston Symphony Orchestra, remaining until 1969.

Morton Subotnick composes *Silver Apples of the Moon,* the first classical work commissioned by a record label, Nonesuch Records.

1968

The Blossom Music Center is founded in Cuyahoga Falls, Ohio.

The album *Switched-On Bach,* by Wendy Carlos, is released.

Three New York concerts of Philip Glass's music bring Glass widespread attention as a minimalist composer.

Conductor Charles Munch dies.

Pianist Rudolf Serkin becomes director of the Curtis Institute, remaining in that position until 1975.

1969

Conductor Leonard Bernstein resigns as music director of the New York Philharmonic, taking the title laureate conductor.

Conductor Georg Solti becomes music director of the Chicago Symphony Orchestra, beginning one of the great associations in orchestral history. He remains in Chicago until 1991.

The Juilliard School moves to Lincoln Center.

Pianist Vladimir Horowitz begins his third retirement from the concert stage, this one lasting until 1974.

The Los Angeles Chamber Orchestra is founded.

George Szell replaces Leonard Bernstein as music director of the New York Philharmonic, remaining for a single season.

1970

Conductor John Barbirolli dies.

Conductor Thomas Schippers is named music director of the Cincinnati Symphony Orchestra, remaining until his death in 1979.

Conductor Antal Dorati becomes music director of the National Symphony Orchestra, remaining until 1977.

Pianist Garrick Ohlsson becomes the first American to win the Chopin International Piano Competition.

Conductor Seiji Ozawa becomes music director of the San Francisco Symphony, remaining until 1976. Ozawa also becomes artistic director of Tanglewood this year.

Pianist David Saperton dies.

Writer Harold C. Schonberg's book *The Lives of the Great Composers* is published.

Conductor George Szell dies.

Ragtime composer Scott Joplin's opera *Treemonisha* is produced for the first time since its completion in 1911.

1971

The Kennedy Center for the Performing Arts opens.

Leonard Bernstein's Mass is premiered at the gala inauguration of the Kennedy Center for the Performing Arts.

Conductor and composer Pierre Boulez is named music director of the New York Philharmonic, where he remains until 1977.

Conductor Michael Tilson Thomas becomes music director of the Buffalo Philharmonic, remaining until 1979.

Conductor and composer Lukas Foss becomes music director of the Brooklyn Philharmonic, remaining until 1990.

The Pittsburgh Symphony Orchestra moves into Heinz Hall.

Conductor James Levine becomes music director of the Ravinia Festival.

Composer Carl Ruggles dies.

1972

Leonard Bernstein makes his conducting debut at the Metropolitan Opera.

Schuyler Chapin becomes general manager of the Metropolitan Opera, remaining until 1975.

Conductor Lorin Maazel succeeds George Szell as music director of the Cleveland Orchestra, remaining until 1984.

Aaron Copland stops composing, in one of the most abrupt cessations of creative energy in music history.

Composer Ferde Grofé dies.

Pianist, actor, and humorist Oscar Levant dies.

The chamber orchestra Orpheus is founded.

Composer Stefan Wolpe dies.

1973

The American Composers Forum is founded.

Philharmonic Hall in Lincoln Center is renamed Avery Fisher Hall.

Conductor Seiji Ozawa is named music director of the Boston Symphony Orchestra, remaining until 2004.

The Brandenburg Ensemble is founded.

Conductor Otto Klemperer dies.

The Kronos Quartet is founded.

James Levine becomes principal conductor of the Metropolitan Opera.

Bass Samuel Ramey makes his New York City Opera debut.

The clarinet quartet Tashi is founded.

1974

The American String Quartet is founded by students of the Juilliard School.

Pianist Emanuel Ax wins the first Arthur Rubinstein International Piano Competition.

The Cincinnati Chamber Orchestra is founded.

Composer Harry Partch dies.

Composer Roger Sessions wins a Pulitzer Prize career award.

1975

Cellist Lynn Harrell wins the first Avery Fisher Prize.

The Society for American Music is founded as the Sonneck Society.

Tenor Richard Tucker dies.

1976

Pianist Alexander Brailowski dies.

Conductor Dean Dixon dies.

Philip Glass completes his first opera, *Einstein on the Beach*. It is premiered by the Metropolitan Opera.

An outdoor concert presented by the Boston Pops under Arthur Fiedler is attended by 400,000, the largest single live audience for a classical concert in history.

Pianist and teacher Rosina Lhévinne dies.

Conductor Jean Martinon dies.

Conductor Max Rudolf is named music director of the New Jersey Symphony Orchestra, where he remains for a single season.

Cellist Gregor Piatigorsky dies.

Composer Walter Piston dies.

Conductor and composer André Previn becomes music director of the Pittsburgh Symphony Orchestra, remaining until 1984.

Pianist Arthur Rubinstein retires from the concert stage at age 89.

Clarinettist Richard Stoltzman wins the Avery Fisher Award.

Ragtime composer Scott Joplin posthumously wins a Pulitzer Prize for his opera *Treemonisha*, composed in 1911.

1977

The American Composers Orchestra is founded.

Soprano Maria Callas dies.

Conductor Antal Dorati is named music director of the Detroit Symphony Orchestra, holding the position until 1981.

Cellist and conductor Mstislav Rostropovich succeeds Antal Dorati as music director of the National Symphony Orchestra, remaining until 1996.

Conductor Edo de Waart becomes music director of the San Francisco Symphony, remaining until 1985.

Conductor Thomas Schippers dies.

Conductor Leopold Stokowski dies.

1978

Trumpeter and conductor Gerard Schwarz becomes director of the Los Angeles Chamber Orchestra, holding the position until 1986.

Conductor Carlo Maria Giulini becomes music director of the Los Angeles Philharmonic, holding the post until 1984.

Cellist Yo-Yo Ma wins the Avery Fisher Prize.

Conductor Zubin Mehta becomes music director of the New York Philharmonic, holding the position until 1991.

Elmar Oliveira becomes the first and only American violinist to win the Tchaikovsky International Competition.

Conductor William Steinberg dies.

Composer William Grant Still dies.

1979

Abravanel Hall is completed for the Utah Symphony Orchestra.

Pianist Emanuel Ax wins the Avery Fisher Prize.

Educator and composer Nadia Boulanger dies.

Conductor Arthur Fiedler dies.

Violinist Hilary Hahn is born.

Composer Roy Harris dies.

Conductor Neville Mariner becomes music director of the Minnesota Orchestra, remaining until 1986.

Conductor and composer André Previn becomes music director of the Pittsburgh Symphony Orchestra, remaining until 1984.

1980

Violinist Sarah Chang is born.

The Cleveland Chamber Symphony Orchestra is founded.

Conductor André Kostelanetz dies.

Violinist William Kroll dies.

1981

Composer Samuel Barber dies.

Violinist Joshua Bell makes his debut with the Philadelphia Orchestra.

Composer and arranger Robert Russell Bennett dies.

Composer Howard Hanson dies.

Soprano Rosa Ponselle dies.

The Women's Philharmonic is founded.

1982

Philip Glass composes the popular and controversial film score to *Koyaanisqatsi*.

Pianist Horacio Gutiérrez wins the Avery Fisher Prize.

Composer Conlon Nancarrow wins the MacArthur Foundation Award.

Pianist Arthur Rubinstein dies.

1983

Peter Mennin, composer and arts administrator, dies.

Conductor, Alfred Wallenstein dies.

Composer Ellen Taafe Zwilich becomes the first woman to receive a Pulitzer Prize in music, for her Symphony no. 1.

1984

Trumpeter and conductor Gerard Schwarz becomes music director of the Seattle Symphony Orchestra.

Conductor Christoph von Dohnanyi becomes music director of the Cleveland Orchestra, remaining until 2002.

Trumpeter Wynton Marsalis becomes the first recording artist to win Grammy Awards for both a classical and a jazz recording in the same year.

Bass Samuel Ramey makes his Metropolitan Opera debut, after singing for many years at the New York City Opera.

Cellist Leonard Rose dies.

Composer Randall Thompson dies.

1985

The Lark Quartet is founded.

Composer and conductor André Previn becomes music director of the Los Angeles Philharmonic, remaining until 1989.

Conductor Hugh Wolff is appointed music director of the New Jersey Symphony Orchestra, holding the post until 1991.

Conductor Eugene Ormandy dies.

Composer Roger Sessions dies.

Violinist Efram Zimbalist dies.

1986

Pianist and teacher Sascha Gorodnitzky dies.

Pianist Gary Graffman becomes director of the Curtis Institute.

Conductor Edo de Waart becomes music director of the Minnesota Orchestra, holding the position until 1995.

1987

Composer Morton Feldman dies.

Violinist Jascha Heifetz dies.

Pianist and showman Liberace dies.

Composer Vincent Persichetti dies.

1988

Conductor Antal Dorati dies.

Conductor Christoph Eschenbach becomes music director of the Houston Symphony Orchestra, remaining until 1999.

Pianist Raymond Lewenthal dies.

Conductor Lorin Maazel is named music director of the Pittsburgh Symphony Orchestra, holding the position until 1996.

Conductor Michael Tilson Thomas founds the New World Symphony Orchestra.

Conductor Keith Lockhart becomes music director of the Utah Symphony.

1989

Conductor and pianist Daniel Barenboim is named successor to Georg Solti as music director of the Chicago Symphony Orchestra.

Pianist Vladimir Horowitz dies.

Composer Virgil Thomson dies.

Soprano June Anderson makes her Metropolitan Opera debut.

1990

Composer Ernst Bacon dies.

Conductor and composer Leonard Bernstein dies.

Pianist Jorge Bolet dies.

Composer Aaron Copland dies.

Conductor Werner Janssen dies.

Conductor Neeme Järvi becomes music director of the Detroit Symphony Orchestra.

1991

Soprano Renée Fleming makes her Metropolitan Opera debut.

Pianist John Kirkpatrick dies.

Conductor Kurt Masur is named music director of the New York Philharmonic, succeeding Zubin Mehta. Masur remains until 2002.

Pianist Rudolf Serkin dies.

1992

Composer Stephen Albert dies.

Composer John Cage dies.

Pianist William Masselos dies.

Violinist Nathan Milstein dies.

Conductor Esa-Pekka Salonen is named music director of the Los Angeles Philharmonic.

Composer William Schuman dies.

Choral director Robert Shaw receives the National Medal of Arts.

1993

Conductor Maurice Abravanel dies.

Contralto Marian Anderson dies.

Conductor Erich Leinsdorf dies.

Conductor Wolfgang Sawallisch becomes music director of the Philadelphia Orchestra, remaining until 2003.

Philanthropist Alice Tully dies.

1994

Pianist Artur Balsam dies.

Soprano Kathleen Battle is fired from the Metropolitan Opera for "unprofessional actions."

Composer William Bergsma dies.

Conductor Christoph Eschenbach succeeds James Levine as music director of the Ravinia Festival, remaining until 2005.

1995

Conductor Keith Lockhart becomes conductor of the Boston Pops Orchestra.

Pianist and teacher Adele Marcus dies.

Conductor Max Rudolf dies.

Conductor Michael Tilson Thomas becomes music director of the San Francisco Symphony.

1996

Composer Jacob Druckman dies.

Composer and conductor Morton Gould dies.

Composer Otto Luening dies.

Conductor Leonard Slatkin is appointed music director of the National Symphony Orchestra.

Composer David Tudor dies.

1997

Arts administrator Rudolf Bing, former general manager of the Metropolitan Opera, dies.

Composer Ross Lee Finney dies.

Violinist Joseph Fuchs dies.

Composer Conlon Nancarrow dies.

Conductor Georg Solti dies.

Composer Hugo Weisgall dies.

1998

Conductor JoAnne Falletta becomes music director of the Buffalo Philharmonic.

Choral director Margaret Hillis dies.

1999

Conductor Leon Barzin dies.

Violinist Yehudi Menuhin dies.

Choral director Robert Shaw dies.

2000

Pianist and humorist Victor Borge dies.

Composer Vivian Fine dies.

Composer Alan Hovhaness dies.

Violinist Oscar Shumsky dies.

2001

Conductor Boris Goldovsky dies.

Conductor Paarvo Järvi becomes music director of the Cincinnati Symphony Orchestra.

The Kimmel Center for the Performing Arts opens as the new home of the Philadelphia Orchestra.

Conductor Robert Spano becomes music director of the Atlanta Symphony Orchestra.

Violinist Isaac Stern dies.

2002

Composer Earle Brown dies.

Conductor Franz Welser-Möst is named music director of the Cleveland Orchestra.

Conductor Lorin Maazel is named music director of the New York Philharmonic.

Composer Ralph Shapey dies.

2003

Composer Arthur Berger dies.

Pianist John Browning dies.

Zankel Hall opens in the Carnegie Hall building.

Conductor Christoph Eschenbach is named music director of the Philadelphia Orchestra.

Composer Lou Harrison dies.

Pianist Eugene Istomin dies.

Music critic Harold C. Schonberg dies.

Pianist Rosalyn Tureck dies.

Conductor Osmo Vänskä is named music director of the Minnesota Orchestra.

2004

Conductor James Levine becomes music director of the Boston Symphony Orchestra, succeeding Seiji Ozawa.

Conductor Neeme Järvi becomes music director of the New Jersey Symphony Orchestra.

2005

Conductor James Conlon becomes music director of the Ravinia Festival.

Glossary of Music Terms

a cappella   Literally "in the chapel." Used generally to describe unaccompanied vocal music.

accent   Extra emphasis given to a note in a musical composition.

alto   (1) The lowest female voice, below mezzo-soprano and SOPRANO. (2) In musical instruments, an instrument with a range of either a fourth or fifth below the standard range; the viola is tuned a fifth below the violin, for example. (3) The alto CLEF (also known as the C clef) used for notating music for alto instruments and voices.

arpeggio   A broken CHORD; the notes of the chord played in succession, rather than simultaneously.

ballad   (1) In folk traditions, a multiversed song that tells a narrative story, often based on historic or mythological figures. (2) In popular music, a slow lament, usually on the subject of lost love.

bar   See MEASURE.

baritone   (1) The male voice situated between the BASS (lowest) and TENOR (highest). (2) Baritone is sometimes used to describe musical instruments that play an octave below the ordinary range.

barrelhouse   An aggressive two-handed piano style suitable for a piano player working in a noisy room, a bar, or a brothel. The same word is used to describe such a venue.

bass   (1) The lowest male vocal range. (2) The deepest-sounding musical instrument within a family of instruments, such as the bass violin. (3) The lowest instrumental part.

beat   The basic rhythmic unit of a musical composition. In common time (most frequently used in popular music), there are two basic beats to the measure; the first is given more emphasis, and therefore is called the *strong* beat, the second is less emphasized and thus is called the *weak* beat.

bebop   A form of jazz that developed in the late 1940s and 1950s played by small ensembles or combos, which emphasized rapid playing and unusual rhythmic accents. Many bebop musicians took common CHORD PROGRESSIONS of popular songs and composed new melodies for them, allowing the accompanying instruments (piano-bass-drums) a form that could be easily followed while the melody parts (trumpet, saxophone) improvised.

bending notes   Technique used on stringed instruments where the musician pushes against a string with the left hand, causing the note to rise in pitch. On an electric guitar, which has light gauge strings, the pitch may rise as much as a whole tone (two frets).

big band jazz   A popular jazz style of the 1930s and 1940s featuring larger ensembles divided into parts (brass, reeds, rhythm). Riffs, or short melodic phrases, were traded back and forth between the melody instruments.

"Blue Moon" progression   A sequence of four chords associated with the song "Blue Moon," popularized in 1935 by Benny Goodman and others. The chords are I, VI minor, IV (or II minor), and V. In the key of C, they would be: C, A minor, F (or D minor), and G. Each chord might be held for two, four, or eight beats, but they appear in sequence. The progression is very common in doo-wop music.

blues An African-American vocal and instrumental style that developed in the late 19th to early 20th centuries. The "blues scale" usually features a flattened third and seventh, giving the music a recognizable sound. The classic 12-bar blues features three repeated lines of four bars each, with the first two lines of lyrics repeated, followed by a contrasting line. The chord progression is also fairly standardized, although many blues musicians have found ways to extend and improvise around these rules.

boogie-woogie Boogie-woogie is a way of playing BLUES on the piano that was first recorded in the 1920s. Its chief characteristic is the left-hand pattern, known as eight-to-the-bar (a note is played on every one of the eight possible eighth notes in a measure of four beats), which provides a propulsive rhythm that seems to have been influenced by the sound of trains. Boogie-woogie became a fad after the 1938 and 1939 From Spirituals to Swing concerts, and was adapted into big band swing, pop, and country music. From there it became part of ROCK 'N' ROLL. To boogie in general slang (as in "I've got to boogie now") means to leave somewhere in a hurry. In musical slang, to boogie means to maintain a repetitive blues-based rhythmic foundation, particularly one associated with the style of John Lee Hooker, similar to the figure in his song, "Boogie Chillen."

brass Traditionally, musical instruments whose bodies are made out of brass (although sometimes today they are made out of other metals). Usually used to refer to members of the horn family, including trumpets and trombones.

British invasion Popular groups of the 1960s that dominated the American pop charts. The Beatles led the charge in 1964, but were quickly followed by many soundalike bands, as well as more distinctive groups like the Rolling Stones, The Who, the Kinks, and many others.

cadence A melodic or harmonic phrase usually used to indicate the ending of a PHRASE or a complete musical composition.

capo A metal or elastic clamp placed across all of the strings of a guitar that enables players to change key, while still using the same chord fingerings as they would use without the capo.

CD (compact disc) A recording medium developed in the mid-1980s that enables music to be encoded as digital information on a small disc, and that is "read" by a laser. Various forms of CDs have been developed since to contain higher sound quality and/or other materials (photographs, moving images, etc.)

chord The basic building block of HARMONY, chords usually feature three or more notes played simultaneously.

chord progression A sequence of chords, for example in the key of C: C, F, and G7.

chorus Most commonly used in popular songs to indicate a repeated STANZA that features the same melody and lyrics that falls between each verse. Perhaps because members of the audience might "sing-along" with this part of the song, it came to be known as the chorus (a chorus literally being more than one voice singing at the same time). See VERSE.

clef The symbol at the beginning of a notated piece of music indicating the note values assigned to each line of the STAFF. The three most common clefs used in popular music are the G clef (or treble clef), usually used to notate the melody; the F clef (or bass clef), usually used for harmony parts; and the less-frequently seen C clef (or tenor clef), used for notating instruments with special ranges, most usually the viola.

country and western (C&W) A category developed by the music industry in the late 1940s to distinguish folk, cowboy, and other musical styles aimed at the white, rural, working-class listener (as opposed to R&B, aimed at black audiences, and pop, aimed at urban whites). Later, the *western* was dropped.

cover versions   The music business has always been competitive, and even before recordings were possible, many artists would do the same song, as can be seen by the multiple editions of the sheet music for certain hits, each with a different artists' photo on the front. In the 1950s the practice of copying records was rampant, particularly by bigger companies, which had more resources (publicity, distribution, influence) and which used their artists to cover songs from independent labels that had started to show promise in the marketplace. A true cover version is one that attempts to stay close to the song on which it is based. Interpretations of existing songs are often called covers, but when artistry is involved in giving an individual treatment to an existing song, that effort is worthy of being considered more than a cover version.

crescendo   A gradual increase in volume indicated in music notation by a triangle placed on its side below the STAFF, like this <.

crossover record   A record that starts in one musical category, but has a broader appeal and becomes popular in another category. For example B. B. King's "The Thrill Is Gone" started out as an R&B record, but crossed over to the pop category.

cut a record   Recording a record.

decrescendo   A gradual decrease in volume indicated in music notation by a triangle placed on its side below the STAFF, as in >.

Delta blues   Blues music originating in the Mississippi Delta and typically featuring the use of a slide, intense vocal performances, an aggressive, sometimes strummed guitar style with bass notes "popped" by the thumb for a snapping sound.

diatonic harmony   The CHORDS implicit in the major scale. The sequence of triads is I major, II minor, III minor, IV major, V major, VI minor, and VII diminished. Because the diminished chord is unstable, it is virtually never used in this context. Because major chords are more common, many songs use only them: I, IV, and V.

disco   A dance form of the 1970s developed in urban dance clubs, consisting of a heavily accented, repeated rhythmic part.

Dixieland jazz   Jazz style popularized in New Orleans at the beginning of the 20th century by small combos, usually including three horns: a clarinet, a trumpet, and a trombone. The rhythm section includes a banjo, a tuba, a simple drum set, and a piano, and occasionally a saxophone, string bass, or guitar is added.

DIY (Do-It-Yourself)   An emphasis on homemade music and recordings, which began with the PUNK movement but outlived it. The message was that everyone could make their own music, and record and market it on their own, using simple, inexpensive instruments and technology.

DJ (deejay)   The person who plays records at a dance club or on a radio station. DJs began to create musical compositions by stringing together long sequences of records, and then further manipulated them using techniques such as backspinning (rapidly spinning a turntable backward while a record is being played) and scratching (moving the turntable back and forth rapidly to emphasize a single note or word).

DVD (digital video disc)   A form of optical disc designed to hold video or film, but also sometimes used for higher-quality music reproduction. See CD (COMPACT DISC).

easy listening   See MOR (MIDDLE-OF-THE-ROAD).

eighth note   See NOTE VALUES.

electronic music   Music created using electronic means, including SYNTHESIZERS, SEQUENCERS, tape recorders, and other nontraditional instruments.

falsetto   A high register vocal sound producing a light texture. Often used in soul music.

finger-picking   A style of guitar playing that keeps a steady bass with the thumb while playing melody on the treble strings.

flat   A symbol in music NOTATION indicating that the note should be dropped one-half step in PITCH. Compare SHARP.

flat pick   A pick held between the thumb and first finger of the right hand that is very effective for playing rapid single note passages or heavy rhythm guitar.

flip side   The other side of a 45 rpm record, typically the nonhit song.

folk music   Traditional music that is passed down from one person to another within a family or a community. Often the original composer or songwriter is unknown.

45   A record that plays at 45 revolutions per minute (rpm). Developed in the 1950s by RCA, the 45 or "single" was the main way of promoting individual songs on the pop and R&B charts through the CD era.

gospel music   Composed black religious music.

half note   See NOTE VALUES.

harmony   Any musical composition with more than one part played simultaneously. In popular music the harmony is usually the accompanying part, made up of CHORDS, that complement the MELODY.

heavy metal   Rock style of the mid-1970s and later that emphasized a thunderous sound, simplified chord progressions, subject matter aimed to appeal to teenage boys (primarily), and flamboyant stage routines. Other variants (death metal, speed metal) developed over the coming decades.

hip-hop   The music (rap), dance (breakdancing), and visual expression (graffiti art) originating in urban areas in the mid-1970s.

holy blues   Songs that combine religious words with blues melodies and accompaniments.

hook   A recurrent musical or lyric phrase that is designed to "hook" the listener into a particular song or record. It is often also the title of a song.

interval   The space between two PITCHES. The first note of a SCALE is considered the first interval; the next note, the second; and so on. Thus, in a C major scale, an "E" is considered a third, and a G a "fifth." The I-III-V combination makes up a major CHORD.

jukebox   A machine designed to play records. Commonly found in bars (known as "juke joints" in the South), these replaced live music by

the mid-1950s, and were a major means of promoting hit records. Customers dropped a "nickel in the jukebox" to hear their favorite song.

key   Indicates the range of notes (or SCALE) on which a composition is based.

key signature   The symbol at the beginning of a piece of notation that indicates the basic KEY of the work.

looping   Repeating a short musical PHRASE or RHYTHM. SEQUENCERS can be programmed to "loop" or repeat these parts indefinitely.

LP   A "long-playing" record, playing at 33 revolutions per minute (rpm). Developed in the late 1940s, the LP enabled record companies to present more or longer compositions on a single disc (the previous time limit of 78s was 3 to 5 minutes, while an LP could hold 20 to 25 minutes per side).

major   One of the two primary SCALES used in popular music. The relation between the seven notes in the major scale is whole step (WS)-WS-half step (HS)-WS-WS-WS-HS. Each scale step has a related CHORD defining major harmony. Compare MINOR.

measure   A unit of musical time in a composition defined by the time signature. In 4/4 time, for example, each measure consists of four beats (and a quarter note is equal to one beat). The bar line (a vertical line across all five lines of the STAFF) indicates the beginning and end of a measure.

melody   Two or more musical tones played in succession, called the "horizontal" part of a musical composition because the notes move horizontally across the staff (as opposed to the HARMONY which is called the "vertical" part because the harmony notes are stacked vertically on the staff). In popular music the melody of a song is the most memorable part of the composition.

meter   The repeated pattern of strong and weak rhythmic pulses in a piece of music. For example, in a waltz, the oom-pah-pah meter is the defining part of the music's style.

MIDI (Musical Instrument Digital Interface) A common programming language that enables SYNTHESIZERS, computers, and SEQUENCERS to communicate with one another.

minor One of the two primary SCALES used in popular music. The relation between the seven notes in the major scale is whole step (WS)-half step (HS)-WS-HS-WS-WS. (There are two variations of this basic pattern found in scales known as the "harmonic" and "melodic" minor.) Each scale step has a related CHORD defining major harmony. Compare MAJOR.

minstrel Performance of African-American songs and dances by white performers in blackface, burnt cork rubbed on their faces beginning in the mid-19th century. Later, black minstrels appeared. Minstrel shows included songs, dances, and humorous skits. Many of these skits and songs made fun of African Americans.

modes A type of SCALE. The two common scales used today (the MAJOR and MINOR) are two types of mode. In the Middle Ages, a system of eight different modes was developed, each with the same intervals but beginning on a different note. The modes are sometimes still heard in folk music, some forms of jazz, and some forms of contemporary classical music.

MOR (middle-of-the-road) Pop music aimed at a wide audience, designed to be as inoffensive and nondisturbing as possible. This term is often used pejoratively by critics. Also sometimes called "easy listening."

movement A section of a longer musical composition.

notation A system developed over many centuries to write down musical compositions using specific symbols to represent PITCH and RHYTHM.

note values The time values of the notes in a musical composition are relational, usually based on the idea of a quarter note equaling one beat (as in ⁴⁄₄ time). In this time signature, a quarter note fills a quarter of the time in the measure; a half-note equals two beats (is twice as long) and a whole note equals four beats (a full measure). Conversely, shorter time values include an eighth-note (half a single beat), a sixteenth (¼ of a single beat), a thirty-second (⅛ of a single beat), etc.

octave An INTERVAL of eight notes, considered the "perfect" consonance. If a string is divided perfectly in half, each half will sound an octave above the full string, so that the ratio between the two notes is expressed as 1:2.

opus A numbering system used in classical composition to indicate the order in which pieces were composed. Some composers only give opus numbers to works they feel are strong enough to be part of their "official" canon.

percussion Instruments used to play the rhythmic part of a composition, which may be "unpitched" (such as drums or cymbals) or "pitched" (such as bells, chimes, and marimbas).

phonograph A mechanical instrument used to reproduce sound recordings. A phonograph consists of some form of turntable, needle, tone arm, amplifier, and speaker. A record is placed on a turntable, a disc that is set to revolve at specific speeds. The needle "reads" the grooves cut into the record itself. The vibrations then are communicated through the tone arm (in which the needle is mounted) into an amplifier (which increases the volume of the sound). A speaker projects the sound out so that it can be heard.

phrase A subsection of the MELODY that expresses a complete musical thought.

Piedmont blues A form of blues from the Carolinas, Georgia, Florida, and Alabama that uses a restrained style of fingerpicking and soft vocal performances. It also often uses ragtime CHORD PROGRESSIONS.

pitch The note defined by its sound; literally, the number of vibrations per second (of a string, air column, bar, or some other vibrating object) that results in a given tone. Pitch is relative; in most tuning systems, a specific note is chosen as the pitch against which others are tuned. In modern music, this is usually A above middle C, defined as vibrating at 440 vps.

pop music   Any music that appeals to a large audience. Originally, the pop charts featured records aimed at white, urban listeners (as opposed to R&B, aimed at blacks, and C&W or country, aimed at rural, lower-class whites). Today, "pop" is applied to any recording that appeals across a wide range of listeners, so that Michael Jackson or Shania Twain could equally be defined as "pop" stars.

power chords   Played on the low strings of an electric guitar, power chords use only the root and the fifth (and often a repeat of the root an octave higher) of a triad, leaving out the third of the CHORD. With no third, the chord is neither MAJOR or MINOR. With only two notes, it is technically not even a chord, but an interval. The use of power chords was pioneered by Link Wray ("Rumble") and the Kinks ("You Really Got Me"), and used extensively in hard rock (Deep Purple's "Smoke on the Water"), heavy metal (Metallica), and grunge (Nirvana's "Smells Like Teen Spirit").

power trio   Three instruments—guitar, bass, and drums—played at loud volumes.

psychedelic   Popular ROCK style of the late 1960s-early 1970s that featured extended musical forms, "spacey" lyrics, and unusual musical timbres often produced by synthesizers. Psychedelic music was supposed to be the "aural equivalent" of the drug experience. See also SYNTHESIZER; TIMBRE.

punk   A movement that began in England and travelled to the United States in the mid-1970s emphasizing a return to simpler musical forms, in response to the growing commercialization of ROCK. Punk also encompassed fashion (including spiked hair, safety pins used as body ornaments, etc.) and sometimes a violent, antiestablishment message.

quarter note   See NOTE VALUES.

race records   Music industry name for African-American popular music recorded in the 1920s until around 1945.

ragtime   Music dating from around the 1890s and usually composed in three or four different sections. The most famous ragtime pieces were for piano, but the style was also adapted in a simplified form for the banjo and the guitar.

record producer   The person in charge of a recording session.

register   The range in notes of a specific part of a musical composition. Also used to define the range of an individual musical instrument or vocal part.

resonator guitar   Guitars with a metal front and back, often used in playing slide guitar, and prized during the 1930s for their volume.

rhythm   The basic pulse of a musical composition. In $4/4$ time, the 4 beats per measure provide the pulse that propels the piece. Compare METER.

rhythm and blues (R&B)   Black popular music that emerged around 1945 and peaked in popularity in the 1960s. It usually included gospel-influenced vocal performances, and a rhythm section of piano, bass, and drums. The lead instruments were often guitar and saxophone.

riff   A short, recognizable melodic phrase used repeatedly in a piece of music. Commonly heard in big band jazz or in electric guitar solos.

rock   An outgrowth of ROCK 'N' ROLL in the 1960s that featured more sophisticated arrangements, lyrics, and subject matter. The BRITISH INVASION groups—notably the Beatles and the Rolling Stones—are sometimes credited with extending the style and subjects treated by rock 'n' roll. Rock itself has developed into many different substyles.

rockabilly   Mid-1950s popular music that combined BLUES and COUNTRY music.

rock 'n' roll   The popular music of the mid-1950s aimed at teenage listeners. Popular rock 'n' roll artists included Elvis Presley, Chuck Berry, Little Richard, and Carl Perkins. Compare ROCK.

royalties   Payments to recording artists based on the sales of their records.

salsa   Literally "spice." A form of Latin dance music popularized in the 1970s and 1980s.

scale   A succession of seven notes. The most common scales are the MAJOR and MINOR.

score   The complete notation of a musical composition.

sequencer   An electronic instrument that can record a series of pitches or rhythms and play them back on command.

78   The first form of recorded disc, that revolved on a turntable at 78 revolutions per minute (rpm). The first 78s were 10 inches in diameter and could play for approximately three minutes per side; later, 12-inch 78s were introduced with slightly longer playing times.

sharp   A symbol in a piece of music indicating that a pitch should be raised one half-step in PITCH. Compare FLAT.

side   One side of a recording disc.

slide guitar   Style of guitar in which the player wears a metal or glass tube on one finger or uses a bottle neck to play notes. It creates a distinctive crying sound. Also called bottleneck guitar.

songster   A turn-of-the-20th-century musician with a varied repertoire that included different styles of music.

soprano   The highest female voice, or the highest pitched instrument in a family of instruments.

soul   A black musical style developed in the 1960s that combined elements of GOSPEL MUSIC with RHYTHM AND BLUES.

spirituals   Traditional religious music found in both white and African-American traditions.

staff   The five parallel lines on which the symbols for notes are placed in a notated piece of music. The CLEF at the beginning of the staff indicates the pitch of each note on the staff.

stanza   In poetry, the basic lyrical unit, often consisting of four or six lines. The lyrics to both the VERSE and CHORUS of a popular song follow the stanza form.

strings   Instruments that produce musical sound through the vibration of strings, made out of animal gut or metal. Violins and guitars are stringed instruments.

suite   In classical music, a group of dances played in succession to form a larger musical composition.

symphony   In classical music, a defined form usually consisting of three parts, played Fast-Slow-Fast.

syncopation   Accenting the unexpected or weaker BEAT. Often used in RAGTIME, jazz, and related styles.

synthesizer   An electronic instrument that is capable of creating different musical pitches and timbres.

tempo   The speed at which a piece of music is performed.

tenor   The highest male voice.

theme   A recognizable MELODY that is often repeated within a musical composition.

thumb picks and finger picks   Guitar picks made of metal or plastic worn on the player's right hand fingers and thumb in order to play louder.

timbre   The quality of a PITCH produced by a musical instrument or voice that makes it distinctive. The timbre of a guitar is quite different from that of a flute, for example.

time signature   In notation, the symbol at the beginning of each STAFF that indicates the basic metric pulse and how many beats are contained in a measure. For example, in 4/4 time, a quarter-note is given one beat, and there are four beats per measure; in 6/8 time, an eighth-note is given one beat, and there are six beats in a measure.

Tin Pan Alley   The center of music publishing on West 28th Street in New York City from the late 19th century through the 1930s (so-called because the clatter from competing pianists working in different buildings sounded to passersby like rattling tin pans). Used generally to describe the popular songs of this period.

tone   See PITCH.

tremolo   The rapid repetition of a single note to give a "quivering" or "shaking" sound. Compare VIBRATO.

turnaround   A musical phrase at the end of a verse that briefly outlines the CHORDS of the song before the start of the next verse.

12-bar blues   A 12-bar BLUES has 12 measures of music, or bars, and is the most common blues format, though eight bars and 16 bars are also used.

vamp   A short segment of music that repeats, usually two or four CHORDS. Two chord vamps are common in GOSPEL and ROCK, especially the I and IV chords (C and F in the key of C).

vanity records   Recordings that are conceived and financed by the artists involved. They are called "vanity records" because the motivation comes from the person or group themselves, not from a record company. The reason is to realize a creative project, to promote a career, or just to boost the ego. Previously, singers and musicians would pay to go into a studio and to cover the costs of backup musicians, mixing, mastering, and manufacturing. This continues, but with the rise of home studios, these steps can be done at home, with computerized recording and CD burning. Vanity records now represent perhaps the majority of recordings being made and are more likely to be called independent productions.

verse   The part of a song that features a changing lyric set to a fixed MELODY. The verse is usually performed in alternation with the CHORUS.

vibrato   A rapid moving up and down slightly in PITCH while performing a single note as an ornament. Compare TREMOLO.

walking bass   A style of bass playing that originated in jazz on the upright bass. The bassist plays a new note on every beat, outlining the CHORDS as they pass by in a CHORD PROGRESSION. Chord notes are primary, but passing notes and other decorations enliven the bass line, as well as brief rhythmic variations enliven the bass line. A rock example is Paul McCartney's bass part in the Beatles' "All My Loving" (1964).

whole note   See NOTE VALUES.

woodwinds   A class of instruments traditionally made of wood, although the term is now used for instruments made of brass or metal as well. Clarinets, flutes, and saxophones are usually classified as woodwinds.

Bibliography

Books

Clarke, Garry E. *Essays in American Music.* Westport, Conn.: Greenwood Press, 1977.

Gann, Kyle. *American Music of the Twentieth Century.* New York: Schirmer Books, 1997.

Heyman, Barbara B. *Samuel Barber: The Composer and His Music.* New York: Oxford University Press, 1992.

Kenneson, Claude. *Musical Prodigies: Perilous Journeys, Remarkable Lives.* Portland, Oreg.: Amadeus Press, 1998.

Kingman, Daniel. *American Music, A Panorama.* New York: Schirmer Books, 1979.

McCue, George. *Music in American Society, 1776–1976.* New Brunswick, N.J.: Transaction Books, 1977.

Mueller, John H. *The American Symphony Orchestra.* Bloomington: Indiana University Press, 1951.

Randel, Don Michael, ed. *The Harvard Biographical Dictionary of Music.* Cambridge, Mass.: Harvard University Press, 1996.

Ritter, Frédéric Louis. *Music in America.* New York: Johnson Reprint Corporation, 1970.

Rockwell, John. *All American Music.* New York: Alfred A. Knopf, 1983.

Sadie, S., and J. Tyrrell, eds. *The New Grove Dictionary of Music and Musicians.* London: Macmillan, 2001.

Struble, John Warthen. *The History of American Classical Music.* New York: Facts On File, 1995.

Tawa, Nicholas E. *The Coming of Age of American Art Music.* New York: Greenwood Press, 1991.

Waters, Edward N. *Victor Herbert: A Life in Music.* New York: Macmillan, 1955.

Articles

Agence France Presse. "Pierre Boulez, Un Musicien Très Demandé." *Agence France Presse French,* 7 August 2002.

Aldrich, Richard. "Antonin Dvorak and His Music." *New York Times,* 8 May 1904, p. SM3.

Ambache, Diana. "Marion Bauer (1882–1955)." *Women of Note.* Available online. URL: http://www.ambache.co.uk/wBauer.htm. Downloaded on July 21, 2004.

American Composers Orchestra. "Gerard Schwarz, conductor." Available online. URL: http://www.americancomposers.org/bios110198.htm. Downloaded on August 13, 2004.

American Music Center. "Leslie Bassett, Biography." Available online. URL: http://www.amc.net/member/Leslie_Bassett/bio.html. Downloaded on July 21, 2004.

Anthony, Michael. "A Three-Alarm Career." *Minneapolis Star Tribune,* 20 July 2003.

———. "Music Man; the Most Popular American Composer under 40, Aaron Jay Kernis Is a Present-day Bernstein." *Minneapolis Star Tribune,* 12 May 1996.

Ardoin, John. "A Unique Gift for Making the Music Sing." Great Pianists of the 20th Century (liner notes), 1998.

———. "Violinist Kelly Barr Pays Tribute to Pioneering Musician Maud Powell." *Arlington Heights Daily Herald,* 22 September 2000.

Art:21. "Laurie Anderson: Biography." Available online. URL: http://www.pbs.org/art21/artists/anderson. Downloaded on February 10, 2004.

Artur Balsam Foundation for Chamber Music. "About Artur Balsam." Available online. URL: http://www.arturbalsam.org/aboutartur.htm. Downloaded on June 21, 2004.

Associated Press. "Coroner Cites AIDS in Liberace Death." *New York Times,* 10 February 1987, p. A17.

———. "Earle Brown, 75, Composer of Experimental Scores." *Newsday,* 9 July 2002.

———. "Edward B. Hill, 87; Composer and Teacher." *New York Times,* 10 July 1960, p. 72.

———. "Grammy-winning Pianist John Browning Dead at 69." *AP Worldstream,* 29 January 2003.

———. "Harold Bauer Dies; Concert Pianist, 77." *New York Times,* 13 March 1951, p. 31.

———. "Mitropoulos Dies in Milan at 64; Stricken at La Scala Rehearsal." *New York Times,* 3 November 1960, p. 1.

———. "Serge Koussevitzky Is Dead at 76; Conducted in Boston for 25 Years." *New York Times,* 5 June 1951, p. 1.

———. "Ulysses Kay, 78, Classical Composer." *Newsday,* 24 May 1995.

Daniel Barenboim Official Web Site. "Daniel Barenboim Biography." Available online. URL: http://www.daniel-barenboim.com. Downloaded on July 8, 2004.

Barron, James. "Liberace, Flamboyant Pianist, Is Dead." *New York Times,* 5 February 1987, p. B6.

Bauer, Ross. "Ross Bauer, Composer." Available online. URL: http://music.ucdavis.edu/empyrean/ross. Downloaded on July 21, 2004.

Bauman, Richard. "Piano Player Made Music Using One Hand." *Grit,* 13 April 2003.

Berlin, Edward A. "A Biography of Scott Joplin." The Scott Joplin International Ragtime Foundation. Available online. URL: http://www.scottjoplin.org/biography.htm. Updated 1998.

Block, Adrienne Fried. "How to Write an American Symphony: Amy Beach and the Birth of *Gaelic Symphony.*" American Composers Orchestra. Available online. URL: http://www.americancomposers.org/beach_article.htm. Updated 1999.

Bornstein, Lisa. "Musical Dissent: 'Cradle' Composer Clashed with Mores of His Day." *Denver Rocky Mountain News,* 29 March 2000.

Buechner, Alan C. "Oscar Sonneck and Recent Developments in the Study of American Music." Society for American Music Web site. Available online. URL: http://www.american-music.org/sam/SocietyHistory.htm. Downloaded on August 15, 2004.

California Artists Management. "Robert Taub." Available online. URL: http://members.aol.com/CAMartists/taub.html. Updated on September 20, 2001.

Cooke, Nym. "The Performing Arts in Colonial American Newspapers, 1690–1783: Text Database and Index (Review)." *Notes,* 1 December 1999.

Davidson, Justin. "At 80, Earl Wild Still Sounded Like a Youngster." *Newsday,* 29 November 1995.

———. "Playing to the Masses: Mark Blitzstein, a Communist and Composer of 'The Cradle Will Rock,' Just Wanted to Craft a Broadway Hit." *Newsday,* 12 December 1999.

Davis, Peter G. "Gregor Piatigorsky Dies; Virtuoso of Cello was 73." *New York Times,* 7 August 1976, p. 47.

Downes, Olin. "Barere Dies Giving Concert Here; Collapses at Piano in Carnegie Hall." *New York Times,* 3 April 1951, p. 1.

———. "George Whitefield Chadwick; Passing of Dean of American Composers Marks End of Epoch in Native Tonal Art." *New York Times,* 12 April 1931, p. X7.

———. "Gershwin Caused New Jazz Values." *New York Times,* 12 July 1937, p. 20.

———. "A Lonely American Composer." *New York Times,* 29 January 1939, p. X7.

———. "Opera Makes Bow at the City Center." *New York Times,* 22 February 1944, p. 26.

———. "When Critics Disagree." *New York Times,* 20 October 1935, p. X7.

———. "Works of Arthur Foote." *New York Times,* 18 April 1937, p. 171.

Dunning, Jennifer. "Leon Barzin, 98, Conductor of Ballets and Music Educator." *New York Times,* 9 May 1999, p. 39.

Eichler, Jeremy. "Giving Voice to Art: Meredith Monk Blends Sound, Movement and Visual Imagery to Create Her Idiosyncratic Works." *Newsday,* 14 July 2000.

Ericson, Raymond. "Andre Kostelanetz, 78, Conducted Symphonic and Popular Music Too." *New York Times,* 15 January 1980, p. A1.

———. "Maria Callas, 53, Is Dead of Heart Attack, in Paris." *New York Times,* 17 September 1977, p. 49.

———. "Rosina Lhévinne, Pianist, Is Dead; Noted Teacher of Juilliard Students." *New York Times,* 11 November 1976, p. 44.

———. "William Steinberg, Orchestral Conductor, Dies at 78." *New York Times,* 17 May 1978, p. B2.

Flanders, Alan. "Sissieretta Jones: The Voice of an Angel." *Virginia Pilot,* 29 January 2004.

Fowler, Glenn. "Ernst Bacon, a Composer Known for Echoing America, Dies at 91." *New York Times,* 18 March 1990, p. 32.

Frankel, Max. "U.S. Pianist, 23, Wins Soviet Contest." *New York Times,* 14 April 1958, p. 1.

Friederich, Otto. "Where the Old Joins the New: William Bolcom Thrives by Mixing Pop and Classical." *Time,* 29 January 1990.

Gates, David. "A Requiem From a Heavyweight." *Newsweek,* 30 September 2004.

Gershwin, George. "Rhapsody in Catfish Row." *New York Times,* 20 October 1935, p. X1.

Gowen, Bill. "Lyric Opera of Chicago Takes Steps to Trim Its Budget and Hold Off Deficit." *Arlington Heights Daily Herald,* 13 December 2002.

Green, Adolph. "Oscar Levant, 1906–1972." *New York Times,* 27 August 1972, p. D3.

G. Schirmer, Inc. "André Previn." Available online. URL: http://www.schirmer.com/composers/previn/bio.html. Updated on October 15, 2004.

———. "Bright Sheng." Available online. URL: http://www.schirmer.com/composers/sheng_bio.html. Updated on February 7, 2004.

———. "Ellen Taaffe Zwilich." Available online. URL: http://www.schirmer.com/composers/zwilich/. Updated on July 20, 2000.

———. "Ferd Grofé." Available online. URL: http://www.schirmer.com/composers/grofe/works.html. Downloaded on June 22, 2004.

———. "George Antheil." Available online. URL: http://www.schirmer.com/composers/antheil_bio.html. Updated on July 17, 2002.

———. "Gian Carlo Menotti." Available online. URL: http://www.schirmer.com/composers/menotti/bio.html. Updated on March 25, 2002.

———. "Gunther Schuller." Available online. URL: http://www.schirmer.com/composers/schuller_bio.html. Updated on April 5, 2002.

———. "John Adams." Available online. URL: http://www.schirmer.com/composers/adams_bio.html. Updated on July 12, 2002.

———. "John Corigliano." Available online. URL: http://www.schirmer.com/composers/corigliano_bio.html. Updated on July 17, 2004.

———. "John Harbison." Available online. URL: http://www.schirmer.com/composers/harbison_bio.html. Updated on April 28, 2004.

———. "Lee Hoiby." Available online. URL: http://www.schirmer.com/composers/hoiby/bio.html. Updated on January 9, 2004.

———. "Leon Kirchner." Available online. URL: http://www.schirmer.com/composers/kirchner/bio.html. Updated December 13, 2001.

———. "Milton Babbitt." Available online. URL: http://www.schirmer.com/composers/babbitt_bio.html. Updated on March 3, 1998.

———. "Morton Gould." Available online. URL: http://www.schirmer.com/composers/gould_bio.html. Updated on April 5, 2002.

———. "Peter Lieberson." Available online. URL: http://www.schirmer.com/composers/lieberson_bio.html. Updated on September 26, 2003.

———. "Stephen Albert." Available online. URL: http://www.schirmer.com/composers/albert_bio.html. Updated on July 30, 2001.

———. "Virgil Thomson." Available online. URL: http://www.schirmer.com/composers/thomson_bio.html. Updated on November 3, 2003.

———. "Wallingford Riegger." Available online. URL: http://www.schirmer.com/composers/riegger_bio.html. Updated on May 4, 1999.

Hall, Ann P. "Celebrating John Knowles Paine's Legacy." Available online. URL: http://www.news.harvard.edu/gazette/2000/05.04/paine.html. Updated on May 4, 2000.

Hansen, Lianne. "Harry Partch Biography." *Weekend Sunday (NPR Transcript)*, 19 April 1998.

———. "Profile: Remembering Harry Partch." *Weekend Edition (NPR Transcript)*, 24 June 2001.

Henahan, Donal. "Carl Ruggles, Composer, Is Dead at 95." *New York Times*, 26 October 1971 p. 45.

———. "George Szell, Conductor, Is Dead." *New York Times*, 31 July 1970, p. 1.

———. "Leonard Bernstein, 72, Music's Monarch, Dies." *New York Times*, 15 October 1990, p. A1.

———. "Music: A Wolpe Tribute." *New York Times*, 18 February 1972, p. 22.

———. "Richard Tucker, the Met Tenor, Is Dead." *New York Times*, 9 January 1975, p. 73.

———. "Roger Sessions, a Composer and Professor, Is Dead at 88." *New York Times*, 18 March 1985, p. A1.

———. "Roy Harris, Prolific Composer of Americana, Dies." *New York Times*, 4 October 1979, p. B19.

———. "Rudolf Serkin, 88, Concert Pianist, Dies." *New York Times*, 10 May 1991, p. A1.

———. "Samuel Barber, Composer, Dead; Twice Winner of Pulitzer Prize." *New York Times*, 24 January 1981, p. 1.

———. "Sir John Barbirolli, Conductor, Dead." *New York Times*, 30 July 1970, p. 28.

———. "Thomas Schippers Is Dead at 47; Conductor of Opera, Symphony." *New York Times*, 17 December 1977, p. 27.

Herron, Frank. "Austrian Pianist Lost Arm to World War I; Found His Art." *Syracuse Post-Standard*, 17 October 2003.

Hewett, Ivan. "The Music That Makes Itself." *London Daily Telegraph*, 29 June 2004.

Hilary Hahn Web site. "Bio." Available online. URL: http://www.hilaryhahn.com/bio.shtml. Downloaded on July 10, 2004.

Holden, Stephen. "Victor Borge, 91, Comic Piano Virtuoso, Dies." *New York Times*, 24 December 2000, p. 31.

Holland, Bernard. "Peter Mennin, Juilliard President and Prolific Composer, Dies at 60." *New York Times*, 18 June 1983, p. 11.

———. "Raymond Lewenthal, 62, Pianist of Romantic 19th Century Pieces." *New York Times*, 24 November 1988, p. D24.

———. "Vladimir Horowitz, Titan of the Piano, Dies," *New York Times*, 6 November 1989, p. A1.

———. "Erich Leinsdorf, 81, a Conductor of Intelligence and Unity, Is Dead." *New York Times*, 12 September 1993, p. 59.

Hudson, Edwards. "Walter Piston Dies; Composer Won Two Pulitzers." *New York Times*, 13 November 1976, p. 21.

Hughes, Allen. "Arthur Fiedler, 84, Conductor of Boston Pops 50 Years, Dies." *New York Times*, 11 July 1979, p. A1.

———. "Eugene Ormandy Is Dead at 85 in Philadelphia." *New York Times*, 13 March 1985, p. A1.

———. "Leopold Stokowski Is Dead of a Heart Attack at 95." *New York Times*, 14 September 1977, p. 1.

———. "Nadia Boulanger, Teacher of Top Composers, Dies." *New York Times*, 23 October 1979, p. A1.

———. "Rosa Ponselle, Dramatic Soprano, Dies." *New York Times*, 26 May 1981, p. C24.

Ivry, Benjamin. "A Composer of Grand Gestures." *Christian Science Monitor*, 4 January 2002.

Janof, Tim. "Conversation with Bernard Greenhouse." Available online. URL: http://www.cello.org/Newsletter/Articles/greenhouse.htm. Downloaded on June 22, 2004.

Jeannero, Napolean Sarony. "Josef Hofmann, Pianist, 81, Dies." *New York Times*, 18 February 1957, p. 1.

John F. Kennedy Center for the Performing Arts. "Biography of Hugh Wolff," Available online. URL: http://www.kennedy-center.org/calendar/index.cfm?fuseaction=showIndividual&entity_id=5023&source_type=A. Updated on April 10, 2003. "Biography of Joseph Kalichstein." Available online. URL: http://www.kennedy-center.org/ calendar/index.cfm?fuseaction=showIndividual &entity_id=3776&source_type=A. Updated on June 14, 2002.

Jones, David. "Sir John Barbirolli." Available online. URL: http://www.st-and.demon.co.uk/JBSoc/ Biography/Biog1.html. Downloaded on July 9, 2004.

Jones, Randye L. "Kathleen Battle, Biography." *Afrocentric Voices.* Available online. URL: http:// www.afrovoices.com/battle.html. Downloaded on July 9, 2004.

———. "Leontyne Price (b. 1927)." *Afrocentric Voices.* Available online. URL: http://www.afro voices.com/price.html. Updated on February 14, 1999.

King College. "Biography: John Antes." Available online. URL: http://www.king.edu/MusicResearch/ Antes/biography.htm. Updated on July 17, 2001.

Knight, Michael. "Sardonic Humorist." *New York Times,* 15 August 1972, p. 38.

Allan Kozinn. "Alexander Schneider, Violin Virtuoso, Dies at 84." *New York Times,* 4 February 1993, p. B10.

———. "Artur Balsam, a Pianist Known for Chamber Work, Dies at 88." *New York Times,* 2 September 1994, p. A23.

———. "Conlon Nancarrow Dies at 84; Composed for the Player Piano." *New York Times,* 12 August 1997, p. B9.

———. "David Tudor, 70, Electronic Composer, Dies." *New York Times,* 15 August 1996, p. D23.

———. "Georg Solti, Master Who Shaped Chicago Symphony, Is Dead at 84." *New York Times,* 6 September 1997, p. 1.

———. "Harold C. Schonberg, 87, Dies; Won Pulitzer Prize as Music Critic for the Times." *New York Times,* 27 July 2003.

———. "John Cage, 79, a Minimalist Enchanted With Sound, Dies." *New York Times,* 13 August 1992, p. A1.

———. "Marian Anderson Is Dead at 93; Singer Shattered Racial Barriers." *New York Times,* 9 April 1993, p. A1.

———. "Mel Powell, Atonal Composer Who Won Pulitzer, Dies at 75." *New York Times,* 27 April 1998, p. 23.

———. "Ross Finney, 90, Composer of the Modern and Lyrical." *New York Times,* 7 February 1997, p. D18.

———. "Shura Cherkassky, 84, Pianist of Romantic School, Dies." *New York Times,* 29 December 1995, p. A30.

———. "Sir Yehudi Menuhin, Violinist, Conductor and Supporter of Charities, Is Dead at 82." *New York Times,* 13 March 1999, p. A1.

———. "Violinist Isaac Stern Dies at 81; Led Efforts to Save Carnegie Hall." *New York Times,* 23 September 2001, p. A1.

Lambert, Bruce. "William Schuman Is Dead at 81; Noted Composer Headed Juilliard." *New York Times,* 16 February 1992, p. 48.

Lehr, John. "Composer Gestures with Sound." *Toronto Star,* 6 March 2001.

London Daily Telegraph. "Obituary of Leo Ornstein." *London Daily Telegraph* 8 March 2002.

Lovely Music. "Robert Ashley." Available online. URL: http://www.lovely.com/bios/ashley.html. Downloaded on December 11, 2003.

Magil, Joseph. "Maud Powell: 1904–1917." *American Record Guide,* 1 July 2002.

Marin, Alsop. "Biography" and "Timeline." Available Online. URL: http://www.marinalsop.com. Updated on April 21, 2004.

———. "The Maestro." Maurice-Abravanel.com. Available online. URL: http://www.maurice-abravanel.com/the_maestro_.html. Updated on June 9, 2004.

Mayer, Martin. "Janos Starker." Cello.org. Available online. URL: http://www.cello.org/cnc/starker/ mayerbio.htm. Downloaded on August 12, 2004.

McLellan, Joseph. "Marlboro: Young Stars, Mature Music." *Washington Post,* 22 February 2002.

Miller, Sarah Bryan. "Skeptics Are Won Over by 'Treemonisha.'" *St. Louis Post-Dispatch,* 23 May 2000.

Moody, James, and Susan Malus. "Beverly Sills: Red Hair and Low-cut Dresses." *Horizon Magazine.* Available online. URL: http://www.horizonmag.com/2/sills.htm. Downloaded on August 19, 2004.

Morrison, Bryce. "A Virtuoso of Finesse and Temperament." Great Pianists of the 20th Century (liner notes), 1999.

National Public Radio . "About Ned." Nedrorem.com. Available online. URL: http://nedrorem.com/index1.html. Updated on July 4, 2004.

———. "Composer George Crumb Still in Demand for His Music at Age 73." *Weekend Edition [transcript]*, 23 November 2002.

New Albion. "Lukas Foss." Available online. URL: http://www.newalbion.com/artists/fossl/. Downloaded on August 12, 2004.

New York Daily Times. "Thalberg's Second Concert." *New York Daily Times*, 12 November 1856, p. 4.

New York Philharmonic Insight Series. "André Kostelantez." Available online. URL: http://www.newyorkphilharmonic.org/kostelanetz. Posted on March 2, 2003.

New York Times. "Arthur Farwell, composer, 79, Dies." *New York Times*, 21 January 1952, p. 15.

———. "Arthur Rubinstein Dies in Geneva at 95." *New York Times*, 21 December 1982, p. A1.

———. "Artur Rodzinski, Conductor, Dead." *New York Times*, 28 November 1958, p. 27.

———. "Bruno Walter, Conductor, Dies; Lcd Philharmonic and the Met." *New York Times*, 18 February 1962, p. 1.

———. "David Saperton, Concert Pianist." *New York Times*, 6 July 1970, p. 31.

———. "Dean Dixon, 61, Dies; Conductor in Exile." *New York Times*, 5 November 1976 p. 18.

———. "Deems Taylor Dies; Composer Was 80." *New York Times*, 4 July 1966, p. 1.

———. "Douglas Moore, Composer, Dead." *New York Times*, 28 July 1969, p. 31.

———. "Ernest Bloch, 78, Composer, Is Dead." *New York Times*, 16 July 1959, p. 27.

———. "E. S. Kelley, Dean of U.S. Composers." *New York Times*, 13 November 1944, p. 19.

———. "Edgard Varese, Composer, Dead." *New York Times*, 7 November 1965, p. 89.

———. "Eugene Ysaye Dies; A Famous Violinist." *New York Times*, 12 May 1931, p. 23.

———. "Fritz Reiner, Conductor, Dead; Led U.S. Orchestras 40 Years." *New York Times*, 16 November 1963, p. 22.

———. "George Antheil, Composer, Dead." *New York Times*, 13 February 1959, p. 17.

———. "George Gershwin, Composer, Is Dead." *New York Times*, 12 July 1937, p. 1.

———. "Irving Fine Dies; Composer Was 47." *New York Times*, 24 August 1962, p. 22.

———. "John Philip Sousa, Band Leader, Dies in Hotel at Reading." *New York Times*, 6 March 1932, p. 1.

———. "Josef Hofmann's Debut." *New York Times*, 30 November 1887, p. 5.

———. "Minnie Hauk Dies in Switzerland." *New York Times*, 7 February 1929, p. 22.

———. "Nadia Reisenberg Dies at 78; Concert Pianist and Teacher." *New York Times*, 12 June 1983, p. 44.

———. "Randall Thompson, Teacher; Composed Works for Chorus." *New York Times*, 10 July 1984, p. B6.

———. "Rodzinski to Lead 10 Radio Concerts." *New York Times*, 31 March 1937, p. 28.

———. "Seymour Shifrin, 53, Chamber Composer and Brandeis Teacher." *New York Times*, 28 September 1979, p. D15.

———. "Victor Herbert Dies on Way to Physician." *New York Times*, 27 May 1924, p. 1.

———. "Vincent Persichetti Dies at 72; Composer of Wide Repertory." *New York Times*, 15 August 1987, p. 33.

———. "William Masselos Is Dead at 72; A Pianist Who Loved Diversity." *New York Times*, 24 October 1992, p. 11.

———. "Wittgenstein, 73, Concert Pianist." *New York Times*, 4 March 1961, p. 23.

Nordlinger, Jay. "Earl Wild at 85." *New Criterion* 1 January 2001.

Oestreich, James R. "Robert Shaw, Choral and Orchestral Leader, Is Dead at 82." *New York Times,* 26 January 1999, p. A21.

———. "Rudolf Firkusny, an Elegant and Patrician Pianist, Is Dead at 82." *New York Times,* 20 July 1994, p. B20.

Ornstein, Severo. "About Leo Ornstein." Poonhill. com. Available online. URL: http://www.poonhill. com/leo_ornstein.html. Downloaded on August 15, 2004.

Pace, Eric. "William Bergsma, A Music Professor and Composer, 72." *New York Times,* 21 March 1994, p. B10.

Page, Tim. "At 60, John Browning Is Still a Vital Piano Force." *Newsday,* 27 October 1993.

———. "Efrem Zimbalist, Violinist, Dies at 94." *New York Times,* 23 February 1985, p. 1.

———. "Leonard Rose, Cellist, Dies; Key Performer and Teacher." *New York Times,* 19 November 1984, p. D14.

———. "Pulitzer-Prize Winning Composer Stephen Albert, 51." *Newsday,* 29 December 1992.

———. "Charles Tomlinson Griffes." Available online. URL: http://www.pbs.org/wnet/ihas/ composer/griffes.html. Downloaded on June 22, 2004.

Peyser, Joan. "Wolpe: A Thoroughly Modern Maverick." *New York Times,* 6 February 1972, p. D17.

Piatigorsky Foundation. "Gregor Piatigorsky (1903– 1976)." Available online. URL: http://www.piati gorsky foundation.org/Gregor.cfm. Downloaded on July 15, 2004.

Pitcher, John. "On Wuorinen's Wavelength." *Washington Post,* 30 October 2000.

Potter, Keith. "Obituary: Earle Brown; Innovative and Influential Composer." *The Independent,* 5 July 2002.

Jones, Randye L. "Marian Anderson (1897–1993)." *Afrocentric Voices.* Available online. URL: http:// www.afrovoices.com/anderson.html. Updated on April 15, 2004.

Patricia Rice. "Dutch Conductor to Lead Symphony." *St. Louis Post-Dispatch,* 13 January 1995.

Rockwell, John. "Antal Dorati, Who Led Orchestras for Over 50 Years, Is Dead at 82." *New York Times,* 15 November 1988, p. D26.

———. "Claus Adams, Cellist, Is Dead; Played with Juilliard String Quartet." *New York Times,* 6 July 1983, p. B9.

———. "Copland, The Dean of U.S. Music, Dies at 90." *New York Times,* 3 December 1990, p. CN29.

———. "Morton Feldman Dies at 61; An Experimental Composer." *New York Times,* 4 September 1987, p. D15.

———. "Peter Herman Adler, TV Opera Pioneer and Conductor, 91." *New York Times,* 3 October 1990, p. B7.

———. "Virgil Thomson, Composer, Critic, and Collaborator With Stein, Dies at 92." *New York Times,* 1 October 1989, p. 1.

———. "Vladimir Ussachevsky, 78, Electronic Composer." *New York Times,* 5 January 1990, p. B5.

———. "Why Aaron Copland and American Music Are Synonymous." *New York Times,* 4 December 1990, p. C15.

Roger Sessions Society. "Biography." Available online. URL: http://www.uncwil.edu/music/sessions society/. Downloaded on August 13, 2004.

Ross, Alex. "Maurice Abravanel, 90, Utah Symphony Leader." *New York Times,* 23 September 1993, p. D22.

Ruhe, Pierre. "Biography." Ruthlaredo.com. Available online. URL: http://www.ruthlaredo.com/bio. html. Posted on March 14, 2002.

———. "A Bland Spot for Modern Music." *Atlanta Journal and Constitution,* 14 April 2002.

Saxon, Wolfgang. "Robert Russell Bennett, 87; Orchestrated Top Musicals." *New York Times,* 19 August 1981, p. D19.

Schlosberg, Daniel. "A First-String Player: Elmar Oliveira Revives Violin Repertoire." *Newsday,* 19 September 2002.

Schmidt, Barbara. "Archangels Unaware." Twain quotes.com. Available online. URL: http://www. twainquotes.com/archangels.html. Downloaded on August 13, 2004.

Schonberg, Harold C. "Howard Hanson Is Dead; Composer and Teacher." *New York Times,* 28 February 1981, p. 19.

———. "Jascha Heifetz Is Dead at 86; A Virtuoso Since Childhood." *New York Times,* 12 December 1987, p. 1.

———. "Jorge Bolet, Pianist, Is Dead at 75." *New York Times,* 17 October 1990, p. D24.

———. "Moral Force in Music." *New York Times,* 18 February 1962, p. 94.

———. "Musical Logician: Hindemith, an Anti-Romantic, Carried Baroque Tradition Into 20th Century." *New York Times,* 30 December 1963, p. 17.

———. "Paul Zukofsky, 13, Heard in Recital." *New York Times,* 1 December 1956, p. 17.

———. "Champion of American Composers." *New York Times,* 14 August 1955, p. X7.

———. "Maker of Homespun Music." *New York Times,* 4 October 1979, p. B19.

———. "Nathan Milstein Dies at 88; An Exalted Violin Virtuoso." *New York Times,* 22 December 1992, p. B10.

Shehori, Mordecai. "Simon Barere, Piano." Cembal d'Amour. Available online. URL: http://www.cembaldamour.com/artistsbios.html. Downloaded on July 8, 2004.

Shepard, Richard F. "Horowitz Tickets Are Sold Out in Two Hours." *New York Times,* 27 April 1965, p. 39.

Shirodkar, Marco. "Alan Hovhaness Biographical Summary." Available online. URL: http://www.hovhaness.com/hovhaness.html. Downloaded on July 19, 2004.

Sony Classical. "Bio." EmanuelAx.com. Available online. URL: http://www.emanuelax.com. Updated 2003.

———. "Kathleen Battle, Biography." Available online. URL: http://www.sonyclassical.com/artists/battle/bio.html. Downloaded on July 21, 2004.

Steinberg, Martin. "NY Philharmonic Premieres John Adams' Sept. 11 Tribute 'On the Transmigration of Souls.'" *AP Worldstream,* 20 September 2002.

Summers, Kim. "Gary Graffman." Allmusic Guide. Available online. URL: http://www.allmusic. com/cg/amg.dll?p=amg&sql=11:09d7yl4jxp9b~T1. Downloaded on July 17, 2004.

Swafford, Jan. "Charles Edward Ives." Charlesives.org. Available online. URL: http://www.charlesives.org/02bio.htm. Updated 1998.

Taubman, Howard. "A Winner on His Merits; Van Cliburn's Approach in Line with Style Liked by Russians." *New York Times,* 17 April 1958, p. X9.

———. "History's Loss." *New York Times,* 24 February 1957, p. 113.

Teachout, Terry. "How Good Was Leonard Bernstein?" *Commentary,* 1 October 1994.

Theodore Presser Company. "Ralph Shapey." Available online. URL: http://www.presser.com/Composers/info.cfm?Name=RALPHSHAPEY. Downloanded on March 11, 2004.

Thirteen.org. "Ruggiero Ricci." Thirteen.org: Legendary Violinists. Available online. URL: http://www.thirteen.org/publicarts/violin/ricci.html. Downloaded on August 14, 2004.

Tommasini, Anthony. "Jacob Druckman, 67, Dies; A Composer and Teacher." *New York Times,* 27 May 1996, p. 44.

———. "Otto Luening, the Composer and Innovator, Is Dead at 96." *New York Times,* 5 September 1996, p. D21.

University of Akron Bierce Library. "Robert Ashley." Smith Archives. Available online. URL: http://www.uakron.edu/ssma/composers/Ashley.shtml. Updated on October 12, 1998.

Walsh, Michael. "Giving the Devil His Due; At Home and Abroad, Samuel Ramey Is Opera's Satanic Majesty." *Time,* 8 June 1987.

Whitman, Alden. "About William Schuman." Available online. URL: http://www.williamschuman.org/frames/fr_about.htm. Downloaded on August 12, 2004.

———. "Joseph Szigeti, Violinist, Dead; Exponent of Classical Tradition." *New York Times,* 21 February 1973, p. 89.

Willis, Cherie. "History of Maurice Abravanel." Online Utah. Available online. URL: http://www.onlineutah.com/abravanelhistory.shtml. Downloaded on June 9, 2004.

Woods, Audrey. "Violinist Yehudi Menuhin Dies." *Associated Press Online,* 12 March 1999.

Editorial Board of Advisers

Richard Carlin, general editor, is the author of several books of music, including *Southern Exposure, The Big Book of Country Music, Classical Music: An Informal Guide,* and the five-volume *Worlds of Music.* He has also written and compiled several books of music instruction and songbooks and served as advisory editor on country music for the American National Biography. Carlin has contributed articles on traditional music to various journals, including the *Journal of Ethnomusicology, Sing Out!, Pickin', Frets,* and *Mugwumps.* He has also produced 10 albums of traditional music for Folkways Records. A longtime editor of books on music, dance, and the arts, Carlin is currently executive editor of music and dance at Routledge Publishers. He previously spent six years as executive editor at Schirmer Books and was the founding editor at A Cappella Books, an imprint of the Chicago Review Press.

Barbara Ching, Ph.D., is an associate professor of English at the University of Memphis. She obtained a graduate certificate in women's studies and her doctorate in literature from Duke University. Dr. Ching has written extensively on country music and rural identity, and she is the author of *Wrong's What I Do Best: Hard Country Music and Contemporary Culture* (Oxford University Press) and *Knowing Your Place: Rural Identity and Cultural Hierarchy* (Routledge). She has also contributed articles and chapters to numerous other works on the subject and has presented papers at meetings of the International Association for the Study of Popular Music.

Ronald D. Cohen, Ph.D., is professor emeritus of history at Indiana University–Northwest (Gary). He obtained a doctorate in history from the University of Minnesota–Minneapolis. Dr. Cohen has written extensively on the folk music revival and is the coproducer, with Jeff Place, of *The Best of Broadside: 1962–1988: Anthems of the American Underground from the Pages of Broadside Magazine* (five-CD boxed set with illustrated book, Smithsonian Folkways Recordings, 2000), which was nominated for a Grammy Award in 2001. He is also the author of *Rainbow Quest: The Folk Music Revival and American Society, 1940–1970* (University of Massachusetts Press) and the editor of *Alan Lomax: Selected Writings, 1934–1997* (Routledge). He is also the editor of the Scarecrow Press book series American Folk Music and Musicians.

William Duckworth is the composer of more than 100 pieces of music and the author of six books and numerous articles, the most recent of which is "Making Music on the Web" (*Leonardo Music Journal,* vol. 9, December 1999). In the mid-1990s he and codirector Nora Farrell began *Cathedral,* a multiyear work of music and art for the Web that went online June 10, 1997. Incorporating acoustic and computer music, live Web casts by its own band, and newly created virtual instruments, *Cathedral* is one of the first interactive works of music and art on the Web. Recently, Duckworth and Farrell created Cathedral 2001, a 48-hour World Wide Web event, with 34 events streamed live from five continents.

Duckworth is currently a professor of music at Bucknell University in Pennsylvania.

Kevin Holm-Hudson, Ph.D., received his doctorate of musical arts (composition with ethnomusicology concentration) from the University of Illinois at Urbana-Champaign. He is an assistant professor of music at the University of Kentucky and is an editor/contributor to *Progressive Rock Reconsidered* (Routledge). Dr. Holm-Hudson is also the author of numerous articles that have appeared in such publications as *Genre* and *Ex Tempore* and has presented papers on a wide variety of topics at conferences, including "'Come Sail Away' and the Commodification of Prog Lite," at the inaugural Conference on Popular Music and American Culture in 2002.

Nadine Hubbs, Ph.D., is associate professor of music and women's studies at the University of Michigan (Ann Arbor). She has written extensively on classical and popular music, particularly in relation to gender and sexuality. Dr. Hubbs is the author of *The Queer Composition of America's Sound: Gay Modernists, American Music, and National Identity* (University of California Press) and various essays, including "The Imagination of Pop-Rock Criticism" in *Expression in Pop-Rock Music* (Garland Publications) and "Music of the 'Fourth Gender': Morrissey and the Sexual Politics of Melodic Contour," featured in the journal *Genders.*

Craig Morrison, Ph.D., holds a doctorate in humanities with a concentration in music from Concordia University (Montreal, Quebec). He is currently a professor of music at Concordia, where he teaches a course titled "Rock and Roll and Its Roots." Dr. Morrison is the author of *Go Cat Go! Rockabilly Music and Its Makers* (University of Illinois Press) and contributed to *The Encyclopedia of the Blues* (Routledge). He has presented many papers on elements of rock and roll.

Albin J. Zak III, Ph.D., earned a doctorate in musicology from the Graduate Center of the City University of New York and is currently chairman of the music department at the University at Albany (SUNY). His publications include *The Velvet Underground Companion* (Schirmer Books) and *The Poetics of Rock: Cutting Tracks, Making Records* (University of California Press). Dr. Zak is also a songwriter, recording engineer, and record producer.

Index

Page numbers in **bold** indicate main entries. Page numbers in *italic* indicate illustrations; page numbers denoted with a *c* indicate chronology entries, while those with a *g* indicate glossary entries.

A

Abas, Matyas 163
Abbey, Henry 154, 155
ABC network 239
Abrams, Miriam 241
Abravenel, Maurice *1*, **1–2**, *2*, 231, 261*c*, 267*c*, 270*c*, 279*c*
Abravenel Hall *1*, **2**, 231, 277*c*
academia xxv
Academy of St.-Martin-in-the-Fields 24, 148
a cappella (definition) 283*g*
accent (definition) 283*g*
Adagio for Strings (Samuel Barber) **2**, 17, 267*c*, 268*c*
Adams, Claus 2
Adams, John **2–3**, 270*c*
    recommended listening 251
    Saint Paul Chamber Orchestra 197
    San Francisco Conservatory of Music 198
    On the Transmigration of Souls **168–169**
Adler, Kurt Herbert **3**, 198
Adler, Peter Herman **3–4**, 260*c*
Adler, Samuel **4**, 265*c*
administrators. *See* music administration
Aeolian Hall 188
African-American music vii, xxiv
African Americans viii, 257*c*, 268*c*, 269*c*
    Marian Anderson **9–10**
    Kathleen Battle **21**
    Thomas (Blind Tom) Bethune **28–29**

Henry Burleigh **40**
James DePreist **67**
Dean Dixon **68–69**
Lawrence Freeman **82**
Sissieretta Jones **119–120**
Scott Joplin **120**
Ulysses Kay **124**, *124*
Leontyne Price **184**
William Grant Still **215**
Aftertones of Infinity (Joseph Schwantner) **4**
Aida (Verdi) 155
AIDS 138
Air Music (Ned Rorem) **4**
Albeneri Trio **4–5**, 16, 123, 200, 270*c*
Albert, Stephen **5**, 268*c*, 279*c*
Albrecht, Charles **5**
Alice Tully Hall **5**
    American String Quartet 7
    Emanuel Ax 14
    Chamber Music Society of Lincoln Center 48
    Sharon Isbin 112
    Alice Tully 228
Alkan, Valentin 136
Aller, Eleanor **5**, 105, 209, 210
Alsop, Marin **5–6**, 41, 272*c*
alto (definition) 283*g*
Amahl and the Night Visitors (Gian Carlo Menotti) xxv–xxvi, 4, **6**, 152, 200, 271*c*
American Bach Soloists **6**
American Brass Quintet **6–7**, 203, 273*c*
American Composers Forum **7**, 134, 276*c*
American Composers Orchestra **7**, 277*c*
    Robert Ashley 13
    Robert Beaser 23
    Dennis Russell Davies 65
    Francis Thorne 224
American Conservatory (Chicago)
    Ruth Crawford Seeger 60
    Frederick G. Gleason 90

Gail Kubik 131
Leo Sowerby 212
American Festival Overture (William Schuman) **7**, 268*c*
American Five 23
American Indians. *See* Native Americans
An American in Paris (George Gershwin) **7**, 87, 265*c*
An American in Paris (movie) 135
American Music (journal) **7**
American Music Center **7**, 268*c*
    Marion Bauer 22
    Otto Luening 143
    Lester Trimble 227
    Hugo Weisgall 237
American String Quartet **7–8**, 276*c*
American Symphony Orchestra **8**, 35, 203, 217, 273*c*
American Symphony Orchestra League 2, **8**, 269*c*
American Youth Orchestra 270*c*
Amherst College 213
Ancient Voices of Children (George Crumb) **8**
Andante online listening service 251
Anderson, June **8**, *8–9*, 271*c*, 279*c*
Anderson, Laurie **9**, 270*c*
Anderson, Marian **9–10**, *10*, 260*c*, 264*c*, 266*c*, 268*c*, 269*c*, 274*c*, 279*c*
Annan, Kofi 153
Antek, Samuel 163
Antes, John **11**, 253*c*, 254*c*
Antheil, George **11–12**, 16, 260*c*, 265*c*, 269*c*–270*c*, 273*c*
Antony and Cleopatra (Barber) 18, 155, 274*c*
Apollo's Fire **12**
Appalachian Spring (Aaron Copland) **12**, 57, 147, 270*c*
Arabesque Records 97
Archer, Frederick 179
Argento, Dominick **12**, *82*, 134, 265*c*